Learn Cocoa Touch for iOS

Jeff Kelley

Apress®

Learn Cocoa Touch for iOS

ISBN-13 (pbk): 978-1-4302-4269-7

ISBN-13 (electronic): 978-1-4302-4270-3

President and Publisher: Paul Manning
Lead Editor: Michelle Lowman
Development Editor: Douglas Pundick
Technical Reviewer: Scott Gardner
Editorial Board: Steve Anglin, Ewan Buckingham, Gary Cornell, Louise Corrigan, Morgan Ertel, Jonathan Gennick, Jonathan Hassell, Robert Hutchinson, Michelle Lowman, James Markham, Matthew Moodie, Jeff Olson, Jeffrey Pepper, Douglas Pundick, Ben Renow-Clarke, Dominic Shakeshaft, Gwenan Spearing, Matt Wade, Tom Welsh
Coordinating Editors: Jennifer L. Blackwell and Jill Balzano
Copy Editor: Kim Wimpsett
Compositor: Bytheway Publishing Services
Indexer: SPi Global
Artist: SPi Global
Cover Designer: Anna Ishchenko

Distributed to the book trade worldwide by Springer Science+Business Media New York, 233 Spring Street, 6th Floor, New York, NY 10013. Phone 1-800-SPRINGER, fax (201) 348-4505, e-mail orders-ny@springer-sbm.com, or visit www.springeronline.com.

For information on translations, please e-mail rights@apress.com, or visit www.apress.com.

Apress and friends of ED books may be purchased in bulk for academic, corporate, or promotional use. eBook versions and licenses are also available for most titles. For more information, reference our Special Bulk Sales–eBook Licensing web page at www.apress.com/bulk-sales.

Any source code or other supplementary materials referenced by the author in this text is available to readers at www.apress.com. For detailed information about how to locate your book's source code, go to www.apress.com/source-code.

To my wife, Amanda. I love you.

Contents at a Glance

About the Author x

About the Technical Reviewer xi

Acknowledgments xii

Introduction xiii

Chapter 1: Getting Started 1

Chapter 2: Objective-C in a Nutshell 15

Chapter 3: Managing On-Screen Content with View Controllers 41

Chapter 4: Saving Content in Your App 79

Chapter 5: Handling User Touches 109

Chapter 6: Integrating Networking and Web Services 141

Chapter 7: Writing Modern Code with Blocks 181

Chapter 8: Managing What Happens When 209

Chapter 9: User Interface Design 243

Chapter 10: Hardware APIs 277

Chapter 11: Media in Your App: Playing Audio and Video 309

Chapter 12: Localization and Internationalizion 351

Appendix A: Running Code on an iOS Device 371

Index 375

Contents

About the Author.. x

About the Technical Reviewer xi

Acknowledgments xii

Introduction xiii

Chapter 1: Getting Started... 1

Summary 13

Chapter 2: Objective-C in a Nutshell 15

Object-Oriented Programming...15

Getting and Setting Data 24

Properties 27

Writing Your Code for You 28

Memory Management...29

Garbage Collection 30

Reference Counting 30

Autorelease Pools...31

Automatic Reference Counting..32

ARC and Properties..33

Categories 34

Class Extensions...35

Protocols...36

Conforming to Protocols 37

Model-View-Controller Programming: Well-Designed Code.................................38

Summary 40

Chapter 3: Managing On-Screen Content with View Controllers 41

View Controller Life Cycle..42

Implementing Application Logic with Controls 46

Providing Lists of Content with Table Views...49

Providing Data to Your Table View 52

Providing Custom Table View Cells 53

Nib Loading In Depth 54

Loading Table View Cells from Nibs 55

iPhone and iPad Nibs..56

Parent and Child View Controllers 57

    Modal View Controllers 57
    Navigation Controllers 57
    Tab Bar Controllers 58
    Split View Controllers 59
    Page View Controllers 59

Passing Data Between View Controllers 60

    Passing Data from a Parent View Controller to a Child View Controller 70
    Passing Data to and from a Modal View Controller 71
    Passing Data Between View Controllers with a Delegate Protocol 74

Summary 78

Chapter 4: Saving Content in Your App 79

Moving Data Around Your App 79

    Delegate Chains 80
    Key-Value Observing 80
    Notifications 88
    Singletons 90

Persisting Data to a File 92

    NSUserDefaults...92
    NSCoding 100
    Manual File Handling 104
    SQLite Databases 105
    File Locations on iOS 106
    Core Data 107

Summary 108

Chapter 5: Handling User Touches 109

The Responder Chain...109

Custom Views 111

UIGestureRecognizer 112

    More Target-Action Methods 113
    Gesture Recognizer Life Cycle 113
    Built-in Gesture Recognizers 113
    Custom UIGestureRecognizers 115

Scroll Views...118

Implementing UI Changes..120

    Adding Pictures to Possessions..120
    Using UIActionSheet 132
    Implementing "Edit" for Table Views 135
    Implementing Table View Reordering...137

Summary 139

Chapter 6: Integrating Networking and Web Services 141

Loading Data from the Network 142

    Creating a URL Request...142
    Creating a URL Connection 142
    Interpreting the Response 143
    Using Received Data..145

Asynchronous Operation 148
    URL Connection Delegate Methods 149
    Asynchronous Networking Concerns 152
Parsing JSON and XML from Web Services 153
    Parsing XML...154
    Parsing JSON 157
    Creating JSON Representations 158
    Parsing Foundation Objects into Model Objects 159
Downloading Files 162
    When to Cache Files 164
    Downloading Images 165
Sending Data Across the Network 165
Creating a Twitter Client 166
Summary 180

Chapter 7: Writing Modern Code with Blocks 181
What Are Blocks? 181
    Blocks Are Encapsulated Functions 182
    Readable Block Declarations with Typedefs 183
    Block Memory Management...184
    Blocks Are Objects 185
    Blocks Capture Scope 186
    Blocks Retain Objects 188
    Using Blocks as Parameters to Methods 189
Why Should We Use Blocks? 190
    UIView Animations...190
    Using Blocks for Asynchronous Callbacks 193
    Using Blocks for Enumeration 194
    Using Blocks to Sort Arrays 199
Using Blocks in Your Code 201
Updating TwitterExample with Blocks 203
    Adding a Completion Handler 203
    Adding Activity Indicators 206
Summary 208

Chapter 8: Managing What Happens When 209
Sending Messages 209
    Messages Under the Hood..210
    Performing Selectors Manually 211
Scheduling Code with Timers...215
Run Loops..219
Multithreaded Code 222
    Running Code on Another Thread 222
    Thread Safety 223
Grand Central Dispatch..230
    Dispatching Code...231
    Using Global Dispatch Queues..233
    Dispatch Objects...236

Summary 242

Chapter 9: User Interface Design 243

Coloring Interface Elements with UIColor...244

Fonts and Text Size 249

Using Images 255

View Layout 257

    View Hierarchy 258

    View Coordinate Systems..258

    View Display Properties 260

    View Layout in UIView Subclasses 263

    View Layout on Retina Display Devices 264

    View Layout on iPad 265

View Animation...266

Example: Reddit Photo Browser 268

Summary 276

Chapter 10: Hardware APIs...277

Using the Camera 278

    Using UIImagePickerController for Photos...278

    Using UIImagePickerController for Videos...282

    Using UIVideoEditorController for Video 284

Using the Accelerometer 285

    Accelerometer Events..285

    Device Orientation Notifications 287

    Using Raw Accelerometer, Gyroscope, and Magnetometer Data with Core Motion....288

Using Location Data..293

    Using CoreLocation..293

    Using MapKit 295

Bring Your Own Device 307

Requiring Devices in Your App 307

Summary 308

Chapter 11: Media in Your App: Playing Audio and Video 309

Playing Audio 309

    System Sound Services..310

    AVAudioPlayer 314

    Other Sound APIs...317

    Example: SoundBoard 317

    Playing Music 322

    Example: TitularSongs..327

Playing Video 333

    Using MPMoviePlayerController 333

    Example: CustomPlayer 338

Summary 349

Chapter 12: Localization and Internationalizion 351

Internationalization 352

    Using Numbers 353

Example: LocaleNumbers 354
Using Dates 359
Processing User Input 361
Localization 363
Localizing Text 365
Example: HelloLocalization 366
Localizing Resources 369
Localizing Nibs 369
Summary 370

Appendix A: Running Code on an iOS Device **371**

The iOS Developer Program 371
iOS Application Security 372
Obtaining a Certificate 372
iOS Application Provisioning 373

Index **349**

About the Author

Jeff Kelley started programming for the iPhone with iPhone OS 2 and has seen it evolve into the iOS we know and love today. Jeff has developed dozens of apps for clients both large and small in a wide variety of industries, as well as several apps for his own use. He's been programming since using BASIC in grade school, with his professional start coming in the Mac IT world in education. Today he does iOS programming full-time, as well as speaking engagements at conferences and the local chapter of CocoaHeads.

About the Technical Reviewer

Scott Gardner is an Apple technology evangelist, consultant, and developer. He combines insight gained from the field and continuous study of iOS to develop apps that are beneficial and intuitive. Scott resides in the Midwest with his wife and daughter.

Acknowledgments

I'd like to thank everyone at Apress for their hard work on this book—specifically, Scott Gardner as my technical reviewer, who made a number of suggestions that improved the quality of the work, as well as keeping me honest with providing top-tier content. Douglas Pudnick, my development editor, also did a great job guiding the direction of the content, and the other editors, Michelle Lowman, Jennifer Blackwell, Kelly Moritz, and Jill Balzano, were all a great help with this book. I'd also like to thank the Detroit Labs crew, specifically cofounders Paul Glomski, Henry Balanon, Nathan Hughes, and Dan Ward, for being understanding with the challenges of writing apps by day and a book by night, as well as for giving me an awesome place to work. At home, a great deal of thanks goes to my wife, Amanda, who put up with me writing this book while also pregnant with our first child, something she deserves endless credit for. Finally, I'd like to thank my parents for helping me get my start in programming; my mom would copy BASIC programs from a book when I was in kindergarten so that I could mess with them when I got home, and later in grade school my dad bought me a copy of Visual Studio—the first app I ever wrote for someone else was a retirement calculator he could keep on his screen at work to count down the seconds until retirement. I've had a lot of help along the way in getting this book published, so to everyone, mentioned here or not, thank you.

Introduction

With every successive release of iOS and its related hardware products, Apple and journalists the world over spout hyperbolic statements about "revolutionary" features, "insanely great" devices, and "unbelievable" sales. The numbers don't disappoint, with hundreds of millions of iOS devices having been sold and billions of dollars sent to developers in revenue. As we enter the post-PC era, we do so using our smartphones and tablets. Apple's iOS is consistently the most user-friendly, powerful platform for these new devices, and developers the world over benefit from offering their products on the App Store. That being said, it is a market that continues to grow every day, especially when customers can obtain an iPhone for next to nothing up front with a two-year contract. As the barrier to entry to the smartphone market declines and the user base goes up, opportunity skyrockets. This book will allow you to take advantage of that opportunity. We'll get up and running using Xcode on Mac OS X, we'll create applications as we learn Objective-C (the language in which you'll be developing your apps), and we'll tour the frameworks that make Cocoa Touch one of the best development environments in the world.

As you should get used to when programming for an Apple environment, there are rules. As such, there are some things you'll need to go through this book: a Mac with an Intel processor running Mac OS X 10.7 (Lion) or newer, with Xcode 4.3 or newer (available from the Mac App Store), and ideally an iOS device running iOS 5.1 or newer. While older versions of Mac OS X, Xcode, and iOS may still be in use, screenshots and step-by-step instructions in this book may not work for other versions.

Who This Book Is For

This book assumes a basic level of programming knowledge. You don't have to be an expert, but any experience you have with C, C++, or even Java will be useful to help frame concepts explained in the early stages of the book. You should also be familiar with the basics of Apple's Mac OS X and iOS operating systems, enough to get around the filesystem in Mac OS X and launch Xcode and enough to launch apps and understand typical app behavior on iOS.

How This Book Is Structured

In general, chapters in this book will begin with more abstract concepts. Where there has been evolution in the development frameworks and libraries, we'll start with the older, more complicated ways and lead in to the newer way of doing things in order to better understand why things have developed the way they have. As each chapter progresses, we'll switch from the abstract to the concrete, with sample projects and example code. We'll develop two apps in multiple chapters, with other smaller examples in addition.

Chapter 1 gets you up and running with Xcode and creating a "Hello, World!" app.

Chapter 2 covers the Objective-C language in detail, including memory management, best practices, and the latest additions to the language.

Chapter 3 discusses working with view controllers, one of the most important types of objects you'll use in iOS development.

Chapter 4 covers handling your data, from moving it around inside the app to saving and loading from disk.

Chapter 5 details handling user touches and basic app flow.

Chapter 6 covers networking and web services, including parsing JSON and XML.

Chapter 7 introduces blocks, Apple's new addition to the C language that encapsulates code.

Chapter 8 explains more about the message dispatch process in iOS, leading to a discussion of multithreaded code.

Chapter 9 covers user interface design in your app.

Chapter 10 details the multitude of hardware APIs available on iOS devices, including the accelerometer, gyroscope, and magnetometer, as well as location services using GPS.

Chapter 11 outlines using media in your app, both audio and video.

Chapter 12 covers the internationalization and localization processes, which help give your app a broader reach.

Downloading the Code

The code for the examples shown in this book is available on the Apress web site, `www.apress.com`. You can find a link on the book's information page under the Source Code/Downloads tab. This tab is located underneath the Related Titles section of the page.

Contacting the Author

Send your questions, comments, criticisms, and lame puns (*especially* lame puns) to me on Twitter as `@SlaunchaMan` or by e-mail at `SlaunchaMan@gmail.com`. Read my blog at `http://blog.slaunchaman.com`, and check out my professional work at `www.detroitlabs.com`.

Getting Started

While apps for your iPhone are a relatively new phenomenon, they're based on decades-old technologies present also on your Mac. Mac OS X introduced a new set of APIs and frameworks collectively known as Cocoa. While iOS shares many lower-level system frameworks and APIs with Mac OS X, the APIs relating to its touch-based user interface, telephone capabilities, and iOS-only functionality reside in the Cocoa Touch layer, an analog to Cocoa for mobile devices. One of the similarities Cocoa Touch has with its desktop counterpart is the tools used for development, including the same IDE, Xcode. In fact, SDKs for iOS and Mac OS X development are included when you download the developer tools. In this chapter, we'll take a closer look at these tools and get started using them.

Installing Xcode

Before you get started writing your applications, you'll need to install Apple's developer tools. While there are many individual applications, libraries, and utilities you'll use over the course of app development, the main one you'll use is Apple's IDE, Xcode.

> **NOTE:** Unlike the iPhone and other Apple products, the leading X in Xcode is capitalized.

There are two ways to install Xcode. The easiest, best-supported, and most up-to-date way is to download Xcode from the Mac App Store. When the download finishes, Xcode will be in your /Applications directory, with no further installation required.

> **NOTE:** By default, the Xcode installer installs developer tools to the /Applications folder on your hard drive. It is possible to install Xcode to a different location, but recent versions of the installer have not exposed that option to users. I recommend installing the App Store version of Xcode to /Applications and installing any beta versions you may use to other folders.

The second way to install Xcode is by downloading an installer from Apple's developer site. While Apple doesn't always release each final shipping version of Xcode this way, this is how you'll install prerelease versions of the tool set. Once you log in with your developer credentials, you'll download a disk image containing an Installer package for the developer tools. Run that package to install Xcode. As of this writing, the latest version of Xcode is 4.3; while older versions may work on your Mac, versions older than 4.0 are significantly different, enough so that it may be difficult to follow along with the tutorials in this book.

Either way, you should know going in that Apple's tool set is a large download, usually more than several gigabytes. There has been some progress on separating individual components into something that Xcode can update without redownloading the whole set of tools, but the initial download is something you probably can't do at your local coffee shop.

The Developer Tools

The developer tools you've installed center around Xcode, but there are some other components that you'll use a lot over the course of this book:

- Instruments allows you to inspect the performance of your application, finding memory leaks, discovering computational bottlenecks, and even breaking down the 3D rendering of games with ease.

- The iOS Simulator runs your iOS applications in a simulated environment. It's important to note the difference between a *simulator* and an *emulator*. In a simulator, your code is compiled for the platform the *simulator* is running on. In the case of an iOS app, the code is compiled for your Mac and runs in a fake, iPhone-*like* environment. In an emulator, the code is compiled the same for the emulator and the platform you're writing *for*. There is no iOS emulator available, but if there were, code compiled for the emulator would be the same as code compiled for the device. This is important in testing because the processor architectures are different on different platforms; your Mac has an Intel processor, but an iPhone has an ARM processor. For this reason, you should always test on the device before releasing an app to ensure that there aren't any device-specific bugs.

- Xcode allows you to download local copies of the entire documentation set usually available at http://developer.apple.com; this documentation allows you to see help inline in Xcode while you write.

- Finally, the tools include compilers, linkers, and other tools needed to turn your code into an actual, functioning application. If you're comfortable with the command line, you can now use gcc and related tools to compile applications. Xcode 4 replaced GCC with Clang running on the LLVM infrastructure, a more modern compiler and the new default. For most cases, LLVM can replace GCC with no loss in functionality—in fact, the gcc command-line utility is really just a symlink to LLVM in recent tool set distributions.

To get started, launch Xcode. By default, the path will be /Applications/Xcode.app. With Xcode installed and launched, let's make our first application.

Hello, World!

When you first start Xcode, you'll see a welcome screen (Figure 1-1). From here, you can open recent projects, launch Apple's developer web site, open the Xcode user guide (which you should definitely read at some point), download source code from a revision control system, and create a new project. Since we haven't created one yet, click "Create a new Xcode project."

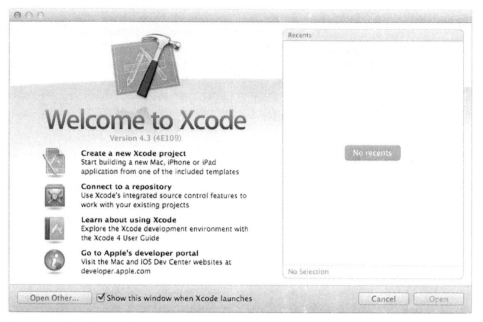

Figure 1-1. *The Xcode welcome screen*

When you create a new project, Xcode presents a wizard, seen in Figure 1-2, that starts with a list of the types of projects it can make. Xcode uses templates to speed the development of common types of applications. On the left, you can see the categories of templates that are currently installed. If it isn't already selected, select Application under iOS on the left to display all of the iOS templates. Our simple application will have only one screen, so select Single View Application and click Next.

Figure 1-2. *Selecting a template from the Xcode New Project Wizard*

The next screen gives you some options to set the metadata for the project and to further refine which template Xcode uses. Since this is our first project, we'll create a "Hello, World!" iOS application. "Hello, World!" is a tradition nearly as old as programming itself wherein the first thing you do in a new language or on a new platform is make a program that displays the words "Hello, World!" to the user. Enter **HelloWorld** for Product Name. The Company Identifier value should be a reverse-DNS label for your company name (if you have one). If you don't have one, your personal web site will do. If you don't have one, consider getting one before releasing any apps to the App Store.) Since my web site is at `http://learncocoatouch.com`, I use `com.learncocoatouch` as my company identifier. This reverse-DNS style listing is used often in iOS to differentiate between applications and other identifiable things, typically with your application ID affixed to the end. For me, the HelloWorld project has the identifier of `com.learncocoatouch.HelloWorld`. App IDs must be unique in the App Store, and installing an app on a device with the same ID as another app will overwrite the existing one.

The class prefix is used to identify code that you create and differentiate it from code that others write. Typically you'll use your initials. This is important to ensure that two developers don't create things with the same name. If your initials happen to be the same as another developer's or what a system framework uses for a prefix, you can use three letters, letters from your company name, or any combination of letters you like. For *Learn Cocoa Touch*, I'll use LCT.

> **NOTE:** You can find an unofficial list of "claimed" prefixes at www.cocoadev.com/index.pl?ChooseYourOwnPrefix. Claim yours now!

The next options affect the template that the project will use. Leave Device Family set to iPhone for now. If you're creating an app for iPad or a Universal app that supports both devices, this is where you set it. Uncheck Use Storyboard and Include Unit Tests, but check Automatic Reference Counting. We'll go over what those mean in more detail later. Once those are set, we're finally ready to create our application. Your screen should look like Figure 1-3. Click Next.

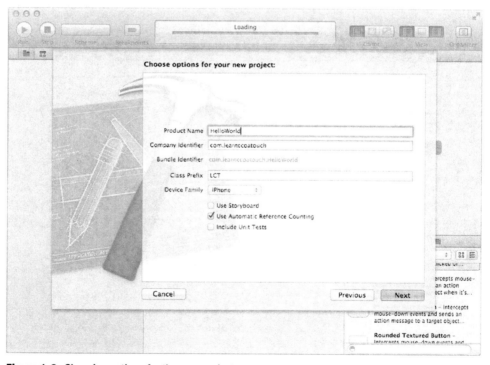

Figure 1-3. *Choosing options for the new project*

Xcode will prompt you to select a location for the project on your hard disk, as well as give you the option to create a local Git repository while it creates the project. If you know and use Git, feel free to select that option; otherwise, it's unneeded for this project. While going through this book, you may find it useful to create a separate directory somewhere in your Home folder for the various apps we'll be writing, such as ~/Projects/Learn Cocoa Touch/.

Once you select a location, Xcode creates your project. The initial screen, shown in Figure 1-4, shows you your project settings. Here we can modify project metadata such as supported resolutions, which iOS version(s) the project will run on, the version number of the application, which device orientations it supports, the icons to use, and so on. We'll leave these alone for now.

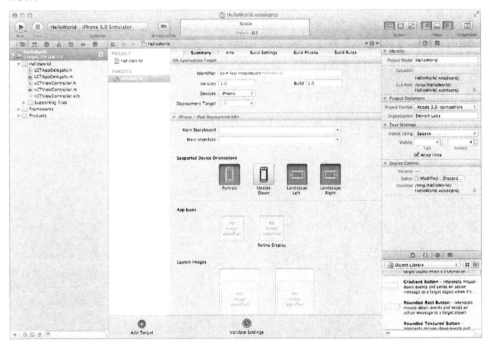

Figure 1-4. *This is the initial layout of the Xcode window once you've created a project.*

To run your application in the iOS Simulator, click the Run button at the upper-left corner of the Xcode window (the one that looks like the iTunes Play button). Since we haven't modified the code at all, it won't look like much. Figure 1-5 shows what you should see at this point when you run your app.

NOTE: If the text to the right of the Run button says iOS Device, change the selection to the iPhone Simulator.

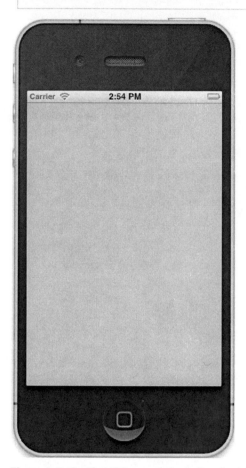

Figure 1-5. *Our first iOS app running in the simulator*

Now that we have the application set up and ready to modify, let's take a look at our goal for this application:

Goal: Build an app that says "Hello, world!" to the user.

Ready to modify the app? Good. Quit the iOS Simulator and head back to Xcode. Press Command+1 to open the File browser on the left pane. Find the file under HelloWorld that ends in ViewController.xib and select it. Note that it will start with your class prefix—in my case, it's called `LCTViewController.xib` by default. The file will open in an Interface Builder view: a visual layout of your application's interface. Right now, it's the same gray view that you saw in the iOS Simulator. Let's change that. The bottom-right corner of the screen contains the Object Library, a collection of user interface elements that you can add to the view. You can switch to its search field by pressing Control+Option+Command+3. Figure 1-6 shows what your screen should look like with the Object Library visible.

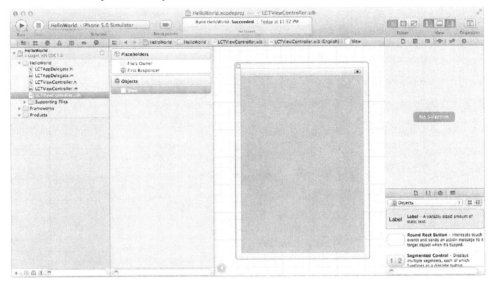

Figure 1-6. *The Xcode window using Interface Builder with the object library visible.*

To add an object to your view, either drag it from the Object Library to your view or double-click it. Drag two objects to your view: a Label and a Round Rect Button. Double-click the button to add a title; let's make this one read "Say Hello." Notice that the button resizes itself when you add the title. You can get labels and buttons to resize themselves to their content by pressing Command+=. Double-click the label and remove the text, and then make it stretch across the view. Once you remove the text, the label will appear to be invisible; if you can't find it, click Editor ➤ Canvas ➤ Show Bounds Rectangles, which will outline the label for you. When you're done, it should look something like Figure 1-7. If so, now is a good time to save your work. Xcode isn't perfect, and if it crashes, your unsaved changes go with it, so getting into a habit of saving often is recommended.

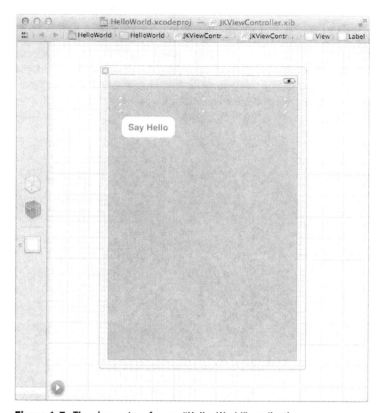

Figure 1-7. *The view set up for our "Hello, World" application*

Now let's add some code to this application. We want the label to say "Hello, World!" when the user presses the button. To do that, we'll add a *method* to our view controller. *Method* is Objective-C's word for function. If you're familiar with object-oriented programming, then methods will be familiar. If not, follow along in this chapter; we will discuss Objective-C later in much more detail.

The view controller's *header file* is a file that *describes* it. Headers are the "public" portion of your code; they describe what the code will do without actually showing how it works. When you receive source code that's already been compiled, typically you'll also receive the headers associated with it. In the file browser, select the file ending in ViewController.h with your prefix before it. In the header, we define the methods that we will create. By default, it should look like this (with some comments at the top):

```
//
//  LCTViewController.h
//  HelloWorld
//
//  Created by Jeff Kelley on 1/28/12.
//  Copyright (c) 2012 Jeff Kelley. All rights reserved.
//

#import <UIKit/UIKit.h>

@interface LCTViewController : UIViewController

@end
```

The first part of creating a method is *declaring* it, that is, telling the code that there will be a method. So, add this line between the @interface and @end lines and save your changes:

```
- (IBAction)sayHelloButtonPressed:(id)sender;
```

We'll go into more detail later on what each part of this line means. For now, you should know that the name of the method is sayHelloButtonPressed:. Now that we've declared it, we can go back to the view and tell our app to run our method when the button is pressed. Head back to the view by opening LCTViewController.xib and select the button. Open the right utilities pane to the Connections Inspector, either by clicking the rightmost icon at the top of the pane or by pressing Command+Option+6. You'll see a list of empty circles on the right side of the list under Sent Events. We're interested in the event Touch Up Inside. These events represent different points of interaction the user has with the button. When they first place their finger on the button, the Touch Down event occurs, and when they lift it, the Touch Up Inside event occurs. Typically on iOS, we use the Touch Up Inside event for user interaction; that way, the user can cancel pressing the button by moving their finger away.

To connect the Touch Up Inside event to the method we created, click the empty circle next to it and drag. We're connecting it to the object called File's Owner, which looks like a transparent box and is to the left of our view. With File's Owner highlighted, release the mouse button, and a list of methods will pop up. The method we created should be the only one in the list. Select it, and the button is now connected to the method. It should look like Figure 1-8.

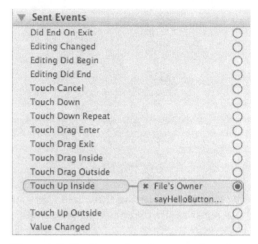

Figure 1-8. *The Connections Inspector view after we've connected the button to the method*

The next step is writing the code that will happen when we press the button. First, we need to create a way to get to the label from our code. Much like creating the method, we'll modify the header first and then connect the view to it. Modify the header to add this line:

```
#import <UIKit/UIKit.h>

@interface JKViewController : UIViewController {
        IBOutlet UILabel *helloWorldLabel;
}

- (IBAction)sayHelloButtonPressed:(id)sender;

@end
```

Now, we need to connect the label in our view to the IBOutlet we created. Select the label in your view, and then open the Connections Inspector. Drag the circle next to New Referencing Outlet to File's Owner and select helloWorldLabel. Now that we've done that, we can use helloWorldLabel in our code to refer to the label.

We have everything set up for our method, so let's create it. We define our methods in the view controller's *implementation* file, which ends in .m. Open the file and add the lines in bold:

```
#import "JKViewController.h"

@implementation JKViewController

// Other methods will be defined here
```

```
- (IBAction)sayHelloButtonPressed:(id)sender
{
        [helloWorldLabel setText:@"Hello, World!"];
}
```

@end

This code calls a method on your label, setText:, with the text "Hello, World!" Now that we've *implemented* our method, click Run again to run the application. Xcode will build the app and run it in the iOS Simulator. You'll see the button. Click it, and the label will say "Hello, World!"

Summary

While creating a "Hello, World!" app is an important beginner's task in any language, it's not going to sell too many copies in the App Store. It doesn't really access too many features of the device, and it doesn't push the envelope with an engaging user interface. It's a good step toward making a quality app, however, and that's what counts. In this chapter, we covered installing and using Xcode, as well as the beginnings of using it for programming. Now that we've created a simple app in Xcode, let's learn more about Objective-C, the programming language we'll be using throughout the book.

Chapter 2

Objective-C in a Nutshell

Objective-C is the primary language you'll be using to create iOS apps using Cocoa Touch. This chapter will walk you through the basics of the language, covering new developments in its evolution as well as tried-and-true methods that are decades old. In this book, I'm assuming that you have at least a basic understanding of the C programming language. If you're coming from a Java or C++ background, you can probably get by just fine, but if you're new to C-like languages altogether, I recommend familiarizing yourself with it. Some excellent books on the subject are *The C Programming Language* by Brian Kernighan and the late Dennis Ritchie, who originally designed the language; *Programming in C* by Stephen Kochan; *C Programming* by K. N. King; and *Learn C on the Mac* by Dave Mark.

Object-Oriented Programming

Objective-C is an object-oriented language, as are Java and C++, but Objective-C is unique in that it is a *superset* of C; that is, anything that is valid in C is also valid in Objective-C. C++ gets close, but not quite there. This means that if you already have code written in C, you can use it as is for iOS. You can also use existing C data structures, functions, and preprocessor macros. The more interesting parts, however, are those that Objective-C adds to turn C into an object-oriented programming language.

An *object* in Objective-C is used much like other data types (integers, floating-point values, characters, and so on) in C, but typically you'll use a pointer to refer to it. The following line is an example of creating an object in Objective-C:

```
NSString *myString = @"Hello, World!";
```

In that line, we created the object myString. Its *class*, or the *kind* of object it is, is NSString. myString is an *instance* of NSString. The asterisk (*) signifies that we're creating a pointer—technically speaking, myString isn't the object itself but rather a pointer *to* an instance of NSString.

> **NOTE:** We created myString as a constant string. The @ followed by a string in quotes signifies this to the compiler.

To declare a class, use the following syntax:

```
@interface ClassName : SuperClassName
```

The @interface is a *compiler directive*—that is, a special command to the compiler that gives it instructions on how to compile your code. In this case, @interface begins the class definition for a class. The SuperClassName is the name of another class from which the class you're creating will *inherit* variables and methods. The root object for most of the objects you'll create is NSObject (the *NS* stands for NeXTStep, NeXT's operating system). While there are technically other base classes, you're free to create your own. For now we'll use NSObject; it contains many functions that Cocoa Touch relies on.

> **NOTE:** The reason the *NS* prefix remains from NeXTStep has to do with the history of Mac OS X. Apple purchased NeXT Software, Inc., in 1996, and the NeXTStep operating system formed the basis of Mac OS X, introduced in 2001. iOS shares many of its system-level frameworks, including Objective-C and the Foundation framework, which contains NSObject and other essential classes, with Mac OS X, thereby inheriting the shared legacy of NeXTStep's *NS* prefix. One advantage of this is that in most cases, classes that begin with an *NS* prefix are also available on the Mac, so if you're interested in programming in Cocoa (the Mac OS X equivalent of Cocoa Touch), learning Cocoa Touch is a great first start.

To help explain this, we'll work toward a goal instead of talking in the abstract the whole time. Our goal is going to be to create an address book. Let's create a class that represents an entry in the address book. Each entry corresponds to an individual person, so we'll name the class Person:

```
@interface Person : NSObject
```

Now, what should we store in our address book? Obvious candidates are the person's first and last names. We can use the Objective-C class NSString that we used earlier to store those values as strings. To add variables, we use this syntax:

```
@interface Person : NSObject {
        NSString *firstName;
        NSString *lastName;
}

@end
```

There are a few new syntactical intrigues to cover in that last sample. First, note that variables are declared inside curly braces ({ and }). These variables are called *instance variables*, meaning that each *instance* of Person—that is, every Person object we create—will have firstName and lastName variables associated with it. Objective-C does not have class-level storage, so instance variables are the only kind you can create for an object. Second in our new syntaxes is the definition of the variables themselves; you'll notice the * character before their names. This declares those variables as a *pointer*. Instead of storing an NSString object, firstName is a *pointer to* an NSString object. This means that firstName contains the memory address of an NSString object. This may be a difficult concept to grasp at first, but for now, just remember to always refer to Objective-C objects with a pointer. You almost never need to refer to them without a pointer. Finally, notice the @end compiler directive; this signifies that the class definition is complete.

Objects can have primitive variables as instance variables. Suppose we want to store the person's birth year. We can store that as an integer. While int will work to declare an integer, just like in C, Apple platforms support the use of NSInteger, which is *not* an object. Instead, NSInteger is a way of defining an integer that's safer to use on different architectures. Don't worry about that for now; just know that NSInteger, despite the *NS* prefix, is not an object. Let's add a birth year to our Person object:

```
@interface Person : NSObject {
        NSString *firstName;
        NSString *lastName;
        NSInteger birthYear;
}

@end
```

Great. You can use any primitive C type as an instance variable in your Objective-C class, even custom structures, unions, and arrays.

So, how do we use this object we've created? We'll create an instance of our Person class and call it someone:

```
Person *someone = [[Person alloc] init];
```

The square brackets are usually the first thing programmers notice about Objective-C as being "weird" compared to other languages. This is how you send messages in Objective-C, with the pattern defined as [receiver message]. When you send a message, the Objective-C runtime looks up the corresponding method (if it exists) in the receiver's class and executes it. Message sending, therefore, is like calling a function, but with the key difference that in Objective-C the function isn't resolved until runtime. In the previous example, first we evaluate the inner message call: [Person alloc]. This is the alloc message sent to the Person class, which allocates enough memory for a new Person object and returns a pointer to it. The next message, init, is then sent to the object at the pointer returned by alloc. If we wanted, we could write it as follows:

```
Person *someone = [Person alloc];
someone = [someone init];
```

> **NOTE:** This pattern of calling alloc and init is common enough that Objective-C supports the new message to do both, but in practice, it isn't used. It is extremely rare to use one without the other, so unless you have a very good reason to do so (and even if you do), you probably shouldn't separate the calls.

Now that we've done this, we can use our new object. But what messages can we send it? Since Person inherits from NSObject, we can send it any message that NSObject defines, but nothing very exciting. Let's add a method to our class so that we can call it on our object. We add a method in the class declaration after the instance variables are declared (and outside of the curly brace) but before the @end symbol. We'll add a method called displayName, which will return the first and last names in one string. Note that method names start with a lowercase letter and use camelCase; this isn't a language requirement, just a convention. Similarly, it's named displayName, not getDisplayName as you might see in other languages. Here's what the declaration looks like:

```
@interface Person : NSObject {
        NSString *firstName;
        NSString *lastName;
        NSInteger birthYear;
}

- (NSString *)displayName;
```

```
@end
```

The first character is a hyphen (-) because `displayName` is an *instance method*, that is, a message that you send to an *instance* of a class. *Class methods*, which you call on the class directly (like `alloc`) begin with a plus (+). Next, in parentheses, is the return type of the method. We're returning a pointer to an `NSString` object in this method. Finally, we have the name, ending with a semicolon. This method doesn't take any parameters—we'll get to methods that take parameters later.

To implement any of this, even an empty class with no methods, we need to define the *implementation* of our class. We made the *interface* with the `@interface` compiler directive, so it should come as no surprise that the implementation begins with `@implementation`. Here's how we implement our class, as well as the method:

```
@implementation Person

- (NSString *)displayName
{
    NSString *name = [NSString stringWithFormat:@"%@, %@", lastName, firstName];

    return name;
}

@end
```

We've written our interface and implementation pieces for this class, but we haven't actually *done* anything with them yet. Let's change that. Open your "Hello, World!" example project and click File ➤ New ➤ File... (or, just press ⌘+N). When the new file dialog appears, select Cocoa Touch in the left column and then Objective-C Class on the right (see Figure 2-1).

Figure 2-1. *The new file dialog*

On the next screen, enter **Person** for Class and **NSObject** for Subclass of. Click Next, and then choose the path (the default should be fine for now). (See Figure 2-2.)

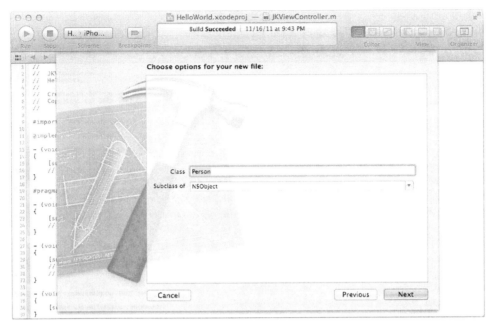

Figure 2-2. *Filling in class information in the new file dialog*

Xcode has been nice enough to fill in some basic things for us in two files:
Person.h and Person.m. The former, Person.h, is the *header file* and is where we
place our @interface block. The latter, Person.m, is the *implementation file*
(hence the *m* in the file name) and contains our @implementation block. To fill in
the rest of the class, open Person.h and add the lines in bold:

```
//
//  Person.h
//  HelloWorld
//
//  Created by Jeff Kelley on 1/28/12.
//  Copyright (c) 2012 Jeff Kelley. All rights reserved.
//

#import <Foundation/Foundation.h>

@interface Person : NSObject  {
    NSString *firstName;
    NSString *lastName;
    NSInteger birthYear;
}

- (NSString *)displayName;
```

```
@end
```

Next, open `Person.m` and add the implementation for `displayName` (in bold):

```
//
//  Person.m
//  HelloWorld
//
//  Created by Jeff Kelley on 1/28/12.
//  Copyright (c) 2012 Jeff Kelley. All rights reserved.
//

#import "Person.h"

@implementation Person

- (NSString *)displayName
{
    NSString *name = [NSString stringWithFormat:@"%@, %@", lastName,
firstName];

    return name;
}

@end
```

We'll want to modify our application to display the result of the `displayName` method instead of "Hello, World!" To do that, however, we need to be able to see the first and last names of a `Person` object. One way to do this is by creating a new `init` method. This will be called the *designated initializer* of our class, that is, the initializer that we'll use when creating new `Person` objects by default. This method will take three parameters: the first name, the last name, and the birth year. Here's how we declare the method in our interface. Add the following method declaration to `Person.h`, before the declaration for `displayName`:

```
- (id)initWithFirstName:(NSString *)firstName lastName:(NSString *)lastName
birthYear:(NSInteger)birthYear;
```

You may notice that the return type is id, *not* a pointer to an object like you might expect. Actually, id *is* just a pointer to an object; it's a good stand-in for when you can use any object. We use it in the `init` methods so that if we create a class that inherits from `Person`, we don't have to redefine the return type. We can also split this declaration into multiple lines to look better. (By convention, we align the colons, which Xcode will do for you automatically if you press the Return key to insert a carriage return before the parameter name. If you modify the text and find it misaligned, Xcode will correct your alignment if you select the code and press Control+I.)

```objc
- (id)initWithFirstName:(NSString *)firstName
              lastName:(NSString *)lastName
             birthYear:(NSInteger)birthYear;
```

You may also have noticed that the three parameters have text before the colon, the type in parentheses, and then a name. The part before the colon is actually part of the method's name. We would call this method `initWithFirstName:lastName:birthYear:`. The three parameters are named according to the text after their type until a space. To implement the method, add the following lines to `Person.m` before the @end compiler directive:

```objc
- (id)initWithFirstName:(NSString *)fName
              lastName:(NSString *)lName
             birthYear:(NSInteger)bYear
{
    self = [super init];

    if (self) {
        firstName = fName;
        lastName = lName;
        birthYear = bYear;
    }

    return self;
}
```

> **NOTE:** In the implementation, I changed the names of the method's parameters in order to avoid a conflict with the names of the instance variables. One convention to get around this is to prefix your instance variables with an underscore (_). Be careful, however; prefixing *anything* with two underscores is reserved for Apple and may break your app in mysterious ways if you accidentally choose a name that Apple has already used. Because Objective-C lacks namespaces, this can happen even if you don't use a double-underscore prefix, so you must be careful to avoid repeating names.

The first line of this method has two names you haven't seen yet: `self` and `super`. Since this is an instance method (it operates on an *instance* of `Person`), `self` refers to the instance that received the message. `super` refers to the class that `Person` inherits from—in this case, `NSObject`. This isn't calling a class method, however; when you call `[super init]`, you're sending the message to the same object that received the current message, but you're using the `init` method from its superclass. We assign this value back to `self` in case the superclass's implementation returns a modified value.

The next piece of code checks to see whether self is not nil and, if it isn't, sets the instance variables according to the parameters. Finally, it returns self. We can use this method in our code like so:

```
Person *person = [[Person alloc] initWithFirstName:@"Jeff"
                                          lastName:@"Kelley"
                                         birthYear:1986];
```

This creates and returns a new instance of Person with my name and birth year. Calling [person displayName] will return the string "Kelley, Jeff." Let's put this to use. In your "Hello, World!" example project from Chapter 1, open the main view controller implementation file (LCTViewController.m). At the top, add this line:

```
#import "Person.h"
```

This lets us use our Person class in this file. Without importing the header, the compiler won't know about the class. Now, modify the method called sayHelloButtonPressed: to create a Person:

```
- (IBAction)sayHelloButtonPressed:(id)sender
{
    Person *person = [[Person alloc] initWithFirstName:@"Jeff"
                                              lastName:@"Kelley"
                                             birthYear:1986];
    [helloWorldLabel setText:[person displayName]];
}
```

Build and run the application. When you click the Hello, World! button, the text field should display the person's name formatted as "Last Name, First Name."

Getting and Setting Data

One thing you may notice about our Person class is that there's no way to get to the instance variables (firstName, lastName, and birthYear) from outside the class. To get these variables and set them, we can add some methods to the class. Open Person.h and add these methods before the @end directive:

```
@interface Person : NSObject  {
    NSString *firstName;
    NSString *lastName;
    NSInteger birthYear;
}

- (id)initWithFirstName:(NSString *)firstName
               lastName:(NSString *)lastName
              birthYear:(NSInteger)birthYear;
```

```
- (NSString *)firstName;
- (NSString *)lastName;
- (NSInteger)birthYear;
- (NSString *)displayName;
```

@end

There's no issue of a name conflict with the name of the method being the same as the name of the instance variable. To implement these methods, add the following code to `Person.m`:

```
@implementation Person

- (id)initWithFirstName:(NSString *)fName
               lastName:(NSString *)lName
              birthYear:(NSInteger)bYear
{
    self = [super init];

    if (self) {
        firstName = fName;
        lastName = lName;
        birthYear = bYear;
    }

    return self;
}


- (NSString *)displayName
{
    NSString *name = [NSString stringWithFormat:@"%@, %@", lastName, firstName];

    return name;
}


- (NSString *)firstName
{
    return firstName;
}

- (NSString *)lastName
{
    return lastName;
}

- (NSInteger)birthYear
{
    return birthYear;
```

```
}
```

```
@end
```

Now we can get the first name from a `Person` by sending it the `firstName` message. To be able to *set* the values, we'll define some other methods. Add the following method declarations to `Person.h`:

```objc
@interface Person : NSObject  {
    NSString *firstName;
    NSString *lastName;
    NSInteger birthYear;
}

- (id)initWithFirstName:(NSString *)firstName
               lastName:(NSString *)lastName
              birthYear:(NSInteger)birthYear;

- (NSString *)firstName;
- (void)setFirstName:(NSString *)firstName;
- (NSString *)lastName;
- (void)setLastName:(NSString *)lastName;
- (NSInteger)birthYear;
- (void)setBirthYear:(NSInteger)birthYear;
- (NSString *)displayName;

@end
```

The convention is to prepend `set` to the name of the variable, with the first letter capitalized. Implementing these is also straightforward, but we have to rename the parameter to avoid it having the same name as the instance variable. There's a lot of back-and-forth between the header and the implementation file in Objective-C. One thing that can help, if your Mac's display is wide enough, is the Assistant editor in Xcode. Open `Person.m` and select View ➤ Assistant Editor ➤ Show Assistant Editor, or press ⌘+Control+Return. A secondary editing pane will open on the right side of the screen. If the Assistant Editor doesn't have `Person.h` open, press ⌘+Shift+Option+Z to switch to Counterparts mode, which will automatically open the header file for the implementation you're looking at. Now that you have both files open, adding a method declaration in your header and then implementing it in your implementation file is much easier. With `Person.h` open, add the implementations for our three setter methods:

```objc
- (void)setFirstName:(NSString *)name
{
    firstName = name;
}
```

```
- (void)setLastName:(NSString *)name
{
    lastName = name;
}

- (void)setBirthYear:(NSInteger)year
{
    birthYear = year;
}
```

@end

While creating these methods is easy enough, it's tedious. There's a lot of typing and switching files, and if you want to change the name of something, there are a lot of places where you need to do so. When Objective-C was in its early years, this was the best it got. Some developers would use third-party applications to create these methods to get and set their instance variables, which is a sign of how tedious it was. Thankfully, Apple added some new features to the language to make this easier.

Properties

Properties are a way to define accessor methods in your class. Instead of defining a getter and a setter for an instance variable, you can use a property to do so. Here's an example of a property:

`@property (nonatomic, copy) NSString *firstName;`

The declaration tells us a few things. First, it tells us the type and name of the variable. This line in the header is the equivalent of these two lines:

```
- (NSString *)firstName;
- (void)setFirstName:(NSString *)firstName;
```

With the property declared, we can refer to these methods (and implement them) without declaring them by name. Second, the words in the parentheses define some information about how the variable is used. We use nonatomic to define access rules for threading. It's not important to learn now, but in general atomic is safer for multithreaded applications but slower than nonatomic. Most of the time, you'll use nonatomic. The next word is copy, which indicates that we'll make a copy of the string when setting it. We typically use copy for strings to ensure that the string is not modified after we set it. Instead of copy, there are some things we can use for memory management, but we'll discuss that in a bit. You can also pass a third word, either readonly or readwrite. If you use readonly, then the setter will not be created (readwrite is the default). For future reference, Table 2-1 lists the attributes you can set (the bold options are the default).

Table 2-1. *Attributes for Objective-C Properties*

Memory Management Semantics	Read/Write Semantics	Atomicity
`assign`	`readwrite`	Atomic
weak (iOS 5+ with ARC enabled and Xcode 4.2 or newer) __unsafe_unretained (iOS 4.3 and older and Xcode 4.2 or newer)	readonly	Nonatomic
strong (iOS 5+ and Xcode 4.2 or newer) retain (iOS 4.3 and older)		
copy		

As you can see, weak, __unsafe_unretained, and strong all require Xcode 4.2. To use weak, you must be using ARC, which is a type of memory management automation. We'll discuss ARC in more detail in just a bit.

You can also define the names for the getter and setter methods if you want to change them. If you don't, then they will be assumed to be the default names, but if, for instance, your variable is a Boolean type (BOOL), then you might want the getter to use the word is. This is such a property declaration line in a header:

```
@property (getter = isFoo) BOOL foo;
```

This line is the equivalent of the following lines:

```
- (BOOL)isFoo;
- (void)setFoo:(BOOL)foo;
```

Similarly, if you want to change the name of the setter methods, you can use setter = with the name you'd like to use (though this is rare in practice). Using the attributes, you can use properties to declare most, if not all, of the accessor methods your objects will need.

Writing Your Code for You

Properties are nice, but they only take care of the method declaration for you. There's still the matter of *implementing* the methods with boilerplate code that just sets the variables as needed. Luckily, when Apple added properties to the language, it also added a way to implement these methods: the @synthesize compiler directive. Inside an implementation block, you can use @synthesize to tell the compiler to generate those methods for you. It will use the property attributes you set to generate the methods appropriately. If you don't have an instance variable to store the property, using @synthesize will create one for you. The following class is an object with one property, completely implemented without explicitly implementing a single method:

```
@interface BoolWrapper: NSObject {
    BOOL _value;
}
@property BOOL value;
@end

@implementation BoolWrapper
@synthesize value = _value;
@end
```

This defines a BOOL property value, using the instance variable _value as storage for the value. If we had omitted declaring _value as an instance variable, the @synthesize line would have created it for us. We can send an instance of BoolWrapper the value and setValue: messages, never having written them. This is where properties really shine. Not only do you not have to implement boilerplate code, but if you ever need to refactor your code, it makes it much easier. It also makes your code much less likely to have errors in it, since the code generated by the compiler is very well-tested—and the compiler doesn't make typos or get tired.

Memory Management

Memory is a precious resource on iOS devices. The original iPhone had 128MB of RAM, most of which was used by the OS. Four years later, the iPhone 4S has 512MB of RAM, still much less than modern systems running Mac OS X. That being the case, how we use the memory available to us is very important. While this section might not be exciting, understanding how memory management on iOS works is crucial to troubleshooting performance problems.

The memory on the device is split up into two types: stack memory and heap memory. The *stack* is filled up as your code executes; when one function calls another, it *pushes* a *stack frame* onto the stack: its local variables and storage required for it. When the function is done, that stack frame is *popped* off of the stack, and that space is reclaimed for future use. Stack space is very limited, and when you run out, the program crashes, having caused a *stack overflow* (hence the name of the popular programming Q&A site). While stack memory is convenient, there's a huge drawback: when the stack frame is popped, everything on it disappears. This doesn't really work well with objects. Typically, when we create an object in a method, we'll want that object to still be available after that method completes. If the object is created on the stack, though, it will be destroyed at the end of the method.

For this reason, all Objective-C objects are created on the *heap*. While it's possible to manually override object creation and create objects on the stack, in practice this is unnecessary. *Heap memory* is different from stack memory in that we have to request it from the operating system. In C, we use the `malloc()` function to allocate a portion of memory. You may notice the similarity with the `alloc` message you sent to your classes to create new objects.

Unlike the stack, the heap does not clean itself up once we're done; all memory allocated with `malloc()` must be cleared with `free()`. Once you free a block of memory that you've manually allocated, that space is once again available for use. Objects are created on the heap, as well, but it's more difficult than allocating arbitrary memory. We know we want objects to stick around, but how can we tell how long they should stick around for in order to free their memory?

Garbage Collection

One way to do this is called *garbage collection*. Java, used on Android and other managed systems, uses garbage collection, which works by keeping track of your objects and periodically destroying them when it can tell that they're no longer being used. While this sounds easy, there's a trade-off: your app is paused while the garbage collector runs, causing performance issues. There are some ways to mitigate that, but none of them is perfect. Another problem is that if two objects reference one another, the garbage collector can't tell when they are no longer used, because either one might be using the other. This is called a *retain cycle*, and the net effect is large swaths of memory taken up by unusable objects. Apple briefly introduced garbage collection into Objective-C on Mac OS X with mixed results, and today its use is discouraged.

Reference Counting

Objective-C uses another method for keeping track of objects: *reference counting*. Reference counting works by counting the number of references there are to an object and destroying the object when that number reaches 0. In Objective-C, this is called the *retain count* of the object. All objects start their life with a retain count of 1, and when it reaches 0, the object is destroyed, and its memory is returned to the system. Here is an example of a typical retain-counting scenario:

```
- (void)doSomething
{
    MyObject *foo = [[MyObject alloc] init];

    [foo doAnImportantTask];

    [foo release];
}
```

In this example, foo is created with a retain count of 1; then before we're done, we send it the release message, which decrements the retain count. One crucial thing to note, however, is that we don't actually *know* that foo will be destroyed at this point. Before sending it the release message, we sent foo the doAnImportantTask message. In that method, foo could have been retained (by being sent the retain message), which increments its retain count. The general rule is that in any given method, we have to balance calls to retain and release. Since allocating foo gave it a retain count of 1, we sent it the release message to go down to 0 before the method finished. We need to release an object only if we have retained it or created it. In Cocoa Touch, there is a naming convention that indicates when you need to release an object: if the method name begins with alloc, new, copy, or create, then it is expected that the object will be returned with a +1 retain count, and you will need to release it when you're done. All other methods should return objects that do not need releasing.

Autorelease Pools

While reference counting systems are effective, sometimes you want to return an object and release it at the same time. You often see class methods that are factories for an object:

```
+ (MyObject *)object;
```

The object method returns an instance of MyObject, but since its name doesn't begin with a prefix that indicates ownership, we shouldn't return an object with a +1 retain count. To get around that, object is implemented thusly:

```
 + (MyObject *)object
{
    MyObject *object = [[MyObject alloc] init];

    return [object autorelease];
}
```

At first glance, this seems like `object` will be deallocated immediately: it's created with a retain count of 1 and then sent an `autorelease` message, with seems like something that would decrement its retain count, causing it to go to 0 and be deallocated. Autoreleasing an object *does* decrement its retain count...just not yet. It's not too important *when* the object is actually released, because that depends on how busy the system is and how your code is written, but the important thing is that it won't happen until your stack frames are gone, so autoreleased objects are OK to use for the duration of the method.

Automatic Reference Counting

Looking back at the code we wrote for the "Hello, World!" sample application, you may notice something: you never called `retain` or `release` on an object. In fact, there's no memory management code in them at all! Consider yourself a very lucky person; you're learning memory management in an era where all the code is written for you.

Just as properties and `@synthesize` write your getters and setters for you, automatic reference counting writes your memory management code for you. How does it work? Consider the general goal of balancing calls to `retain` and `release`. Generally speaking, an object's retain count should be the same at the end of a method as it is at the beginning of the method. What automatic reference counting (ARC) does is to retain objects when a pointer to them is created and release objects when that pointer falls out of scope. This code:

```
{
    MyObject *object = [MyObject object];
}
```

will produce this code through ARC:

```
{
    MyObject *object = [[MyObjet object] retain];
    [object release];
}
```

ARC knows which methods return already retained objects and deals with those accordingly. It can even use its knowledge of the memory management code to optimize an app's memory usage and speed execution. The calls to retain and release that it generates are also faster than the messages you would send. All in all, ARC, like properties, transfers work from you, the programmer, to the compiler. And believe me, the less time you spend writing memory management code, the better. The largest portion of crashes on pre-ARC iOS applications is incorrect memory management code. Consider this fragment:

```
- (void)importantTask
```

```
{
    MyObject *object = [[MyObject alloc] init];

    [object doSomething];
    [object release];

    [object doSomethingElse];
}
```

Assuming that doSomething does not incorrectly retain object, we have a problem. The call to release will cause object's retain count to go to 0, destroying it, but *after* that, we call doSomethingElse on object. Since object is just a *pointer* to an object, it still has the memory address of the object stored in it. If you try to access that memory, the system knows that it's already taken it back from you. Since you aren't allowed to access memory that the system has not given to you, this call to doSomethingElse causes the application to crash. ARC nearly eliminates these types of errors, saving untold hours of developer heartache.

ARC and Properties

One thing you do need to understand about memory management with ARC is how to use it with properties. One category of attributes you can set on a property is its memory management semantics. Using the attribute strong will cause the property to be retained when it's set and not released until the object is deallocated. This is the most common use of properties. One common problem, however, is that if two objects have a strong reference to one another, neither will ever be released, just like with garbage collection. The solution is for one of them to have a reference to the other but *not* retain it. Before iOS 5, the assign attribute was used for this. The trouble here, though, is that if you use assign, you can have a reference to an object after it's been released, crashing the app when you try to use it. In iOS 5, Apple introduced the weak attribute, which is a reference to an object that does not retain it. When the referenced object is deallocated, however, the weak reference goes away, so you can't try to call methods on deallocated objects. Weak references allow you to temporarily store pointers to objects without worrying about affecting their life cycle or being affected by it.

When a weak referenced object is destroyed, all weak pointers to it are set to nil, Objective-C's equivalent to a null object. Sending messages to nil is OK, so with weak references, you don't need to check to see if the reference points to an object. Messages sent to nil that return a return value will return nil for all object types and 0 for all primitive types.

Categories

Sometimes, instead of writing your own class, you just want to add a method to an existing class. Let's say, for instance, that you want a quick way to double a string by appending it to itself. It would be nice if you could write the following code:

```
NSString *myString = @"Hello, World!";
NSString *doubleString = [myString doubleString];
```

Unfortunately, the doubleString method does not exist on NSString. One way to get it would be to create a subclass of NSString that implements the method. This isn't perfect, however, because then we have to replace our NSStrings with the subclass everywhere we want to use the new method. Fortunately, Objective-C categories allow us to add the method to the *existing* class! Here's how we would create a category:

```
@interface NSString (DoubleString)
- (NSString *)doubleString;
@end
```

This looks like creating a new class, but instead of the superclass, we specify a category name—in this case, DoubleString. Then, in our implementation, we specify the same name:

```
@implementation NSString (DoubleString)
- (NSString *)doubleString
{
    return [self stringByAppendingString:self];
}
@end
```

Note that we can still access self while in the category. Categories make it very easy to extend classes without modifying the original class or subclassing them. Another useful thing you can do with categories is to use them to separate functionality. If you have an object that can be used in a Mac OS X app as well as an iOS app, for instance, you might have one category that draws it on-screen on a Mac and another for iOS. One example of Apple doing this is the UIKitAdditions category on NSString, which has plenty of useful methods for determining how a string will be drawn on iOS. Since NSString is shared between Mac OS X and iOS and those methods are useful only on the latter, a category is a good way to separate those concerns.

Categories are not without risk, however. In the previous example where we implemented the doubleString method, we made an important assumption: that there was not already a doubleString method declared on NSString. If there was, then one of the implementations would override the other, which is clearly not what we want. Even worse, it's not always clear *which* implementation will "win," so you don't even know what code is running! Another scenario that we want to avoid is the case where Apple also decides to add the same functionality. If, in a future iOS release, Apple added the `doubleString` method, the same problem would occur. To avoid this, it's always considered a best practice to declare your category methods using a prefix. In this case, I would change `doubleString` to `LCT_doubleString`. While this isn't quite as elegant, it serves the important purpose of protecting the code from being broken by somebody else's. The naming convention for category files is `<ClassName>+<CategoryName>.[h/m]`. For our string doubling category, we could name the files `NSString+Doubling.h` and `NSString+Doubling.m`.

> **NOTE:** One other caveat of categories is that you cannot declare new instance variables in a category. This would change the internal memory layout of the object, and since the original class can't always be recompiled, we can't modify the layout of its memory.

Class Extensions

Unlike other languages, Objective-C does not offer private methods. Any method can be called at any time by anyone. In fact, it's possible to query an object at runtime and obtain a list of every method that can be called on it. That being said, there is still some usefulness in hiding a method from other developers. Generally speaking, any method declared in your header file should be a method that can be called from other classes on your object. If you want to declare a method that is only to be used inside your class, you can do so with a special type of category: a class extension. Since we don't want this to be public, the interface declaration of the class extension goes in the implementation (`.m`) file for your class, not the header (`.h`). Here's an example of a class extension being declared:

```
@interface MyClass()
- (void)superSecretMethod;
@end
```

As you can see, a class extension is declared with the class name and then an empty set of parentheses. Unlike with categories, you are allowed to define new instance variables in a class extension, making them a good place to store internal variables that you don't want to expose outside of the class.

> **NOTE:** Like methods, there is no way to truly make an instance variable secret. It is possible to query an object at runtime and obtain a list of its instance variables.

The methods that you declare in a class extension are implemented alongside the regular methods for the class. A typical implementation file with a class extension might look like this:

```
#import "MyClass.h"

@interface MyClass() {
    NSString *secretString;
}
- (void)mySuperSecretMethod;
@end

@implementation MyClass
- (void)mySuperSecretMethod
{
    // Implement super-secret method here.
}
…
@end
```

Protocols

When programming with more than one developer, often you'll be working on two classes simultaneously that, while separate from one another in many respects, need to work together to accomplish a task. This is where header files come in; one developer creates the header file for the class, and the other looks at the header to determine what methods are available. Often, though, you won't care about the other class, other than what you need to know in order to work with it. Protocols are a way to abstract a group of methods away from a class. When we create a protocol, we define a list of methods. Objects that *conform* to this protocol must then implement those methods. One common example is one class sending a message to another class when it has finished a long-running task. Let's create a class called Worker with a long-running task:

```
@interface Worker: NSObject
- (void)longRunningTask;
@end
```

What we want to happen is for the worker to notify some other object when the task is complete. In Objective-C, it's common to refer to these helper objects as *delegates*. The practice of using them is called *delegation*, and it's one of the more common design patterns used in Objective-C. To create the protocol, we'll create a new header file, WorkerDelegate.h:

```
// WorkerDelegate.h

@class Worker;

@protocol WorkerDelegate
@required
- (void)workerDidFinish:(Worker *)worker;
@end
```

> **NOTE:** The @class compiler directive is called a *forward declaration*. This allows us to use the Worker class without actually importing the Worker class's header file. In general, it's better to import as few headers as needed; whenever any header your implementation files includes is changed, the file will need to be recompiled, even if its contents are unchanged. Even without the compile-time speedup, it's better to avoid including unneeded headers to keep your code clean and organized.

The compiler directive @protocol signifies the creation of a protocol, with the name following. The naming convention is to capitalize the first letter and to use camelCase throughout. Next, we use @required to indicate that any methods following *must* be implemented by objects that conform to the WorkerDelegate protocol. You can also use @optional to signify methods that are declared but do not need to be implemented. Methods are now declared as optional by default, which wasn't always an option. Because of that prior limitation, some older classes use "informal protocols," which aren't protocols in the language sense of the word. Informal protocols are simply one or more methods that you can implement in your code to be called from other objects, like a regular protocol, but aren't enforced by any header.

Conforming to Protocols

To conform to a protocol, we create a list after the declaration of a class. We'll create a new class, Delegate, to conform to the protocol:

```
#import "WorkerDelegate.h"

@interface Delegate : NSObject <WorkerDelegate>

@end
```

The syntax is to use angle brackets (< and >) to indicate the beginning and end of the list of protocols the class conforms to; multiple protocols are separated by a comma and space. If you create a new class and leave its header like that without implementing the required method, you'll get a compiler warning that you haven't yet implemented the `workerDidFinish:` method.

> **NOTE:** It is common practice to group all of a protocol's methods together in your implementation file for a class that conforms to the protocol.

Next, we need to modify `Worker` to store a pointer to the delegate:

```
#import "WorkerDelegate.h"

@interface Worker : NSObject

@property (weak) id <WorkerDelegate> delegate;

@end
```

Typically delegates are created with type `id`, since we don't care what kind of object it is, only that it conforms to the `WorkerDelegate` protocol. Then, in our long-running task method, we can use the delegate like so:

```
- (void)longRunningTask
{
    // Perform task.

    [[self delegate] workerDidFinish:self];
}
```

Protocols allow you to keep your code clean and separate different areas of functionality in your classes. Apple uses protocols all over Cocoa Touch, especially using the delegation design pattern, so they are something every iOS developer should know extremely well.

Model-View-Controller Programming: Well-Designed Code

The design philosophy behind much of Apple's code (and, in fact, much *modern* code) is called Model-View-Controller (MVC). MVC dictates a separation of your code between the *model*, or the *data* that your application deals with; the *view*, or the *presentation* of that data; and the *controller*, which mediates between the two. Consider, for instance, an address book. In an address book, the *model* is the address data: people, addresses, phone numbers, and so on. The *view* is the layout of the app: lists of people, buttons for editing information, and so on. The belief behind MVC is that the model code should never have any view code in it. If, for instance, you're writing a cross-platform address book, then the code that draws the window for the address book on Mac OS X should not be in the model code, nor should the code to draw it on iOS. On the other hand, code that affects the model should not be in the view; while the view might display an alphabetized list of people, it should not contain code for changing someone's name. Figure 2-3 illustrates the separate nature of the MVC paradigm.

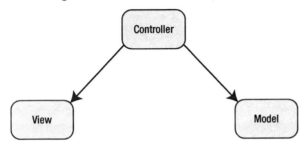

Figure 2-3. *The separation of concerns in the Model-View-Controller paradigm*

The benefits of MVC programming often occur not when writing an app for the first time but when adding features to it. By turning your code into more modular pieces, it's easier for it to be modified or swapped. The more modular the code, the easier this is. If tomorrow Apple were to release an API for writing apps for the Apple TV, you wouldn't want to have to sift through iOS button-creating code to get important pieces of the address book for an Apple TV version. In general, assume that the view can be anything: a screen on iOS, a window on Mac OS X, a web site, or perhaps even output on a physical LCD screen! If your model code concentrates on storing data and your view code concentrates on displaying data to the user and receiving input from the user, your code will have a head start on the road to greatness.

MVC is achieved using the *controller*, an invisible intermediary between the model and view. The controller reads the first and last names from the model and sends them to the view, as well as receiving user input in the view and updating the model accordingly. Controllers are the least-reusable portion of MVC code, because they're often tied both to the model code and to the view code. iOS uses the concept of controllers so much that Apple has created a special class for them: `UIViewController`. We'll discuss view controllers more in-depth as we build our first real app in the next chapter.

Summary

In this chapter, we went over the basics of Objective-C. You should now be comfortable creating classes, declaring and implementing methods, using properties, and conforming to protocols, as well as using Xcode and the other developer tools to achieve these goals. Thanks to ARC, you'll also be writing perfect memory-management code, since you won't be writing any! Your "Hello, World!" example project from Chapter 1 now has a Person class in it that you've used to display a sample person. You should also be starting to think about the Model-View-Controller paradigm to get ready for Chapter 3.

Managing On-Screen Content with View Controllers

By and large, iOS apps deal with their content one screen at a time. The Contacts app, for instance, has a list of contacts on one screen. It has one function: to display a list of contacts. When you tap a contact, another screen of content is displayed, this time detailing the contact you selected. Safari displays one web page at a time, the Settings app displays one group of settings at a time, and Mail displays a folder at a time and then displays one message when you select it. This trend of displaying content one screenful at a time is necessary when dealing with screens as small as the iPhone's; with a resolution of only 320x480, there simply isn't much room for multiple groups of information.

The screens that do appear in iOS applications have some common features. Often the application has a navigation bar at the top with the name of the screen that's being displayed and a Back button on the left side. Other apps use a black tab bar on the bottom to switch between different screens. Some behaviors are common to all screens of content: loading them when they're needed, disposing of them when they aren't, and presenting them to the user. This common behavior and these common tasks are encapsulated in one of the most important classes in all of Cocoa Touch: `UIViewController`. A view controller manages a single view, usually a screenful of content. This view can have many subviews in a complex hierarchy, but a view controller deals directly with one view—its view property—as its primary piece of content.

In this chapter, we'll take a tour through UIViewController, learning how and when to use them, as well as some subclasses of it in UIKit that allow you to take advantage of framework code instead of writing it yourself. We'll cover all of the major types of view controllers, as well as the nib loading system that loads user interfaces for the view controllers from files that you create. We'll also start MyStuff, an app that we'll be working on for a few chapters that serves as a home inventory system.

View Controller Life Cycle

The life cycle of a view controller begins when your app creates one. You might think that as part of its creation process, the view controller creates its view. In fact, to preserve memory, the view is created only at the last possible second; if you were to create 1,000 view controllers but display only one to the user, only one view would be created. Creating a view controller is easy:

```
UIViewController *viewController = [[UIViewController alloc]
initWithNibName:@"MyViewController" nibBundle:nil];
```

The "nib name" portion of that refers to one of the more powerful tools at your disposal as a Cocoa Touch developer: Interface Builder. Formerly a stand-alone application outside of Xcode, Interface Builder now refers to the interface you see in Xcode when working on your app's UI. A nib, which today has the .xib file extension, is a view that's been archived in XML onto the disk. When the view controller needs its view, it opens that XML file and loads the view from it. The real strength of Interface Builder–created nibs, however, is the way you create them. Instead of writing tedious UI layout code wherein you manually position every element of your view hierarchy, Interface Builder allows you to manually drag and drop user interface elements into a live representation of your view, as you can see in Figure 3-1. You can modify the view's properties directly, tweaking settings with immediate visual feedback of how it's going to look in your app.

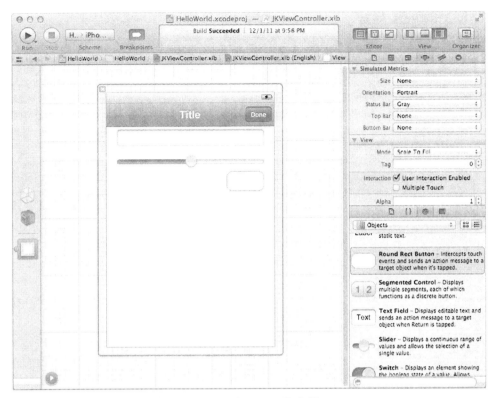

Figure 3-1. *Using Interface Builder to create a view controller's UI*

Laying out your views without writing a line of code is convenient enough, but Interface Builder goes a step further. When you create a view and add it to your interface, sometimes you need a pointer to it in your code. Other times, especially with user interface elements like buttons, sliders, and switches, you need the view to call a method when it's pressed or its value changes. Interface Builder uses two special keywords to denote these use cases: IBOutlet and IBAction. An IBOutlet is a pointer that will get filled in when the nib is loaded. To create one, simply add IBOutlet to your property declaration:

```
@property (strong, nonatomic) IBOutlet UILabel *titleLabel;
```

> **NOTE:** You can also use the IBOutlet keyword when declaring instance variables.

One you've defined the outlet, you can use Interface Builder to "fill it in." Simply hold Control and drag from File's Owner on the left side of the view to your outlet, as shown in Figure 3-2. This makes the connection between the view and your code. Now, when the nib is loaded, it will call setTitleLabel: on your view controller with the label you've created.

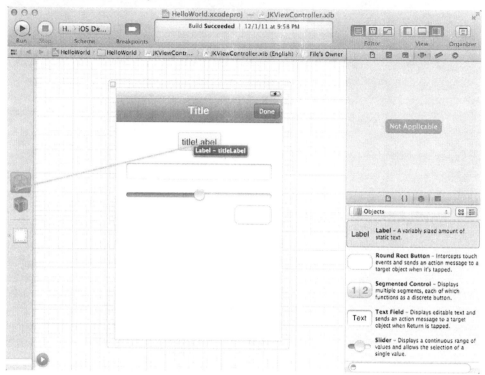

Figure 3-2. *Connecting the view controller to the title label*

Using IBOutlets allows us to change user interface elements dynamically, making them essential to effective UI design. When we need to go from the UI to the code, we use IBActions. Replace void with IBAction as the return type for your method:

```
- (IBAction)doneButtonPressed:(id)sender;
```

The parameter on the method, sender, will be a pointer to the button that was pressed. Just like you connected your view controller to the title to connect the title label to its property, you connect from the button to the view controller to connect it to the method. Xcode will automatically link the method to the proper control event and call your method when the user presses it.

Once your view has been created in Interface Builder and loaded into the view controller's view property, the rest of the view controller life cycle begins. Not all view controllers' views are created in Interface Builder, however. If you prefer to create the view in code, you can implement the loadView method in your subclass of UIViewController and do it there. Sometimes creating your views in code is easier, especially if their contents are highly dynamic or if you use many custom subclasses of UIView.

Regardless of how you load the view, the next step in the life cycle is the viewDidLoad method. You can use this method to do any further setup of your view needs, such as filling in labels with values from your objects or starting a network request.

> **NOTE:** In all of the view controller life cycle methods that you implement in UIViewController subclasses, be sure to call the superclass's implementation. For viewDidLoad, for instance, you'd call [super viewDidLoad].

There are a few more places where you can customize your view controller's behavior. The life cycle methods viewWillAppear:, viewDidAppear:, viewWillDisappear:, and viewDidDisappear: are fairly self-explanatory. Typically, if you're going to perform custom animations when your view appears on the screen, you do that in the viewWillAppear: method and then begin the animations in the viewDidAppear: method. If your view has long-running or repeating animations, you might stop them in viewDidDisappear:. Most of the time you can get away without implementing these methods, but they're always available if you need them.

When the view is unloaded, your view controller subclass will receive the viewDidUnload message. This is one of the more important methods to override in a view controller, because one view controller might load and unload its view multiple times in its life. Anything you set up in viewDidLoad must be reversed, as well as anything that was set up in the nib, such as your outlets. Before iOS 5, it was necessary to set all of your outlets to nil in your viewDidUnload method to release them when your view was released. If you're using ARC and targeting only iOS 5 and newer, you can use a weak reference for your IBOutlets:

```
@property (weak) IBOutlet UILabel *myLabel;
```

Once your view is deallocated, the label will be released, and when it in turn is deallocated, the weak pointer to it is reset to nil. This allows you to avoid having huge implementations of viewDidUnload just to release all of your outlets. Xcode will set these outlets to nil in your viewDidUnload method if you create the outlets by Control+dragging, but you aren't obligated to do so yourself.

You might be asking when a view controller would release its view but not be deallocated. The answer is when memory pressure forces it to do that. Since iOS devices have much less memory than desktop computers have, memory is a very constrained resource. The system takes every opportunity possible to reclaim it. When memory gets low, the system sends out a notification, and all view controllers respond by calling their didReceiveMemoryWarning methods. This method can figure out if the view controller's view is on the screen; if it isn't, then the view controller will release its view to reclaim that memory. Subclasses of UIViewController can implement didReceiveMemoryWarning to take that opportunity to release large objects. If you have large objects that are easily re-created, use this method to release them and set pointers to them to nil to help the application reclaim some memory. If you don't release enough, the system will quit your application if there isn't enough memory for it to run.

The final view controller life cycle method we'll look at is shouldAutorotateToInterfaceOrientation:. This long-winded method is called when the user rotates their device. Its one parameter is interfaceOrientation, which is one of four orientations. To support rotation, simply return YES for orientations your view controller supports, and return NO for orientations it doesn't. The system will take care of animating your view during the rotation, but if you need more control over the process, such as if you need to adjust your view's layout depending on the rotation, you can implement various methods to manage it.

> **NOTE:** For iPhone, it is uncommon to support the
> UIInterfaceOrientationPortraitUpsideDown orientation, but for iPad you
> should try to support all four orientations.

Implementing Application Logic with Controls

View controllers play a central role in your application's behavior. iOS applications respond to user touches on user interface elements such as buttons, sliders, and so forth. Instead of implementing the logic to respond to those touches in the views themselves, you should use view controllers to receive those user actions and respond. This makes user interface elements more reusable, keeping application-specific logic in your view controllers. Apple's user interface elements support this pattern, implemented in the abstract class UIControl. Common examples include UIButton, UISlider, UISwitch, and, with iOS 5, UIStepper.

Apple's controls use the concepts of "targets" and "actions" to call back to your code when the user interacts with them. This is set up automatically when you use Interface Builder, but it's fairly easy to set up in code. To get a button to call didTapButton: in our code, we would write the following code:

```
[myButton addTarget:self
            action:@selector(didTapButton:)
  forControlEvents:UIControlEventTouchUpInside];
```

The final parameter is a bitmask of control events. For buttons, the convention is to use UIControlEventTouchUpInside, which is fired when the user lifts their finger off the device when it was touching the button. Another common event is UIControlEventValueChanged, which is called when, for instance, the user adjusts the value of a slider.

The UIButton class is easy to customize. It has several control states, which allow you to customize its behavior based on how the user is currently interacting with it. To make a button have red text by default but blue text when touched, two lines of code will suffice:

```
[button setTitleColor:[UIColor redColor] forState:UIControlStateNormal];
[button setTitleColor:[UIColor blueColor] forState:UIControlStateHighlighted];
```

> **NOTE:** The UIColor class defines several helpful class-level methods to quickly create common colors.

Creating buttons is easy, too. Most of the time, your designer will want a custom button, because iOS's typical buttons are rather uninspiring. This is best accomplished with a background image. When you create a button, you use the buttonWithType: class method on UIButton, passing one of several types. Creating a custom button with a background image is straightforward:

```
UIButton *myButton = [UIButton buttonWithType:UIButtonTypeCustom];
[myButton setBackgroundImage:myBackgroundImage forState:UIControlStateNormal];
```

By default, iOS will darken the button when the user taps it, but you may also specify an image for UIControlStateHighlighted to customize that.

Need a button with multiple sections? Use a UISegmentedControl. Instead of providing a title, you provide multiple titles, one for each segment on the control.

Another typical user interface element is a UISlider. Sliders have a button (referred to as the *thumb*) that moves on a track from a minimum value to a maximum value. So, if you wanted to make a slider to change a value between 1 and 100 that calls the method sliderValueChanged: when its value changed, you would write the following code:

```
UISlider *slider = [[UISlider alloc] init];
[slider setMinimumValue:0];
[slider setMaximumValue:100];
[slider addTarget:self
           action:@selector(sliderValueChanged:)
 forControlEvents:UIControlEventValueChanged];
```

As the user adjusts the slider, you will receive messages constantly, unless you set its continuous property to NO. You can also customize the appearance of the slider, providing custom images for the thumb, minimum track (to the left of the thumb), and maximum track. In iOS 5 and newer, you can also change the tint color of the slider to fit your app's color scheme.

Sometimes you need to interrupt the user to get input. In those cases, you can present the user with an alert using the UIAlertView class. Alert views are created with a title, message, and one or more buttons, examples of which you can see in Figure 3-3. To receive the button that the user selected, implement the UIAlertViewDelegate protocol. Creating an alert view is easy:

```
UIAlertView *alert = [[UIAlertView alloc] initWithTitle:@"Title"
                                                message:@"Message"
                                               delegate:self
                                      cancelButtonTitle:@"Cancel"
                                      otherButtonTitles:@"OK", nil];
```

Figure 3-3. *A UIAlertView with two buttons*

Showing an alert view is as easy as calling its show method. Once the user taps a button, it calls its delegate's alertView:clickedButtonAtIndex: method with the index of the button that the user tapped. Alert views are best used for situations where you need the user to select between two or three actions before continuing. Using too many as notifications will simply annoy your users.

Providing Lists of Content with Table Views

One of the most basic interfaces you'll use in an iOS application is the table view, implemented in the UITableView class. Nearly every application that has a list of items the user must pick from uses a table view, and for good reason: they perform well, they're easy to create, and they provide common behavior that the user expects. A table view consists of sections, each of which contains zero or more rows. Each row is drawn using a UITableViewCell, a reusable class that performs the drawing work for each row. Table views have only one column, so be sure to maximize the horizontal space your data uses. The more vertical space each cell uses, the fewer cells will fit on the screen. There are two styles to table views, illustrated in Figure 3-4.

Figure 3-4. *A prototypical* `UITableView`. *On the left is a table view with the "plain" style, and on the right is the "grouped" style.*

Instead of subclassing `UITableView`, you implement two protocols: `UITableViewDataSource` and `UITableViewDelegate`. Since a view controller that solely consists of a table view and implements both of these protocols is such a common pattern, you can use the built-in subclass `UITableViewController`, which will perform the initial setup for you. Implementing the table view protocol methods follows a pattern for every table view.

First, the data source method `numberOfSectionsInTableView:` is called. Like every table view protocol method, the first parameter is a pointer to the table view. Next, the table view gets the number of rows in its sections in the `tableView:numberOfRowsInSection:` method. Finally, we're ready to create a cell. The table view calls the `tableView:cellForRowAtIndexPath:` method on its data source, which returns a `UITableViewCell` object. This process is heavily optimized, however, since table view performance is so important. Table views should be smooth and responsive even when the user is scrolling through hundreds of cells as quickly as they can, so the operations in this method need to be as fast as possible. One of the shortcuts taken here is that the table view cells are reused as the user scrolls. When one cell moves past the top of the screen, it is reused as the next cell coming up from the bottom. To accomplish this, each cell has a string property called `reuseIdentifier`, which should be unique for each *kind* of cell in your table view. When you're creating a cell, first try to get a cell that's ready for reuse. A typical implementation of this method might look like this:

```
- (UITableViewCell *)tableView:(UITableView *)tableView
cellForRowAtIndexPath:(NSIndexPath *)indexPath
{
    UITableViewCell *cell = [tableView
dequeueReusableCellWithIdentifier:@"CellIdentifier"];

    if (cell == nil) {
        cell = [[UITableViewCell alloc]
initWithStyle:UITableViewCellStyleDefault
                                    reuseIdentifier:@"CellIdentifier"];
    }

    [[cell textLabel] setText:[NSString stringWithFormat:@"Row %d", [indexPath
row]]];

    return cell;
}
```

> **NOTE:** Table views use the `NSIndexPath` class with table view–specific extensions to represent a row in the table. Use the `section` and `row` methods to retrieve the desired values.

By calling `dequeueReusableCellWithIdentifier:` on the table view, we might get a cell that's ready to use. If not, we get `nil` back and have to create one ourselves. There are several built-in styles to use, or you can use your own subclass of `UITableViewCell`. By reusing these cells, the table view avoids having to create and destroy them, saving what would otherwise be an expensive operation.

Once a table view's contents grow beyond a reasonable quantity, it's difficult for the user to navigate it. One solution is a search bar at the top of the table view that narrows the list of content to that which matches the user's search term. Another is to separate the content into letters, such as sorting a list of people by last name and then to allow the user to tap a letter on the right margin of the table view to jump to that letter's section. To accomplish this, provide an array of letters in the data source's `sectionIndexTitlesForTableView:` method, and specify which titles correspond to which sections in the `tableView:sectionForSectionIndexTitle:` method. This is a quick and easy way to help users navigate your app without getting frustrated from seemingly endless scrolling.

Another way to provide more information to the user is to provide header and footer text for the sections, using the `tableView:titleForHeaderInSection:` and `tableView:titleForFooterInSection:` methods. Depending on the style of the table view, the titles are rendered differently; by default, the "plain" table view style pins the header of the topmost section to the top of the table view. You may also specify custom views for your header and footer using the table view delegate's `tableView:viewForHeaderInSection:` and `tableView:viewForFooterInSection` methods.

Until now we've used only the data source methods, but once we want to respond to the user's actions, we use the delegate methods. The most common one to implement is `tableView:didSelectRowAtIndexPath:`, which is called when the user taps a row. In many applications, this is where you would transition to a new view controller to display the details of the item the user tapped. It's important to let the user know that they can select a row, and one common way to do so is to use the table view cell's `accessoryType` property. Setting it to `UITableViewCellAccessoryDisclosureIndicator` adds an icon to the right of the cell that indicates to the user that tapping the cell will cause an action to occur.

Providing Data to Your Table View

One common pattern for table views is to store an array of objects, one per row. The number of objects in the array is the number of rows in the table view's first (and usually only) section.

By storing your data in an array, you can use its ordered nature to allow the array to represent the state of the table view, obtaining your object by calling `[myArray objectAtIndex:[indexPath row]]`. This holds up well when you edit the data, because the changes you make in the array can be reflected in the table view, and vice versa.

These methods are enough to provide great table views that allow your users to navigate information quickly, but sometimes you'll need to modify the contents of a table view. Perhaps you're syncing with the cloud in the background and more items have been added to the list, or the user needs to delete one. Whenever you need to modify the order of a table view or manage its contents, it's a two-step process: first, tell the table view what changes are being made, and second, modify the data to reflect those changes. The exact order doesn't matter, but when you reorder the table view, the values it receives from its data source must match up; if you delete a row in section 2, the number of cells you return for section 2 must be one fewer.

Deleting a cell or inserting a cell is a matter of a method call on the table view: either `deleteRowsAtIndexPaths:withRowAnimation:` or `insertRowsAtIndexPaths:withRowAnimation:`. If you have a few different changes to make, you can tell the table view to wait before making any changes by sending it the `beginUpdates` method at the beginning and the `endUpdates` method at the end. You could alternatively call `reloadData` on the table view to reload all data, but it's less efficient and isn't animated. Finally, if you need to move cells around, use the `moveRowAtIndexPath:toIndexPath:` method or, for large changes, the `moveSection:toSection:` method.

Table views can support the reordering of rows by displaying a reordering control on the right of the cell. To do this, the table view must enter "editing" mode, done by calling `setEditing:animated:` on the table view. For each row, the table view calls the data source method `tableView:canMoveRowAtIndexPath:` and, if it returns `YES`, displays the control. When the user drags the cell to reorder it and releases it, the table view will call its data source method `tableView:moveRowAtIndexPath:toIndexPath:`, in which the data source should update the data model (in our case, the array of objects) to reflect the user's changes. As the user is dragging the cell around, you can restrict which locations it can move to by implementing `tableView:targetIndexPathForMoveFromRowAtIndexPath:toProposedIndexPath:` in your table view's delegate.

Editing mode also allows you to display delete buttons, add buttons, and further adjust the appearance of your table view. To learn more about these customizations, refer to the `UITableView`, `UITableViewDataSource`, and `UITableViewDelegate` documentation.

Providing Custom Table View Cells

While Apple's provided table view cells are good enough for many uses, often you'll want your table views to have a specific look to them or to have a heavily customized internal view hierarchy. In that case, you have two options: create a subclass of `UITableViewCell` or implement a table view cell in a nib. If you're creating a subclass of `UITableViewCell`, you can add subviews in the `initWithStyle:reuseIdentifier:` method. Much like any other custom `UIView` subclass, override `layoutSubviews` to lay out your cells programmatically. One extra step for table view cells is the `prepareForReuse` method, which will be called when the table view is ready to reuse your cell for a new row. In this method, you should return your table view cell to its initial state. This is especially important if the table view cell doesn't always use the same subviews; you wouldn't want information from one row to be displayed elsewhere.

Whether you're creating your cells in code or in a nib, the cell has a subview accessible with the `contentView` property. Your subviews should be inserted into the content view, which will resize when the table view enters editing mode or when accommodating cell accessories.

If you need to adjust the height, there are two ways. The first (and easy) way is the `rowHeight` property on `UITableView`. In cases where you want every cell to have the same height, this is easy and works well. You might think that specifying a dynamic height for each cell would be easy. It's not impossible, but doing so can be quite involved. The first step is implementing the `tableView:heightForRowAtIndexPath:` method in your table view's delegate. In this method, you will return the correct value for the height of that particular cell. If you're trying to size your cells based on text content, however, you have to figure out how tall the text is based on the width of the table view. With complicated layouts, you essentially need to lay out the subviews of your cell to figure out how tall the cell needs to be. There isn't an easy solution for this problem—and it's worse if you have localized content—but thankfully, it's uncommon to use table views with large pieces of text.

Nib Loading In Depth

If you need to load a table view cell from a nib, there are a few ways to do it. Before we talk about table view cells specifically, let's talk about how nibs work. As we've established before, each one is a collection of one or more views in an array, archived to disk in an XML-formatted `.xib` file. When your app is compiled for release, the `.xib` file is compiled into a `.nib` file, which is why it's called a *nib*. When you open the `.xib` file in Xcode, one of the objects it displays on the left side of the interface has an ethereal, mostly transparent style to its icon and the name File's Owner. The style of the icon indicates that the object does not exist in the nib but is referenced from outside of it. This object is the "owner" of the nib when it's loaded. For view controllers, you'll notice that the File's Owner object is set up as a member of your view controller subclass.

When the view is loaded by a view controller, it connects the outlets and actions set up via Interface Builder. The same thing happens when you manually load a nib, but you must specify the owner:

```
[[NSBundle mainBundle] loadNibNamed:@"MyNib"
                              owner:self
                            options:nil];
```

By passing `self` as the owner, we can specify how the connections from Interface Builder will be made.

Loading Table View Cells from Nibs

For a table view cell, one common pattern is to use an `IBOutlet` as temporary storage for a table view cell, which allows you to use Interface Builder to connect the cell to the outlet. In your table view controller's header, add a property for the cell:

```
@property (strong) IBOutlet UITableViewCell *incomingCell;
```

Then, when it's time to create the cell, load it from a nib:

```
- (UITableViewCell *)tableView:(UITableView *)tableView
cellForRowAtIndexPath:(NSIndexPath *)indexPath
{
    UITableViewCell *cell = [tableView
dequeueReusableCellWithIdentifier:@"CellIdentifier"];

    if (cell == nil) {
        [[NSBundle mainBundle] loadNibNamed:@"MyCellNib"
                                      owner:self
                                    options:nil];

        cell = [self incomingCell];
        [self setIncomingCell:nil];
    }

    return cell;
}
```

This can be confusing at first, mostly because of the odd role that `incomingCell` plays. It's a temporary storage area for the cell used to capture the outlet in the nib. Once you have the cell, you assign it to `cell` and then set `incomingCell` to `nil` since you're done with it. A slightly more straightforward method relies on the fact that the `loadNibName:owner:options:` method returns an `NSArray` of the top-level objects in the nib:

```
- (UITableViewCell *)tableView:(UITableView *)tableView
cellForRowAtIndexPath:(NSIndexPath *)indexPath
{
    UITableViewCell *cell = [tableView
dequeueReusableCellWithIdentifier:@"CellIdentifier"];

    if (cell == nil) {
        NSArray *nibObjects = [[NSBundle mainBundle] loadNibNamed:@"MyCellNib"
                                                   owner:nil
                                                   options:nil];

        cell = [nibObjects objectAtIndex:0];
    }

    return cell;
}
```

This method relies on the cell being the only object in the nib, but it doesn't use any sleight of hand with outlets like the former method. I prefer doing it this way, but the net effect is the same in either case: a nib you can use to adjust your cell's layout without spending all of your time writing layout code.

iPhone and iPad Nibs

When you're writing an app that works on iPhone and iPad, you will typically reuse some view controllers. Often, however, you'll want to change the layout of the view controller to better fit the device the app is running on. Writing this in code is easy; the class `UIDevice` has a property called `userInterfaceIdiom` that will tell you whether you're on an iPad, allowing you to lay out views manually depending on the idiom the current device uses. In nibs for view controllers' views, it's even easier: simply provide two nibs. In fact, the default `UIViewController` implementation will look for nibs automatically. If the name of your view controller class is `MyViewController`, name your iPhone-sized nib `MyViewController.xib` and your iPad-sized nib `MyViewController~ipad.xib`. Then, when you create your view controller, don't specify a name:

```
[[MyViewController alloc] initWithNibName:nil bundle:nil];
```

Since the nibs are named properly, they will be loaded automatically. This allows you to manage the user interface for each device without writing any code to do so.

Parent and Child View Controllers

Thus far in this chapter, we have focused on one view controller at a time. Apps with a single view controller are rare, however, but you need a way to move between them. One way is to call `setRootViewController:` on your app's window, but this doesn't give you animation or keep a reference to both view controllers. Depending on your needs, there are three built-in ways to switch between view controllers in Cocoa Touch, as well as some other uses for parent and child view controllers.

Modal View Controllers

If you want a view controller to be displayed on top of your current view controller modally, `UIViewController` has a built-in method, `presentModalViewController:animated:`, that will do exactly that. Since modal view controllers prevent the user from accessing the first view controller, they are best used where the user must take action to continue, such as a login screen for a web service. The modal view controller animates in from the bottom of the screen and, on iPhone, completely covers it. On iPad, you can set the property `modalPresentationStyle` to adjust how it's displayed. Once you're done with the view controller, call `dismissModalViewControllerAnimated:` on the parent view controller, which will animate it away, revealing your first view controller underneath. You could alternatively call `dismissModalViewControllerAnimated:` on the modal view controller, which will forward the message to the parent view controller, but since the message must eventually reach the parent, it's best to call it on the parent directly if you can.

> **NOTE:** You can specify the animation a view controller uses to animate onto the screen with its `modalTransitionStyle` property.

Navigation Controllers

Navigation controllers are probably the most used view controller in all of Cocoa Touch. They provide common functionality that many apps use: a title bar at the top of the screen, a Back button that moves the user back in the view controller hierarchy, and animation between view controllers. The `UINavigationController` class provides this functionality and manages the presentation of your view controller's view for you. The navigation controller maintains a stack of view controllers, with the visible view controller as the topmost item on the stack. To move to a new view controller, call `pushViewController:animated:` on the navigation controller, and to go back, call `popViewControllerAnimated:`. Pressing the built-in Back button will automatically pop the current view controller off the stack. One of the best things about these transitions is that the animations are built-in, so the behavior is consistent across all of a user's apps. If you need to manage the view controller hierarchy manually, perhaps to initialize it to a known state, the navigation controller exposes a `viewControllers` array that you can use to modify the stack of view controllers directly. If you need to go all the way back to the beginning, you can call `popToRootViewControllerAnimated:`.

Navigation controllers are also integrated into `UIViewController` through the `UINavigationItem` object. The navigation item is created on demand by the view controller and customizes how the view controller interacts with the navigation controller. The most common use is its `title` property, which controls the title displayed on the navigation controller's navigation bar (the bar at the top of the navigation controller's view), as well as the default text for the Back button when the view controller is next-to-highest in the navigation controller's view controller hierarchy. You can also specify the `leftBarButtonItem` and `rightBarButtonItem` properties to control the buttons that appear on the navigation bar. Like with `UIButton`, these buttons, instances of the `UIBarButtonItem` class, use the target-action paradigm to send messages. You can create them two ways: with system-provided bar button items or with a custom title.

Navigation items also allow you to manage the behavior of the Back button. When a view controller is *behind* the topmost view controller in the stack, its Back button is displayed, because it's what will be displayed when the user taps the Back button. Set the `backBarButtonItem` property to a bar button item with a custom image or title, and you can customize the appearance of the Back button.

Tab Bar Controllers

Tab bar controllers are used less but are still popular objects for navigation between view controllers. A `UITabBarController` maintains an array of view controllers, each represented by a `UITabBarItem`. It displays buttons along the bottom of its view representing each view controller. Tapping the buttons highlights them and shows the view controller's view above the tab bar. If the tab bar controller cannot display a button for every view controller because of the width of the screen, it replaces the last one it can display with a More button. Tapping this button displays a view controller that allows the user to select between the remaining view controllers, as well as edit which ones appear in which positions. A canonical example of using a tab bar controller is the Music app on iOS.

Often you'll want to combine navigation controllers and tab bar controllers. This usually works well, but you should be sure that the root view controller is the tab bar controller, not a navigation controller. Switching between tabs should switch between different navigation controllers, allowing them each to maintain their own navigation hierarchies. The Phone app on iPhones behaves this way.

Split View Controllers

On iPad, the increased screen real estate from iPhone relaxes the "one view controller per screenful of content" rule established earlier. The screen is more than large enough to display two sets of information. One common use for this is the split view controller. When the iPad is in landscape orientation, the split view controller displays a list of items on the left in a table view and displays a detail view on the right. In portrait orientation, the list on the left disappears by default but can be summoned again with a button on the detail view's navigation bar. Mail on iPad is the canonical example of this behavior, and it's a good example of the ideal use of this controller: sorting through a list of items on one side while viewing them one at a time in large detail on the other.

Page View Controllers

Another built-in view controller that manages multiple view controllers is `UIPageViewController`. New in iOS 5, it allows you to flip between two view controllers like a book in iBooks without writing the complex OpenGL code to curl the page. The page view controller, like the table view, has `dataSource` and `delegate` properties. Instead of rows of data, the data source for `UIPageViewController` provides view controllers, one for each page. Instead of using an index path or something similar, the page view controller's data source protocol is two methods: `pageViewController:viewControllerBeforeViewController:` and `pageViewController:viewControllerAfterViewController:`. It's up to you to keep track of the view controllers and figure out which ones to pass—just return `nil` if there is no view controller before or after the one it sends as the final parameter.

Another nifty feature of the page view controller is that it exposes some of its inner workings to you, enabling you to further customize its behavior. It has objects that manage the user's interaction with it called *gesture recognizers*. These recognizers can be added to other views, allowing you to create a page view controller in a frame that the user can interact with by dragging from the frame into the page. We'll discuss gesture recognizers in more detail later.

Passing Data Between View Controllers

As you've read, there are plenty of ways to show the user different view controllers. The next step in building a great app is to send data from one view controller to another. There are some common patterns here, too, depending on the relationship between the view controllers. One thing to keep in mind as a goal is to *reduce coupling*, that is, to prevent as much as possible situations in which your view controller class is directly integrated into the other view controller class. Generally, it's OK for a view controller to use methods specific to view controllers that it creates—it has to create them, after all—but the reverse should be avoided. We'll examine how this works with a typical master-detail application that we'll work on for a few chapters: a home inventory system called MyStuff.

Open Xcode and create a new project. In the template chooser, select Empty Application. For the Product name, enter **MyStuff**. Enter your class prefix; I'll use LCT in this book. For Device Family, select iPhone. Check the Use Automatic Reference Counting box but not the other two. Save the project to your hard drive, and we're ready to go!

The project as defined doesn't have any view controllers, nor does it have any data. Let's make a new class to represent a possession in our house. In Xcode, select File ➤ New ➤ New File…, and in the dialog that opens, select Cocoa Touch on the left side, followed by "Objective-C class" on the right. Select Next, and for the name of the class, enter **Possession**. For Subclass Of, specify **NSObject**. Save it to disk, and it will open in Xcode.

In `Possession.h`, add two properties:

```
#import <Foundation/Foundation.h>

@interface Possession : NSObject

@property (copy) NSString *name;
@property (strong) NSNumber *value;

@end
```

Implement those properties in the 'Possession.m':

```
#import "Possession.h"

@implementation Possession
```

```
@synthesize name = _name;
@synthesize value = _value;
```

```
@end
```

As you can see, this is a very simple class, but it's a good starting point for us. Let's create a view controller to serve as our master list view controller. Create a new file, but this time select "UIViewController subclass" instead of "Objective-C class." Name it **PossessionListViewController** and make it a subclass of UITableViewController. Uncheck the "With XIB for user interface" box. The view for a view controller this simple is pretty much just a table view, so we won't need to customize it further. In the implementation file (PossessionListViewController.m), import the Possession header so we can use the Possession class by entering the line in bold:

```
#import "PossessionListViewController.h"
```

`#import "Possession.h"`

Next, let's create an array to store our possessions into. Other classes don't need to access this array, so instead of creating it as a property, we'll add it as an instance variable in the implementation file using a class extension. We'll also add a method for retrieving a possession at an index in the array. Add all of the following lines before the existing @implementation line:

```
@interface PossessionListViewController() {
    NSMutableArray *_possessions;
}

- (Possession *)possessionAtIndex:(NSUInteger)index;

@end
```

We'll make it a mutable array so we can add to it later, and the _ prefix is convention for instance variables. Next up, let's implement our table view methods to get a basic implementation together. Remove the existing methods between @implementation and @end and replace them with following lines in bold:

```
@implementation PossessionListViewController

- (NSInteger)numberOfSectionsInTableView:(UITableView *)tableView
{
    return 1;
}

- (NSInteger)tableView:(UITableView *)tableView
 numberOfRowsInSection:(NSInteger)section
```

```
{
    return [_possessions count];
}

- (UITableViewCell *)tableView:(UITableView *)tableView
        cellForRowAtIndexPath:(NSIndexPath *)indexPath
{
    NSString *cellIdentifier = @"PossessionCell";

    UITableViewCell *cell = [tableView
dequeueReusableCellWithIdentifier:cellIdentifier];

    if (cell == nil) {
        cell = [[UITableViewCell alloc]
initWithStyle:UITableViewCellStyleValue1
                                    reuseIdentifier:cellIdentifier];
    }

    Possession *possession = [self possessionAtIndex:[indexPath row]];

    [[cell textLabel] setText:[possession name]];
    [[cell detailTextLabel] setText:[[possession value] stringValue]];

    return cell;
}

- (Possession *)possessionAtIndex:(NSUInteger)index
{
    return [_possessions objectAtIndex:index];
}

@end
```

In Xcode, click Run and…you'll see a white screen. We need to add the view controller to the view hierarchy. Click Stop in Xcode, and open your app delegate's implementation file (remember, it uses your class prefix if you have one; mine is LCTAppDelegate.m), and import your view controller's header:

```
#import "LCTAppDelegate.h"

#import "PossessionListViewController.h"

…
```

In the application:didFinishLaunchingWithOptions: method, just before the return YES; line, add the following code to create and display your view controller:

```
PossessionListViewController *listViewController =
[[PossessionListViewController alloc] initWithNibName:nil
                                          bundle:nil];

[[self window] setRootViewController:listViewController];
```

Now when you click Run in Xcode, you'll see an empty table view. This is expected, since we never added any items to our list! Go back to PossessionListViewController.m and implement an init method after the @implementation line:

```
@implementation PossessionListViewController;

- (id)initWithNibName:(NSString *)nibNameOrNil
            bundle:(NSBundle *)nibBundleOrNil
{
    self = [super initWithNibName:nibNameOrNil
                        bundle:nibBundleOrNil];

    if (self) {
        Possession *iPhone = [[Possession alloc] init];
        [iPhone setName:@"iPhone 4S"];
        [iPhone setValue:[NSNumber numberWithInt:649]];

        Possession *iPad = [[Possession alloc] init];
        [iPad setName:@"iPad 2"];
        [iPad setValue:[NSNumber numberWithInt:499]];

        _possessions = [NSMutableArray arrayWithObjects:iPhone, iPad, nil];
    }

    return self;
}
```

This will initialize our array to include two sample items. Feel free to put whatever values you'd like in there. Click Run and, as you can see in Figure 3-5, success!

Figure 3-5. *Our application showing some data*

As you can see, the values for our possessions are displaying correctly, but so far the user interface is a bit spartan. Let's spice it up a bit. First let's embed it in a navigation controller. Open up the app delegate (LCTAppDelegate.m for me), remove the lines that have been struck through, and add the code in bold in application:didFinishLaunchingWithOptions::

```
PossessionListViewController *listViewController =
[[PossessionListViewController alloc] initWithNibName:nil
                                                bundle:nil];

UINavigationController *navigationController =
[[UINavigationController alloc]
initWithRootViewController:listViewController];

[[self window] setRootViewController:listViewController];
[[self window] setRootViewController:navigationController];

return YES;
```

Now we have a navigation bar at the top of our screen, but it has no title. In our view controller, add the line in bold to the init method:

```
- (id)initWithNibName:(NSString *)nibNameOrNil
              bundle:(NSBundle *)nibBundleOrNil
{
    self = [super initWithNibName:nibNameOrNil
                           bundle:nibBundleOrNil];

    if (self) {
        [self setTitle:@"Item Details"];
    }

    return self;
}
```

Now we have a navigation bar and a title. Lookin' better already! Just a few more tweaks and we'll be ready for venture capital....

The next thing to create is our detail view controller. This screen should allow us to edit the name of the possession and its value. In Xcode, create a new view controller by selecting File ➤ New ➤ New File…, name it **PossessionDetailViewController**, and create it as a subclass of UIViewController. Check the box to create a XIB this time. Save it to disk and open the nib, which will be named PossessionDetailViewController.xib. Drag two labels onto the view from the right side's object list, as well as two text fields. If you don't see the object list, press ⌘+Option+1 or select View ➤ Utilities ➤ Show Object Library; the object library will appear in the Utilities pane on the right portion of the Xcode window, on the bottom half. Change the text on the labels to read Name and Value (either by double-clicking them or by selecting them, opening the Attributes inspector in the Utilities pane by pressing ⌘+Option+4 or selecting View ➤ Utilities ➤ Show Attributes Inspector and changing the value for Text) and arrange them as shown in Figure 3-6.

Figure 3-6. *Our beautiful detail page layout*

Next, create two IBOutlets in your header for the text fields:

```
@interface PossessionDetailViewController : UIViewController

@property (weak) IBOutlet UITextField *nameField;
@property (weak) IBOutlet UITextField *valueField;

@end
```

Don't forget to add corresponding @synthesize calls in your implementation file (PossessionDetailViewController.m):

```
@implementation PossessionDetailViewController

@synthesize nameField = _nameField;
@synthesize valueFeild = _valueField;
```

Next, connect the views to these outlets in your nib. To do that, open the nib (PossessionDetailViewController.xib). Holding the Control key, drag from the File's Owner object on the left side of the editor pane to your text fields, one at a time. When you release the mouse button, you'll see a window appear with the various destinations for the connection. Choose nameField for the text field next to the Name label and valueField for the text field next to Value. If you accidentally connect the text field to the wrong outlet, you can fix it in the Connections Inspector. To open it, select the text field you incorrectly connected and press ⌘+Option+6 or select View ➤ Utilities ➤ Show Connections Inspector. The Connections Inspector, as shown in Figure 3-7, lists the connections you've made to the text field under Referencing Outlets. The outlet in Figure 3-7 is correct. If you connect it to the wrong outlet, press the small x to the left of the referencing object's name (in Figure 3-7, it's File's Owner) to disconnect it.

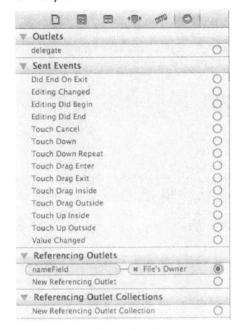

Figure 3-7. *The Connections Inspector*

Once you've connected your text fields' outlets, let's add another property to our view controller: a pointer to the possession we're showing details for. Open PossessionDetailViewController.h, and add the lines in bold:

@class Possession;

@interface PossessionDetailViewController : UIViewController

@property (weak) IBOutlet UITextField *nameField;
@property (weak) IBOutlet UITextField *valueField;
@property (strong) Possession *possession;

@end

We use a forward declaration of the `Possession` class (the `@class Possession;` line) to ensure that other classes that import the `PossessionDetailViewController.h` header don't also import the `Possession.h` header. This is important with larger projects, because you may have circular references through header files that are tough to resolve. It also speeds compilation to import as few header files as possible. You won't get Xcode's code completion for the name of the class when you create a forward declaration, but that's OK. To use the `Possession` class in your view controller's implementation, you do need to import the `Possession` header, even with the forward declaration in the view controller's header.

Don't forget to add the `@synthesize` line for possession in the view controller's implementation file. Open `PossessionDetailViewController.m`, and add the line in bold:

```
@implementation PossessionDetailViewController

@synthesize nameField = _nameField;
@synthesize valueFeild = _valueField;
@synthesize possession = _possession;
```

Now that we have our header straightened out, let's write some methods in the implementation file. We'll need a Done button to get back to the list, and we'll need to populate the fields with the correct values. The following code block is the entire implementation file except for the comments at the top; the lines we're adding now are bold.

```
#import "PossessionDetailViewController.h"

#import "Possession.h"

@interface PossessionDetailViewController()

- (void)doneButtonPressed:(id)sender;

@end

@implementation PossessionDetailViewController

@synthesize nameField = _nameField;
@synthesize valueField = _valueField;
@synthesize possession = _possessionField;

- (id)initWithNibName:(NSString *)nibNameOrNil
            bundle:(NSBundle *)nibBundleOrNil
{
    self = [super initWithNibName:nibNameOrNil
                           bundle:nibBundleOrNil];
```

```objc
    if (self) {
        [self setTitle:@"Item Details"];

        UIBarButtonItem *doneButtonItem =
        [[UIBarButtonItem alloc]
initWithBarButtonSystemItem:UIBarButtonSystemItemDone
                                                      target:self

action:@selector(doneButtonPressed:)];

        [[self navigationItem] setRightBarButtonItem:doneButtonItem];
    }

    return self;
}

- (void)viewWillAppear:(BOOL)animated
{
    [super viewWillAppear:animated];

    [[self nameField] setText:[[self possession] name]];
    [[self valueField] setText:[[[self possession] value] stringValue]];
}

- (void)doneButtonPressed:(id)sender
{
    if ([[possession name] isEqualToString:[[self nameField] text]] == NO)
{
        [possession setName:[[self nameField] text]];
    }

    NSNumber *newValue = [NSNumber numberWithInt:[[[self valueField] text]
intValue]];

    if ([[possession value] isEqualToNumber:newValue] == NO) {
        [possession setValue:newValue];
    }

    [[self navigationController] popViewControllerAnimated:YES];
}

@end
```

Passing Data from a Parent View Controller to a Child View Controller

This code will change the values of possession when the Done button is pressed and go back to the list. We're almost at the point where we can use it, but we need to add some code to get to the detail view controller. Open the list view controller (PossessionListViewController.m), and add the line in bold (the ellipsis indicates that there is code between these two sections that I've omitted):

```objc
#import "PossessionListViewController.h"

#import "Possession.h"
#import "PossessionDetailViewController.h"

...

- (UITableViewCell *)tableView:(UITableView *)tableView
        cellForRowAtIndexPath:(NSIndexPath *)indexPath
{
    NSString *cellIdentifier = @"PossessionCell";

    UITableViewCell *cell = [tableView
dequeueReusableCellWithIdentifier:cellIdentifier];

    if (cell == nil) {
        cell = [[UITableViewCell alloc] initWithStyle:UITableViewCellStyleValue1
                                      reuseIdentifier:cellIdentifier];
    }

    Possession *possession = [self possessionAtIndex:[indexPath row]];

    [[cell textLabel] setText:[possession name]];
    [[cell detailTextLabel] setText:[[possession value] stringValue]];

    [cell setAccessoryType:UITableViewCellAccessoryDisclosureIndicator];

    return cell;
}

- (void)tableView:(UITableView *)tableView
didSelectRowAtIndexPath:(NSIndexPath *)indexPath
{
    [tableView deselectRowAtIndexPath:indexPath animated:YES];

    PossessionDetailViewController *detailViewController =
    [[PossessionDetailViewController alloc] initWithNibName:nil
                                                     bundle:nil];
```

```
    [detailViewController setPossession:[self possessionAtIndex:[indexPath
row]]];

    [[self navigationController] pushViewController:detailViewController
                                          animated:YES];
}

…

@end
```

Now run your application. When you select the first item, you'll see its detail view controller push onto the screen, and when you hit Done, it'll take you back to the master list. At this point, the Back button does not save our changes, but the Done button does. If you change values, however, you won't see them immediately on the list view controller. If you scroll that item offscreen and back on, the values will be updated. This is because we never told our table view to reload any rows. For now, we can fix that with a single method in our list view controller:

```
- (void)viewWillAppear:(BOOL)animated
{
    [super viewWillAppear:animated];

    [[self tableView] reloadData];
}
```

This is a bit heavy-handed for this purpose, because it forces the table view to reload all of its contents every time, but it will work for our purposes. In future chapters, we'll go over better ways to pass data around the application. For now, though, we need to implement one more feature to make our first app complete: the ability to add new items to the list.

Passing Data to and from a Modal View Controller

Let's add a button to the navigation bar on the list view to add a new item, along with declaring a method for it to call in our class extension by adding the lines in bold in PossessionListViewController.m:

```
@interface PossessionListViewController() {
    NSMutableArray *_possessions;
}
```

```
- (void)addItemButtonPressed:(id)sender;
- (Possession *)possessionAtIndex:(NSUInteger)index;

@end

@implementation PossessionListViewController

- (id)initWithNibName:(NSString *)nibNameOrNil
               bundle:(NSBundle *)nibBundleOrNil
{
    self = [super initWithNibName:nibNameOrNil
                           bundle:nibBundleOrNil];

    if (self) {
        Possession *iPhone = [[Possession alloc] init];
        [iPhone setName:@"iPhone 4S"];
        [iPhone setValue:[NSNumber numberWithInt:649]];

        Possession *iPad = [[Possession alloc] init];
        [iPad setName:@"iPad 2"];
        [iPad setValue:[NSNumber numberWithInt:499]];

        _possessions = [NSMutableArray arrayWithObjects:iPhone, iPad, nil];

        [self setTitle:@"My Stuff"];

        UIBarButtonItem *addItemButton =
        [[UIBarButtonItem alloc]
initWithBarButtonSystemItem:UIBarButtonSystemItemAdd
                                                        target:self
action:@selector(addItemButtonPressed:)];
        [[self navigationItem] setRightBarButtonItem:addItemButton];
    }

    return self;
}
```

This creates a nice-looking button for us with a plus sign in it. To get it to work, let's have it create a new PossessionDetailViewController and present it modally. We'll begin with a basic implementation; add the following code to PossessionListViewController.m, before the @end directive:

```
- (void)addItemButtonPressed:(id)sender
{
    PossessionDetailViewController *detailViewController =
    [[PossessionDetailViewController alloc] initWithNibName:nil
                                                     bundle:nil];
```

```
    [self presentModalViewController:detailViewController
                          animated:YES];
}
```

Run your app after putting this method in, and you'll quickly discover that this needs a bit more. For starters, there's no way to get out of the modal view controller. To get another navigation bar for this view controller, we'll create another navigation controller and present *it* modally. Modify the method you just created with the line in bold:

```
- (void)addItemButtonPressed:(id)sender
{
    PossessionDetailViewController *detailViewController =
    [[PossessionDetailViewController alloc] initWithNibName:nil
                                                bundle:nil];

    UINavigationController *navigationController =
    [[UINavigationController alloc]
initWithRootViewController:detailViewController];

    [self presentModalViewController:navigationController
                          animated:YES];
}
```

This is better, but the Done button won't work, because there's no view controller behind it to pop to in the navigation stack. We'll need to modify the Done button's behavior to determine what it should do. To properly encapsulate the behavior, we need to make sure that the *list* view controller determines the behavior of the detail view controller, since the list view controller creates it for different purposes. Let's create a flag we can set on the detail view controller that we can use for this purpose. In PossessionDetailViewController.h, add the line in bold after the other @property lines:

```
@property (weak) IBOutlet UITextField *nameField;
```

```
@property (weak) IBOutlet UITextField *valueField;
```

```
@property (strong) Possession *possession;
```

@property (getter = isModal) BOOL modal;

Add the @synthesize line to the detail view controller's implementation file (PossessionDetailViewController.m) by adding the line in bold:

```
@synthesize nameField = _nameField;
```

```
@synthesize valueField = _valueField;
```

```
@synthesize possession = _possession;
```

@synthesize modal = _modal;

Next, modify this file's doneButtonPressed: method by replacing the struck-out line with the bold lines:

```
- (void)doneButtonPressed:(id)sender
{
    if ([[possession name] isEqualToString:[[self nameField] text]] == NO) {
        [possession setName:[[self nameField] text]];
    }

    NSNumber *newValue = [NSNumber numberWithInt:[[[self valueField] text]
intValue]];

    if ([[possession value] isEqualToNumber:newValue] == NO) {
        [possession setValue:newValue];
    }

    [[self navigationController] popViewControllerAnimated:YES];
    if ([self isModal]) {
        [self dismissModalViewControllerAnimated:YES];
    } else {
        [[self navigationController] popViewControllerAnimated:YES];
    }
}
```

This will use the value of the modal property to determine the proper closing behavior. Back in our list view controller, we'll set this to YES when creating it from the Add button. Open PossessionListViewController.m, and modify the addItemButtonPressed: method with the line in bold:

```
- (void)addItemButtonPressed:(id)sender
{
    PossessionDetailViewController *detailViewController =
    [[PossessionDetailViewController alloc] initWithNibName:nil
                                                      bundle:nil];

    [detailViewController setModal:YES];

    ...
```

Passing Data Between View Controllers with a Delegate Protocol

Now the detail view controller appears and disappears properly in either case, but adding an item still won't work, since possession is nil in the detail view controller when we add a new item. To accomplish this, we need to inform our list view controller when a new item has been added. We don't want the detail view controller to rely on any details about how the list view controller works, because this allows it to be reusable. If we were to call a method on the list view controller directly from the detail view controller, we'd have to rewrite the detail view controller if we replaced the list view controller later. To avoid that, we'll create a protocol that the list view controller can conform to. In Xcode, create a new file by selecting File ➤ New ➤ New File…. This time, use "Objective-C protocol" in the Cocoa Touch category and name it **PossessionDetailViewControllerDelegate**. We'll define one required method that we'll call whenever the detail view controller finishes editing an item. Open your new header file, `PossessionDetailViewControllerDelegate.h`, and add the lines in bold:

```
#import <Foundation/Foundation.h>

@class Possession;
@class PossessionDetailViewController;

@protocol PossessionDetailViewControllerDelegate <NSObject>

@required

- (void)possessionDetailViewController:(PossessionDetailViewController
*)detailViewController
                    didEditPossession:(Possession *)possession;

@end
```

Now, in the list view controller's header, we can import this protocol's header and declare that the list view controller conforms to it. Open `PossessionListViewController.h`, and add the code in bold:

```
#import <UIKit/UIKit.h>

#import "PossessionDetailViewControllerDelegate.h"

@interface PossessionListViewController : UITableViewController
<PossessionDetailViewControllerDelegate>

@end
```

For the implementation, we'll simply add the possession to our _possessions array if it isn't already in the array. Open `PossessionListViewController.m`, and add the following method in bold before the @end directive:

```
- (void)possessionDetailViewController:(PossessionDetailViewController
*)detailViewController
                    didEditPossession:(Possession *)possession
{
```

```
    if ([_possessions containsObject:possession] == NO) {
        [_possessions addObject:possession];
    }
}

@end
```

Now, we need to tell the detail view controller what to call when it's done editing. We also need to create a new possession when the possession detail view controller is done editing and its possession property is nil. We'll start by giving the detail view controller a delegate property. Open PossessionDetailViewController.h, and add both the header import and property declaration lines in bold:

```
#import <UIKit/UIKit.h>


#import "PossessionDetailViewControllerDelegate.h"


@class Possession;


@interface PossessionDetailViewController : UIViewController


@property (weak) IBOutlet UITextField *nameField;

@property (weak) IBOutlet UITextField *valueField;

@property (strong) Possession *possession;

@property (getter = isModal) BOOL modal;

@property (weak) id <PossessionDetailViewControllerDelegate> delegate;


@end
```

Next, open the detail view controller's implementation file (PossessionDetailViewController.m), and add the line in bold to import synthesize accessor methods for the delegate:

```
@implementation PossessionDetailViewController

@synthesize nameField = _nameField;
@synthesize valueField = _valueField;
@synthesize possession = _possession;
@synthesize modal = _modal;
```

```
@synthesize delegate = _delegate;
```

Next, in the detail view controller's doneButtonPressed: method, add the code in bold to call the delegate method, as well as create new possessions as necessary:

```
- (void)doneButtonPressed:(id)sender
{
    if ([self possession] == nil) {
        [self setPossession:[[Possession alloc] init]];
    }

    if ([[[self possession] name] isEqualToString:[[self nameField] text]] ==
NO) {
        [[self possession] setName:[[self nameField] text]];
    }

    NSNumber *newValue = [NSNumber numberWithInt:[[[self valueField] text]
intValue]];

    if ([[[self possession] value] isEqualToNumber:newValue] == NO) {
        [[self possession] setValue:newValue];
    }

    [[self delegate] possessionDetailViewController:self
                                didEditPossession:[self possession]];

    if ([self isModal]) {
        [self dismissModalViewControllerAnimated:YES];
    } else {
        [[self navigationController] popViewControllerAnimated:YES];
    }
}
```

Now, the final piece will be to set the list view controller as the delegate of the detail view controller. Open PossessionListViewController.m. In both places where a PossessionDetailViewController is created by calling [[PossessionDetailViewController alloc] initWithNibName:nil bundle:nil], add the lines in bold:

```
- (void)tableView:(UITableView *)tableView didSelectRowAtIndexPath:(NSIndexPath
*)indexPath
{
    [tableView deselectRowAtIndexPath:indexPath animated:YES];

    PossessionDetailViewController *detailViewController =
    [[PossessionDetailViewController alloc] initWithNibName:nil
                                                bundle:nil];

    [detailViewController setDelegate:self];
```

```
    [detailViewController setPossession:[self possessionAtIndex:[indexPath
row]]];

    [[self navigationController] pushViewController:detailViewController
                                    animated:YES];
}
…
- (void)addItemButtonPressed:(id)sender
{
    PossessionDetailViewController *detailViewController =
    [[PossessionDetailViewController alloc] initWithNibName:nil
                                    bundle:nil];

    [detailViewController setDelegate:self];
    [detailViewController setModal:YES];

    UINavigationController *navigationController =
    [[UINavigationController alloc]
initWithRootViewController:detailViewController];

    [self presentModalViewController:navigationController
                        animated:YES];
}
```

Run your app, and add a new item. If you've done everything properly, it's been added to the list! We now have a fully functional way to add items to the list. Ship it. You may notice, however, that possessions are not saved between launches of the app. We'll expand on this app in the next chapter to add that and other additional functionality.

Summary

This chapter covered a lot of ground on view controllers. We went over their life cycle, how to implement application logic using them, and how to load content with nibs. By now, you should be familiar with creating and using view controllers. You should also be able to pass data from one view controller to another in an app. In the next chapter, we'll expand on this idea, passing data not only between view controllers but between launches of the app by persisting it to disk.

Saving Content in Your App

No matter how great your Cocoa Touch app is, your users aren't going to be using it forever. They'll be getting phone calls, switching to other apps, downloading new ones, and even getting new devices. When they come back to your app, they want—and expect—everything to be just as they left it the last time they used it. Their data should be there (and unchanged), and even their user interface should be just as it was the last time they opened the app. Some of this you get by virtue of the app remaining in memory while it isn't open, but when iOS removes it from memory to reclaim space, you need to be prepared to re-create that data on demand. In this chapter, we'll discuss how to persist your app's data to the disk to save it between launches. Since you have to walk before you run, though, let's first discuss how to move data around *inside* the app; if you can't move it inside the app, it's going to be difficult to move it *outside* of the app. Once we discuss moving data around inside your app, we'll discuss how to persist that data to disk to make it available between launches.

Moving Data Around Your App

So far, your experience with moving data around has been very basic. When you created a list of possessions in our sample app, MyStuff, the only data you passed around was a possession the user tapped to display a detail view controller. Passing a pointer to said possession was simple and easy between the two view controllers, because they had a direct parent-child relationship, but it won't always be so easy. Often you won't have a direct link between two objects but need to pass data between them. The simplest way is what you did in MyStuff: passing the object directly and using a delegate the other way. In this section, we'll discuss how to pass data between different sections of your app using this and other methods.

Delegate Chains

When you pass a pointer to an object from a parent view controller to its child and then pass it back to the parent using a delegate protocol, the flow of the data is neatly contained. If you need to add more steps to the process, however, things get more complicated. Suppose your detail view controller needed to present a second detail view controller to modify some specific detail of the object. The solution would be to pass a pointer to the object from the detail view controller to a new child view controller. Once that view controller was done, it would then notify its parent through a delegate message, which would in turn notify its parent the same way. As you can probably see, it's possible to extend this *ad infinitum*, creating an unbroken chain of view controllers passing objects to their children and receiving messages in return. This works fine, but it's not the most elegant solution, especially for complicated view controller hierarchies, and it also works only when there's a direct connection between two view controllers, such as this parent-child relationship.

Key-Value Observing

When we wrote the delegate protocol for our detail view controller in MyStuff, the goal was to tell the parent view controller that we were done editing the object, which in turn allowed us to update the user interface and display the new values. To our parent view controller, which is just a list of objects, it doesn't matter where these objects are modified; we simply want to always present the most up-to-date information possible. You might, for example, later implement a website that syncs objects across devices and then update from that website in the background. In these circumstances, since we care about the value of an object changing, we can use an Objective-C paradigm called *Key-Value Observing* (KVO) to receive notifications when the values change.

Key-Value Observing is implemented in the root NSObject class, which means that it works with nearly every object you'll ever use in Objective-C code on an Apple platform, including Cocoa Touch on iOS. What it allows us to do is observe the value of an object and receive notifications when that value changes. The value is most often a property of the object, though later we'll look at other uses.

Using KVO

To register for a notification when a property changes, call the
addObserver:forKeyPath:options:context: method on the object you want to
observe:

```
[someObject addObserver:self

            forKeyPath:@"propertyName"

              options:NSKeyValueObservingOptionNew

              context:NULL];
```

This adds self as an observer on someObject whenever its property named
propertyName changes. The options argument is a bitmask specifying how
you'd like to be notified. Passing NSKeyValueObservingOptionNew results in the
notification including the new value when the value changes. The context
argument allows you to specify a void pointer for a custom context, but in
practice it's rarely used. When you're programming with ARC, the compiler
forbids you from using an object as the context pointer, which was one use
before ARC was commonplace. When the value changes, it calls the following
method:

```
- (void)observeValueForKeyPath:(NSString *)keyPath
                    ofObject:(id)object
                      change:(NSDictionary *)change
                     context:(void *)context
{
    // Write code here that reacts to the change.
}
```

You're responsible for implementing this method for any class that acts as an
observer. In our example, the keyPath argument will be propertyName, and the
object argument will be someObject, but you should always inspect those values
to be sure you've observed the correct change. To observe the value of a flag
property on self, you would first call this method:

```
[self addObserver:self
      forKeyPath:@"flag"
         options:0
         context:NULL];
```

To make sure you're responding to the correct change, you'll want to verify
these values when you observe the change:

```
- (void)observeValueForKeyPath:(NSString *)keyPath
                    ofObject:(id)object
                      change:(NSDictionary *)change
                     context:(void *)context
```

```
{
    if (object == self) {
        if ([keyPath isEqualToString:@"flag"]) {
            // Respond to the change here
        }
    }
}
```

The two consecutive `if` statements help future-proof your app, because the `observeValueForKeyPath:ofObject:change:context:` method might be called by several different changes.

The change dictionary will contain different values based on the options we specified when adding the observer; for `NSKeyValueObservingOptionNew`, the new value will be in the dictionary for the key `NSKeyValueChangeNewKey`. In this method, you should respond to the change appropriately, whether that means updating your UI, saving your content, or triggering further changes.

> **NOTE:** It's very important that you remember to always remove your observers when you're done with them by calling `removeObserver:forKeyPath:` on the object. If you've specified a context pointer, you can use the `removeObserver:forKeyPath:context:` method to remove the observer just for that context pointer. You should do this when you no longer need the observer to be called, or in `dealloc` for objects that need to be notified of changes for their entire life cycle. If you don't, you may wind up receiving a notification after your object has been released, crashing your app.

How KVO Works

Something you'll notice fairly quickly as you begin to use KVO in your day-to-day programming is that if you create your own objects and use KVO on their properties, you didn't have to write any code to get these notifications, so long as you set the properties using the synthesized setter methods. How does this work? It takes advantage of the dynamic nature of Objective-C. Since the Objective-C runtime allows you to create classes while the program is running, that's exactly what it does. The runtime creates a subclass of the class you're observing, overriding the setter method for the property you're observing. That setter method calls the original setter method and then sends out your notifications. Once this new class is created, the runtime does one sneaky trick: it changes the class pointer on the observed object to the new class. This isn't something I recommend doing yourself, but in the case of KVO, it's perfectly safe.

Manual KVO Implementations

What we've covered of KVO so far works extremely well for changing a single property at a time. More complicated objects, however, need special treatment. A common case where KVO falls short is if your custom setter has other side effects. A class that represents a home loan, for instance, will probably have a principal property, an interestRate property, and a monthlyPayment property, with the last one being read-only. When you change the interestRate property, the monthlyPayment property will need to be re-computed. In that case, you *could* call another property setter, triggering *another* KVO notification, but in the event where monthlyPayment is not a writable property, we can trigger the notification manually:

```
- (void)setInterestRate:(float)newInterestRate
{
    [self willChangeValueForKey:@"interestRate"];
    interestRate = newInterestRate;
    [self didChangeValueForKey:@"interestRate"];

    [self willChangeValueForKey:@"monthlyPayment"];
    monthlyPayment = MonthlyPaymentForInterestRate(interestRate);
    [self didChangeValueForKey:@"monthlyPayment"];
}
```

As you can see, each call to willChangeValueForKey: is balanced with a call to didChangeValueForKey: with the same key path argument. If you implement this, you should also override the class method automaticallyNotifiesObserversForKey:, returning NO for the key path for which you're manually sending notifications. Suppose you have a class with two properties, subtotal and taxRate, which are used to calculate a third, read-only property, totalDue. You would first implement automaticallyNotifiesObserversForKey: to avoid automatically returning notifications for totalDue:

```
+ (BOOL)automaticallyNotifiesObserversForKey:(NSString *)key
{
    if ([key isEqualToString:@"totalDue"]) {
        return NO;
    }

    return [super automaticallyNotifiesObserversForKey:key];
}
```

Next, when you set the `subtotal` or `taxRate` values, you would manually notify observers of a change in `totalDue`:

```
[self willChangeValueForKey:@"totalDue"];
_totalDue = [self subtotal] + ([self subtotal] * [self taxRate]);
[self didChangeValueForKey:@"totalDue"];
```

Using this method, you can control when the observation methods are called and provide custom logic for your data.

KVO In Action

Let's put what we've learned about KVO into action in our MyStuff app. Remove the following line from `PossessionListViewController.m`:

```
- (void)viewWillAppear:(BOOL)animated
{
    [super viewWillAppear:animated];

    [[self tableView] reloadData];
}
```

We'll use KVO to update the table cells' contents automatically instead of reloading the entire contents of the table view every time the view appears. This will result in new items not immediately showing up, but we'll fix that later in this chapter. In Xcode, create a new file (File ➤ New ➤ New File…) and select Objective-C Class from Cocoa Touch on the left column. Click Next, name the class `PossessionListTableViewCell`, and make it a subclass of `UITableViewCell`. Save it to disk, and Xcode will add it to the project. Open the header (`PossessionListTableViewCell.h`), and add the following lines in bold:

```
#import <UIKit/UIKit.h>

@class Possession;

@interface PossessionListTableViewCell : UITableViewCell

@property (strong, nonatomic) Possession *possession;

@end
```

Switch to the header (`Possession.h`) by pressing ⌘, Control, and the up-arrow key simultaneously (or selecting it in Xcode's file browser), and remove the methods created by Xcode's template. Add the following code in bold (we'll walk through it afterward):

```
#import "PossessionListTableViewCell.h"
```

```objc
#import "Possession.h"

static NSString * const kPossessionNameKeyPath = @"name";
static NSString * const kPossessionValueKeyPath = @"value";

@implementation PossessionListTableViewCell {
    BOOL isObservingPossession;
}

@synthesize possession = _possession;

- (void)dealloc
{
    if (isObservingPossession == YES) {
        [_possession removeObserver:self
forKeyPath:kPossessionNameKeyPath];
        [_possession removeObserver:self
forKeyPath:kPossessionValueKeyPath];
        isObservingPossession = NO;
    }
}

- (void)setPossession:(Possession *)possession
{
    if (isObservingPossession == YES) {
        [_possession removeObserver:self
forKeyPath:kPossessionNameKeyPath];
        [_possession removeObserver:self
forKeyPath:kPossessionValueKeyPath];
        isObservingPossession = NO;
    }

    _possession = possession;

    if (_possession != nil) {
        [_possession addObserver:self
                      forKeyPath:kPossessionNameKeyPath
                         options:(NSKeyValueObservingOptionInitial |
                                  NSKeyValueObservingOptionNew)
                         context:NULL];

        [_possession addObserver:self
                      forKeyPath:kPossessionValueKeyPath
                         options:(NSKeyValueObservingOptionInitial |
                                  NSKeyValueObservingOptionNew)
                         context:NULL];

        isObservingPossession = YES;
    }
}
```

```
- (void)prepareForReuse
{
    [self setPossession:nil];

    [super prepareForReuse];
}

- (void)observeValueForKeyPath:(NSString *)keyPath
                      ofObject:(id)object
                        change:(NSDictionary *)change
                       context:(void *)context
{
    if (object == [self possession]) {
        if ([keyPath isEqualToString:kPossessionNameKeyPath]) {
            [[self textLabel] setText:[change
objectForKey:NSKeyValueChangeNewKey]];
        }
        else if ([keyPath isEqualToString:kPossessionValueKeyPath]) {
            [[self detailTextLabel] setText:[[change
objectForKey:NSKeyValueChangeNewKey] stringValue]];
        }
    }
}

@end
```

When we set the value of possession, we add an observer for its name and value properties. Whenever we set the observer, we set the value of isObservingPossession to YES to keep track of whether we need to remove it. If we didn't do this, we would run the risk of crashing the app by removing an observer that wasn't registered. When we add the observer, we specify the given options to get a notification immediately with the initial value, as well as on any subsequent changes. Finally, when we observe the change, we set the values in the table view cell. This class is done, so save your work and open PossessionListViewController.m. Add a line with the other #import declarations at the top of the file to import your table view cell class:

#import "PossessionListTableViewCell.h"

Next, modify the tableView:cellForRowAtIndexPath: method to use our new table view cells:

```
- (UITableViewCell *)tableView:(UITableView *)tableView
        cellForRowAtIndexPath:(NSIndexPath *)indexPath
{
    static NSString *CellIdentifier = @"Cell";
    NSString *cellIdentifier = @"PossessionCell";
```

```
    UITableViewCell *cell = [tableView
dequeueReusableCellWithIdentifier:CellIdentifier];
    PossessionListTableViewCell *cell = (PossessionListTableViewCell
*)[tableView dequeueReusableCellWithIdentifier:cellIdentifier];

    if (cell == nil) {
        cell = [[PossessionListTableViewCell alloc]
initWithStyle:UITableViewCellStyleValue1

reuseIdentifier:cellIdentifier];
    }

    Possession *possession = [self possessionAtIndex:[indexPath row]];

    [cell setPossession:possession];

    [cell setAccessoryType:UITableViewCellAccessoryDisclosureIndicator];

    return cell;
}
```

Run the app and edit a possession. You'll see the list's table view cell being updated automatically after you edit its item. While this looks the same as it did before, it's much more efficient, because only the parts that needed to change did, whereas before, every on-screen table view cell was being reloaded. For a larger app with complicated table view cells that require a lot of processor time to create, this can be the difference between a well-performing app and a slow, unpopular app.

Using Key-Value Observation is a great way to control the flow of your app's data. By using KVO to update UI elements, you can decouple the code that updates the model object from the code that updates the UI; now that we've set these table view cells up, we can modify our Possession class instances at will without remembering to update the table view cell. We do still have a problem: new items aren't being added. For that, we can modify the detail view controller's delegate method to inform the table view of the changes. Open PossessionListViewController.m, and modify the possessionDetailViewController:didEditPossession: method as follows:

```
- (void)possessionDetailViewController:(PossessionDetailViewController
*)detailViewController
                    didEditPossession:(Possession *)possession
{
    if ([_possessions containsObject:possession] == NO) {
        [_possessions addObject:possession];
        NSIndexPath *newIndexPath = [NSIndexPath
indexPathForRow:[_possessions indexOfObject:possession]
                                        inSection:0];
```

```
    NSArray *indexPaths = [NSArray arrayWithObject:newIndexPath];

    [[self tableView] insertRowsAtIndexPaths:indexPaths
withRowAnimation:UITableViewRowAnimationAutomatic];
    }
}
```

Now, when you add a new item, the table view will add a row for it automatically without reloading the other rows, which is more efficient. This works well for us in a delegate method, because we already have a connection between these two view controllers. If we didn't, how would we get notified when a new item was added? The answer is another way to move data around in your app: notifications.

Notifications

A common pattern in good code design, as we've mentioned, is decoupling. While delegate protocols are great for this, they still require a one-to-one relationship between the object and its delegate. Notifications, on the other hand, allow you to broadcast a message across your entire app without knowledge of which objects are listening. Notifications are handled by the NSNotificationCenter class, which is a singleton—an object that is designed to have only one instance. You access the singleton instance like so:

```
NSNotificationCenter *nc = [NSNotificationCenter defaultCenter];
```

Registering for Notifications

Like many other APIs in Cocoa Touch, using NSNotificationCenter usually involves setting a target and an action; in this case, the observer is the target. To receive a notification, much like with KVO, you need to register for it:

```
static NSString * const kNotificationName = @"notificationName";

[nc addObserver:self
      selector:@selector(handleNotification:)
         name:kNotificationName
       object:nil];
```

The four arguments begin with the observer, followed by a selector specifying the message to send to the observer when the notification fires. Next is the notification name. This is just a string that identifies the notification. In your own apps, it's better to define the name in a string constant, as shown earlier with kNotificationName, than to retype it every time you use it; it's quite embarrassing to spend a few hours hunting down a bug only to realize that you've misspelled the notification name (not that I've ever done that!). The final argument allows you to specify which object you'd like to receive notifications from. Typically you'll pass nil here, which tells the NSNotificationCenter to send the message when *any* object fires the notification.

> **NOTE:** Just like with Key-Value Observing, it's important to remove an observer for NSNotificationCenter before it's deallocated, lest you run the risk of your app crashing when a deallocated object is sent a message. You'll typically do this in your dealloc method.

You may notice that the selector passed to NSNotificationCenter in that example code ended in a colon, signifying an argument. The argument is of type NSNotification, and it contains some useful information about the notification. Notifications have three instance methods you can use to get this information: name, the name of the notification; object, the object that posted the notification; and userInfo, an NSDictionary containing whatever key-value pairs were included with the notification when it was posted. The userInfo dictionary is one of the more useful features of using NSNotifications, and several system notifications give useful information this way. You can also craft your own userInfo dictionaries when you create your own notifications to pass whatever data you need along with them.

Posting Your Own Notifications

When you want to post a notification, instead of creating your own NSNotification objects, just use one of NSNotificationCenter's convenience methods: either postNotificationName:object: or postNotificationName:object:userInfo:. The first argument, like with registering an observer, is the name of the notification, and the second argument is the object that's posting the notification (almost always self). You can create your own notification objects if you prefer; just use the postNotification: method instead. Creating a notification might look like this:

```
NSDictionary *userInfo = [NSDictionary dictionaryWithObject:@"Fido"
                                                     forKey:@"dogName"];

[nc postNotificationName:@"notificationName"
                  object:self
                userInfo:userInfo];
```

One of the more powerful reasons to use notifications is that you don't need to know anything about the objects that are receiving them. Unlike with delegate messages, you can have multiple objects receive a single notification, so if your app has multiple view controllers that all display the contents of a single object, you can send one notification to inform all of them that the object has been updated.

Common System Notifications

There are some very useful notifications available for your objects to listen for in iOS. Paramount among these is UIApplicationDidReceiveMemoryWarningNotification, which is sent whenever the system is running low on available memory. You've seen this before in view controllers, but if you have an object outside of a view controller that uses large quantities of memory, such as an image cache, you can use this notification to tell you when to purge that memory. Another helpful notification is UIApplicationSignificantTimeChangeNotification, which will be posted when, for instance, daylight saving time takes effect. Any calendar-like application would do well to respond to that notification. There are, of course, more notifications in iOS that are helpful, but it won't do to simply list them here. Instead, you can refer to the developer documentation for more details.

> **NOTE:** As you can see from the two earlier examples, Apple's naming conventions for notification names seem to make them as long as possible. If in other platforms you've tried to keep your code in 80- or 100-character wide screens, if possible, you may have trouble keeping up that style when using Cocoa Touch. Apple errs on the side of verbosity over ambiguity, so long names are common.

Singletons

NSNotificationCenter is a great example of a singleton. Put simply, a singleton is an object designed to have a single instance that lives forever. Singletons are useful for any object that coordinates data for multiple objects, serving as a single point of reference for a common set of functionality. Another example of a singleton is NSFileManager, which is used to access the filesystem of the device, something you'll be doing later in this chapter. Many programmers have a low opinion of singletons, because there is a danger of using them too frequently; if your singletons are never deallocated, they'll use memory indefinitely, so using too many will have adverse performance effects. In Cocoa Touch, singletons are used frequently, but be sure to think about when singletons make sense in your code before you use them.

A typical singleton has a shared instance that's accessed with a class method. A prototypical singleton might look like this:

```
@interface Singleton : NSObject

+ (id)sharedInstance;

@end

@implementation Singleton

static Singleton *_sharedInstance = nil;

+ (id)sharedInstance
{
    if (_sharedInstance == nil) {
        _sharedInstance = [[self alloc] init];
    }

    return _sharedInstance;
}

@end
```

> **NOTE:** Although we initialized _sharedInstance to nil in its declaration line in the previous code, this is not strictly necessary if you're using ARC, because it will be initialized with nil by default. If you aren't using ARC, you'll need to initialize it to nil, because immediately after declaration it will point to a garbage value.

Singletons created in this manner will never be deallocated, because the _sharedInstance variable will always be a reference to it. With ARC's weak references, you could define it as a weak reference, therefore allowing it to be deallocated when it's not in use, but if your singleton is expensive to create (in performance terms), it's probably not worth it.

Some websites may direct you to override the retain, release, and retainCount methods for singletons, allowing you to prohibit the creation of more than one. While this is impossible under ARC, because you can't override those methods, it wasn't the best advice before ARC, either. Sometimes, for performance reasons, you might want to create a separate instance of NSNotificationCenter or NSFileManager that isn't a singleton at all; in that case, using the regular alloc and init methods returns an object just like any other with a normal life cycle.

Another common use for singletons is to manage resources, such as a network connection. Instead of having every view controller in your app loading data from the network, it can be helpful to funnel those operations through a single point, preventing you from trying to load multiple connections at once. This is good for performance and for battery life. We'll cover some more techniques for networking later.

Persisting Data to a File

So far in this chapter we've covered various ways to move data around your application. They all share one large disadvantage: they don't save data in a way that outlives the application. When your app quits, Key-Value Observing notifications cease to fire, system notifications don't reach your code, and your delegates are gone. Ideally, you would save your user's data to disk before the app quits and load it in when the app starts, allowing their work to outlive the app's session. There are a few ways to save data, each with their own advantages and limitations. We'll start with the simplest of these: user defaults. We'll also cover saving data to files using archiving, as well as writing files directly.

NSUserDefaults

If you've been a long-time Mac user, then you've probably wanted to enable hidden preferences for some applications before. For instance, to view hidden files in Finder, the trick is to open Terminal and issue the following command:

```
defaults write com.apple.finder AppleShowAllFiles TRUE
```

Restart the Finder, and you're all set. The defaults command on your Mac is interacting with the user defaults system of Mac OS X, which exists on iOS as well. On the Mac, in your home folder, application preferences can be found at the directory ~/Library/Preferences/. Each file corresponds to an application's preferences, and they contain key-value pairs, just like an NSDictionary. Instead of saving, loading, and managing these files manually, NSUserDefaults manages them for you, allowing you to set persistent values. It's just as easy on iOS. To save a value into a key called userName, simply call the NSUserDefaults singleton:

```
[[NSUserDefaults standardUserDefaults] setObject:@"Jeff" forKey:@"userName"];
```

From that point forward, unless you delete that key or the user deletes the app, you can always get the value of userName just as easily:

```
NSString *userName = [[NSUserDefaults standardUserDefaults]
objectForKey:@"userName"];
```

> **NOTE:** If the key you ask for doesn't exist in the user defaults dictionary, you'll get
> nil back. Be sure to account for this possibility.

Not all objects can be saved using NSUserDefaults. Those that can are NSArray,
NSData, NSDate, NSDictionary, NSNumber, and NSString. These are the types of
objects that iOS knows how to write into a *property list*, which is a special XML-
based file that encodes these objects. The code you just saw to save userName
to the user defaults would result in the following property list file being written:

```
<?xml version="1.0" encoding="UTF-8"?>
<!DOCTYPE plist PUBLIC "-//Apple//DTD PLIST 1.0//EN"
"http://www.apple.com/DTDs/PropertyList-1.0.dtd">
<plist version="1.0">
<dict>
    <key>userName</key>
    <string>Jeff</string>
</dict>
</plist>
```

"Property list" is abbreviated as plist here. In between the opening <plist>
and closing </plist> tags is a hierarchy of objects. Property lists have one root
object, usually either an array or a dictionary, specified here with dict. A
dictionary has key-value pairs, specified by alternating <key> tags with value
tags. Since we specified a string, the value tag is <string>, but other types can
also appear. Dictionaries and arrays can nest one another. This is a property list
containing two dictionaries in an array:

```
<?xml version="1.0" encoding="UTF-8"?>
<!DOCTYPE plist PUBLIC "-//Apple//DTD PLIST 1.0//EN"
"http://www.apple.com/DTDs/PropertyList-1.0.dtd">
<plist version="1.0">
<array>
    <dict>
        <key>userName</key>
        <string>Jeff</string>
    </dict>
    <dict>
        <key>userName</key>
        <string>Amanda</string>
    </dict>
</array>
</plist>
```

As you can see, the two dictionaries appear one after the other in the array. There's no special syntax between objects in an array, just a series of them.

Using User Defaults to Save App Data

Let's modify MyStuff to save data to disk using `NSUserDefaults`. Open `PossessionListViewController.m` in Xcode. We'll declare two new methods in our class extension. Add the lines in bold:

```
@interface PossessionListViewController() {
    NSMutableArray *_possessions;
}

- (void)addItemButtonPressed:(id)sender;
- (Possession *)possessionAtIndex:(NSUInteger)index;
- (void)savePossessionsToDisk;
- (void)loadPossessionsFromDisk;

@end
```

First, we'll implement savePossessionsToUserDefaults. Since we can't save a Possession object directly to the user defaults, we'll convert it to an NSDictionary first. Add the new method in the @implementation block of the file:

```
- (void)savePossessionsToDisk
{
    NSMutableArray *possessionsAsDictionaries =
    [NSMutableArray arrayWithCapacity:[_possessions count]];

    for (Possession *possession in _possessions) {
        NSDictionary *possessionRepresentation =
        [NSDictionary dictionaryWithObjectsAndKeys:
          [possession name], @"name",
          [possession value], @"value", nil];

        [possessionsAsDictionaries addObject:possessionRepresentation];
    }

    [[NSUserDefaults standardUserDefaults] setObject:possessionsAsDictionaries
                                        forKey:@"possessions"];
    [[NSUserDefaults standardUserDefaults] synchronize];
}
```

This code creates a mutable array with enough capacity for each possession. A mutable array is simply an array that can be modified after it's created. Next, we iterate through our array of possessions. For each one, we create a dictionary with keys to match the properties of the object. Then we add the dictionary to the mutable array and move to the next possession. When this is all done, we save the array to the user defaults database for the key possessions. We'll use that key in our loading method. Finally, we send the synchronize method to the user defaults singleton. This forces it to save our changes to disk. If you omit this, you may find that the application is killed by the system before NSUserDefaults periodically writes its in-memory cache to the filesystem. Calling synchronize forces your changes to be persisted. This is especially helpful while debugging an app, since killing the iPhone Simulator will almost always quit the app before NSUserDefaults saves automatically.

The method to load possessions from the user defaults is similarly simple. Add this method after the previous one:

```
- (void)loadPossessionsFromDisk
{
    NSArray *possessionDictionaries =
    [[NSUserDefaults standardUserDefaults] objectForKey:@"possessions"];

    _possessions = [NSMutableArray array];

    for (NSDictionary *dictionary in possessionDictionaries) {
        Possession *possession = [[Possession alloc] init];

        [possession setName:[dictionary objectForKey:@"name"]];
        [possession setValue:[dictionary objectForKey:@"value"]];

        [_possessions addObject:possession];
    }
}
```

In this method, first we load the array of possessions from NSUserDefaults. Even though we saved it from an NSMutableArray, it's actually saved as an immutable array. Next, we set _possessions to an empty mutable array to prepare it for loading our possessions in. We iterate over the dictionaries in the array from NSUserDefaults, creating a new Possession value for each one and filling in its values from the dictionary and then adding it to our possessions array.

Now that we've written this array, we need to save it. Modify the possessionDetailViewController:didEditPossession: method to save the array:

```
- (void)possessionDetailViewController:(PossessionDetailViewController
*)detailViewController
                didEditPossession:(Possession *)possession
{
    if ([_possessions containsObject:possession] == NO) {
        [_possessions addObject:possession];
        NSIndexPath *newIndexPath = [NSIndexPath indexPathForRow:[_possessions
indexOfObject:possession]
```

```
                                                       inSection:0];
        NSArray *indexPaths = [NSArray arrayWithObject:newIndexPath];

        [[self tableView] insertRowsAtIndexPaths:indexPaths
withRowAnimation:UITableViewRowAnimationAutomatic];
    }

    [self savePossessionsToDisk];
}
```

Next, we need to load our items when the app starts. Modify
initWithNibName:bundle: to do so, removing our test data from earlier:

```
- (id)initWithNibName:(NSString *)nibNameOrNil
              bundle:(NSBundle *)nibBundleOrNil
{
    self = [super initWithNibName:nibNameOrNil
                           bundle:nibBundleOrNil];

    if (self) {
        Possession *iPhone = [[Possession alloc] init];
        [iPhone setName:@"iPhone 4S"];
        [iPhone setValue:[NSNumber numberWithInt:649]];

        Possession *iPad = [[Possession alloc] init];
        [iPad setName:@"iPad 2"];
        [iPad setValue:[NSNumber numberWithInt:499]];

        _possessions = [NSMutableArray arrayWithObjects:iPhone, iPad, nil];

        [self loadPossessionsFromDisk];

        [self setTitle:@"My Stuff"];

        UIBarButtonItem *addItemButton =
        [[UIBarButtonItem alloc]
initWithBarButtonSystemItem:UIBarButtonSystemItemAdd
                                                  target:self
action:@selector(addItemButtonPressed:)];
        [[self navigationItem] setRightBarButtonItem:addItemButton];
    }

    return self;
}
```

Run the app again, and you'll notice that your list of items is empty. Add a new
one, and then quit the iPhone Simulator. Run the app again, and there's your

item! You now have an app that persists data between launches. If you added two sample items and examined the preferences file, it would look like this:

```
<?xml version="1.0" encoding="UTF-8"?>
<!DOCTYPE plist PUBLIC "-//Apple//DTD PLIST 1.0//EN"
"http://www.apple.com/DTDs/PropertyList-1.0.dtd">
<plist version="1.0">
<dict>
    <key>possessions</key>
    <array>
        <dict>
            <key>name</key>
            <string>iPhone 4S</string>
            <key>value</key>
            <integer>649</integer>
        </dict>
        <dict>
            <key>name</key>
            <string>iPad 2</string>
            <key>value</key>
            <integer>499</integer>
        </dict>
    </array>
</dict>
</plist>
```

Notice that the array of possessions is itself in a dictionary. The top-level object of all preference files is a dictionary. This is a good example of the nesting that occurs in property lists, because we have two dictionaries in an array in another dictionary.

Using NSUserDefaults to persist data works well enough, but it isn't really designed to store *all* of your app's data. It would be better if we could archive our possessions to a separate file, leaving NSUserDefaults for preferences in our app. This is actually fairly easy to do, because both NSArray and NSDictionary support writing their contents to disk directly as a property list. This still means, however, that we can't save our objects directly, so we'll still have to convert our Possession objects to NSDictionary objects. First, we'll need a location to save the file. Add a new method declaration in the class extension in PossessionsListViewController.m by adding the line in bold:

```
@interface PossessionListViewController() {
    NSMutableArray *_possessions;
}

@property (strong) NSMutableArray *possessions;

- (void)addItemButtonPressed:(id)sender;
- (Possession *)possessionAtIndex:(NSUInteger)index;
```

```
- (NSString *)possessionsArchivePath;
- (void)savePossessionsToDisk;
- (void)loadPossessionsFromDisk;

@end
```

Next, add the following lines in bold in the class implementation to implement the method:

```
- (NSString *)possessionsArchivePath
{
    NSString *documentsPath =
    [NSSearchPathForDirectoriesInDomains(NSDocumentDirectory,
                                         NSUserDomainMask,
                                         YES) objectAtIndex:0];
    return [documentsPath
stringByAppendingPathComponent:@"possessions.plist"];
}
```

To save our objects to disk, we simply need to call a single method on the temporary array of dictionaries we've created. Modify the savePossessionsToDisk method by removing the lines that are struck out and adding the lines in bold:

```
- (void)savePossessionsToDisk
{
    NSMutableArray *possessionsAsDictionaries =
    [NSMutableArray arrayWithCapacity:[_possessions count]];

    for (Possession *possession in _possessions) {
        NSDictionary *possessionRepresentation =
        [NSDictionary dictionaryWithObjectsAndKeys:
         [possession name], @"name",
         [possession value], @"value", nil];

        [possessionsAsDictionaries addObject:possessionRepresentation];
    }

    [[NSUserDefaults standardUserDefaults] setObject:possessionsAsDictionaries
                                    forKey:@"possessions"];
    [[NSUserDefaults standardUserDefaults] synchronize];
    [possessionsAsDictionaries writeToFile:[self possessionsArchivePath]
                            atomically:YES];
}
```

The writeToFile:atomically method of NSArray will take care of creating a property list file for you. The atomically argument, if passed YES, will create the file in a temporary location and move it into place once it's done. This helps avoid having an unfinished file in that location if there's an error saving it, preventing further errors when you're loading the file.

Loading from this file is a quick change. Modify the loadPossessionsFromDisk method by removing the lines that have been struck out and adding the lines in bold:

```
- (void)loadPossessionsFromDisk
{
    NSArray *possessionDictionaries =
    [[NSUserDefaults standardUserDefaults] objectForKey:@"possessions"];
    NSArray *possessionDictionaries =
    [NSArray arrayWithContentsOfFile:[self possessionsArchivePath]];

    _possessions = [NSMutableArray array];

    for (NSDictionary *dictionary in possessionDictionaries) {
        Possession *possession = [[Possession alloc] init];

        [possession setName:[dictionary objectForKey:@"name"]];
        [possession setValue:[dictionary objectForKey:@"value"]];

        [_possessions addObject:possession];
    }
}
```

Just like that, we're saving and loading to our own file. In fact, you can even open this file and edit it on your Mac. Run the application, save some content into it, and quit the iPhone Simulator. The file that's been saved is on your filesystem, but it's in a hidden-by-default location on Lion: your Library folder. Open a Finder window on your Mac, and select Go ➤ Go to Folder… in the menu bar or press Shift+⌘+G; then enter ~/Library/Application Support/iPhone Simulator in the dialog box that appears. Select the subfolder that matches the version of iOS you've been using (check Xcode if you're unsure) and then the Applications folder contained inside. All of the apps in your iPhone Simulator are represented as a folder with a long, nonsensical UUID for a name. Select them until you see the one that has MyStuff inside. In *that* folder, look in the Documents subfolder, and you'll see possessions.plist. You can open this file in Xcode, which has an editing mode for property lists. Figure 4-1 shows the file opened in Xcode.

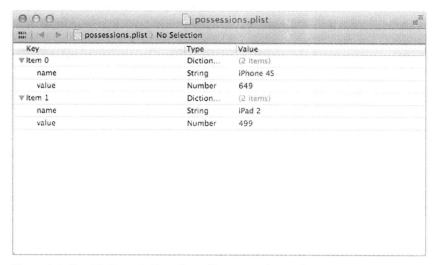

Figure 4-1. *Xcode's Property List editor with* `possessions.plist` *open*

You can see that each dictionary has a drop-down element on the left, with items listed underneath while expanded. For the dictionary, you can edit the key, type, and value from within Xcode. Try it yourself—change one of the values, save the file, and then run your app from Xcode. This ability to open property lists and edit those values directly is an excellent debugging tool.

NSCoding

As good as our file-saving solution is, we still have to go through the trouble of converting our objects to an `NSDictionary` when we save them and from a dictionary back to an object when we load them. Fortunately, there is a protocol we can conform to, NSCoding, that helps with this. We still have to do some work, but we don't have to create any temporary arrays or dictionaries. Let's implement NSCoding in MyStuff to simplify how we save and load files. Open the header file for `Possession`, `Possession.h`, and declare your conformity to this protocol by adding the code in bold:

```
@interface Possession : NSObject <NSCoding>
```

There are two methods to implement in `Possession.m`. First, we'll set up some string constants that we'll refer to. These constants are the keys we'll use to archive properties to disk. Add the following lines in bold before the implementation:

```
static NSString * const kNameKey = @"name";
static NSString * const kValueKey = @"value";
```

```
@implementation Possession
```

Then, we'll implement `initWithCoder:`, which is called to load your object from disk by adding the code in bold to the implementation:

```
- (id)initWithCoder:(NSCoder *)aDecoder
{
    self = [self init];

    if (self) {
        [self setName:[aDecoder decodeObjectForKey:kNameKey]];
        [self setValue:[aDecoder decodeObjectForKey:kValueKey]];
    }

    return self;
}
```

You'll notice that this looks just like a regular `init` method, albeit with this `NSCoder` argument. The `NSCoder` is a helper object that transfers values from the file to your object. Saving an object is shorter. Add an `encodeWithCoder:` method by adding the following code in bold after `initWithCoder:` in your implementation:

```
- (void)encodeWithCoder:(NSCoder *)aCoder
{
    [aCoder encodeObject:[self name]
                  forKey:kNameKey];
    [aCoder encodeObject:[self value]
                  forKey:kValueKey];
}
```

> **NOTE:** When you have many properties that you're saving to disk, the potential for typos is high. It's recommended you use string constants for all of your keys so that if you do make a typo, you make it in a way that'll be consistent. There's no rule that says you have to save a property to a key that matches its name, so if you mistype it, the compiler won't complain.

To write your object to disk, open `PossessionListViewController.m`, and modify the `savePossesionsToDisk` method:

```
- (void)savePossessionsToDisk
{
    [NSKeyedArchiver archiveRootObject:_possessions
                               toFile:[self possessionsArchivePath]];

    NSMutableArray *possessionsAsDictionaries =
```

```
        [NSMutableArray arrayWithCapacity:[_possessions count]];

        for (Possession *possession in _possessions) {
            NSDictionary *possessionRepresentation =
            [NSDictionary dictionaryWithObjectsAndKeys:
            [possession name], @"name",
            [possession value], @"value", nil];

            [possessionsAsDictionaries addObject:possessionRepresentation];
        }

        [possessionsAsDictionaries writeToFile:[self possessionsArchivePath]
                                    atomically:YES];
}
```

This introduces the NSKeyedArchiver object, which you'll use in conjunction with any class that conforms to the NSCoding protocol. When we pass it our array of possessions, it simply iterates over them and archives them to a file using the NSCoding methods we wrote. And, as you can see, the amount of code it took to write the file in this method was drastically reduced. The story is similar for loading objects from the file. Modify loadPossessionsFromDisk as follows:

```
- (void)loadPossessionsFromDisk
{
    NSArray *possessionDictionaries =
    [NSArray arrayWithContentsOfFile:[self possessionsArchivePath]];

    _possessions = [NSMutableArray array];
    _possessions = [NSKeyedUnarchiver unarchiveObjectWithFile:[self
possessionsArchivePath]];

    if (_possessions == nil) {
        _possessions = [NSMutableArray array];
    }

    for (NSDictionary *dictionary in possessionDictionaries) {
        Possession *possession = [[Possession alloc] init];

        [possession setName:[dictionary objectForKey:@"name"]];
        [possession setValue:[dictionary objectForKey:@"value"]];

        [_possessions addObject:possession];
    }
}
```

This is also less code, but you'll notice that we added a check to see whether _possessions is nil after loading. If the file doesn't exist, the NSKeyedUnarchiver object will return nil, and in that case, we create an empty array so that we can still add to it. If you run the app now and you had previously saved data, it'll

crash, since what existed before in possessions.plist isn't what
NSKeyedUnarchiver expects. This is a good lesson for your app in general:
between versions, if you switch file names, be sure to anticipate the old file
names existing and potentially being in a different format. To get around this,
let's switch from using the plist file extension to the archive file extension. In
PossessionListViewController.m, remove the struck-out line and add the line in
bold to the possessionsArchivePath method:

```
- (NSString *)possessionsArchivePath
{
    NSString *documentsPath =
    [NSSearchPathForDirectoriesInDomains(NSDocumentDirectory,
                                        NSUserDomainMask,
                                        YES) objectAtIndex:0];
    return [documentsPath stringByAppendingPathComponent:@"possessions.plist"];
    return [documentsPath
stringByAppendingPathComponent:@"possessions.archive"];
}
```

Technically, what NSKeyedArchiver saves *is* a property list, but it isn't one that
you'd ever want to modify by hand. Figure 4-2 displays the property list as
opened in Xcode.

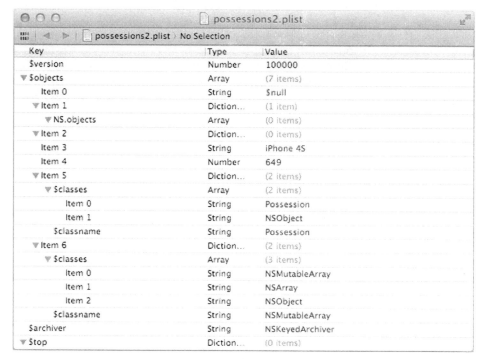

Figure 4-2. *A property list as saved by an* `NSKeyedArchiver`

Even if you were able to figure out the format Apple's using for this property list, there's no guarantee that it won't change drastically in the next version of Mac OS X or iOS, so trying to parse it on your own is probably a fruitless endeavor.

The process of saving a file to disk in this manner is called *serialization*. The idea is that an object that's been *serialized* to disk should be indistinguishable from an object that's *deserialized* from disk. This is usually the case with objects that implement `NSCoding`, unless you don't encode key information when encoding it. It's also how nibs work; a nib is just an XML property list containing serialized objects. When you load a nib from the disk in your app, the view is simply deserialized from the file. In effect, when you drag a label onto your view when using the nib editor in Xcode, you're creating that object directly and then saving it into a form from which it can be restored when the app is running.

Manual File Handling

Using `NSCoding` or property list objects to save your data to disk has some important advantages. First, the code is very well-tested. Because Apple relies on it for implementations of iOS frameworks, it has unit tests around it and a whole team of engineers capable of fixing it. Second, it's portable, which means that instead of saving the binary data of your objects to a file, it saves a representation of the data that's independent of the processor architecture of the computer it's running on. The details are a fairly advanced topics, but it should suffice to know that different processors store data in memory differently, and if you tried to save that data to disk directly as the processor stores it or transmit that data to another computer as the processor stores it, you might wind up trying to open data that isn't saved in the format *your* computer expects it to be. Code that gets around this is called *portable*, and using NSCoding methods to save your data does this for you.

Sometimes, perhaps for performance reasons, to save disk space, or to work with a proprietary file format, you may want to read from and write to files on disk directly, without using higher-level helper objects like NSKeyedArchiver and the like. To do that, you can use the NSFileHandle object, which will allow you to read and write bytes directly to the file. While using higher-level APIs to save data is usually recommended, there are other options if you can't.

SQLite Databases

There are several important drawbacks to the way we've approached saving content in our app so far. One of the more serious problems you'll encounter as your app gets more complex is that your model objects will begin to eat up a lot of memory. While our possessions array is miniscule with a handful of objects, a user who has a lot of things—say, in the order of millions—will present a problem. When we reach this point, we need to implement a solution that saves our objects to disk and also allows us to load a portion of them at a time without loading the entire array. We also need to be able to save our array of possessions without loading the entire array into memory.

One way you might solve this problem would be to save each possession to its own file and then use a directory containing them as a container instead of an array. A better implementation, however, would be to use a database technology to store the data instead of flat files. iOS supports SQLite out of the box, so if you're familiar with SQL databases, you can apply that technology to your iOS apps with very little effort. We won't go into it here, but it would be trivial to use a SQLite database in MyStuff, enabling us to persist data using the database instead of property lists, which would allow the app to store much more data. SQLite is also very good performance-wise, which will be important when your app reaches a point where you need to add SQLite for scaling reasons.

File Locations on iOS

We've talked a lot about files but not really about where those files go. You may have seen a bit of the filesystem hierarchy of your app while poking around in the Finder and inspecting the iPhone Simulator's files. Let's take a step back and talk about how your iOS app will interact with files. One important concept to understand is that your app is *sandboxed*: it can't access the files, passwords, preferences, or images of any other app. There are well-defined places where your app is allowed to save files, with different implications and conventions for saving files in each. Files included with your app are in the *app bundle*.

The App Bundle

The app bundle is a directory that contains everything your app includes when users download it from the App Store: images, videos, the executable file, and so on. The app bundle is strictly read-only, and its integrity is verified with code signing. Because of the code-signing requirement, changing anything in the app bundle would invalidate the code signature, rendering your app unusable. To get a file out of the app bundle, you can use the NSBundle class. Here's some code you would write to get the path to the file Catalog.pdf from the bundle:

```
NSString *path = [[NSBundle mainBundle] pathForResource:@"Catalog"
                                        ofType:@"pdf"];
```

Loading files from the bundle will obviously work only if you've included the file in the app. If you have many files or if they're especially large, you may not want to include them in your application bundle. There are two other main locations to store files: the Documents directory and the Caches directory.

The Documents Directory

The Documents directory on iOS is the main place where you'll store user-generated files. Files that are placed in the Documents directory are backed up when the device is backed up using iCloud or iTunes, so it's important to store files that can't easily be re-created in Documents to avoid losing them. To get the path to the Documents directory, use the NSSearchPathForDirectoriesInDomains function:

```
NSArray *documentsDirectories =
NSSearchPathForDirectoriesInDomains(NSDocumentDirectory,
                                    NSUserDomainMask,
                                    YES);
```

NSSearchPathForDirectoriesInDomains returns an array of paths, so to get the path, just get the first object from the array. The first argument is the most important to specify; in this case, it specifies that you're looking for the Documents directory.

The Caches Directory

The Caches directory is different from the Documents directory in a few key ways. First, it isn't backed up. Files that you place in Caches will be deleted if the user gets a new phone and transfers their information to it. With that restriction, it's important to only put files in the Caches directory that you can either re-create or re-download, since at any time they may cease to exist. iOS 5 added a feature that automatically cleans caches when the device runs short on memory, much to the chagrin of apps that were relying on those files persisting, though Apple has since added a way to mark a file in Caches as one that the system should not automatically purge, which will be covered later in this book. Getting the Caches directory is just like getting the Documents directory:

```
NSArray *cacheDirectories =
NSSearchPathForDirectoriesInDomains(NSCachesDirectory,
                                    NSUserDomainMask,
                                    YES);
```

Like with the Documents directory, this returns an array of directories, of which there will be one.

Core Data

Managing files across the filesystem, a database in SQLite, and moving objects in and out of memory is a lot of work, and it's hard to get right. You may be removing objects from memory too aggressively (or not aggressively enough), your database code may not be optimized, and your filesystem access might be a huge, unorganized mess. Data persistence is also a common problem. Nearly every app needs to manage objects, store them, and find them. Apple's answer to this problem is Core Data, a framework available on Mac OS X and iOS that manages your data persistence for you. Core Data can save your app's data in a SQLite database, which is the default, in XML or binary formats, or simply save it in memory; Core Data can also automatically save large files such as images and videos in external files to improve database performance. The centerpiece of Core Data is the *managed object model*, which is a document that describes your data. Using a visual layout in Xcode, you can define classes and the relationships between them. For instance, an app that tracks books might have a Book class and an Author class. Using Core Data, you would create an object diagram that looks like Figure 4-3.

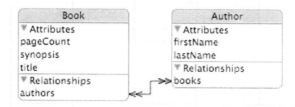

Figure 4-3. *Editing* Book *and* Author *classes in Core Data*

This configuration would create the two classes. The Book class would have pageCount, synopsis, and title properties, as well as an NSSet of Authors. The Author class would have a firstName and lastName properties, as well as an NSSet of Books. This alone makes Core Data a convenient tool, just for object modeling. Core Data also manages the object life cycle for you, from creating an object to saving it to disk. Finally, Core Data can search for objects for you, even automating the management of table views to display your search results. It's a powerful tool. For more information, there are excellent books that cover Core Data: *More iOS 5 Development* and *Pro Core Data for iOS, Second Edition*.

Summary

In this chapter, we talked about what to do with your data. Whether you're moving it around in your app with Key-Value Observing or sending NSNotifications, there are several ways to get a pointer to an object from point A to point B. We've also talked about using NSUserDefaults to store preferences and simple key-value pairs to persist data. For larger amounts of data, we covered creating property lists, as well as using the NSCoding protocol to store archived data. Now that we've covered what to do with your data, in the next chapter we'll cover how to let the user interact with it.

Handling User Touches

The iPhone was a drastic change from every computing platform that came before it in many ways, but none more so than its lack of a mouse or keyboard. Instead of responding to keyboard key presses, mouse clicks, and mouseover events, the iPhone responds to *touch*. Designing a user interface around touch is more than converting from clicks to taps. The iPhone offers *direct manipulation*: when you place your finger on a message in Mail and move it down an inch, the contents of the message move down an inch as well. Direct manipulation effectively removes a layer of abstraction between the user and the content dating back to the very first graphical user interfaces (GUIs): the scroll bar. As a result, iOS and other touchscreen operating systems are easier to use and more intuitive than their desktop predecessors. This chapter will show you how you can use touch in your apps, transforming a stale user experience into a rich, immersive app that users will love. We'll talk about various ways you can make your application respond to user touches, including custom views and gesture recognizers, as well as update our MyStuff example app with some new user interface elements.

The Responder Chain

If you look at the UIView documentation, you'll see that UIView inherits from UIResponder. To find the documentation, open the Organizer window in Xcode by pressing ⌘+Option+2 or by selecting Window ➤ Organizer. Select the Documentation icon on the toolbar, and you'll be in the documentation browser. To find the UIView documentation, we'll search the documentation library for it. To open the search panel, click the magnifying glass icon in the left pane, press ⌘+Option+2, or select Help ➤ Documentation and API Reference. Type UIView in the search box to start searching. If you don't find any results, you might not be searching the iOS library; click the hourglass icon in the search field text box, and then select Show Find Options. Ensure that an iOS library is enabled in the drop-down list that appears next to Doc Sets.

A responder is simply any object that responds to user input. Since UIView inherits from UIResponder, we know that it can receive user input. In Cocoa Touch, user touches are a kind of UIEvent that get passed to a UIResponder object to be dealt with. UIEvents can be more than just touches, too: they're generated when the user shakes the device or when the user uses a remote control, like the volume controls on Apple-branded earbuds.

When the user taps the screen, the system figures out what the topmost view is at that location and sends it a UIEvent object containing one or more UITouch objects. Most of the time, the user inputs only one touch at a time but occasionally (more so on iPad, with its larger screen) may be using two or more fingers to touch simultaneously. Once the event has been sent to the topmost UIView object, it has entered what's known as the *responder chain*. Each object in the responder chain is responsible for either handling the event, therefore consuming it, or sending it to the *next* object in the chain. Every object in the chain inherits from UIResponder, giving them all a common set of methods to use in evaluating the touch(es). UIResponder also declares the nextResponder method, which returns the next responder in the responder chain.

Let's follow the user's tap up the responder chain to see where it goes. First, the user taps the screen, creating UITouch and UIEvent objects. The system analyzes the current view hierarchy on the screen, determines the topmost view that contains the coordinates at which the user touched, and sends it a message with the touch and the event as arguments (we'll get into the specifics of this message later). If the view does not respond to the touch, it calls nextResponder on itself. The UIView implementation of nextResponder returns the view's view controller if it has one—UIViewController also inherits from UIResponder. If not, it returns its superview, which is the view it's contained in. If the view controller doesn't consume the touches, it returns the view's superview in its nextResponder implementation. So, a touch many levels deep in the view hierarchy could pass through a view, a few levels of superviews, a view controller, back to another view, and so on. Eventually, the nextResponder method of UIView will return the topmost view in any application, the UIWindow. If the window doesn't consume the view, its next responder is the UIApplication object that represents the foreground application. While it's possible to subclass UIApplication to do custom event handling, the practice is very rare and best avoided. Instead, beginning in iOS 5, your application delegate can inherit from UIResponder instead of NSObject, giving you a better place to respond to events at an application level.

For touch events, it's easy for the application to determine which view a user probably meant to tap, since it knows the location of the touch. For other events, it's not so clear. When the user shakes the device or taps the on-screen keyboard, this generates an event with no obvious way to determine which object should receive it. The answer in Cocoa Touch is called the *first responder*. When an object becomes the first responder, it becomes the starting point for events such as these. In fact, to get the on-screen keyboard to appear, you can call the becomeFirstResponder method on a UITextField object, and you can force it to disappear by calling resignFirstResponder on the text field. The first responder can also be useful if, say, you want to implement a view that changes color when you shake the device.

Custom Views

The most direct route to handling user input is to create your own custom UIView subclass. While this is the most direct route, it's also the most involved. In a subclass of UIResponder, you can implement the touch methods directly. The touch methods, which correspond to four phases of the touch, are as follows:

```
- (void)touchesBegan:(NSSet *)touches withEvent:(UIEvent *)event;
- (void)touchesCancelled:(NSSet *)touches withEvent:(UIEvent *)event;
- (void)touchesEnded:(NSSet *)touches withEvent:(UIEvent *)event;
- (void)touchesMoved:(NSSet *)touches withEvent:(UIEvent *)event;
```

It's important to implement all four of these methods, because the UIKit framework expects a UIView to handle the entire set of touch events. Each method has in common an NSSet of touches and a UIEvent object to which they belong. An NSSet is a collection class like an NSArray but is unordered. An important difference between a set and an array is that an object can be in a set only once but can be in an array at multiple locations. Attempting to add an object to a set it's already in will have no effect. There's also the NSOrderedSet class, introduced in iOS 5, which is ordered like an array but enforces unique objects like a set. Let's look at an example implementation for a view. To call the method didReceiveTap when the user taps the view, you would need to put code only in the touchesEnded:withEvent: method, though you would implement all four methods:

```
- (void)touchesBegan:(NSSet *)touches withEvent:(UIEvent *)event
{
}

- (void)touchesMoved:(NSSet *)touches withEvent:(UIEvent *)event
```

```
{
}

- (void)touchesEnded:(NSSet *)touches withEvent:(UIEvent *)event
{
    [self didReceiveTap];
}

- (void)touchesCancelled:(NSSet *)touches withEvent:(UIEvent *)event
{
}
```

The fourth method in this list, touchesCancelled:withEvent:, is called when the system interrupts the touch. If you were creating a painting app, for instance, and the user received a phone call while painting, this method would be called. The key difference between it and touchesEnded:withEvent: is that the former is triggered by the system while the latter is triggered by the user.

While implementing a tap is easy, more advanced touch patterns require significant effort to code. To implement a swipe to the right, you have to track all touches, measure the distance between them, and decide how close to a horizontal line to allow the user to draw and still trigger a swipe gesture. To implement a pinch, you need to track two or more lines of movement. A common problem with these is that since you're implementing all of this code yourself, what one developer does will differ from what another does. My code may be more forgiving than yours on calling a crooked swipe a horizontal one, while yours may allow for slower double-taps than mine. What's worse, we both had to spend the time writing touch-handling code! Luckily, beginning in iOS 3.2 with the introduction of the iPad, Apple introduced the UIGestureRecognizer class, which delivers a solution to touch-handling woes.

UIGestureRecognizer

A UIGestureRecognizer is a helper object designed to take the guesswork and manual coding out of touch recognition. There are several premade subclasses available to use, and together they form a powerful suite. You can create as many gesture recognizers as you want and even use multiple gesture recognizers with a single view. You can subclass UIGestureRecognizer to implement custom gestures in an efficient and reusable manner, or even mix them with your own manual touch-handling code.

More Target-Action Methods

Like the UIControl subclasses we looked at earlier, UIGestureRecognizers operate using the target-action paradigm. Unlike UIControl, there are not multiple control events or different actions to send; a gesture recognizer performs the action on the target only when it has successfully recognized its gesture. You can use the addTarget:action: method to add multiple objects as targets for a single gesture recognizer.

Gesture Recognizer Life Cycle

Gesture recognizers are created like any object and initialized with the initWithTarget:action: method. Since it doesn't make any sense to recognize a gesture and do *nothing* with it, you can't create a gesture recognizer without specifying at least one target-action pair. Once you create it, you add it to a view using the UIView method addGestureRecognizer:. Gesture recognizers operate on a specific view, so while you can't add one gesture recognizer to two views, you *can* add it to a superview they have in common.

Once the gesture recognizer has been added to a view, it transitions through a series of states (accessible through its state property). At the beginning, the state is *possible*. When the gesture is finished, the state is either *recognized* or *failed*, depending on whether the received touches matched the gesture. If the state is *recognized*, then the gesture recognizer calls the action method of its target.

Some gesture recognizers are *continuous*, which means that instead of detecting one discrete gesture, they send constant updates when they receive touches. If you wanted to track touches in a painting app, for instance, you could use a continuous gesture recognizer to get immediate updates while the user moves a finger. For a continuous gesture recognizer, there are additional states: *began*, called when the touches start, *changed*, called every time they change, and *ended*, which is equivalent to *recognized* on a noncontinuous gesture recognizer.

Built-in Gesture Recognizers

Apple provides six built-in gesture recognizers with iOS 5, all of them subclasses of UIGestureRecognizer. In order of increasing complexity, they are as follows:

▨ UITapGestureRecognizer: A tap gesture recognizer recognizes taps. You can customize it by modifying the numberOfTapsRequired property to enforce multiple taps, as well as the numberOfTouchesRequired property to enforce multiple fingers doing the touching.

▨ UILongPressGestureRecognizer: A long press is a tap that isn't released immediately. The long press gesture recognizer shares the numberOfTapsRequired and numberOfTouchesRequired properties with UITapGestureRecognizer but also has the minimumPressDuration property, allowing you to specify the amount of time that qualifies as a long press, and has the allowableMovement property that defines the maximum distance a touch can move before canceling the long press. One advantage of the long press gesture recognizer is that these two values are set to sensible defaults, making apps that use them consistent with one another.

▨ UISwipeGestureRecognizer: A swipe gesture recognizer recognizes when the user swipes up, left, right, or down, exposed in the direction property, and allows you to specify the numberOfTouchesRequired property. A swipe gesture recognizer is *not* continuous, so you won't receive any messages from it until the user has completed the swipe.

▨ UIPanGestureRecognizer: A pan gesture recognizer also recognizes the motion of the user's finger but in a continuous manner. You can specify the maximumNumberOfTouches and minimumNumberOfTouches properties to customize its behavior, and there are two methods to query its values: translationInView: and velocityInView:. The translation allows you to reposition a view based on the user dragging their finger, for instance, while the velocity (measured in points per second) allows you to add cool features like throwing a view with inertia.

▨ UIPinchGestureRecognizer: A pinch gesture recognizer measures continuous finger movement toward and away from the center of all touches. It uses the relative change in location to adjust its scale property, which you could use, for instance, to resize the view. The pinch gesture recognizer also provides the velocity property.

⬚ UIRotationGestureRecognizer: Like the pinch gesture
recognizer, the rotate gesture recognizer measures two
touches continuously, but instead of scale, gives you rotation
in radians, allowing you to rotate the view based on user input.

These classes allow for significant customization of your UI's behavior. By
combining gesture recognizers, you can implement complicated user interfaces
and patterns without writing a line of code that directly handles user touches.
Add that to the consistent behavior users expect that you gain when using
system-provided gesture recognizers, and you get a recipe for UI success.

Custom UIGestureRecognizers

Despite the depth of the built-in gesture recognizers' support for most of the
gestures you'll want to use in your apps, occasionally you'll need one that does
something that's just a bit different. In that situation, you can create your own
subclass of UIGestureRecognizer to recognize it for you. If, for instance, you
wanted a gesture recognizer that recognized a downward gesture in the shape
of a greater-than sign (>), you could implement it yourself.

> **NOTE:** To create a subclass of UIGestureRecognizer, you must import an extra
> header in your implementation file: UIGestureRecognizerSubclass.h. This file
> contains redefinitions of some of the regular header's properties, allowing you to set
> them.

We'll call the example UIGestureRecognizer subclass
LCTGreaterThanGestureRecognizer. The header doesn't need any modification:

```
//
//  LCTGreaterThanGestureRecognizer.h
//  GreaterThanGesture
//
//  Created by Jeff Kelley on 2/2/12.
//  Copyright (c) 2012 Jeff Kelley. All rights reserved.
//

#import <UIKit/UIKit.h>

#import <UIKit/UIGestureRecognizerSubclass.h>

@interface LCTGreaterThanGestureRecognizer : UIGestureRecognizer

@end
```

In the implementation, we'll track the user's touches and maintain some state to determine where in the gesture they are. To that end, we'll define some instance variables in the implementation file:

```
@implementation LCTGreaterThanGestureRecognizer {
        CGPoint _beginningPoint;
        CGPoint _midPoint;
        BOOL _receivedDownRightSwipe;
        BOOL _receivedDownLeftSwipe;
}
```

_beginningPoint refers to the point the user began touching at. We'll save it so we can compare against it later:

```
- (void)touchesBegan:(NSSet *)touches withEvent:(UIEvent *)event
{
        UITouch *touch = [touches anyObject];

        _beginningPoint = [touch locationInView:[self view]];
}
```

Since NSSets are unordered, there is no first or last object, so we use the first one it returns. Once we have the beginning point, we compare future points against it. To match our gesture, we need to track two motions: moving down and to the right and then down and to the left. Once we've traveled a minimum distance down and to the right, we mark _receivedDownRightSwipe as YES and store the location to _midPoint. The user might keep going in this direction, though, so as they continue moving down and to the right, we continue to set _midPoint until they reverse direction. Once that occurs, we can begin tracking down and to the left until they complete the gesture. If any of these things fail to happen, we set the gesture recognizer's state to Failed, ending the tracking of touches:

```
#define CGPointDistanceFromPoint(p1, p2) (sqrtf(powf((p2.x - p1.x), 2.0f) +
powf((p2.y - p1.y), 2.0f)))

// The minimum amount a user's finger must move to trigger one half of the
swipe.
static const CGFloat kMinimumSwipeDistance = 50.0f;

- (void)touchesMoved:(NSSet *)touches withEvent:(UIEvent *)event
{
        UITouch *touch = [touches anyObject];

        CGPoint newPoint = [touch locationInView:[self view]];

        if (_receivedDownRightSwipe == NO) {
                if (newPoint.x >= _beginningPoint.x &&
                        newPoint.y >= _beginningPoint.y) {
```

```
                        CGFloat distance = CGPointDistanceFromPoint(newPoint,
_beginningPoint);

                        if (distance >= kMinimumSwipeDistance) {
                            _midPoint = newPoint;
                            _receivedDownRightSwipe = YES;
                        }
                }
                else {
                    [self setState:UIGestureRecognizerStateFailed];
                }
        }
        else if (newPoint.x >= _midPoint.x &&
                        newPoint.y >= _midPoint.y) {
                // Still going in the original direction, don't start looking
for new distance.
                _midPoint = newPoint;
        }
        else if (newPoint.x <= _midPoint.x &&
                        newPoint.y >= _midPoint.y) {
                CGFloat distance = CGPointDistanceFromPoint(newPoint,
_midPoint);

                if (distance >= kMinimumSwipeDistance) {
                        _receivedDownLeftSwipe = YES;
                }
        }
        else {
                [self setState:UIGestureRecognizerStateFailed];
        }
}
```

There are a few more things to do before finishing this implementation. First, if
_receivedDownRightSwipe and _receivedDownLeftSwipe are both YES when
touches end, we mark the gesture as recognized; otherwise, we mark it as
failed:

```
- (void)touchesEnded:(NSSet *)touches withEvent:(UIEvent *)event
{
        if (_receivedDownRightSwipe && _receivedDownRightSwipe) {
                [self setState:UIGestureRecognizerStateRecognized];
        }
        else {
                [self setState:UIGestureRecognizerStateFailed];
        }
}
```

If touches are canceled, then the gesture fails:

```
- (void)touchesCancelled:(NSSet *)touches withEvent:(UIEvent *)event
{
```

```
        [self setState:UIGestureRecognizerStateFailed];
}
```

Finally, the gesture recognizer will reset itself using the `reset` method. We'll reset our state there, being sure to call `super`'s implementation:

```
- (void)reset
{
        [super reset];

        _beginningPoint = CGPointZero;
        _midPoint = CGPointZero;
        _receivedDownRightSwipe = NO;
}
```

And there you have it: a fully functional gesture recognizer to capture your custom gesture. While this may not seem like it has much use, gestures can actually be quite handy for giving power users shortcuts or even as part of a game! For most cases, however, you'll want to use built-in user interface components with built-in gesture recognizers. One of the more common components you'll use for interactivity is `UIScrollView`.

Scroll Views

`UIScrollView` is a common type of `UIView` that scrolls content inside itself. Both `UITableView`, which we've covered before, and `UIWebView`, use `UIScrollView` to move their contents around. To use `UIScrollView`, do two things: first, add the content you'd like to scroll as subviews of the scroll view. Second, set the `contentSize` property on the scroll view to reflect the size of the content. Now, when the user moves their finger around on the scroll view, its contents will automatically shift to match the finger's movements. The scroll view's `contentOffset` property tells you how much the scroll view has moved from its starting location; you can also set it to scroll the scroll view programmatically. See Figure 5-1 for how `UIScrollView` works. If you've ever done view programming on Mac OS X, you may notice a key difference between Mac OS X and iOS: in iOS, the origin of the coordinate system is at the top left of the view, but in Mac OS X, the origin is at the bottom left of the view.

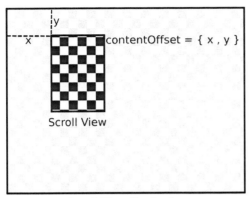

Scroll View Contents

Figure 5-1. *A typical scroll view. The* `contentOffset` *of the scroll view is {* `x, y` *}, and the visible portion is the darker checkerboard pattern inside the scroll view.*

One convenient feature of `UIScrollView` is its `pagingEnabled` property (accessible via the `isPagingEnabled` method). When this is set to YES, the scroll view snaps to even multiples of its width as you scroll left and right and of its height as you scroll up and down. If you're using a scroll view to display multiple pieces of content that are all the same size, you can use this to achieve a page-scrolling effect. For instance, if you have an array of images called images, this is how you could create a scroll view to pan between them:

```
UIScrollView *scrollView = [[UIScrollView alloc] initWithFrame:CGRectMake(0.0f,
0.0f, 320.0f, 480.0f)];
[scrollView setPagingEnabled:YES];

CGFloat xValue = 0.0f;

for (UIImage *image in images) {
        UIImageView *imageView = [[UIImageView alloc]
initWithFrame:CGRectMake(xValue, 0.0f, 320.0f, 480.0f)];
        [imageView setImage:image];
        [scrollView addSubview:imageView];
        xValue += 320.0f;
}

[scrollView setContentSize:CGSizeMake([images count] * 320.0f, 480.0f)];
```

This code sample will allow you to scroll horizontally, paging between images. It's a very typical use of `UIScrollView`, one that allows you to quickly make a very interactive layout for pictures, text, or any other content your app displays.

Implementing UI Changes

Let's use this newfound user interface knowledge in MyStuff. Right now our UI is very vanilla, and for iOS apps, users expect something that pops a bit more. It isn't enough to be a useful app; instead, we should try to make a useful app that also looks good. First we should support pictures of our items.

Adding Pictures to Possessions

Let's add a property to Possession for the image. Open Possession.h and add the line in bold:

```
@interface Possession : NSObject <NSCoding>

@property (strong) UIImage *image;
@property (copy) NSString *name;
@property (strong) NSNumber *value;

@end
```

Next, we'll have to modify how it saves itself to disk. UIImage, a UIKit class to represent images of many formats, did not conform to the NSCoding protocol before iOS 5. To save it to disk on iOS 4, we can't encode it directly. Luckily, we *can* convert it to an NSData object, which we can then save to disk directly. A first pass at saving it will encode it directly as data. Open Possession.m and edit the NSCoding methods, adding the lines in bold:

```
@synthesize image;
@synthesize name;
@synthesize value;

- (id)initWithCoder:(NSCoder *)aDecoder
{
    self = [self init];

    if (self) {
        [self setImage:[UIImage imageWithData:[aDecoder
decodeObjectForKey:@"image"]]];
        [self setName:[aDecoder decodeObjectForKey:@"name"]];
        [self setValue:[aDecoder decodeObjectForKey:@"value"]];
    }

    return self;
}

- (void)encodeWithCoder:(NSCoder *)aCoder
{
```

```
    [aCoder encodeObject:UIImagePNGRepresentation([self image])
                 forKey:@"image"];
    [aCoder encodeObject:[self name]
             forKey:@"name"];
    [aCoder encodeObject:[self value]
             forKey:@"value"];
}
```

The key function that we use here is UIImagePNGRepresentation(). It returns an NSData object from an image, converting it to a PNG representation. You can also use UIImageJPEGRepresentation(), which takes the image as the first argument and a floating-point value for the second argument for the compression quality: 0.0 represents the highest compression (and therefore the lowest quality), while 1.0 represents the lowest compression (and therefore the highest quality).

If you're supporting only iOS 5 and newer, you can encode and decode the UIImage object directly without converting it to an NSData object first.

Now we're ready to add images to our Possession objects. When we get an image, we'll want to display it in the list view. Open PossessionListTableViewCell.m, and add the lines in bold to receive Key-Value Observing notifications when the image is changed:

```
static NSString * const kPossessionImageKeyPath = @"image";
static NSString * const kPossessionNameKeyPath = @"name";
static NSString * const kPossessionValueKeyPath = @"value";

- (void)dealloc
{
    if (isObservingPossession == YES) {
        [_possession removeObserver:self
forKeyPath:kPossessionImageKeyPath];
        [_possession removeObserver:self forKeyPath:kPossessionNameKeyPath];
        [_possession removeObserver:self forKeyPath:kPossessionValueKeyPath];
        isObservingPossession = NO;
    }
}

- (void)setPossession:(Possession *)possession
{
    if (isObservingPossession == YES) {
        [_possession removeObserver:self
forKeyPath:kPossessionImageKeyPath];
        [_possession removeObserver:self forKeyPath:kPossessionNameKeyPath];
        [_possession removeObserver:self forKeyPath:kPossessionValueKeyPath];
        isObservingPossession = NO;
    }
```

```
        _possession = possession;

    if (_possession != nil) {
        [_possession addObserver:self
                        forKeyPath:kPossessionImageKeyPath
                           options:(NSKeyValueObservingOptionInitial |
                                     NSKeyValueObservingOptionNew)
                           context:NULL];

        [_possession addObserver:self
                        forKeyPath:kPossessionNameKeyPath
                           options:(NSKeyValueObservingOptionInitial |
                                     NSKeyValueObservingOptionNew)
                           context:NULL];

        [_possession addObserver:self
                        forKeyPath:kPossessionValueKeyPath
                           options:(NSKeyValueObservingOptionInitial |
                                     NSKeyValueObservingOptionNew)
                           context:NULL];

        isObservingPossession = YES;
    }
}
```

Next, we'll add a line in the observation method to put the image in the table
view cell:

```
- (void)observeValueForKeyPath:(NSString *)keyPath
                      ofObject:(id)object
                        change:(NSDictionary *)change
                       context:(void *)context
{
    if (object == [self possession]) {
        if ([keyPath isEqualToString:kPossessionImageKeyPath]) {
            [[self imageView] setImage:[change
objectForKey:NSKeyValueChangeNewKey]];
        }
        else if ([keyPath isEqualToString:kPossessionNameKeyPath]) {
            [[self textLabel] setText:[change
objectForKey:NSKeyValueChangeNewKey]];
        }
        else if ([keyPath isEqualToString:kPossessionValueKeyPath]) {
            [[self detailTextLabel] setText:[[change
objectForKey:NSKeyValueChangeNewKey] stringValue]];
        }
    }
}
```

Now that we've added these methods, images will display in our table view and
save to our archive when they're set—we just need a way to add images to our

objects. We'll do this in our detail view controller. Open
`PossessionDetailViewController.h`, and add an outlet for an image view we'll
use to show the image:

```
@interface PossessionDetailViewController : UIViewController

@property (weak) IBOutlet UIImageView *imageView;
@property (weak) IBOutlet UITextField *nameField;
@property (weak) IBOutlet UITextField *valueField;
@property (strong) Possession *possession;
@property (getter = isModal) BOOL modal;
@property (weak) id <PossessionDetailViewControllerDelegate> delegate;

@end
```

Next, you'll need to synthesize setter and getter methods for the `imageView`
property. Open `PossessionDetailViewController.m`, and add the line in bold:

```
@implementation PossessionDetailViewController

@synthesize imageView;
@synthesize nameField;
@synthesize valueField;
@synthesize possession;
@synthesize modal;
@synthesize delegate;
```

Save your work, and open the nib file, `PossessionDetailViewController.xib`.
Open the Object Library on the right side of the screen (if it isn't there, you can
open that pane by pressing ⌘+Option+0). Find the Image View object, and drag
one into your view. Control+click from the File's Owner on the left, and drag to
the image view; then connect it to the `imageView` property when the choice pops
up. Now rearrange the UI objects as shown in Figure 5-2.

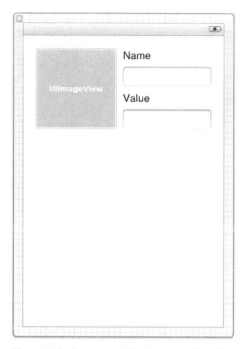

Figure 5-2. *Our new detail view controller nib*

Let's see what this looks like. Build and run the app. If you had saved objects from before or try to add an item, you'll notice that it crashes. The crash is because of our KVO method observing the image value of a Possession object. When we load the possession from disk, it doesn't have an image, so its image property is nil. The Key-Value Observing methods, however, put the values in an NSDictionary to pass to your method, and nil cannot be placed in a dictionary, because it is not an object. To get around this, the Key-Value Observing methods will put an instance of the NSNull class in its place. Our app, as written, will try to place that value in the image view, which will crash. To fix this, we'll make a temporary variable for the new value of the change dictionary and then set that to nil if it's an NSNull instance. Open PossessionListTableViewCell.m, and modify the lines in bold:

```
- (void)observeValueForKeyPath:(NSString *)keyPath
                      ofObject:(id)object
                        change:(NSDictionary *)change
                       context:(void *)context
{
    id newObject = [change objectForKey:NSKeyValueChangeNewKey];

    if ([newObject isKindOfClass:[NSNull class]]) {
```

```
        newObject = nil;
    }

    if (object == [self possession]) {
        if ([keyPath isEqualToString:kPossessionImageKeyPath]) {
            [[self imageView] setImage:[change
objectForKey:NSKeyValueChangeNewKey]];
            [[self imageView] setImage:newObject];
        }
        else if ([keyPath isEqualToString:kPossessionNameKeyPath]) {
            [[self textLabel] setText:[change
objectForKey:NSKeyValueChangeNewKey]];
            [[self textLabel] setText:newObject];
        }
        else if ([keyPath isEqualToString:kPossessionValueKeyPath]) {
            [[self detailTextLabel] setText:[[change
objectForKey:NSKeyValueChangeNewKey] stringValue]];
            [[self detailTextLabel] setText:[newObject stringValue]];
        }
    }
}
```

This code will be more resilient against crashes. Let's build and run again and then look at the detail view controller for a possession. You'll notice that there's no image. This isn't entirely unexpected; we never added an image in the first place! We'll want to enable the user to tap the image view to add an image, but, as you can see in Figure 5-3, it doesn't appear if there is no image in the Possession object. To let the user know that they can add an image, we can add a label underneath the image view. Reopen the nib, PossessionDetailViewController.xib, and add a label. Place the label on top of the image view and resize it so that its frame matches the image view's. Open the Attributes Inspector in the right pane, which can be accessed by pressing Option+⌘+4. The attributes of the label should now be listed down the right side of the window. With the label selected, set the Text property to Tap to Add Image. Next, set the Number of Lines property to 0, which will allow it to wrap the text to multiple lines. Under Alignment, click the middle button, which will center the text. The font size is a little large, so click the down arrow to the right of Font until the size is 13.0. Finally, we need to move this label behind the image view, so that it won't display when there is an image. With the label selected, select Editor ➤ Arrange ➤ Send to Back, which will move the label behind the image view.

The next step is to configure the detail view controller to show the possession's image when it appears. Open PossessionDetailViewController.m, and modify its viewWillAppear: method as follows by adding the following code in bold:

```
- (void)viewWillAppear:(BOOL)animated
{
    [super viewWillAppear:animated];

    [[self imageView] setImage:[[self possession] image]];
    [[self nameField] setText:[[self possession] name]];
    [[self valueField] setText:[[[self possession] value] stringValue]];
}
```

Build and run, add an item, and the app should look like Figure 5-3.

Figure 5-3. *Our new detail view controller*

Unfortunately, tapping the label doesn't yet *do* anything. To do that, we'll add a tap gesture recognizer to the image view. We'll do this in the detail view controller's `viewDidLoad` method. In more recent versions of Xcode, you can also create gesture recognizers in Interface Builder by dragging them onto a view and then connecting them to actions. For now, we'll create them in code. Open PossessionDetailViewController.m, and add the viewDidLoad method:

```
- (void)viewDidLoad
{
    [super viewDidLoad];

    UITapGestureRecognizer *tapGestureRecognizer =
    [[UITapGestureRecognizer alloc] initWithTarget:self

action:@selector(imageViewTapped:)];

    [[self imageView] addGestureRecognizer:tapGestureRecognizer];
    [[self imageView] setUserInteractionEnabled:YES];
}
```

We have to set the userInteractionEnabled: property of imageView to YES, because it's turned off by default for image views, which don't usually receive taps directly. Next we have to add the imageViewTapped: method. Add a declaration for the method to the class extension:

```
@interface PossessionDetailViewController()

- (void)doneButtonPressed:(id)sender;
- (void)imageViewTapped:(UITapGestureRecognizer *)tapGestureRecognizer;

@end
```

When we write the method, we'll use a UIKit class called UIImagePickerController to take a picture of the object. The UIImagePickerController class inherits from UIViewController, so we can create one and present it as a modal view controller. Write the method as follows:

```
- (void)imageViewTapped:(UITapGestureRecognizer *)tapGestureRecognizer
{
    UIImagePickerController *imagePickerController =
    [[UIImagePickerController alloc] init];

    if ([UIImagePickerController
isSourceTypeAvailable:UIImagePickerControllerSourceTypeCamera]) {
        [imagePickerController
setSourceType:UIImagePickerControllerSourceTypeCamera];
    }
    else {
        [imagePickerController
setSourceType:UIImagePickerControllerSourceTypeSavedPhotosAlbum];
    }

    [imagePickerController setDelegate:self];
```

```
    [self presentModalViewController:imagePickerController animated:YES];
}
```

You may notice a compiler warning in this code where you call `setDelegate:` on `imagePickerController`. We'll fix this shortly, so for now, you can ignore it. The image picker controller can be used to take pictures with the device's camera (if it has one) or to get pictures from the user's photo library. In this case, we'll use the camera if it's available but fall back to the user's saved photos album if it isn't. Once we've created it and set its source type, we'll set the detail view controller (`self` in this method) as its delegate in order to receive the image the user selects. Finally, we present it modally. From there the image picker controller takes over, returning control to our code once the user selects (or takes) an image.

> **NOTE:** For testing on the iPhone Simulator, you can't use the camera, but you can use the Saved Photos album. The simplest way to add an image to the iPhone Simulator's Saved Photos album is through Safari; click and hold on an image to save it to the album.

Before we go testing this code, we need to add a delegate to the image picker controller. Interestingly, the `delegate` property of `UIImagePickerController` is defined as conforming to two protocols: `UINavigationControllerDelegate` and `UIImagePickerControllerDelegate`. In Apple's source code, they declare it with the following line (from `UIImagePickerController.h` in the iOS system frameworks):

```
@property(nonatomic,assign) id <UINavigationControllerDelegate,
UIImagePickerControllerDelegate> delegate;
```

Therefore, to prevent the compiler warning our code generated earlier, we'll need to make `PossessionDetailViewController` conform to both the `UINavigationControllerDelegate` and `UIImagePickerControllerDelegate` protocols, even though we won't be implementing any methods defined in `UINavigationControllerDelegate`. Open the header file (`PossessionDetailViewController.h`), and adjust the class declaration accordingly:

```
@interface PossessionDetailViewController : UIViewController
<UIImagePickerControllerDelegate, UINavigationControllerDelegate>
```

The methods we *will* implement come from `UIImagePickerControllerDelegate`. Add these two methods to your implementation of `PossesionDetailViewController`:

```
#pragma mark - UIImagePickerControllerDelegate Protocol Methods

- (void)imagePickerController:(UIImagePickerController *)picker
didFinishPickingMediaWithInfo:(NSDictionary *)info
{
    // We can't save the image to our possession if our possession is nil.
Create one if
    // it does not yet exist and fill in the values the user has already
entered.
    if ([self possession] == nil) {
        [self setPossession:[[Possession alloc] init]];
        [[self possession] setName:[[self nameField] text]];
        [[self possession] setValue:[NSNumber numberWithInt:[[[self
valueField] text] intValue]]];
    }

    UIImage *image = [info
objectForKey:UIImagePickerControllerOriginalImage];

    [[self possession] setImage:image];

    [self dismissModalViewControllerAnimated:YES];
}

- (void)imagePickerControllerDidCancel:(UIImagePickerController *)picker
{
    [self dismissModalViewControllerAnimated:YES];
}
```

```
#pragma mark -
```

To help organize our code, we're using the #pragma mark compiler directive. Using it allows us to label sections of our code, similar to a comment. You can see these sections in the drop-down list of methods that appears in the editor, as in Figure 5-4. #pragma mark - places a horizontal line in the list, while #pragma mark - followed by a text label places that label in the list. If you use a class name or, as we did earlier, a protocol name, you can jump right to the documentation for that symbol by holding Option while clicking it and then clicking the book icon at the top right of the pop-up window that appears. You can also jump right to where a protocol is defined by holding ⌘ and clicking its name in the #pragma mark - note.

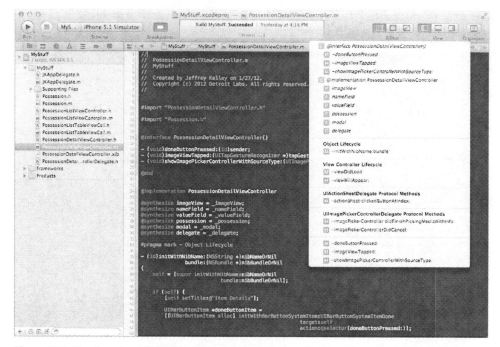

Figure 5-4. *The drop-down list in Xcode's editor (note that my Xcode preferences include a dark background instead of the default white background)*

The second of these methods is called only if the user cancels the image picker, and implementing it merely involves dismissing the modal view controller. The first one is more interesting. First, it ensures that there's a Possession object to store an image into, and if there is not but the user has already entered text, it saves that text to the newly created object. It takes the image the user has selected from the info dictionary passed to it, setting it as the image property of the current Possession object. Once we set the image property, the KVO methods we set up earlier take care of displaying it in both the detail view controller and the list view controller. The NSCoding methods we set up in Possession now save this image to disk, as well, so the next time we run the app, any images you've set will still be there. Build and run the app, setting some images in your items. Once you do, you should see them displayed in both locations, as in Figure 5-5.

Figure 5-5. *MyStuff with images set for its products*

Awesome! Now we have an app people can use to track their belongings, including pictures of each item. We aren't done yet, however. When we created the image picker controller, we assumed that users would want to use their camera (if available) to take a picture. This doesn't support people who want to take pictures of some items but have saved photos of other items. Leave something like this out, and you're sure to get some one-star reviews on the App Store. Let's instead give the user a prompt to select whether they want to use a picture from the camera or from their Photos library. We'll use a UIKit object called UIActionSheet, which shows a modal dialog asking the user to select one of several options.

> **NOTE:** On devices with cameras that shoot high-resolution photos, you may notice a delay when creating a new possession with an image. This delay occurs as the image is saved to disk. In a later chapter, we'll learn about performance and multithreading on iOS. Until then, the delay is normal.

Using UIActionSheet

An instance of UIActionSheet is created with an optional title, a delegate to receive taps, and some button titles. We'll need to make our PossesionDetailViewController class the delegate, which means another protocol to conform to. Open its header, and add the new declaration:

```
@interface PossessionDetailViewController : UIViewController
<UIActionSheetDelegate, UIImagePickerControllerDelegate,
UINavigationControllerDelegate>
```

Now we're ready to add the action sheet. First, though, let's consider the imageViewTapped: method. Right now, it creates and displays a UIImagePickerController, which we still want to do, but we want to do at a different point in our code. We also want the user to specify which source type to use (camera or photo library). To that end, let's declare a new method in the class extension:

```
-
(void)showImagePickerControllerWithSourceType:(UIImagePickerControllerSourceType
)sourceType;
```

In the implementation, we'll do most of the same thing as we did in imageViewTapped:, only using the passed-in source type. Enter this for the method implementation:

```
-
(void)showImagePickerControllerWithSourceType:(UIImagePickerControllerSourceType
)sourceType
{
    UIImagePickerController *imagePickerController =
    [[UIImagePickerController alloc] init];

    [imagePickerController setSourceType:sourceType];

    [imagePickerController setDelegate:self];

    [self presentModalViewController:imagePickerController animated:YES];
}
```

Perfect. Now we can call this whenever we want. Return to the implementation for imageViewTapped: and remove its contents, replacing them with this:

```
- (void)imageViewTapped:(UITapGestureRecognizer *)tapGestureRecognizer
{
    if ([UIImagePickerController
isSourceTypeAvailable:UIImagePickerControllerSourceTypeCamera] &&
        [UIImagePickerController
isSourceTypeAvailable:UIImagePickerControllerSourceTypePhotoLibrary]) {
        UIActionSheet *actionSheet =
        [[UIActionSheet alloc] initWithTitle:nil
                                    delegate:self
                           cancelButtonTitle:@"Cancel"
                      destructiveButtonTitle:nil
                           otherButtonTitles:@"Take Photo", @"Choose From
Library", nil];

        [actionSheet showInView:[self view]];
    }
    else if ([UIImagePickerController
isSourceTypeAvailable:UIImagePickerControllerSourceTypePhotoLibrary]) {
        [self
showImagePickerControllerWithSourceType:UIImagePickerControllerSourceTypePh
otoLibrary];
    }
}
```

In this method, we'll create an action sheet only if multiple source types are available for the UIImagePickerController. If we're on an early-model iPod Touch or the iPhone Simulator, where there is no camera, then we'll skip straight to the method we just created for displaying the image picker controller, because there is no choice for the user to make. If neither is available, then we do nothing.

Next, we have to write the code that responds to the action sheet. Our buttons are displayed as in Figure 5-6: Take Photo, then Choose From Library and finally Cancel.

Figure 5-6. *Adding some UI polish with an action sheet*

Let's implement the delegate method for UIActionSheet,
actionSheet:clickedButtonAtIndex:. The index passed to the delegate will
correspond to the position the button is in, beginning at 0. Therefore, 0 will
correspond to Take Photo, 1 will correspond to Choose From Library, and 2 will
correspond to Cancel. The cancel button index is also a property of
UIActionSheet, cancelButtonIndex. We'll take advantage of that in our method
to exit early if the user pressed Cancel. Implement the delegate method in
PossessionDetailViewController.m:

```
- (void)actionSheet:(UIActionSheet *)actionSheet
clickedButtonAtIndex:(NSInteger)buttonIndex
{
    if (buttonIndex == [actionSheet cancelButtonIndex]) {
```

```
        return;
    }
    else {
        UIImagePickerControllerSourceType sourceType;

        if (buttonIndex == 0) {
            sourceType = UIImagePickerControllerSourceTypeCamera;
        }
        else {
            sourceType = UIImagePickerControllerSourceTypePhotoLibrary;
        }

        [self showImagePickerControllerWithSourceType:sourceType];
    }
}
```

By inspecting the value of the selected index, we can determine which type of image picker controller to show, which we do by calling our helper method we wrote earlier. This action sheet provides a bit of UI polish and friendliness, giving the user a choice instead of deciding for them. It's important to do things like this to let the user feel like they're in control, but we're still not done with our app yet.

Implementing "Edit" for Table Views

We've made MyStuff useful, and we've added a smidge of polish, but we don't do something that's extremely important: letting the user recover from their own mistakes. If they accidentally add a possession or get rid of it later, we have no way to display that! Fortunately, UITableView supports an "editing" mode that adds a delete control next in every row. To enable editing mode, we can add an Edit button on the left of the navigation bar when we're in the list view controller. Open PossessionListViewController.m, and edit initWithNibName:bundle: with the lines in bold:

```
- (id)initWithNibName:(NSString *)nibNameOrNil
            bundle:(NSBundle *)nibBundleOrNil
{
    self = [super initWithNibName:nibNameOrNil
                          bundle:nibBundleOrNil];

    if (self) {
        [self loadPossessionsFromDisk];

        [self setTitle:@"My Stuff"];

        UIBarButtonItem *addItemButton =
```

```
        [[UIBarButtonItem alloc]
initWithBarButtonSystemItem:UIBarButtonSystemItemAdd
                                                target:self

action:@selector(addItemButtonPressed:)];
        [[self navigationItem] setRightBarButtonItem:addItemButton];

        [[self navigationItem] setLeftBarButtonItem:[self editButtonItem]];
    }

    return self;
}
```

Not much new code at all, huh? editButtonItem is a convenience method of
UIViewController that creates a button for you. Figure 5-7 shows you what the
view controller will look like when it's in editing mode:

Figure 5-7. *Our list view controller in Editing mode*

Entering Editing mode animates a few changes for us automatically:

- The disclosure indicator on the right side of the table view slides off the screen to the right.

- The text of the cell moves to the right.

- A delete control fades in and from the left.

Pressing the Delete button pushes the cell's content aside to make room for a red Delete button, but pressing it won't do us much good yet. To respond to that button, we need to implement the table view data source method `tableView:commitEditingStyle:forRowAtIndexPath:`. Add it to the list view controller (`PossessionListViewController.m`) with the following implementation:

```
- (void)tableView:(UITableView *)tableView
commitEditingStyle:(UITableViewCellEditingStyle)editingStyle
forRowAtIndexPath:(NSIndexPath *)indexPath
{
    if (editingStyle == UITableViewCellEditingStyleDelete) {
        [_possessions removeObjectAtIndex:[indexPath row]];

        NSArray *indexPaths = [NSArray arrayWithObject:indexPath];
        [tableView deleteRowsAtIndexPaths:indexPaths

withRowAnimation:UITableViewRowAnimationAutomatic];

        [self savePossessionsToDisk];
    }
}
```

Removing the item is a three-step process. First, we remove it from our model, which in this case is the _possessions array. Next, we tell the table view to delete the cell at that index path. Finally, we save our possessions to disk, which will update the archive to remove that item. Build and run, and try deleting a possession. You should see the row it's in animate away as the others move around. This is another quick bit of polish we can add to the app that gives it a better user experience. The ability to delete an item allows the user to recover from their mistakes, as well as adjust their data set over time. Next, we'll give them more control over how their data is displayed by allowing them to reorder content in the list.

Implementing Table View Reordering

Always remember that the data in the app is not yours, it's your user's. To that end, they may want to change how their data is sorted and displayed. Currently, MyStuff doesn't sort the data in any meaningful way; it's just displayed in the order it was entered. We could sort it ourselves, either alphabetically or by value, but instead let's allow the user to sort their own data. We'll do that through another provided mechanism from UITableView: the reordering control. Figure 5-8 shows what our table view will look like with reordering controls.

Figure 5-8. *Our list table view with reordering controls, in and out of editing mode*

As you can see, the reordering control is a box made up of three lines. When we enter editing mode, it replaces the disclosure indicator as the table view cell's accessory view on the right. To enable the reordering control, we don't set a property on the table view, call a method, or anything like that. Instead, we simply *implement* the method that gets called when the user moves the row; the table view determines that we've implemented that method and displays the control. Open PossessionListViewController.m, and add the following table view data source method:

```
- (void)tableView:(UITableView *)tableView
moveRowAtIndexPath:(NSIndexPath *)sourceIndexPath
     toIndexPath:(NSIndexPath *)destinationIndexPath
{
    id movingObject = [_possessions objectAtIndex:[sourceIndexPath row]];

    [_possessions removeObjectAtIndex:[sourceIndexPath row]];
    [_possessions insertObject:movingObject atIndex:[destinationIndexPath row]];

    [self savePossessionsToDisk];
}
```

In this method, we simply modify the _possessions array to match the change that the user made and then save it to disk to persist their changes. The table view handles all of the UI updates for us automatically.

> **NOTE:** you have a table view where some rows cannot be moved or some destinations are not valid, implement the data source method `tableView:canMoveRowAtIndexPath:` to disable the reorder controls on a row-by-row basis, and implement the long-winded delegate method `tableView:targetIndexPathForMoveFromRowAtIndexPath:toProposedIndexPath:` to adjust the destination row as the user drags.

Now that they can reorder their content, our users are in full control of their data, so we're well on our way to having a good app that people will like. MyStuff still has a long way to go in the look-and-feel department, but its functionality is solid.

Summary

In this chapter we covered a lot of ways to make your app more responsive to user touch. From implementing your own UIView subclasses to handle touches to using UIGestureRecognizers, there are plenty of options for you to create great user experiences. We also covered several built-in user experiences that you can use to provide the user with functionality that's consistent across their applications, giving you the benefit of users who already know how to use your app. We'll put this to good work in our next chapter, wherein we'll use the device's network connectivity to create the next great Twitter client.

Integrating Networking and Web Services

The iPhone ushered in a new era of always-connected apps. Nearly every iOS app in the App Store uses the network connection in some way, whether it's to load graphics, post high scores to a Game Center leaderboard, or just report analytics data to its developer. At the same time, however, as developers, we must be judicious about how *much* data we use, what we send, and how we send it. Many customers are not on expensive, unlimited-data plans—especially those outside of the United States—and therefore won't appreciate an app that downloads a few hundred megabytes of images at launch. Understanding how to use the networking functionality of these devices is a fundamental requirement of a Cocoa Touch developer.

Hand in hand with learning how to use networking services is the knowledge of how to integrate with web services. It isn't enough to simply read data from the Internet; that data must also be parsed, and the app must run accordingly. Data on the Web is in various formats, from XML to JSON to custom formats, and comes from various places, from static files to complex web applications. Invariably, these web services will also require you to send data back to them, which itself is a series of challenges, from text encoding to image representations. This chapter will walk you through all of these scenarios, from loading simple data from the network to uploading files and data to web services. Along the way, we'll use our newfound skills to create a Twitter client.

We'll start with something easy: getting some simple data from the network into our app.

Loading Data from the Network

Whole categories of apps wouldn't be very useful without being able to read data from the network. Weather apps, movie ticket apps, and news-reading apps would be impossible to make useful. Fortunately, we can use the network on iOS devices. Let's look at a quick example of using the NSURLConnection class to get weather data from a web service. To get the weather data, we first need to identify the web service we'll use. There are various weather services out there, each with its own license agreement and terms of use. For this book, I'll use the Yahoo! Weather service. You can read more about it at http://developer.yahoo.com/weather/. The actual URL we'll use to get weather data is http://weather.yahooapis.com/forecastrss?p=48226. In this case, "48226" is the ZIP code for Detroit, Michigan, passed as a parameter to the URL. There are three steps to this process. First, we have to make a URL request.

Creating a URL Request

The NSURLRequest object encapsulates everything that the NSURLConnection object will need to make the request: the URL we're connecting to, the cache settings for the request, and any HTTP headers that need to be sent along with the request. To create the NSURLRequest object, we first need to create an NSURL object to represent the URL. Creating the request looks like this:

```
NSURL *weatherURL = [NSURL
URLWithString:@"http://weather.yahooapis.com/forecastrss?p=48226"];
NSURLRequest *urlRequest = [NSURLRequest requestWithURL:weatherURL];
```

The default settings for the URL request are good enough for this simple task, so we won't do any further configuration.

Creating a URL Connection

Once we've created the request, we're almost ready to create the connection and get data. We'll be using the NSURLConnection class method sendSynchronousRequest:returningResponse:error:, which synchronously loads data from the network. The first parameter is the request we just created, but the second two need to be created beforehand.

> **NOTE:** In practice, it's generally a bad idea to use synchronous URL connections. They stop execution while waiting for the connection to finish. If you have a slow connection or are loading a large amount of data, using synchronous requests can cause your app to hang until the connection is complete. Later in this chapter we'll cover asynchronous requests, which are a much better way to handle loading data, and in Chapter 7 we'll cover performance issues like this in a more general manner.

This method is declared in the system header NSURLConnection.h:

```
+ (NSData *)sendSynchronousRequest:(NSURLRequest *)request
returningResponse:(NSURLResponse **)response error:(NSError **)error;
```

As you can see, the second two parameters are not regular pointers to objects but instead pointers to *pointers* to objects, which is why they have the two asterisks. This can be confusing at first, but in reality it's just a way for this method to give you a pointer. You'll create a pointer for each and initialize it to point to nil:

```
NSURLResponse *urlResponse = nil;
NSError *error = nil;
```

With these two pointers created, you can call the method and create the connection:

```
NSData *receivedData = [NSURLConnection sendSynchronousRequest:urlRequest
                                        returningResponse:&urlResponse
                                                    error:&error];
```

Prepending an ampersand (&) before urlResponse and error passes a pointer to the pointer instead of the pointer itself. When this method finishes, these pointers will point to the appropriate objects. By passing pointers this way, we can receive multiple return values from one method.

Interpreting the Response

When this method returns, the receivedData object will contain the data we got back from the server in an NSData object. As it is, a plain NSData object isn't too useful. Since we know that this service returns text, not other data like an image, let's convert it to an NSString object:

```
NSString *receivedText = [[NSString alloc] initWithData:receievedData
                                                encoding:NSUTF8StringEncoding];
```

> **NOTE:** You may have noticed that we used `NSUTF8StringEncoding` as the second parameter. The string encoding of the data you receive will depend on the server you're connecting to. Most services use either UTF8 or ASCII text encoding. For more information on different encoding types and when to use them, check out Joel Spolsky's article on the topic at `www.joelonsoftware.com/articles/Unicode.html`.

Now we have a string containing the server's response to our request. This isn't immediately useful to us, because it's in XML, but it's a start. Once you have the data from the server, it's just a matter of parsing it. We can also glean some information from our `urlResponse` object. Since this is an HTTP connection (our URL began with `http://`), the response object is actually an instance of `NSHTTPURLResponse`, which is a subclass of `NSURLResponse`. The HTTP-specific subclass gives you additional data, such as the status code of the response. If, for instance, you were writing an iOS app to interface with a network-enabled coffee pot over HTTP—a well-defined use of the protocol—and you wanted to respond appropriately to HTTP status code 418 ("I'm a teapot," which you would get if you accidentally connected to a teapot, not a coffee pot), the code might look like this:

```
if ([urlResponse isKindOfClass:[NSHTTPURLResponse class]]) {
    NSInteger statusCode = [(NSHTTPURLResponse *)urlResponse statusCode];

    if (statusCode == 418) {
        // Oops, it's a teapot!
        NSLog(@"Accidentally messaged a teapot.");
    }
}
```

While this example seems pretty trivial, it offers an opportunity to discuss how we handle a tricky situation in Objective-C. We want to use the status code of the response, but it's available only if the response is an `NSHTTPURLResponse` object; any other `NSURLResponse` object won't do. We use the `isKindOfClass:` method to check the class of `urlResponse`. If it is an `NSHTTPURLResponse`, then we know we can check the status code. To call the `statusCode` method on it, we first cast it to an `NSHTTPURLResponse` object using parentheses. This lets the compiler know our assumption and will enable code completion in Xcode.

Generally speaking, an HTTP status code that's above or equal to 200 and below 300 is considered "successful," with some common errors in the 400- and 500-level range. Some web services require the status code to return 200 on success, which you can use to your advantage when programming against them. Another useful method on NSHTTPURLResponse is allHeaderFields, which returns the headers sent with the response. This can be useful if, for instance, the headers specify caching information for the returned data.

If there was a problem with your connection, often the error object will be set to an NSError upon returning from sendSynchronousRequest:returningResponse:error:. The NSError class defines a number of useful methods you can use to get more information about the error. The localizedDescription method returns text that's localized for displaying to the user. The code method returns an error code, specific to the domain returned by the domain method. Finally, there may be more information in the NSDictionary returned by the userInfo method. These errors can be invaluable when trying to troubleshoot the network connection.

Using Received Data

Once you receive a response from the server you've connected to, you'll have an NSData object containing the response body. Depending on the service you're connecting to, this might be text, an image, a video, or a proprietary binary format. If it's text, it might be plain text, comma- or tab-delimited text databases, JSON- or XML-formatted data, or a proprietary textual format. Whatever format it's in, your app should handle it appropriately. We'll cover images, JSON, and XML later in this chapter. For now, instead of parsing the data, we'll just use the NSLog() macro to display it in the console. First, let's make an actual app to put this code we've just covered in. Open Xcode and make a new project by selecting File ➤ New ➤ Project…. Select Application under iOS on the left side of the dialog and then Empty Application from the list of templates. For Product Name, enter **SimpleWeather**. Fill in the Company Identifier and Class Prefix fields, select iPhone from the Device Family drop-down box, uncheck Use Core Data and Include Unit Tests, and leave Use Automatic Reference Counting checked. When you're done, the settings should match Figure 6-1.

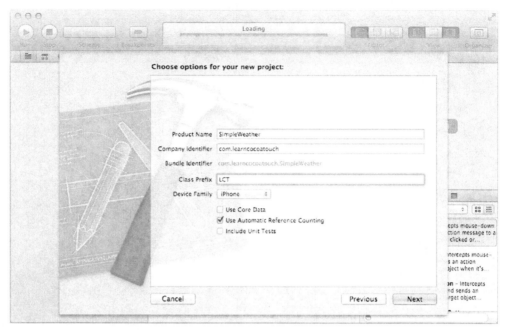

Figure 6-1. *Xcode settings for creating the SimpleWeather app*

> **NOTE:** When you use the Empty Application template, you'll see the following line in the console when you run the app:
>
> ```
> Application windows are expected to have a root view controller
> at the end of application launch
> ```
>
> By the time we're done with this app, our window will have a root view controller, so you won't see this message anymore.

Click Next, and save your project to disk. Open your app delegate implementation file (LCTAppDelegate.m for my class prefix, LCT). Add our networking code in bold to the application:didFinishLaunchingWithOptions: method:

```
- (BOOL)application:(UIApplication *)application
didFinishLaunchingWithOptions:(NSDictionary *)launchOptions
{
    self.window = [[UIWindow alloc] initWithFrame:[[UIScreen mainScreen]
bounds]];
    // Override point for customization after application launch.
```

```
    self.window.backgroundColor = [UIColor whiteColor];
    [self.window makeKeyAndVisible];

    NSURL *weatherURL =
    [NSURL
URLWithString:@"http://weather.yahooapis.com/forecastrss?p=48226"];

    NSURLRequest *urlRequest = [NSURLRequest requestWithURL:weatherURL];

    NSURLResponse *urlResponse = nil;
    NSError *error = nil;

    NSData *receivedData = [NSURLConnection
sendSynchronousRequest:urlRequest

returningResponse:&urlResponse

                                                            error:&error];

    NSString *receivedText = [[NSString alloc] initWithData:receivedData

encoding:NSUTF8StringEncoding];

    NSLog(@"%@", receivedText);

    return YES;
}
```

Run the app. You won't see much in the iPhone Simulator window, but the
Xcode window should show you the data it received. If you don't see the debug
area, select View ➤ Debug Area ➤ Activate Console, or press Shift+⌘+C. The
debug area appears at the bottom of the screen and contains log messages
sent from your app. Figure 6-2 shows an Xcode window with the debug area
open to the console on the bottom and some response data from Yahoo!

displayed. \

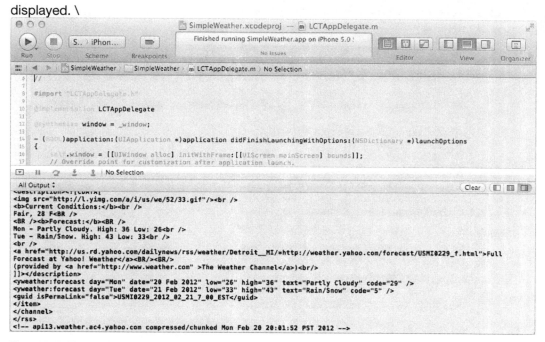

Figure 6-2. *Xcode's Console open in the debug area. My Xcode editor window has a dark background; yours (if you haven't changed it) will have a white background.*

If the network connection succeeded, you should see the response data in the console now. It's XML-formatted data that contains a weather forecast for Detroit, Michigan. The next step is to take that XML data, turn it into a useful format, and display it to the user. Before we do that, however, there's a problem with the way we've done things. By using the `sendSynchronousRequest:returningResponse:error:` method of `NSURLConnection`, we're preventing the app from finishing its launch until we receive a response from the server. This doesn't provide a good experience for the user, and more importantly, if the app takes too long to start, it'll be terminated by the operating system. Let's change that before we deal with the data.

Asynchronous Operation

The method we used earlier is a typical synchronous method that returns three objects: the data, the response, and an error (if one is encountered). `NSURLConnection` also supports using a delegate to receive these objects, which allows you to continue execution before the response is received. Let's modify the code to run asynchronously. Open your app delegate's implementation file (LCTAppDelegate.m for me), and modify the application:didFinishLaunchingWithOptions: method by deleting the struck-out lines and adding the lines in bold:

```
- (BOOL)application:(UIApplication *)application
didFinishLaunchingWithOptions:(NSDictionary *)launchOptions
{
    self.window = [[UIWindow alloc] initWithFrame:[[UIScreen mainScreen]
bounds]];
    // Override point for customization after application launch.
    self.window.backgroundColor = [UIColor whiteColor];
    [self.window makeKeyAndVisible];

    NSURL *weatherURL =
    [NSURL URLWithString:@"http://weather.yahooapis.com/forecastrss?p=48226"];

    NSURLRequest *urlRequest = [NSURLRequest requestWithURL:weatherURL];

    NSURLResponse *urlResponse = nil;
    NSError *error = nil;

    NSData *receievedData = [NSURLConnection sendSynchronousRequest:urlRequest
                                               returningResponse:&urlResponse
                                                          error:&error];

    NSString *receivedText = [[NSString alloc] initWithData:receievedData

encoding:NSUTF8StringEncoding];

    NSLog(@"%@", receivedText);

    NSURLConnection *connection = [[NSURLConnection alloc]
initWithRequest:urlRequest

delegate:self];

    [connection start];

    return YES;
}
```

URL Connection Delegate Methods

You may have noticed that we never opened the app delegate's header to declare our conformance to a protocol. While there *is* a delegate protocol called NSURLConnectionDelegate in Cocoa Touch, the delegate property of

NSURLConnection isn't declared as conforming to it. Historically, the URL connection delegate methods have always been an informal protocol, and the important ones still are. There are four methods you'll want to implement almost every time you use NSURLConnection:

- connection:didReceiveResponse:
- connection:didReceiveData:
- connection:didFailWithError:
- connectionDidFinishLoading:

Similar to the UITableView delegate and data source methods, the first parameter to all of these methods is a pointer to the URL connection. The objects that were all returned from the single synchronous method—the data from the body of the response, the response itself, and an error, if present—are all returned in separate methods, with an extra method that's called when the connection is done. One consequence of this separation is that we need a place to store these values before the connection is done loading. Modify your app delegate's implementation file (LCTAppDelegate.m) with the lines in bold to add private instance variables for these values:

```
#import "LCTAppDelegate.h"

@implementation LCTAppDelegate {
    NSMutableData *_receivedData;
    NSURLResponse *_receivedResponse;
    NSError *_connectionError;
}

@synthesize window = _window;

...
```

You might notice that instead of an NSData object, we're using an NSMutableData object. This is because the URL connection will call connection:didReceiveData: multiple times, so we need to keep track of all the data it's received over its lifetime. With that in mind, in your app delegate implementation file (LCTAppDelegate.m), modify the code with the lines in bold:

```
- (BOOL)application:(UIApplication *)application
didFinishLaunchingWithOptions:(NSDictionary *)launchOptions
{
    self.window = [[UIWindow alloc] initWithFrame:[[UIScreen mainScreen]
bounds]];
    // Override point for customization after application launch.
    self.window.backgroundColor = [UIColor whiteColor];
    [self.window makeKeyAndVisible];
```

```objc
    NSURL *weatherURL =
    [NSURL URLWithString:@"http://weather.yahooapis.com/forecastrss?p=48226"];

    NSURLRequest *urlRequest = [NSURLRequest requestWithURL:weatherURL];

    NSURLConnection *connection = [[NSURLConnection alloc]
initWithRequest:urlRequest

delegate:self];

    _receivedData = [[NSMutableData alloc] init];

    [connection start];

    return YES;
}
- (void)connection:(NSURLConnection *)connection
didReceiveResponse:(NSURLResponse *)response
{
    _receivedResponse = response;
}

- (void)connection:(NSURLConnection *)connection didReceiveData:(NSData
*)data
{
    [_receivedData appendData:data];
}

- (void)connection:(NSURLConnection *)connection didFailWithError:(NSError
*)error
{
    _connectionError = error;
}

- (void)connectionDidFinishLoading:(NSURLConnection *)connection
{
    NSLog(@"Response: %@", _receivedResponse);

    NSString *receivedString = [[NSString alloc] initWithData:_receivedData

encoding:NSUTF8StringEncoding];

    NSLog(@"Body: %@", receivedString);
}
```

Run your application, and you should see similar console output as you saw before. The difference now is that the rest of the application was allowed to continue before the connection finished. Had the connection taken 30 seconds to load, your users would have appreciated not having to wait for it.

Asynchronous Networking Concerns

Before we continue, there are some caveats to using NSURLConnection asynchronously that you should know about. First, there is no built-in queuing mechanism for NSURLConnection operations. If you were to create 50 objects that each fired off an NSURLConnection asynchronously, you would quickly find performance issues as the app tried to open 50 connections. While iOS devices are more than capable from a hardware perspective of maintaining multiple simultaneous connections, any more than a handful can become an issue. A good rule of thumb is to have no more than three simultaneous connections, especially when the user is connected to a cell network.

A second concern with asynchronous networking is that each active connection is given the same priority. If you have an absolutely critical data upload in your app, it may be competing with other code in your app that's downloading an image or content, or even with the Mail app in the background on the device. While this is rarely a serious issue, it's important to think about as you design your app.

Finally, it's difficult to coordinate delegate messages for multiple URL connections. It's certainly possible; each delegate method has a pointer to the URL connection as its first parameter, so you could reference that value before continuing, but this would quickly become tedious, and managing the state of the connections would be tricky.

Fortunately, I'm not giving you all of this bad news without some good news. Other developers have encountered this problem before and created open source solutions around them. Most of them use the built-in queuing mechanism in NSOperationQueue, which we'll discuss in a later chapter. They each have their own uses and advantages, so instead of backing a single project, I'll name three that I have found useful: ASIHTTPRequest, AFNetworking, and MKNetworkKit. When you're building a real application, search the Internet for these solutions and consider leveraging them to help with your asynchronous networking.

Back in our weather-parsing example app, we have received the data from the server and done so in a suitably asynchronous fashion, so let's work on parsing the data into a useful form.

Parsing JSON and XML from Web Services

JSON and XML are two different approaches to the same kind of problem: how do we encapsulate data in a meaningful way to send to another computer? When you connect to the weather service for a ten-day forecast, for instance, it returns a list of high and low temperatures for those days. For your app to be able to use that data, the format that the web service uses to send that data back must be documented somewhere so that you can parse it. What does that all *mean*, though? Put simply, you have to translate between native Objective-C objects and the data from the server.

To explain, let's look at some data in XML. This data, from Yahoo!'s web service, shows a two-day forecast:

```
<yweather:forecast day="Wed" date="22 Feb 2012" low="31" high="39"
text="Rain/Snow Showers Early" code="5" />
<yweather:forecast day="Thu" date="23 Feb 2012" low="32" high="40" text="PM Snow
Showers" code="14" />
```

As you can see, there are two yweather:forecast objects, with the properties day, date, low, high, text, and code. Let's look at what that might look like in JSON:

```
{
  "forecast": [
    {
      "day": "Wed",
      "date": "22 Feb 2012",
      "low": 31,
      "high": 39,
      "text": "Rain/Snow Showers Early",
      "code": 5
    },
    {
      "day": "Thu",
      "date": "23 Feb 2012",
      "low": 32,
      "high": 40,
      "text": "PM Snow Showers",
      "code": 14
    }
  ]
}
```

When JSON is received from a server, it's compacted without line breaks, so it would look like this:

```
{"forecast":[{"day":"Wed","date":"22 Feb
2012","low":31,"high":39,"text":"Rain/Snow Showers
```

```
Early","code":5},{"day":"Thu","date":"23 Feb 2012","low":32,"high":40,"text":"PM
Snow Showers","code":14}]}
```

While these two forms are functionally identical, the first is much more human-readable. It has an array of elements called forecast, each with the same properties as in the XML. We'll learn more about the syntax of each format as we go into parsing it.

Parsing XML

There are two distinct types of XML parsers: streaming and tree-based. Streaming parsers, also called *sequential parsers*, read one element at a time, processing the element's data as it reads. Tree-based parsers read the entire document at once, organizing elements into a hierarchy of objects. Tree parsers can be dangerous to use on iOS devices, because keeping the entire document in memory for the life span of your application can run up against memory limits. For that reason, the built-in parser, NSXMLParser, is something closer to a streaming processor, though it's not considered to be a true streaming parser. While this can be a verbose way to parse your data, it's safer in memory-constrained environments. Let's implement NSXMLParser in our weather example. Open your app delegate's header file (LCTAppDelegate.h using my class prefix) and declare that it conforms to the NSXMLParserDelegate protocol by adding the text in bold:

```
#import <UIKit/UIKit.h>

@interface LCTAppDelegate : UIResponder <NSXMLParserDelegate,
UIApplicationDelegate>

@property (strong, nonatomic) UIWindow *window;

@end
```

To understand how NSXMLParser works, consider the structure of an XML element. An element with the name element and the content content is structured like so:

```
<element>content</element>
```

As the XML parser reads the file, when it reads the <element> tag, it marks off the *beginning* of the element by sending a message to its delegate. It continues to read the text until it finds the </element> tag, at which point it sends another message to its delegate. It saves the text it encounters between the two tags, sending it in another delegate method. There are, therefore, three main delegate methods defined in NSXMLParserDelegate for each element, as well as one to catch errors and two to demarcate the beginning and end of the document:

- `parserDidStartDocument:`

- `parserDidEndDocument:`

- `parser:didStartElement:namespaceURI:qualifiedName:attrib utes:`

- `parser:didEndElement:namespaceURI:qualifiedName:`

- `parser:foundCharacters:`

- `parser:parseErrorOccurred:`

Like a good delegate protocol, the first parameter to each is a pointer to the NSXMLParser object. The third and fourth have additional parameters for namespaces and qualified names, but for simple XML parsing we won't need to use them. If you do advanced XML processing, there are other methods as well to deal with topics such as XML entity declarations and the like. For now, this collection of methods is enough for us to parse the response from Yahoo!. Open your app delegate's implementation file (LCTAppDelegate.m), and modify the connectionDidFinishLoading: method by adding the lines in bold and deleting those that have been stuck out:

```
- (void)connectionDidFinishLoading:(NSURLConnection *)connection
{
    NSLog(@"Response: %@", _receivedResponse);

    NSString *receivedString = [[NSString alloc] initWithData:_receivedData

encoding:NSUTF8StringEncoding];

    NSLog(@"Body: %@", receivedString);

    NSXMLParser *parser = [[NSXMLParser alloc] initWithData:_receivedData];
    [parser setDelegate:self];

    [parser parse];
}
```

In this method, we'll simply create an instance of NSXMLParser, give it a pointer to the data we received from the URL connection, set its delegate to self (here, the app delegate object), and tell it to begin parsing. This hands control of the parsing logic to the XML parser, which will in turn call our delegate methods. The data we're looking for is the yweather:forecast element, which doesn't have any text content. Instead, it uses attributes, and a sample forecast element is as follows:

```
<yweather:forecast day="Fri" date="24 Feb 2012" low="27" high="35" text="Few
Snow Showers" code="14" />
```

The attributes will be passed as the final parameter to
parser:didStartElement:namespaceURI:qualifiedName:attributes:, so we can
use that method to parse the data. First, let's create a mutable array to pass
data into. At the top of the file, add a mutable array to the class's private
instance variable declarations:

```
@implementation LCTAppDelegate {
    NSMutableData *_receivedData;
    NSURLResponse *_receivedResponse;
    NSError *_connectionError;
    NSMutableArray *_forecasts;
}
```

We'll store the attributes we receive in this array. Next, add an implementation
for parser:didStartElement:namespaceURI:qualifiedName:attributes: before
the @end compiler directive at the end of the file. Because all of the data is in the
attributes, we can just add the dictionary to our array:

```
- (void)parser:(NSXMLParser *)parser
didStartElement:(NSString *)elementName
  namespaceURI:(NSString *)namespaceURI
 qualifiedName:(NSString *)qName
    attributes:(NSDictionary *)attributeDict
{
    if ([elementName isEqualToString:@"yweather:forecast"]) {
        [_forecasts addObject:attributeDict];
    }
}
```

We'll also need to implement parserDidStartDocument: to create our array. Add
this method after the previous one but still before the @end compiler directive:

```
- (void)parserDidStartDocument:(NSXMLParser *)parser
{
    _forecasts = [NSMutableArray array];
}
```

Now, when the XML parser encounters a yweather:forecast element, our
delegate methods will save the attribute dictionaries to the _forecasts array.
Implement parserDidEndDocument: after parserDidStartDocument:, and output
the array to the console:

```
- (void)parserDidEndDocument:(NSXMLParser *)parser
{
    NSLog(@"%@", _forecasts);
}
```

Build and run the app. You should see the array's description in the console.
The output should look like this:

```
2012-02-24 23:45:50.078 SimpleWeather[1235:f803] (
        {
        code = 14;
        date = "24 Feb 2012";
        day = Fri;
        high = 35;
        low = 27;
        text = "Few Snow Showers";
    },
        {
        code = 14;
        date = "25 Feb 2012";
        day = Sat;
        high = 33;
        low = 21;
        text = "Few Snow Showers";
    }
)
```

As you can see, the array has two forecasts, each with code, date, day, high, low, and text keys.

> **NOTE:** Although the console output looks similar to JSON, which you'll see in more detail later in the chapter, it isn't. This is just a human-readable output format for logging.

We've successfully parsed the XML data into Foundation objects. The next steps for this application would probably include creating a user interface around these results, maybe displaying the forecasts in a table view or in some custom view. While the streaming XML parser can be complicated, it works quite well for simple tasks such as this. Most new web services, however, use JSON or at least offer JSON as an option. For iOS development with Cocoa Touch, you'll typically use JSON before XML. With that in mind, let's dive into parsing JSON data.

Parsing JSON

JSON is an acronym for JavaScript Object Notation. It comes from the JavaScript language and has emerged as the go-to format for transmitting objects across the network. There are two main structures you'll encounter in JSON: arrays and dictionaries. An array starts with the [character, with elements inside separated by commas, and ends with the] character. In JSON, data objects are simply strings and numbers, so a JSON array of numbers can be defined as such:

```
[1,2,3]
```

Dictionaries start with the { character and end with the } character. Key-value pairs are denoted with the key first, a : character, and then the value, with commas separating the pairs. A simple dictionary can be defined as such:

```
{"value1":10,"value2":42}
```

This dictionary has two keys, value1 and value2, with the values of 10 and 42, respectively. As you can see, JSON notation is as simple as possible, with very few characters defining a simple syntax. You may already be thinking of how you would write a parser for JSON, which would be no small effort. Fortunately, Cocoa Touch supports parsing JSON natively as of iOS 5, so you don't have to! Simply use the NSJSONSerialization class to parse the JSON into NSArray, NSDictionary, NSString, and NSNumber objects. Here's an example of parsing data returned from a web service in a URL connection delegate's connectionDidFinishLoading: method:

```
- (void)connectionDidFinishLoading:(NSURLConnection *)connection
{
    NSLog(@"Response: %@", _receivedResponse);

    // _receivedData is the NSData object received from the connection

    NSError *parseError = nil;
    id responseObject = [NSJSONSerialization JSONObjectWithData:_receivedData
                                                       options:0
                                                         error:&parseError];

    // Handle responseObject here
}
```

As you can see, we use an NSData object with data we've received from the connection to create the responseObject object. The responseObject object will be either an NSArray or NSDictionary, depending on what's in the JSON. There are also some options that can be passed as the second argument to JSONObjectWithData:options:error:, allowing you to create NSMutableArray and NSMutableDictionary objects instead of their immutable counterparts, to create NSMutableString objects instead of NSString objects, or to allow top-level objects that aren't arrays or dictionaries.

Creating JSON Representations

If you need to create your own JSON, it's similarly built-in. The following code snippet creates an array of strings and then creates a JSON string to represent it:

```
NSArray *fruits = [NSArray arrayWithObjects:@"orange", @"apple", @"cherry",
@"pear", nil];

NSError *encodingError = nil;
NSData *jsonData = [NSJSONSerialization dataWithJSONObject:fruits
                                           options:0
                                           error:&encodingError];
NSString *jsonString = [[NSString alloc] initWithData:jsonData
                                        encoding:NSUTF8StringEncoding];
NSLog(@"%@", jsonString);
```

The output of the NSLog() line in this code is as follows:

```
["orange","apple","cherry","pear"]
```

As you can see, it's an array with our four strings in it. This is ideal for uploading your own data to a web service. JSON isn't perfect, however; for instance, there is no built-in type for binary data, so if you want to upload an image to a web service, you'll either have to encode it in a string or find another method of uploading the data.

Parsing Foundation Objects into Model Objects

With both XML and JSON, we've learned how to take the data from the web service and parse it into NSArray and NSDictionary objects containing NSString and NSNumber objects. With Objective-C, however, it's often more desirable to work with native objects. In our Yahoo! Weather example, for instance, we'd ideally create an LCTForecast object to work with. Let's go ahead and create it now, giving it the properties we'd like to use. In Xcode, select File ➤ New ➤ File... or press ⌘+N. Select Cocoa Touch in the left column and Objective-C Class on the right. Click Next, and name the class LCTForecast, as a subclass of NSObject. Click Next and save the file to disk with the Create button. Open the newly created header, LCTForecast.h, and add the properties shown here in bold:

```
#import <Foundation/Foundation.h>

@interface LCTForecast : NSObject

@property (copy) NSString *date;
@property (strong) NSNumber *low;
@property (strong) NSNumber *high;
@property (copy) NSString *text;

@end
```

Next, switch to the implementation file (LCTForecast.m), and add @synthesize directives for the properties after the @implementation directive:

```
@implementation LCTForecast

@synthesize date = _date;
@synthesize low = _low;
@synthesize high = _high;
@synthesize text = _text;

@end
```

Now, all we need is a way to get data into the object. To do this, we're going to create a method called initWithDictionary:, into which we'll pass the dictionary we've parsed from the data we received from the web server. Open the header again (LCTForecast.h), and add a line to declare the method:

```
@interface LCTForecast : NSObject

@property (copy) NSString *date;
@property (strong) NSNumber *low;
@property (strong) NSNumber *high;
@property (copy) NSString *text;

- (id)initWithDictionary:(NSDictionary *)dictionary;

@end
```

Now, switch back to the implementation file (LCTForecast.m) and implement the method. Since the XML data returns strings for every attribute, we'll have to convert low and high to NSNumber objects. We'll do that by using their intValue methods to get an int type and then creating an NSNumber object from the int. Create the method as follows in bold:

```
@implementation LCTForecast

@synthesize date = _date;
@synthesize low = _low;
@synthesize high = _high;
@synthesize text = _text;

- (id)initWithDictionary:(NSDictionary *)dictionary
{
    self = [super init];

    if (self) {
        _date = [[dictionary objectForKey:@"date"] copy];
        _text = [[dictionary objectForKey:@"text"] copy];
```

```
        _low = [[NSNumber alloc] initWithInt:[[dictionary
objectForKey:@"low"] intValue]];
        _high = [[NSNumber alloc] initWithInt:[[dictionary
objectForKey:@"high"] intValue]];
    }

    return self;
}

@end
```

This method will extract the values we want to store from the parsed
NSDictionary, allowing us to turn the output from the web service into native
objects. Let's return to our app delegate and create these objects. Open your
app delegate's implementation file (LCTAppDelegate.m), and import the
LCTForecast header at the top with the line in bold:

```
#import "LCTAppDelegate.h"
#import "LCTForecast.h"
...
```

Next, modify the
parser:didStartElement:namespaceURI:qualifiedName:attributes: method to
create LCTForecast objects and place them in the _forecasts array by adding
the code in bold and removing the code that's been struck out:

```
- (void)parser:(NSXMLParser *)parser
didStartElement:(NSString *)elementName
  namespaceURI:(NSString *)namespaceURI
 qualifiedName:(NSString *)qName
    attributes:(NSDictionary *)attributeDict
{
    if ([elementName isEqualToString:@"yweather:forecast"]) {
        [_forecasts addObject:attributeDict];

        LCTForecast *forecast = [[LCTForecast alloc]
initWithDictionary:attributeDict];
        [_forecasts addObject:forecast];
    }
}
```

Build and run the app again, and the console output should look like this:

```
2012-02-25 00:55:09.876 SimpleWeather[2043:f803] (
    "<LCTForecast: 0x688be90>",
    "<LCTForecast: 0x688c0b0>"
)
```

As you can see, the array has two LCTForecast objects in it, which have been
created by our parser. Now the app is ready to use native Objective-C

paradigms for managing these objects and constructing a useful user interface around them.

> **NOTE:** The debug text printed for the LCTForecast object is a little sparse. You can control what gets printed in the console by implementing the description method, which returns a string, in any class that inherits from NSObject. Here's an example implementation of description for LCTForecast:
>
> ```
> - (NSString *)description
> {
>     return [NSString stringWithFormat:@"%@, date: <%@>, text:
> <%@>, low: <%@>, high: <%@>",
>             [super description],
>             [self date],
>             [self text],
>             [self low],
>             [self high]];
> }
> ```

Downloading Files

So far, we've covered what to do with text data coming from a server, but what about other kinds of data? Your app might download images, music, videos, or documents from a server. In those cases, it's best to save the file to the device's disk. One obvious solution would be to write the data received from the server to a file when the connection is done loading:

```
// Download the Apple favicon image
NSURL *faviconImageURL = [NSURL
URLWithString:@"http://www.apple.com/favicon.ico"];

NSURLRequest *urlRequest = [NSURLRequest requestWithURL:faviconImageURL];
NSURLResponse *urlResponse = nil;
NSError *error = nil;

NSData *imageData = [NSURLConnection sendSynchronousRequest:urlRequest
```

```
                                   returningResponse:&urlResponse
                                               error:&error];
```

```
[imageData writeToFile:@"favicon.ico" atomically:YES];
```

This code snippet downloads the small browser icon for Apple's website and saves it to the file `favicon.ico`. This works well for small images and files—the icon is only 9KB as of this writing—but what if the app had to download a file, perhaps a movie that the app would play back offline, that was larger than the memory capacity of the device? This method wouldn't work, because the `imageData` variable would be too large to store in memory. In those cases, you would implement the URL connection delegate methods and use them to work with just the data that comes in:

```
- (void)connection:(NSURLConnection *)connection didReceiveData:(NSData *)data
{
    NSFileHandle *fileHandle = [NSFileHandle
fileHandleForWritingAtPath:@"favicon.ico"];
    [fileHandle seekToEndOfFile];
    [fileHandle writeData:data];
}
```

Here, we use an `NSFileHandle` to manage writing data at the end of a file. This allows us to keep just the amount of data we need in memory. For large files, however, there is the danger of the connection being interrupted, the user entering a tunnel and losing their connection to the cell tower, and so on. For that reason, you may want to do this atomically, writing the data to a secondary location on disk, and then moving the file to the final location when the connection finishes error-free. The previous code sample could be written as follows to be atomic:

```
- (void)connection:(NSURLConnection *)connection didReceiveData:(NSData *)data
{
    NSString *filePath = @"favicon.ico";
    NSURL *fileURL = [NSURL fileURLWithPath:filePath];

    NSString *tmpFilePath = @"favicon.ico.tmp";
    NSURL *tmpFileURL = [NSURL fileURLWithPath:tmpFilePath];

    NSError *copyError = nil;
    BOOL copySuccess = [[NSFileManager defaultManager] copyItemAtURL:fileURL
                                                        toURL:tmpFileURL

error:&copyError];

    if (copySuccess == YES) {
        NSFileHandle *fileHandle = [NSFileHandle
fileHandleForWritingAtPath:tmpFilePath];
        [fileHandle seekToEndOfFile];
```

```
        [fileHandle writeData:data];

        NSError *moveError = nil;

        BOOL moveSuccess =
          [[NSFileManager defaultManager] replaceItemAtURL:fileURL
                                         withItemAtURL:tmpFileURL
                                        backupItemName:@"favicon.bak"
                                               options:0
                                     resultingItemURL:NULL
                                                 error:&moveError];

        if (moveSuccess == NO) {
            NSLog(@"Error moving item at URL %@ to URL at %@: %@",
                  tmpFileURL,
                  fileURL,
                  [moveError localizedDescription]);
        }
    }
    else {
        NSLog(@"Error copying item at URL %@ to URL at %@: %@",
              fileURL,
              tmpFileURL,
              [copyError localizedDescription]);
    }
}
```

When to Cache Files

When you're saving content to disk, there are two main locations that you'll use: the Documents directory and the Caches directory. The key difference between the two is that the contents of the Caches directory are not backed up and, on iOS 5 and greater, may be emptied by the operating system as the device runs low on free space. For that reason, any file that you can't easily re-create, such as user-generated content, should be saved in the Documents folder to prevent losing it forever. Data that you know you'll be able to redownload easily, such as images and content served from a web service that you maintain, can be saved in the Caches directory. One in-between gray area is content that you can easily redownload but that you don't want the system to purge yet. This could include content the user has saved for offline viewing or large files that the user is currently using. For those, Apple updated iOS 5.0.1 to include a flag that you can set on a file in the Documents directory to prevent it from being backed up. This prevents large, easily redownloaded files from taking up valuable space in the user's iCloud backups, while also preventing iOS from deleting those files when the device is low on disk space. Starting in iOS 5.1, Apple offers NSURL-level APIs for setting this value. Assuming an NSString object currently set to the file's path, you would use the following code to prevent a file from being backed up:

```
NSURL *fileURL = [NSURL fileURLWithPath:pathString];
NSError *error = nil;
[fileURL setResourceValue:[NSNumber numberWithBool:YES]
               forKey:NSURLIsExcludedFromBackupKey
                error:&error];
```

Downloading Images

Special care should be taken when you're downloading images to display to the user. An app that displays image galleries can grow very quickly, especially as the cameras in Apple devices grow in resolution. For that reason, it's good practice to keep track of how large your set of downloaded images has grown and removing cached images yourself before they grow too large. You can use the removeItemAtURL:error: or removeItemAtPath:error: method of the NSFileManager class to delete locally saved images before the cache grows too large.

Another thing to consider when downloading images is that often, such as when you're displaying a thumbnail of a larger image, you'll be displaying the image in a smaller size than the original downloaded size. While a UIImageView object can automatically scale images to display them, the quality of the resized images is less than what you can get if you manually resize them on the device before displaying them. Also, placing the original image in a UIImageView keeps the entire original image in memory. If your app were to display 100 8-megapixel images as 10x10 thumbnails, you would be using a mere 0.00125 percent of the images' pixels to display on the screen, yet keeping 100 percent of them in memory! This is an extreme example, to be sure, but there are real performance gains to be had by resizing images to just the size you need before displaying them. Fortunately, a number of open source libraries exist to do this exact thing; a quick Google search for "resize UIImage" should turn up a suitable library.

Sending Data Across the Network

So far, all of the networking code we've seen has involved loading data *from* a server into the app. Just as important, however, is sending data back *to* the server; any app that consists of user-generated content relies on this functionality. Sending data is akin to receiving it: create an NSURLRequest, set some of its properties, and use an NSURLConnection to perform the request. In fact, the URL connection still returns an NSURLResponse, NSError, and some NSData to represent the server's response, so from that perspective, the process is the same. The key differences is in preparing the URL request. Instead of NSURLRequest, you'll use its mutable subclass, NSMutableURLRequest, which allows you to set the HTTP method, HTTP body, and any HTTP header fields you need to set. The following code sample sends the string "Hello, World!" to a URL at www.example.com/service using the PUT HTTP method:

```
NSString *message = @"Hello, World!";
NSData *bodyData = [message dataUsingEncoding:NSUTF8StringEncoding];
NSString *contentLength = [NSString stringWithFormat:@"%d", [bodyData length]];

NSURL *serviceURL = [NSURL URLWithString:@"http://www.example.com/service"];

NSMutableURLRequest *request = [NSURLRequest requestWithURL:serviceURL];
[request setHTTPMethod:@"PUT"];
[request setHTTPBody:bodyData];
[request setValue:contentLength forHTTPHeaderField:@"Content-Length"];

NSURLResponse *response = nil;
NSError *error = nil;

NSData *responseData = [NSURLConnection sendSynchronousRequest:request
                                    returningResponse:&response
                                                error:&error];
```

We'll be sending plenty of data in our next example app: a fully functioning Twitter client.

Creating a Twitter Client

Twitter's explosive growth in popularity has brought with it a smorgasbord of Twitter clients for iOS. Search for "Twitter" in the App Store, and you'll get more results than you can easily sift through, official Twitter client notwithstanding. Creating a Twitter client, therefore, is something of a rite of passage for today's Cocoa Touch developer. This makes a certain amount of text, because an API for sending 140-character messages can be only so complex.

> **NOTE:** The documentation for Twitter's API, as of this writing, is available at
> http://dev.twitter.com.

A successful Twitter client needs to have some basic functionality:

- Displaying the user's timeline
- Displaying images from a user's timeline

▓ Posting a new tweet

▓ Searching Twitter for posts

To do this, naturally, we have to be able to log in to Twitter. Every API except for search requires that the user is authenticated. Historically, this was a huge pain, because Twitter uses the OAuth standard for authentication. Apps that authenticate to services that use OAuth don't store the user's password directly; instead, they save an "authorization token" that can serve as proof that the user has logged in. The authorization token is just a string that gets passed back to the server whenever you're doing something as that user. While this doesn't sound too bad at first, the devil is in the details.

To log in to an OAuth service, the app first loads a web view pointed at the service's login page. The user types their login and password, and the web view redirects to a success page. This success page typically does one of two things: opens a URL that you've specified as a callback URL, passing the authorization token as an argument in the URL string, or displays a second page with a PIN that the user enters into your app. The PIN is then used to obtain the authorization token. Implementing these features is time-consuming, inefficient, and difficult to learn. What's worse, each service that implements OAuth does so slightly differently, so learning it once isn't enough; you have to learn OAuth as well as each site's quirks.

Another piece to the OAuth puzzle is creating an API key. For each web service for which you want to add OAuth authentication to your app, you have to register with the developers of the service and receive an API key with which you'll authenticate your requests. These API keys often tie in to a rate limit for the service, so your app can't make too many requests and slow down the service for everyone using it.

Luckily for Cocoa Touch developers, once again Apple has stepped in on your behalf. It introduced the Accounts framework in iOS 5, which allows the system to store information about the user's accounts in a central location on the device, rather than having each app store the information. As of iOS 5.0.1, the only service that takes advantage of the Accounts framework is Twitter, which has its own Twitter framework in the OS as well. With the Twitter framework, instead of your app needing to authenticate the user manually, you can use the account they've entered into the system without doing the OAuth dance. Instead of a login screen, the user will have a single alert view to click that gives your app permission to access their Twitter account. If they have multiple Twitter accounts, you'll need to ask which one they want to use, but that's the extent of how you gain Twitter authorization in iOS 5.

Let's get started with our Twitter app. Open Xcode, and select File ➤ New ➤ New Project… or press ⌘+Shift+N. With Application under iOS selected on the left, select Empty Application from the right. Click Next, and then fill in your company identifier and class prefix (I'll use com.learncocoatouch and LCT, respectively). Choose iPhone for Device Family, uncheck Use Core Data, check Use Automatic Reference Counting, and uncheck Include Unit Tests. When you're done, it should look like Figure 6-3. Click Next once more and save the project to disk.

Figure 6-3. *The configuration options for creating our Twitter client*

Now that we've created the project, we need to do some additional configuration. We'll be using the Accounts and Twitter frameworks, so we need to tell Xcode to link our app with them at compile time. Open the file browser by selecting View ➤ Navigators ➤ Show Project Navigator or by pressing ⌘+1. Select the top item, TwitterExample (your project file). Select TwitterExample from the list of targets on the left side of the editor pane, and open the Summary tab. Under the Linked Frameworks and Libraries section, you should see some frameworks already linked: UIKit, Foundation, and CoreGraphics. Click the plus button (+) to bring up a list of frameworks you can add to the project. Select Accounts.framework and click Add, and then click the plus button again and select Twitter.framework. When you're done, the section should look like Figure 6-4.

Figure 6-4. *The TwitterExample app configured to link to the Accounts and Twitter frameworks*

Great. Before we continue, you should enter your Twitter credentials into the iPhone Simulator for testing. Open the iPhone Simulator—if you don't have it in your Dock, build and run this empty app to launch it—and open the Settings app. Select Twitter and enter your username and password. When you're done, it should look like Figure 6-5.

Figure 6-5. *The Twitter settings page in the Settings app, configured with a Twitter account*

Once you have a Twitter account set up, we're ready to get coding. The first thing we're going to do is create a Twitter controller object. This controller, which we'll implement as a singleton, will handle all of the methods that require communication with Twitter's servers. By putting this in a separate class, we can encapsulate these methods appropriately. In Xcode, select File ➤ New ➤ File... or press ⌘+N to create a new file. With Cocoa Touch selected on the left column, select Objective-C Class. Click Next, and name the class `LCTTwitterController`, as a subclass of `NSObject`. Click Next, and save the file to disk. Open the header file (`LCTTwitterController.h`), and add the following method declarations in bold:

```
@interface LCTTwitterController : NSObject
```

```
+ (id)sharedInstance;
```

```
- (void)authorizeAccount;
- (void)getTweetsInUserTimelineWithCompletionHandler:(void(^)(NSArray
*tweets))handler;
```

```
@end
```

We'll use the `sharedInstance` method to get a pointer to the singleton object. The `authorizeAccount` method will ensure that we have a valid account, which we'll need for the other method, `getTweetsInUserTimelineWithCompletionHandler:`, which will return a list of tweets for the user to read. You might be wondering about this odd bit of syntax in its declaration:

```
(void(^)(NSArray *tweets))handler
```

This is a *block*: a piece of code encapsulated in an object that you can pass to a method. This particular block returns void and has one parameter, an NSArray called `tweets`. We'll focus on blocks in particular in the next chapter. For now, just copy the syntax out of the book.

Let's now add implementations for these methods. In Xcode, switch to the Twitter controller's implementation file (LCTTwitterController.m), and add the lines in bold (this is a large block of text, but we'll come back to it later):

```
#import "LCTTwitterController.h"

#import <Accounts/Accounts.h>
#import <Twitter/Twitter.h>

static NSString * const kSavedTwitterAccountKey = @"SavedTwitterAccount";

@implementation LCTTwitterController {
    ACAccountStore *_accountStore;
    ACAccount *_twitterAccount;
}

+ (id)sharedInstance
{
    static id _sharedInstance = nil;

    if (_sharedInstance == nil) {
        _sharedInstance = [[self alloc] init];
    }

    return _sharedInstance;
}
```

```objc
- (id)init
{
    self = [super init];

    if (self) {
        _accountStore = [[ACAccountStore alloc] init];

        // If we've previously saved the account, load it now.
        NSString *accountId =
        [[NSUserDefaults standardUserDefaults]
stringForKey:kSavedTwitterAccountKey];

        if (accountId) {
            _twitterAccount = [_accountStore
accountWithIdentifier:accountId];
        }

    }

    return self;
}

- (void)authorizeAccount
{
    if (_twitterAccount == nil) {
        ACAccountType *accountType = [_accountStore
accountTypeWithAccountTypeIdentifier:ACAccountTypeIdentifierTwitter];

        NSUserDefaults *userDefaults = [NSUserDefaults
standardUserDefaults];

        [_accountStore requestAccessToAccountsWithType:accountType
                                withCompletionHandler:^(BOOL granted,
NSError *error) {
                                    if (granted) {
                                        NSArray *twitterAccounts =
                                        [_accountStore
accountsWithAccountType:accountType];

                                        if ([twitterAccounts count] > 0) {
                                            _twitterAccount =
                                            [twitterAccounts
objectAtIndex:0];

                                            NSString *identifier =
                                            [_twitterAccount identifier];

                                            [userDefaults
```

```
setObject:identifier

forKey:kSavedTwitterAccountKey];
                                          [userDefaults synchronize];
                                      }
                                  }
                          }];
      }
}

- (void)getTweetsInUserTimelineWithCompletionHandler:(void(^)(NSArray
*tweets))handler
{
    NSString *timelinePath =
@"https://api.twitter.com/1/statuses/home_timeline.json";
    NSURL *timelineURL = [NSURL URLWithString:timelinePath];

    TWRequest *timelineRequest = [[TWRequest alloc] initWithURL:timelineURL
                                                     parameters:nil

requestMethod:TWRequestMethodGET];

    [timelineRequest setAccount:_twitterAccount];
    [timelineRequest performRequestWithHandler:^(NSData *responseData,
NSHTTPURLResponse *urlResponse, NSError *error) {
        if (responseData) {
            id topLevelObject = [NSJSONSerialization
JSONObjectWithData:responseData
                                                            options:0

error:NULL];

            if ([topLevelObject isKindOfClass:[NSArray class]]) {
                if (handler != NULL) {
                    handler(topLevelObject);
                }
            }
        }
    }];
}

@end
```

Now that you've written these methods, let's break them down. First, in
sharedInstance, we keep track of a _sharedInstance pointer. Using the static
qualifier ensures that we have only one pointer; every time sharedInstance is
called, the _sharedInstance pointer is the same pointer, though it will point to a
new memory address after we create the shared instance of TwitterController.
The init method loads a saved account ID from the user defaults database (if

there is one), which allows us to cache the user's account to prevent them from needing to authorize our app every time it runs. Next, the authorizeAccount method requests authorization for all Twitter accounts. If it receives authorization, it saves the account information for the first Twitter account it finds in the user defaults database for future retrieval. In a shipping app, you'll want to ask the user which account to use if they have more than one.

The timeline retrieval method performs network connection tasks that should look somewhat familiar to you. It creates a request with a URL, sets some parameters, and then executes the request. The difference is that the request is of type TWRequest, which are specially crafted requests designed to work with Twitter. The setAccount: method takes a Twitter account as its parameter, and this enables the TWRequest object to, among other things, handle all of the authorization code on your behalf, which saves you untold hours of headache and frustration. This method also uses a block to handle the response from the network, from which we use the response data to build an NSArray that we'll later decode into tweets. For now, we pass this NSArray into another function, which has been passed as a block as the parameter to this method. Now that we've created a simple controller for our Twitter functionality, let's create some UI around it.

In Xcode, select File ➤ New ➤ New File… or press ⌘+N. Select Cocoa Touch from the left column and then Objective-C class from the right pane. Click Next, and give this new class the name LCTTimelineViewController, as a subclass of UITableViewController. Leave both Targeted for iPad and "With XIB for user interface" unchecked. Click Next and save the files to disk. Open the implementation file (LCTTimelineViewController.m) and add a line at the top to import the LCTTwitterController header file:

```
#import "LCTTimelineViewController.h"
#import "LCTTwitterController.h"
```

Xcode should have created a class extension for you already underneath the #import lines. If so, copy the code in bold to add an instance variable for our array of tweets; otherwise, copy the entire code block and place it directly under the last #import directive:

```
@interface LCTTimelineViewController () {
    NSArray *_tweets;
}

@end
```

Since we used the UITableViewController template, some of the table view methods should already be present. Find the implementation for numberOfSectionsInTableView: from the template. If this doesn't exist, place the method below in its entirety (save for the crossed-out lines) between the main @implementation and @end directives (*not* the class extension); otherwise, remove the crossed-out code and add the bold code:

```
- (NSInteger)numberOfSectionsInTableView:(UITableView *)tableView
{
#warning Potentially incomplete method implementation.
    // Return the number of sections.
    return 0;
    return 1;
}
```

We're going to have one section in this table view, with each tweet in the timeline represented by a row in the section. Find the existing implementation of tableView:numberOfRowsInSection: and modify it as shown next or, if it isn't present, implement it after numberOfSectionsInTableView:.

```
- (NSInteger)tableView:(UITableView *)tableView
numberOfRowsInSection:(NSInteger)section
{
#warning Incomplete method implementation.
    // Return the number of rows in the section.
    return 0;
    return [_tweets count];
}
```

Here we use the number of tweets in the _tweets array to determine the number of rows in the table view. Finally, find the implementation for tableView:cellForRowAtIndexPath: and modify it as shown next or implement it after tableView:numberOfRowsInSection:.

```
- (UITableViewCell *)tableView:(UITableView *)tableView
         cellForRowAtIndexPath:(NSIndexPath *)indexPath
{
    static NSString *CellIdentifier = @"Cell";
    UITableViewCell *cell = [tableView
dequeueReusableCellWithIdentifier:CellIdentifier];

    if (cell == nil) {
        cell = [[UITableViewCell alloc]
initWithStyle:UITableViewCellStyleSubtitle
                                        reuseIdentifier:CellIdentifier];
    }

    // Configure the cell...

    NSDictionary *tweet = [_tweets objectAtIndex:[indexPath row]];

    [[cell textLabel] setText:[tweet objectForKey:@"text"]];
```

```
    [[cell detailTextLabel] setText:[[tweet objectForKey:@"user"]
objectForKey:@"name"]];

    return cell;
}
```

This method puts the text of the tweet and the user's display name in the cell.

> **NOTE:** The text and name keys may change over time as Twitter modifies their API.
> Consult the Twitter documentation if they don't seem to work.

We need to do two more things before testing this: displaying the view controller and loading tweets into it. First, still in (LCTTimelineViewController.m), implement the viewWillAppear: method after the methods you just created (but before the final @end line):

```
- (void)viewWillAppear:(BOOL)animated
{
    [super viewWillAppear:animated];

    [[LCTTwitterController sharedInstance]
getTweetsInUserTimelineWithCompletionHandler:^(NSArray *tweets) {
        _tweets = tweets;
        [[self tableView] performSelectorOnMainThread:@selector(reloadData)
                                           withObject:nil
                                        waitUntilDone:NO];
    }];
}
```

Again, though the syntax for the block parameter to getTweetsInUserTimelineWithCompletionHandler: may be confusing, we'll cover it in great detail in the next chapter. Furthermore, we'll explain the performSelectorOnMainThread:withObject:waitUntilDone: method in a future chapter about performance and multithreading. Next, let's get this view controller on the screen. Open the app delegate implementation file (LCTAppDelegate.m), and add a line at the top to import the view controller's header:

```
#import "LCTAppDelegate.h"

#import "LCTTwitterController.h"
#import "LCTTimelineViewController.h"
```

Next, modify the application:didFinishLaunchingWithOptions: method with the lines in bold to display the view controller:

```objc
- (BOOL)application:(UIApplication *)application
didFinishLaunchingWithOptions:(NSDictionary *)launchOptions
{
    self.window = [[UIWindow alloc] initWithFrame:[[UIScreen mainScreen]
bounds]];
    // Override point for customization after application launch.
    self.window.backgroundColor = [UIColor whiteColor];
    [self.window makeKeyAndVisible];

    [[LCTTwitterController sharedInstance] authorizeAccount];

    LCTTimelineViewController *viewController =
    [[LCTTimelineViewController alloc]
initWithStyle:UITableViewStylePlain];

    [[self window] setRootViewController:viewController];

    return YES;
}
```

Build and run the application. When the app launches, you'll see a prompt in an alert view asking you to authorize the app to use your Twitter accounts. Once you've authorized it, you should see a table of recent tweets from accounts you follow. Congratulations! You've just made your first Twitter app. There is one small issue, however: if the table view controller loads before the user has authorized the account, it won't load any tweets. To fix this for now, let's add a reload button. In Xcode, return to the method you just modified in the app delegate's implementation file (LCTAppDelegate.m), and embed the view controller in a navigation controller:

```objc
- (BOOL)application:(UIApplication *)application
didFinishLaunchingWithOptions:(NSDictionary *)launchOptions
{
    self.window = [[UIWindow alloc] initWithFrame:[[UIScreen mainScreen]
bounds]];
    // Override point for customization after application launch.
    self.window.backgroundColor = [UIColor whiteColor];
    [self.window makeKeyAndVisible];

    [[LCTTwitterController sharedInstance] authorizeAccount];

    LCTTimelineViewController *viewController =
    [[LCTTimelineViewController alloc] initWithStyle:UITableViewStylePlain];

    UINavigationController *navigationController =
    [[UINavigationController alloc]
initWithRootViewController:viewController];

    [[self window] setRootViewController:navigationController];
```

```
    return YES;
}
```

Now, open the view controller's implementation file
(LCTTimelineViewController.m), and modify the initWithStyle: method:

```
- (id)initWithStyle:(UITableViewStyle)style
{
    self = [super initWithStyle:style];

    if (self) {
        [self setTitle:@"Timeline"];

        UIBarButtonItem *reloadButton =
        [[UIBarButtonItem alloc]
initWithBarButtonSystemItem:UIBarButtonSystemItemRefresh
                                                target:self

action:@selector(reloadButtonPressed:)];
        [[self navigationItem] setLeftBarButtonItem:reloadButton];
    }

    return self;
}
```

Next, declare the reloadButtonPressed: method in the class extension at the
top of this file:

```
@interface LCTTimelineViewController () {
    NSArray *_tweets;
}

- (void)reloadButtonPressed:(id)sender;

@end
```

Finally, let's implement the reloadButtonPressed: method in the main
@implementation block of the object (not the class extension) before the @end
directive:

```
- (void)reloadButtonPressed:(id)sender
{
    [[LCTTwitterController sharedInstance]
getTweetsInUserTimelineWithCompletionHandler:^(NSArray *tweets) {
        _tweets = tweets;

        [[self tableView] performSelectorOnMainThread:@selector(reloadData)
                                    withObject:nil
                                    waitUntilDone:NO];
```

```
    }];
}
```

Build and run your app again, and you should be able to refresh the list using this button. A good Twitter client, however, will also allow the user to *post* tweets to Twitter. Let's add that functionality. To do so, we'll use another class in the Twitter framework, TWTweetComposeViewController. Remaining in the view controller's implementation file, modify the initWithStyle: method once more to create a button for posting a tweet:

```
- (id)initWithStyle:(UITableViewStyle)style
{
    self = [super initWithStyle:style];

    if (self) {
        [self setTitle:@"Timeline"];

        UIBarButtonItem *reloadButton =
        [[UIBarButtonItem alloc]
initWithBarButtonSystemItem:UIBarButtonSystemItemRefresh
                                                   target:self

action:@selector(reloadButtonPressed:)];
        [[self navigationItem] setLeftBarButtonItem:reloadButton];

        UIBarButtonItem *tweetButton =
        [[UIBarButtonItem alloc]
initWithBarButtonSystemItem:UIBarButtonSystemItemCompose
                                                   target:self

action:@selector(tweetButtonPressed:)];
        [[self navigationItem] setRightBarButtonItem:tweetButton];
    }

    return self;
}
```

As before, add a line to the class extension to declare the action method that the button will call:

```
@interface LCTTimelineViewController () {
    NSArray *_tweets;
}

- (void)reloadButtonPressed:(id)sender;
- (void)tweetButtonPressed:(id)sender;

@end
```

Next, at the top of the file, add a line to import the Twitter framework header:

```
#import "LCTTimelineViewController.h"

#import <Twitter/Twitter.h>

#import "LCTTwitterController.h"
```

And finally, implement tweetButtonPressed: underneath reloadButtonPressed: but before the @end directive:

```
- (void)tweetButtonPressed:(id)sender
{
    TWTweetComposeViewController *viewController =
    [[TWTweetComposeViewController alloc] init];

    [self presentModalViewController:viewController animated:YES];
}
```

And that's it! Run your app and click the tweet button. You'll see an entire Twitter UI that you didn't have to write, and tweeting from it will actually work! As you can see, iOS 5's built-in Twitter support greatly simplified making apps that work with Twitter. In the next chapter, we'll look more at blocks and how they work with modern APIs such as the Twitter integration, improving our little Twitter client as we go.

Summary

In this chapter, we've talked a lot about the networking on iOS. We've covered parsing XML and JSON into meaningful model objects, creating and using URL connections, and using them asynchronously. Additionally, we've looked at downloading images from remote sources and sending data back to web services. We've also created a simple Twitter client, to which we'll continue to add features as we progress through this book.

Writing Modern Code with Blocks

If there's a trend to be picking up on with regards to Apple's development of the developer tools and languages surrounding Cocoa Touch's development, it's that Apple is trying to make things as easy as possible for developers to create engaging, easy-to-use apps. It seems that with every new iOS release, there are more ways in which your life gets easier as a Cocoa Touch developer. One such way occurred with iOS 4.0 and Mac OS X Snow Leopard and is actually a new feature added by Apple to the C language: blocks. C language development in general moves at a glacial pace, so any new features are news just by being new features added to C. Blocks are exciting for much more than that; they allow greater freedom, more logical code grouping, and better encapsulation in your code. In this chapter, we'll discuss what blocks are, how they work, and why you'll want to use them. We'll also cover some of Apple's new APIs that require you to use blocks, a glimpse of which you've already gotten in the Twitter example from Chapter 6. Finally, we'll revisit that example to expand on its features, turning it into a much better app. First, let's talk about what blocks even *are*.

What Are Blocks?

Put simply, a block is a piece of code that's self-contained. Like a function or method, blocks take arguments and return values, but unlike functions or method, they're anonymous; that is, you can create and execute a block without it ever having a name. Typically, a block represents a discrete task, whether that's comparing two objects, performing an animation, or resizing an image. In that regard, blocks play a huge role in bringing multithreaded processing to your code; we'll see some of that in this chapter, and even more in the next chapter. Blocks are also used to delay the execution of code; instead of passing a target-action pair or an object and a method selector, you can pass a block to be executed after some other task. This is all convenient and good, but Apple has also added some memory management magic to blocks that make using them with Objective-C all the more beneficial. Now that I've properly talked them up, let's take a look at what a block looks like.

Blocks Are Encapsulated Functions

For our first block, let's take the traditional path and create a "Hello, World!" block. The block, when executed, will print "Hello, World!" to the console and nothing more. It takes no arguments and returns no value, so its return type is void, just like a function or method that returns no value. Creating the block is as follows:

```
void (^helloBlock)(void) = ^ void (void){ NSLog(@"Hello, World!"); };
```

Let's break that down. First, we have the return type, which in this case is void. Then, in parentheses, we have a carat to signify that this is a block, followed by the name of the temporary variable we're storing the block in, so we have (^helloBlock). Finally, another set of parentheses contains a comma-separated list of the arguments the block takes, which in this case is nothing, so it's simply (void). The net result of the left side of the expression is a new temporary variable called helloBlock that contains a block. If you've ever used function pointers in C, you'll notice that the syntax is nearly identical, with the difference being that an asterisk (*) is used for a function, and a carat (^) is used for a block.

The right side of this expression is the block itself. It begins with the carat, followed by the return type (here, void), and then, in parentheses, the argument list, which in this case is simply (void). Then, in between braces ({ and }) is the actual code of the block. Be sure to notice that there are *two* semicolons here. One ends the expression *inside* the block, which is an NSLog() function call, and the second ends the expression that *defines* the block. Forgetting one or both of these semicolons is an incredibly easy way to practice debugging your code. To save on space, you can omit void return types and argument lists from the right side; the previous code could be written as follows:

```
void (^helloBlock)(void) = ^{ NSLog(@"Hello, World!"); };
```

As you can see, this is much more concise. To recap, this line (and the previous version of it) creates a block that calls NSLog() when it executes and then stores the block in a variable called `helloBlock`. Now, how do we execute it? Just like a function, call it:

```
helloBlock();
```

Calling `helloBlock()` will cause the block's code to immediately execute. Interestingly enough, it's not necessary to store the block in a variable before calling it. The following line of code successfully prints "Hello, World!" to the console:

```
^{ NSLog(@"Hello, World!"); }();
```

The merits of this *particular* code sample are few, but it's an interesting example of blocks' anonymity.

Readable Block Declarations with Typedefs

The previous example was about as simple as block declarations get. In practice, block declarations are more complex. Consider a block that returns a `BOOL` value and takes two arguments, of types `id` and `NSError*`. Declaring a variable to store this block called `resultHandler` would be as follows:

```
BOOL (^resultHandler)(id result, NSError *error);
```

This isn't too bad. It's still readable enough to use as-is. What if, however, it had a third argument, which itself was another block? Now things get more complex:

```
BOOL (^resultHandler)(id result, NSError *error, NSString
*(^helperBlock)(void));
```

As you can see, things could quickly get out of hand. To combat this, one thing you can do is define common block types using typedefs, a C method of defining your own types. The first `resultHandler` block shown earlier might be a common enough style of block that you want to refer to it as a discrete type called `ResultHandler`. This can be accomplished with the following line:

```
typedef BOOL (^ResultHandler)(id result, NSError *error);
```

With our newfound type definition, we can declare a variable for this type of block much more succinctly:

```
ResultHandler resultHandler;
```

Pretty simple, eh? Creating the block and storing it in the variable is easy, as well:

```
ResultHandler resultHandler = ^ BOOL (id result, NSError *error) {
    [result performSomeTask];
    return YES;
};
```

As you can see, the block returns a BOOL, takes two arguments, and we return a BOOL in our implementation. You can use one typedef inside of another, too; if we wanted to add a HelperBlock type as a third argument, we could define two types:

```
typedef NSString *(^HelperBlock)(void);
typedef BOOL (^ResultHandler)(id result, NSError *error, HelperBlock helperBlock);
```

This is a quick and easy way to vastly improve your code's readability.

Block Memory Management

One unique feature of blocks is their memory management semantics. Blocks are created on the stack, just like a temporary variable is. When the scope in which they're created ends, the block is destroyed along with the rest of the stack frame. Consider the following example:

```
if (x == 5) {
    void (^myBlock)(void) = ^{
        [self doSomethingCool];
    };
}
```

When the if statement in this code is done, myBlock is destroyed. What if we wanted to use myBlock outside of the if statement? You might think that this would work:

```
void (^myBlock)(void) = NULL;

if (x == 5) {
    myBlock = ^{
        [self doSomethingCool];
    };
}
else {
    myBlock = ^{
        [self doSomethingElse];
    };
}

myBlock();
```

The problem here is that when the block stored in myBlock is created, it's inside either the if statement or the else statement, so the block will still be destroyed when the statement is done. Because of this, the myBlock variable will hold garbage data when we try to execute it, resulting in a crash. To get around this, we need to get the block off the stack and onto the heap. This is done with the

`Block_copy()` function, which copies the block from the stack to the heap. Since it's moving the location of the block in memory, the original block's location is no longer valid. Once you've copied a block, be sure to use only the return value of `Block_copy()`, not the original block. The following is the correct version of the previous code with ARC turned off; we'll discuss ARC and blocks later:

```
void (^myBlock)(void) = NULL;

if (x == 5) {
    myBlock = Block_copy(^{
        [self doSomethingCool];
    });
}
else {
    myBlock = Block_copy(^{
        [self doSomethingElse];
    });
}

myBlock();
Block_release(myBlock);
```

As you can see, we store the returned value from `Block_copy()` in myBlock, moving it to the heap and avoiding its destruction. Blocks are reference-counted, so for every call to `Block_copy()`, we must also call `Block_release()`; just like Objective-C objects, blocks will be destroyed when their retain count reaches 0. You can also call `Block_retain()` on a block to increment its retain count, but it's important to note that calling `Block_retain()` on a stack-based block will *not* copy it to the heap. Similarly, it's important to note that calling `Block_copy()` on a block that's already been copied to the heap will simply increment the retain count; it won't actually make yet another copy of the block. For that reason, using `Block_copy()` alone and never using `Block_retain()` shouldn't cause any problems, but using `Block_retain()` by itself could leave you spending some time debugging your app when it crashes. Just as it does with memory management for Objective-C objects, ARC will help with memory management with blocks. How does it do that? By treating the blocks as objects.

Blocks Are Objects

You may have noticed some similarities between blocks and Objective-C objects. The both have similar, reference-counted memory management environments, and we store blocks into variables much like how we store objects into pointers. These similarities are not just skin deep, either. While they aren't full-fledged objects in the sense that an NSArray is, blocks are compatible with the Objective-C runtime thanks to some behind-the-scenes trickery. This allows you to send a message to a block. The previous code could be written like this (still with ARC turned off):

```
void (^myBlock)(void) = NULL;

if (x == 5) {
    myBlock = [^{ [self doSomethingCool]; } copy];
}
else {
    myBlock = [^{ [self doSomethingElse]; } copy];
}

myBlock();
[myBlock release];
```

As you can see, the block is now a receiver for the copy and release messages, which do the equivalent of Block_copy() and Block_release(), respectively. We could also call retain on a block with the expected effects.

The fact that blocks can also be used as objects has much further-reaching implications than simplifying your memory management code. For one, if you're using ARC, the memory management code is written for you by the compiler, which is smart enough to copy blocks to the heap as appropriate. This alone leads to fewer crashes by eliminating some developer mistakes. Another useful way to take advantage of the situation is by putting blocks into collection classes like NSArray and NSDictionary. This allows for some pretty clever usage patterns for blocks. You can use an NSArray like a stack, pushing and popping blocks onto and off of it for execution, or use blocks in an NSDictionary to bind specific actions to certain keys. If you use a block with an API that isn't expecting a block, such as adding a block to an array, be sure to place a copy of the block in the array, as in the following example:

```
[myArray addObject:[^{
    [self doSomething ];
} copy]];
```

There's a lot of power in this flexibility to be taken advantage of, but what's even more powerful is a bit of extra magic that Apple has infused into the implementation of blocks.

Blocks Capture Scope

The blocks we've seen so far can get data from only one place: their arguments. If you want to write a block that processes an image, resizing it to a certain size, then at the very least you'll want to give it an image argument and a size argument. If that were the *only* way to get data into a block, then not only would argument lists get extremely long for complicated procedures, but also blocks really wouldn't be that much more useful than methods or functions. Fortunately, blocks also have the ability to capture their surrounding scope and use it during their execution! You could create a simple block that pulls in a string and prints it to the console:

```
NSString *message = @"Hello, World!";

void (^blockLog)(void) = ^{
    NSLog(@"%@", message);
};

blockLog();
```

Here, the `blockLog` block uses the value of the `message` variable, but not from an argument! When the block is created, it captures the values from the surrounding scope that have been referenced, eliminating the need to define all of them as arguments. The memory management here is not always straightforward, however; and `int` created as a temporary variable but then referenced in a block should remain accessible to the block for the block's entire lifetime. If the block is copied to the heap, however, it may outlive the stack frame in which the `int` was created, resulting in it having been destroyed. To get around this issue, when you copy a block to the heap, it will copy stack-based variables with it. This is entirely automatic, so you don't need to worry about keeping a list of stack-based variables you've referenced in a block; the compiler will keep that list for you. This is where the benefits of blocks start to show, because capturing scope like this just isn't possible with functions or methods. You'd have to pass every variable in as an argument.

There is one important caveat to mention with blocks capturing scope. By default, a block cannot *modify* a variable that it has pulled in from the surrounding scope. Allowing the block to modify the variable would require much more compiler intervention. When a block gets copied to the heap, if it can modify the variable, then references to the variable must also be changed in order for that value to remain consistent. The compiler is perfectly capable of taking care of this for you, so long as you tell it that you need it to. To do so, you use a *storage qualifier*, which is an attribute you specify when you create the variable. To create an `int` value that a block can write to, prepend `__block` (that's two underscores at the beginning) before `int` in your declaration:

```
__block int myInt = 42;
```

Once you've done that, the block can write to the variable at will, whether or not it gets copied to the heap. Thanks to the `__block` storage qualifier, writing blocks that outlive the method in which they were created is easy and useful. Another useful feature of blocks is how they interact with Objective-C objects.

Blocks Retain Objects

Just like with any other variable, you can reference pointers to Objective-C objects from a block's surrounding scope while you're inside a block. This works as you would expect, even with self when you're in an Objective-C method. Since Objective-C objects, unlike temporary variables like ints, are created on the heap and reference counted, simply copying the pointer to the block is not sufficient, especially if the block itself outlives the original reference to the object. To get around this problem, when you reference an Objective-C object in a block, it's automatically sent the retain message, and it's sent release when the block is destroyed. This allows you to use objects in your blocks without worrying that the object will be deallocated before the block is done using it. You can also combine objects with the __block storage qualifier to create objects inside of blocks with the expected memory management implications.

There is one major caveat to the use of objects with blocks, however: retain cycles. It's possible to get in a situation where a block references an object, thus retaining it, but the object also retains the block, thus causing a situation where neither object will ever be deallocated. Let's look at how that happens and then at how to avoid it. Consider an object with one property: a block that takes no arguments and returns void. We'll name the class BlockHolder:

```
typedef void (^SimpleBlock)(void);

@interface BlockHolder : NSObject

@property (copy) SimpleBlock block;

@end
```

Note that for blocks, we'll use the copy attribute for the property to ensure that it gets copied to the heap. Now let's look at how we might create a retain cycle with a BlockHolder object:

```
BlockHolder *holder = [[BlockHolder alloc] init];

[holder setBlock:^{
    NSLog(@"%@", [holder description]);
}];
```

In this code snippet, we create a new instance of the BlockHolder class and assign it to the holder variable. Next, we create a block to pass in to it that simply prints the object's description to the console. The devil is in the details: since we reference `holder` in the block, it's retained by the block, and since the `BlockHolder` class defines the `block` property with the `copy` attribute, it will retain the block, leading to both objects retaining one another. Because of the retain cycle, neither of these objects will ever be deallocated. There are two ways to combat this, one specific and one general. First, since we wrote the `BlockHolder` class, we can modify the block. Instead of taking no arguments, we can provide a pointer to the block holder as an argument to the block. We'll use `self` as the name to emulate how `self` works in an Objective-C method. The new `SimpleBlock` declaration would be as follows:

```
typedef void (^SimpleBlock)(id self);
```

When we created the block, we would then replace `holder` with `self`:

```
BlockHolder *holder = [[BlockHolder alloc] init];

[holder setBlock:^(id self){
    NSLog(@"%@", [self description]);
}];
```

This avoids a retain cycle quite nicely. `self` might be a little confusing, so you may want to use a different name for the argument, but this is a good way to avoid retain cycles entirely. The second way is more useful if you don't control the code of the object to which you're passing the block. What you'll do is create a weak reference to the object and refer to that in the block, avoiding the retain cycle because weak references do not cause an extra `retain` call. In that case, the code to create the block might look like this:

```
typedef void (^SimpleBlock)(void);

BlockHolder *holder = [[BlockHolder alloc] init];

__weak BlockHolder *safeHolder = holder;

[holder setBlock:^{
    NSLog(@"%@", [safeHolder description]);
}];
```

The __weak qualifier requires iOS 5 and ARC. If you're using ARC and iOS 4.3, use __unsafe_unretained instead.

Using Blocks as Parameters to Methods

One final point I'd like to make about blocks is one about style. A coding pattern that Apple tends to follow is to arrange the parameters to an Objective-C method such that any arguments that are blocks come last. This helps keep things legible, because it's easy to miss a single parameter between two blocks. An example of the incorrect style is as follows:

```
[someObject someMethodWithThisParameter:@"ThisParameter"
                 performingThisBlock:^{
                     NSLog(@"This Block");
                 }
             withThisParameter:YES
                 andThisBlock:^{
                     NSLog(@"Another Block");
                 }];
```

As you can see, it's difficult to tell where one parameter ends and the other begins. This is exacerbated even more when the code inside the blocks is long. An example of the proper style is shown here:

```
[someObject someMethodWithThisParameter:@"ThisParameter"
                 andThisParameter:YES
                 performingThisBlock:^{
                     NSLog(@"This Block");
                 }
                 andThisBlock:^{
                     NSLog(@"Another Block");
                 }];
```

By grouping the blocks at the end, the code is much more readable, at least in my opinion (and Apple's). Now that we've covered what blocks are and how you'll use them, let's cover *why* you'd want to use them at all.

Why Should We Use Blocks?

To talk about why we should use blocks, let's examine a few common scenarios and look at how things were done before blocks existed. We'll then look at how these scenarios are easier or cleaner—or both—when using blocks. While all of the old ways are still valid and still work, new APIs that Apple is releasing with each version of iOS and Mac OS X feature blocks heavily, often without blockless workarounds. Let's begin this analysis with one of iOS's most powerful features: UIView animations.

UIView Animations

The animation system in iOS is extremely powerful. Every view is drawn by an OpenGL-backed layer, allowing very simple code to create extremely performant, hardware-accelerated 2D and 3D animations. This was the case before blocks and is still the case with blocks, but the new, block-based animation APIs that arrived with blocks in iOS 4 make it much simpler. Let's look at a common example: fading out a view. Using the old method, the code would look like this (assuming that the view we want to fade out is called myView):

```
[UIView beginAnimations:@"animationName" context:NULL];
[UIView setAnimationDuration:1.0];

[myView setAlpha:0.0f];

[UIView commitAnimations];
```

The basic idea behind the animation system is that in between calls to beginAnimations:context: and commitAnimations, you simply set properties on your view that you want them to have at the end of the animation; the animation system will automatically interpolate between the current values and the destination values over a period of time defined by setAnimationDuration:. While this is about as simple as animations get, it's still worth looking at the block-based alternative:

```
[UIView animateWithDuration:1.0
              animations:^{
                  [myView setAlpha:0.0f];
              }];
```

As you can see, three UIView class method calls have been replaced by one. Instead of placing your animation methods between two method calls, you simply put them in the block that gets passed as the second parameter. Even this is an improvement in terms of the length of code, but the improvements start to really shine when we add some options to it. First let's say that once the animation is done, we'd like to remove the now-transparent view from its superview. Using the old method, we add two lines in our animation preamble:

```
[UIView beginAnimations:@"animationName" context:NULL];
[UIView setAnimationDuration:1.0];
[UIView setAnimationDelegate:self];
[UIView
setAnimationDidStopSelector:@selector(animationDidStop:finished:context:)];

[myView setAlpha:0.0f];

[UIView commitAnimations];
```

In this code, we call setAnimationDelegate: to give the animation system an object to which it can send a message when the animation is complete. We then provide a selector for it to use when sending the message. The first parameter is a pointer to an NSString with the animation ID (animationName in the previous sample), the second parameter is a BOOL value that corresponds to whether the animation finished (in some cases, such as if the view's superview had been removed from its view hierarchy before the animation finished, this will be NO), and the third argument is a mostly unused context pointer. We aren't done yet, however; we need to implement this new method:

```
- (void)animationDidStop:(NSString *)animationID
                finished:(BOOL)finsihed
                 context:(void *)context
{
    [myView removeFromSuperview];
}
```

We should also add a line to the header file or class extension declaration to declare this method. This is where things start to get pretty verbose. Let's compare it with the equivalent block-based code:

```
[UIView animateWithDuration:1.0
                animations:^{
                    [myView setAlpha:0.0f];
                }
                completion:^(BOOL finished) {
                    [myView removeFromSuperview];
                }];
```

That's already several lines fewer! This method adds one more parameter, a block that runs when the animation is complete. Its sole argument is a BOOL for whether or not the animation finished. Since you're defining the completion handler right where you define the animation, you don't need to keep track of an animation ID.

If that were as complicated as the older-style UIView animations got, the block-based methods would still be a massive improvement. As your code becomes more complex, you may have several different animations in a single class. In that case, without blocks, you'll handle the completion of these animations in the same animationDidStop:finished:context: method, which means you'll need to use the animation ID to ensure that the right code runs for the right animation. The real advantage of using blocks here, however, is that it keeps the completion code right next to the animation code. You don't have to remember to put it in the animationDidStop:finished:context: method or go looking in that method for the right code based on the animation ID. Instead, everything related to a single animation is in the same place. Six months after you write the code, if you have to come back and modify it, you'll be thankful for this code organization, because it makes troubleshooting things much simpler. This is a big reason to prefer using blocks in general and is the focus of the next area we'll investigate: using blocks as callbacks.

Using Blocks for Asynchronous Callbacks

In an earlier chapter, we discussed using asynchronous `NSURLConnection` methods to avoid blocking the main thread, which would in turn make the app unresponsive. This is a good thing to do, but one potential symptom of this is that these callback methods that the URL connection calls are the same for every connection. If you have code that creates 20 URL connections, they will all send the same delegate messages, which means that in those methods you'll need to figure out which URL connection actually sent the message in order to act accordingly. Several open source networking libraries get around this by allowing you to specify a completion handler. Here's what it might look like:

```
[MyNetworkingLibrary loadURLWithRequest:aURLRequest
                completionHandler:^(NSData *receivedData,
                                     NSURLResponse *response,
                                     NSError *error) {
            // Handle the response here
        }];
```

Just like the URL loading we did before, this takes a URL request and sends it along, receiving some data, a response, and potentially an error in return. The exact methods you'll call vary between networking libraries— `MyNetworkingLibrary` isn't a real library name—but the core idea is the same: instead of calling a delegate method when the connection is done, the library simply executes a block provided to it when you made the request.

Like with `UIView` animations, the main advantage here is code organization. The code that handles getting the request is right next to the code that made the request in the first place, which allows you to see at a glance what's happening at both steps in the process. Like with animations, the more connections you have, the more tedious the delegate methods will be, and the harder they'll get to maintain and troubleshoot as the project ages. This advantage isn't just for URL loading, either; any long-running process that doesn't need to block the main thread should be written to take advantage of completion handler blocks. A single object can have multiple blocks associated with it, as well; some of the URL libraries allow you to define a block that's called multiple times to report download progress.

Much like URL loading, another place where the code to run at a later time can be placed in a block is when using `NSNotificationCenter`. Instead of defining a method to be called when the notification is fired, you can use a block to define the code that should be executed right where you register for the notification:

```
NSNotificationCenter *nc = [NSNotificationCenter defaultCenter];
[nc addObserverForName:UIApplicationDidReceiveMemoryWarningNotification
            object:nil
```

```
        queue:nil
usingBlock:^(NSNotification *note) {
    NSLog(@"Received memory warning!");
}];
```

We'll elaborate more on the queue parameter later, but this once again allows you to arrange your code in a much more readable fashion. Instead of finding the method that gets called when the notification fires, you can find the code that will be executed in the supplied block. This results in you having to write less code and, ideally, fewer bugs. As useful as blocks are for callbacks, they have even more utility when enumerating collections, which we'll discuss next.

Using Blocks for Enumeration

Enumerating items from a collection is a task that exists in nearly every programming language produced in the past few decades. The general idea is simple: given a collection of items, obtain a reference to each one in succession, perform some code with it, and then obtain the next, repeating until you've exhausted all of the items. Before we talk about using blocks for this goal, let's look at some tools at your disposal in Cocoa Touch to enumerate objects from collection classes (arrays, dictionaries, and sets).

> **NOTE:** iOS 5 added a new collection class, NSOrderedSet, which has features of an array (its members are ordered) and a set (its members are unique). We won't look at ordered sets specifically here, but you can usually assume that accessing their members works as it does for an array.

For Loops

The most traditional way to enumerate items from a collection, expressed here in Objective-C, is to use a for loop:

```
NSUInteger count = [myArray count];
for (NSUInteger i = 0; i < count; i++) {
    id object = [myArray objectAtIndex:i];

    [object performSomeTask];
}
```

In this example, we obtain the number of objects in the array and process them from first to last, sending a message to them and then moving to the next object. This code has the advantage of being near-universal; people coming from other programming languages are almost always going to know what this code does and how to modify it to get it to behave as desired. For any given object, it's easy to obtain the current index in the array, because that's stored in the i variable. A disadvantage is that the NSArray method objectAtIndex: returns id, so we don't know the class of the objects contained therein, but that's easy to figure out through introspection.

For dictionaries, a for loop isn't quite as easy. This code enumerates all of a dictionary's objects and sends them a message:

```
NSArray *keys = [myDictionary allKeys];
NSUInteger count = [keys count];
for (NSUInteger i = 0; i < count; i++) {
    id key = [keys objectAtIndex:i];
    id object = [myDictionary objectForKey:key];

    [object performSomeTask];
}
```

As you can see, it isn't too different, but it does require obtaining a key from the dictionary's array of keys and using that key to obtain an object. If you have an NSSet, which has no order and therefore no objectAtIndex: method, you'll have to use its allObjects methods to get an array of its objects and then enumerate through the returned array.

NSEnumerator

Instead of going through a collection manually using a for loop, it's also possible to use the Objective-C class NSEnumerator to enumerate the objects. An instance of NSEnumerator continues to return objects from its nextObject method until it's exhausted the collection's objects. For dictionaries, there are two enumerators, one for objects and one for keys. Using an NSEnumerator is as follows:

```
NSEnumerator *objectEnumerator = [myArray objectEnumerator];
id object;

while ((object = [objectEnumerator nextObject])) {
    [object performSomeTask];
}
```

In this code, we obtain an NSEnumerator from the array. The NSArray class defines the objectEnumerator and reverseObjectEnumerator methods, the latter simply traversing the array from its last item to its first. Next, we create a pointer to an object called object. We continue to store the returned value from the nextObject method of the enumerator into object, and if it isn't nil, the while expression will evaluate to true, and we'll call performSomeTask on object.

> **NOTE:** Because using a single equal sign (=) instead of a two (==) for equality in expressions, such as if (a = 42) …, is such a common programming mistake, we use two sets of parentheses around the while statement as a sign to the compiler that we know what we're doing, preventing some compiler versions from warning us about potentially unsafe code.

With an NSEnumerator, there are some trade-offs compared to using a for loop. You don't need to obtain the total count of elements in the collection, but you also need to do some extra work if you want to obtain the index of the current element.

One thing you can't do while using NSEnumerator is to enumerate a mutable collection, such as NSMutableArray, NSMutableDictionary, or NSMutableSet, and change the collection while you're enumerating. If you need to do that, you should either make an immutable copy of the original data and enumerate through the copy or save a list of the changes you need to make and execute them after you're done enumerating. If, for instance, you wanted to remove every odd NSNumber object from a mutable array called myMutableArray, you would do it as follows:

```
NSArray *myArray = [NSArray arrayWithArray:myMutableArray];
NSEnumerator *objectEnumerator = [myArray objectEnumerator];
NSNumber *number;

while ((number = [objectEnumerator nextObject])) {
    if ([number intValue] % 2) {
        [myMutableArray removeObject:number];
    }
}
```

We can't remove an object from myMutableArray while enumerating it, so we enumerate myArray and remove objects from myMutableArray.

Fast Enumeration

Fast Enumeration, added in Mac OS X 10.5 and available in iOS from the beginning, is actually a protocol that the collection classes conform to named NSFastEnumeration. It allows you to use a special syntax for enumerating objects:

```
for (NSString *string in myArray) {
    [string performSomeTask];
}
```

Fast Enumeration is typed, so here we're casting the objects in myArray to NSString objects. This doesn't guarantee that the returned objects will be NSString instances, just that the variable string will be considered by the compiler to be of type NSString *. You should still query the object for its class to ensure that it is, in fact, what you expect.

When using Fast Enumeration with an array or a set, it iterates over the objects in the collection; when using it with a dictionary, it iterates over all of the dictionary's keys. Fast Enumeration, aside from being more efficient than NSEnumerator, is also less code and much more readable. It's similar enough to a foreach loop that programmers coming from other languages are fairly likely to understand what the code does. Inside the loop, you don't have the count of the array or the index of the current object, but you can get those easily if you need them. Before blocks were on the scene, Fast Enumeration was the preferred way of enumerating through Cocoa Touch collection classes, and it's still a pretty good option.

Just as with NSEnumerator, you can't change mutable collections while using Fast Enumeration on them; if you do, the collection will raise an exception, and your app will crash.

Performing Selectors on Members

So far, our rather contrived example use of enumeration has been to send a single message, performSomeTask, to the objects in the collection. If that's all you need to do and you have an NSArray or NSSet of objects, you can use the instance method makeObjectsPerformSelector:. This sends a single message to every member of the collection. There's also a variation that takes an object and sends its as a parameter to the method, called makeObjectsPerformSelector:withObject:. This is useful if you only need to call a method that has one or zero parameters and only if the parameter is an Objective-C object. If you need to do anything more complex, you'll need to use one of the enumeration techniques described here.

Enumerating with Blocks

Introduced in Mac OS X and iOS 4 along with blocks were some methods on the collection classes that you can use to enumerate their objects using blocks. Our example from earlier would be written thusly:

```
[myArray enumerateObjectsUsingBlock:^(id obj, NSUInteger idx, BOOL *stop) {
    [obj performSomeTask];
}];
```

As far as line count goes, this is on par with Fast Enumeration for simplicity. The method takes one parameter, a block, which has three arguments: a pointer to the object, its index in the array, and a pointer to a BOOL value. The third one is interesting. It's actually meant for you to modify if you'd like to stop enumerating. Where you would call break in a for loop to stop enumeration, when using a block, you would set it as follows:

```
*stop = YES;
```

This would fill in the appropriate value and stop enumerating.

On the surface, enumerating through collection classes doesn't appear to be much better or easier than using any of the previous methods. The NSDictionary equivalent, enumerateKeysAndObjectsUsingBlock:, is rather nice, because it passes both the key and the object to the block, but otherwise the methods are not much different. Where the block-based methods shine, however, is in the expanded version of these methods, enumerateObjectsWithOptions:usingBlock:. The first argument is a bit mask of options, chief among with is NSEnumerationConcurrent. This tells the array to enumerate through your items concurrently, which is a huge gain on devices whose processors have multiple cores (though it can also significantly boost performance in some situations on single-core devices). The following code would execute performSomeTask on every object in myArray in a concurrent fashion:

```
[myArray enumerateObjectsWithOptions:NSEnumerationConcurrent
                   usingBlock:^(id obj, NSUInteger idx, BOOL *stop) {
                       [obj performSomeTask];
                   }];
```

Just like that, you can take advantage of iOS's advanced multithreading performance without writing a single line of threading code. The method won't return until all of the objects have been enumerated, but it will expand the enumeration to run as many concurrent instances as is practical. As more and more devices have multiple cores, this method of enumeration should be your default, because it's an easy way to increase the performance of your app without increasing the level of effort required on your part. We'll discuss multicore processing in much greater detail in the next chapter, but this is a good start. For now, use it as a tool to get performance out of your app when enumerating through collection classes. That concludes our tour of why blocks are good for enumeration. A closely related topic that blocks also help with is sorting an array of items.

Using Blocks to Sort Arrays

Much like enumeration, sorting an array is a common task to many programming languages. The basic concept is similar in every language: walk the array in one of many patterns based on the kind of sort you're performing, comparing values and acting accordingly. Which type of sort you use is a matter of great debate, but the need to sort values is something almost every programming language needs to address at some time. Objective-C is no different, and there are a few ways to sort an array.

Sorting Arrays with Comparison Selectors

The most straightforward method to sort an array is to use a comparison method on each object. This is supported with the NSArray instance method sortedArrayUsingSelector:, which takes a comparison selector as its parameter and returns a new NSArray, sorted by calling the selector on each object in the array with another object in the array as its parameter. To sort an array of strings case-insensitively, the code would be as follows:

```
NSArray *sortedArray = [myArray
sortedArrayUsingSelector:@selector(caseInsensitiveCompare:)];
```

Each object in the array will be sent the caseInsensitiveCompare: message with another object as the parameter. This is fairly straightforward, if not very customizable; it will sort an array based on only one method, and for it to work properly, every object in the array must implement that same method.

There is a similar family of sorting methods such as sortedArrayUsingFunction:context: that use C functions to sort the array. While they don't rely on the member objects to implement any functionality, you're still limited to one path of execution for comparison. If you want to sort an array based on multiple criteria, you're better off using sort descriptors.

Sorting Arrays with Sort Descriptors

A sort descriptor is an object that encapsulates the way in which your data is sorted. A single descriptor focuses on one attribute of each object and sorts based on that attribute. To use sort descriptors, you use an array of them to arrange a hierarchy of sort descriptors that will be used to sort your objects. Given an Objective-C class called Person with name and age properties, the following code sorts people first by age, oldest to youngest, and then alphabetically by name:

```
NSSortDescriptor *ageDescriptor = [[NSSortDescriptor alloc] initWithKey:@"age"
ascending:NO];
NSSortDescriptor *nameDescriptor = [[NSSortDescriptor alloc] initWithKey:@"name"
ascending:YES];
NSArray *sortDescriptors = [NSArray arrayWithObjects:ageDescriptor,
nameDescriptor, nil];

NSArray *sortedArray = [myArray sortedArrayUsingDescriptors:sortDescriptors];
```

By default, the sort descriptors will use the compare: method to compare two items, but there is a method you can use while creating them to modify the selector it uses. If you wanted to sort an array of strings with the localizedCaseInsensitiveCompare: method, you could do it as follows:

```
NSSortDescriptor *sortDescriptor =
[NSSortDescriptor sortDescriptorWithKey:nil
                            ascending:YES

selector:@selector(localizedCaseInsensitiveCompare:)];

NSArray *sortDescriptors = [NSArray arrayWithObject:sortDescriptor];

NSArray *sortedArray = [myArray sortedArrayUsingDescriptors:sortDescriptors];
```

Sort descriptors are useful when your data has lots of identical values, prompting you to need a secondary, tertiary, or further sort methods. When you add blocks to the equation, they become even more useful.

Sorting Arrays with Blocks

To use blocks when sorting arrays, you will most often use a defined type of block called NSComparator. The definition of NSComparator is in a system header files as follows:

```
typedef NSComparisonResult (^NSComparator)(id obj1, id obj2);
```

The block returns an NSComparisonResult and takes two arguments, one for each object to compare. There are three possible return values: NSOrderedAscending, for when obj1 is lower than obj2; NSOrderedDescending, for when obj1 is higher than obj2; and NSOrderedSame for when they are equal. The block's implementation can use obj1 and obj2 however you desire, and using an NSComparator to sort an array is straightforward:

```
NSArray *sortedArray = [myArray
sortedArrayUsingComparator:^NSComparisonResult(id obj1, id obj2) {
    return [obj1 caseInsensitiveCompare:obj2];
}];
```

In this case, we simply call the `caseInsensitiveCompare:` method, but you can use whatever logic is appropriate to compare values. You can also create NSSortDescriptor objects with comparator blocks:

```
NSSortDescriptor *nameSortDescriptor =
[[NSSortDescriptor alloc] initWithKey:@"name"
                         ascending:YES
                         comparator:^NSComparisonResult(id obj1, id obj2) {
                             return [obj1 caseInsensitiveCompare:obj2];
                         }];

NSArray *sortDescriptors = [NSArray arrayWithObject:nameSortDescriptor];

NSArray *sortedArray = [myArray sortedArrayUsingDescriptors:sortDescriptors];
```

Here the block is the same, but we can combine it with NSSortDescriptor to take advantage of the ability to have multiple sort criteria.

Just as with enumerating through collections, sorting arrays has an ace up its sleeve when you use blocks. We can automatically sort an array concurrently with the `sortedArrayWithOptions:usingComparator:` method. The following sorts our array of strings concurrently:

```
NSArray *sortedArray = [myArray sortedArrayWithOptions:NSSortConcurrent
                                 usingComparator:^NSComparisonResult(id
obj1, id obj2) {
                                     return [obj1
caseInsensitiveCompare:obj2];
                                 }];
```

Depending on the size of your array, using this method to concurrently sort its contents can offer huge performance gains. As is the case with enumeration, the more processor cores a device has, the faster this will go, so writing your array-sorting code like this now will ensure maximum performance on any future iOS devices, regardless of the number of cores they have.

To recap, blocks allow you to write better code. You can use them to replace callbacks in some situations, keeping the callback code near other related code, to enumerate and sort arrays, and in new APIs that require blocks. Now that I've argued for the use of blocks, let's look at how you can add blocks to your own APIs.

Using Blocks in Your Code

There are two main ways you can use blocks in your own code, and the difference lies in the lifetime of the block. The first, and easiest, way is to simply accept a block as a method parameter and call it at some point in the method:

```
- (void)expensiveOperationWithCompletionHandler:(void(^)(void))handler
{
    [self performExpensiveOperation];

    if (handler != NULL) {
        handler();
    }
}
```

In this method, we use the `handler` parameter to store a block that gets called after the method's main operation. Note that we must check to see whether the block is NULL, because it's perfectly legal to call this method like this:

```
[self expensiveOperationWithCompletionHandler:NULL];
```

If we didn't check for NULL, the app would crash.

> **NOTE:** There has been some debate on whether it's more appropriate to use NULL or nil when talking about a block that points to nothing. In this book I'll stick to NULL, but if you see nil in other code, that's also acceptable.

The reason this method is so simple is that the stack frame never exits while handler is in it. Even if the block was created on the stack and never moved to the heap, it would still be valid here. The second method for calling blocks in your own APIs gets around this problem.

For the second method, you'll first create a property for the block, using the copy attribute to ensure that it gets copied to the heap:

```
@property (copy) void(^completionHandler)(void);
```

The `expensiveOperation` method might then be as follows:

```
- (void)expensiveOperation
{
    [self performExpensiveOperation];

    if ([self completionHandler] != NULL) {
        [self completionHandler]();
    }
}
```

Even when the block is a property, we'll check it against NULL to ensure there's no breakage. Storing the block in a property not only allows you to store it in the heap and call it when necessary, but it also allows you to call the same block from multiple methods, as well as multiple times. One common example is found in several open source networking libraries; when you create a request to load a URL, you can specify a block to run when the progress is updated.

Now that we've covered these methods, let's look at improving our Twitter client from Chapter 6 to take advantage of blocks.

Updating TwitterExample with Blocks

In our TwitterExample code from earlier, there are some optimizations we can make with blocks to clean up the code a little. In our Twitter controller class, we have an `authorizeAccount` method that signs the user in to Twitter and authorizes our app to use their Twitter account. As it currently stands, that method simply returns once it calls the `requestAccessToAccountsWithType:completionHandler:` method of `ACAccountStore`, but it doesn't do anything special once that method is finished. As a result, we attempt to authorize the app while it's loading and hope that it finishes before our view controller loads the tweets. You may have noticed the app loading a blank list of tweets at startup but loading perfectly fine when the user clicks the Reload button; this is why. Let's change that method to take a completion handler of its own so that we can take advantage of blocks to run code when the accounts are authorized.

Adding a Completion Handler

Fire up Xcode and open the TwitterExample project. Open the Twitter controller's header file, `LCTTwitterController.h` (remember, if your class prefix is not LCT, the file name will be different), and modify the declaration for `authorizeAccount` by removing the struck-out lines and adding the lines in bold:

```
@interface LCTTwitterController : NSObject

+ (id)sharedInstance;

- (void)authorizeAccount;
- (void)authorizeAccountWithCompletionHandler:(void(^)(void))handler;
- (void)getTweetsInUserTimelineWithCompletionHandler:(void(^)(NSArray
*tweets))handler;

@end
```

Now, open the corresponding implementation file (`LCTTwitterController.m`), and modify the `authorizeAccount` method by removing the struck-out lines and adding the lines in bold:

```
- (void)authorizeAccount
- (void)authorizeAccountWithCompletionHandler:(void (^)(void))handler
{
    if (_twitterAccount == nil) {
        ACAccountType *accountType = [_accountStore
accountTypeWithAccountTypeIdentifier:ACAccountTypeIdentifierTwitter];

        NSUserDefaults *userDefaults = [NSUserDefaults standardUserDefaults];

        [_accountStore requestAccessToAccountsWithType:accountType
                                withCompletionHandler:^(BOOL granted, NSError
*error) {
                            if (granted) {
                                NSArray *twitterAccounts =
                                [_accountStore
accountsWithAccountType:accountType];

                                if ([twitterAccounts count] > 0) {
                                    _twitterAccount =
                                    [twitterAccounts objectAtIndex:0];

                                    NSString *identifier =
                                    [_twitterAccount identifier];

                                    [userDefaults setObject:identifier
forKey:kSavedTwitterAccountKey];

                                    [userDefaults synchronize];
                                }
                            }

                            if (handler != NULL) {
                                handler();
                            }
                        }];
    }
    else {
        if (handler != NULL) {
            handler();
        }
    }
}
```

One important thing to note is that we must check the value of handler before calling it. If we pass NULL in when we call the method but the method doesn't check to ensure that the value of handler isn't NULL, we'll crash the app when we try to execute the block. This is a simple change, but it allows us to execute arbitrary code once the account is authorized. If we already have an account, then the method will call the completion handler and do nothing else, allowing saved logins to continue to work as before. Before we put it into action, we need to remove the existing call to authorizeAccount, because that method no longer exists. Open the app delegate's implementation file (LCTAppDelegate.m) and remove the line that authorizes the account in the application:didFinishLaunchingWithOptions: method by removing the struck-out line:

```
- (BOOL)application:(UIApplication *)application
didFinishLaunchingWithOptions:(NSDictionary *)launchOptions
{
    self.window = [[UIWindow alloc] initWithFrame:[[UIScreen mainScreen]
bounds]];
    // Override point for customization after application launch.
    self.window.backgroundColor = [UIColor whiteColor];
    [self.window makeKeyAndVisible];

    [[LCTTwitterController sharedInstance] authorizeAccount];

    LCTTimelineViewController *viewController =
    [[LCTTimelineViewController alloc] initWithStyle:UITableViewStylePlain];

    UINavigationController *navigationController =
    [[UINavigationController alloc] initWithRootViewController:viewController];

    [[self window] setRootViewController:navigationController];


    return YES;
}
```

Helpfully, Xcode should already have alerted you to an issue with this line. Now that we aren't using LCTTwitterController in the app delegate, we can remove the #import directive for it. At the top of the file, remove the struck-out line like so:

```
#import "LCTAppDelegate.h"

#import "LCTTwitterController.h"
#import "LCTTimelineViewController.h"
```

Now would be a good time to save your work. Next up, we'll add a step to the view controller life cycle of LCTTimelineViewController to authorize the account before loading tweets. Open LCTTimelineViewController.m, and modify the viewWillAppear: method by adding the lines in bold:

```
- (void)viewWillAppear:(BOOL)animated
{
    [super viewWillAppear:animated];
```

```
    [LCTTwitterController sharedInstance]
authorizeAccountWithCompletionHandler:^{
        [[LCTTwitterController sharedInstance]
getTweetsInUserTimelineWithCompletionHandler:^(NSArray *tweets) {
            _tweets = tweets;

            [[self tableView] performSelectorOnMainThread:@selector(reloadData)
                                               withObject:nil
                                            waitUntilDone:NO];
        }];
    }];
}
```

Here we have a block nested in another block. Once the first method's
completion handler fires, the second method is called, and finally when its
completion handler fires, we reload the table view. Run the app in Xcode; it
should load tweets at startup after authorizing the account. This is pretty good,
but there's no feedback while it's loading, just an empty table view. Let's add
some visual indications that the app is working.

Adding Activity Indicators

One way you can indicate that your app is in the middle of a network call is to
use the network activity indicator on the device's status bar. This is accessed
through the UIApplication class by modifying the
networkActivityIndicatorVisible property. Let's do this while we're loading
tweets. Open LCTTwitterController.m in Xcode, and modify the
getTweetsInUserTimelineWithCompletionHandler: method to use the network
activity indicator by adding the lines in bold:

```
- (void)getTweetsInUserTimelineWithCompletionHandler:(void(^)(NSArray
*tweets))handler
{
    NSString *timelinePath =
@"https://api.twitter.com/1/statuses/home_timeline.json";
    NSURL *timelineURL = [NSURL URLWithString:timelinePath];

    TWRequest *timelineRequest = [[TWRequest alloc] initWithURL:timelineURL
                                                     parameters:nil

requestMethod:TWRequestMethodGET];

    [timelineRequest setAccount:_twitterAccount];

    [[UIApplication sharedApplication]
setNetworkActivityIndicatorVisible:YES];
```

```
    [timelineRequest performRequestWithHandler:^(NSData *responseData,
NSHTTPURLResponse *urlResponse, NSError *error) {
        [[UIApplication sharedApplication]
setNetworkActivityIndicatorVisible:NO];

        if (responseData) {
            id topLevelObject = [NSJSONSerialization
JSONObjectWithData:responseData
                                                            options:0
                                                            error:NULL];

            if ([topLevelObject isKindOfClass:[NSArray class]]) {
                if (handler != NULL) {
                    handler(topLevelObject);
                }
            }
        }
    }];
}
```

Build and run the app, and you should notice the network activity indicator in the status bar. This is a near-universal construct in iOS apps that allows you to inform the user that the app is performing network operations. It's not too noticeable if you're looking at the table view, however. Let's fix that by updating the title of the view controller while we're loading tweets. In Xcode, open LCTTimelineViewController.m, and modify the viewWillAppear: method by adding the lines in bold:

```
- (void)viewWillAppear:(BOOL)animated
{
    [super viewWillAppear:animated];

    LCTTwitterController *twitterController = [LCTTwitterController
sharedInstance];

    NSString *title = [self title];

    [self setTitle:@"Authorizing…"];
    [twitterController authorizeAccountWithCompletionHandler:^{
        [self performSelectorOnMainThread:@selector(setTitle:)
                               withObject:@"Loading Tweets…"
                            waitUntilDone:NO];

        [twitterController
getTweetsInUserTimelineWithCompletionHandler:^(NSArray *tweets) {
            [self performSelectorOnMainThread:@selector(setTitle:)
                                   withObject:title
                                waitUntilDone:NO];

            _tweets = tweets;
```

```
        [[self tableView] performSelectorOnMainThread:@selector(reloadData)
                                           withObject:nil
                                        waitUntilDone:NO];
    }];
  }];
}
```

The first thing we do is save the view controller's current title to the `title` variable. This allows us to change the title we set for the view controller in `initWithStyle:` without also modifying it in this method. Next we change the title to "Authorizing…" while we authorize the account, to "Loading Tweets…" while we load the tweets, and finally back to whatever it was at the beginning once the tweets are loaded. For the second two, we use `performSelectorOnMainThread:withObject:waitUntilDone:` to ensure that the title is only ever changed on the main thread, because calling UI methods from other threads can cause problems on iOS, including crashes and unintended user interface settings. We'll learn more about threads in the next chapter, so it you're not sure what that means, don't worry. Build and run your app, and you should see the title changing along with the network activity indicator. Our Twitter client still has a long way to go before it's complete; in the next chapter, we'll add some more features to it as we talk about performance and concurrency in code.

Summary

This chapter has been a tour of blocks, a new feature added by Apple to the C programming language (and thus, by extension, to the Objective-C programming language). After reading this chapter, you should be comfortable creating and using blocks as well as creating and using APIs that use blocks. You should understand why we use blocks and what their advantages are. Blocks will feature heavily in the next chapter, in which we'll talk about writing code that performs well on devices with multicore processors.

Managing What Happens When

So far in this book, you've made things happen in a fairly regular manner. You send a message to an object, the method corresponding to that message selector runs and then returns, and your code continues. This only scratches the surface of what's possible with Objective-C and Cocoa Touch; you can run code later, run two pieces of code at the same time, or run nothing at all until something else happens. In this chapter, we'll discuss the specifics of how you manage when your code runs, as well as delving into why it matters. We'll cover writing code to take advantage of the latest multicore processors, using timers to repeat the execution of code over time, and run loops, Apple's efficient way to wait for events. Along the way, we'll cover topics such as thread safety and how to optimize your code for speed. First let's discuss what we've done so far in the context of this larger discussion.

Sending Messages

When you send a message to an object, you're running a method. We've been sending messages since Chapter 1, but we haven't really looked at the underpinnings of what makes that work. Let's look at that now; knowing this will help contextualize later discussions. When you send a message, the name of the method is called a *selector*. Selectors, represented by the SEL data type, are just strings that correspond to the method name. Consider the following message, sent to an NSArray object called myArray:

```
[myArray count]
```

The selector in this case is count. When this code executes, the Objective-C runtime looks up the method in a table to find its address. When it finds the address, it executes the method. This is heavily cached to improve performance, but the first time you call a particular method on a class, it will look up the method's address and cache it for later.

Messages Under the Hood

The method's implementation is actually implemented as a C function. This particular method of NSArray, count, returns an unsigned integer, so you might think the representative C function would be declared like this:

```
NSUInteger count();
```

Interestingly, when Objective-C code is compiled, these C functions are created with two extra arguments stuck at the beginning: self and _cmd. self is what you've been using to refer to the object that's executing the method, and _cmd is the selector that was executed, which is helpful for debugging. The count method as a C function would be declared thusly:

```
NSUInteger count(id self, SEL _cmd);
```

When the method is first called, the address of that function is looked up and cached.

Why does this matter? In discussions of programming languages and their various merits when compared with one another, a common claim is that Objective-C is slow compared to C or C++. The fact is, since every Objective-C method is implemented by the compiler as a C function, Objective-C code is actually quite fast. That being said, the cost of looking up the function's address is more than zero. Consider the following if statements:

```
for (NSUInteger i = 0; i < [myArray count]; i++) {
    NSLog(@"%@", [[myArray objectAtIndex:i] description]);
}

NSUInteger count = [myArray count];
for (NSUInteger i = 0; i < count; i++) {
    NSLog(@"%@", [[myArray objectAtIndex:i] description]);
}
```

In the first example, every time the loop repeats, it calls the count method of myArray to check that i is less than the count. In the second example, we store the value returned by count into a temporary variable and then compare against that in the loop. This second example has the potential to be much faster, because it isn't calling a method every trip through the loop. As you write real Objective-C code, be sure to consider cases like this. Much of this chapter will focus on the performance of your app, but no matter how many tricks there are to manage when your code is executed, slow code is still slow code.

Performing Selectors Manually

One of the earliest ways most Cocoa Touch developers learn to manage when their code is called is the target-action paradigm of the UIControl class. When you pass a target and an action to an instance of UIButton and assign it to the UIControlEventTouchUpInside event, it's pretty clear what will happen. You can call methods yourself in this fashion using the performSelector: family of methods on NSObject. The following example calls the reloadData method on a UITableView instance called myTableView:

```
[myTableView performSelector:@selector(reloadData)];
```

Now, this itself has no real advantage of simply calling the reloadData method of myTableView. Some of the variants of performSelector:, however, begin to give this real power. One of the tenets of UIKit classes is that all UI code should run on the main thread of the application; that is, you shouldn't update the UI when you're running on a background thread (if you're not sure what a thread is, don't worry; we'll discuss them in depth later in this chapter). The following line of code sets the text of a label but does so on the main thread:

```
[myLabel performSelectorOnMainThread:@selector(setText:)
                        withObject:@"Hello, World!"
                    waitUntilDone:NO];
```

This is equivalent to calling this line of code while already on the main thread:

```
[myLabel setText:@"Hello, World!"];
```

The waitUntilDone parameter, when set to NO, causes the method to return immediately, which is useful if the selector you're passing corresponds to a very long-running method.

The variants of performSelector: that include an object parameter will only allow you to perform selectors that take one parameter. If the method you're looking to call takes multiple parameters, you won't be able to call it with this method. For those methods, we'll see better ways to call them later in this chapter.

Calling Selectors in the Background

The inverse of calling something on the main thread is to call it on a background thread. If you have some long-running task and you call it on the main thread, your application's UI will hang while the task processes. Not only is this a bad user experience, but if your application's UI is hung for too long, the system will terminate it. This automatic termination forces your hand if you have long tasks. We'll discuss different approaches to running code in the background later in this chapter, but the easiest is another variation of the `performSelector:` method:

```
[myObject performSelectorInBackground:@selector(longRunningTask:)
                           withObject:@"foo"];
```

This line will call the `longRunningTask:` method of `myObject` in the background. While we'll cover thread safety in more detail in the portion of this chapter on threads, be sure that any UI updates in a method you call on the background happen on the *main* thread, using `performSelectorOnMainThread:withObject:waitUntilDone:` as needed.

Calling Selectors Later

So far, everything we've done has run whatever code we specify immediately. This isn't always what you want; perhaps you want to present something to the user for a specific amount of time, or you want to refresh information displayed after some interval. The `performSelector:` family of methods has a method to perform a selector after some delay:

```
[myObject performSelector:@selector(update) withObject:nil afterDelay:5.0];
```

This line will call the `update` method of `myObject` with no parameter after a five-second delay. When you use `performSelector:withObject:afterDelay:`, the method is called on the current thread, so if you call this in a method that you've called in the background, it will also run in the background.

If you need to cancel a selector that you've scheduled to call using the previous method, you can use the `NSObject` class method `cancelPreviousPerformRequestsWithTarget:selector:object:` with the same parameters as you gave when scheduling the selector. To cancel the previous update selector scheduling, you would use this method as such:

```
[NSObject cancelPreviousPerformRequestsWithTarget:myObject
                                         selector:@selector(update)
                                           object:nil];
```

It's important to ensure that the three arguments match, or your scheduled selector won't be canceled.

Example: Scheduling Selectors in TwitterExample

One feature of Twitter apps in general is that if you leave them open, they'll refresh their data automatically. Let's add that feature to the TwitterExample app using selectors. Open the TwitterExample project in Xcode, and navigate to the timeline view controller's implementation file (LCTTimelineViewController.m). Add a method declaration for methods called reloadTweets and scheduleTweetRefresh to the class extension as shown in bold:

```
@interface LCTTimelineViewController () {
    NSArray *_tweets;
}

- (void)reloadButtonPressed:(id)sender;
- (void)reloadTweets;
- (void)scheduleTweetRefresh;
- (void)tweetButtonPressed:(id)sender;

@end
```

Add the implementation code for these methods in the implementation section of this file, between the implementations of reloadButtonPressed: and tweetButtonPressed: as follows:

```
- (void)reloadTweets
{
    LCTTwitterController *twitterController = [LCTTwitterController
sharedInstance];

    [twitterController
getTweetsInUserTimelineWithCompletionHandler:^(NSArray *tweets) {
        _tweets = tweets;

        [[self tableView] performSelectorOnMainThread:@selector(reloadData)
                                    withObject:nil
                                    waitUntilDone:NO];

        [self performSelectorOnMainThread:@selector(scheduleTweetRefresh)
                        withObject:nil
                        waitUntilDone:NO];
    }];
}

- (void)scheduleTweetRefresh
{
    [self performSelector:@selector(reloadTweets)
            withObject:nil
            afterDelay:15.0];
}
```

The scheduleTweetRefresh method causes the reloadTweets method to run 15 seconds after it gets called. When the reloadTweets method is complete, it itself calls scheduleTweetRefresh, causing this to cycle every 15 seconds or so, depending on how long it takes to fetch the tweets from Twitter. To get this to run after our initial load of tweets, add the line in bold in the viewWillAppear: method:

```objc
- (void)viewWillAppear:(BOOL)animated
{
    [super viewWillAppear:animated];

    LCTTwitterController *twitterController = [LCTTwitterController
sharedInstance];

    NSString *title = [self title];

    [self setTitle:@"Authorizing…"];
    [twitterController authorizeAccountWithCompletionHandler:^{
        [self performSelectorOnMainThread:@selector(setTitle:)
                            withObject:@"Loading Tweets…"
                            waitUntilDone:NO];

        [twitterController
getTweetsInUserTimelineWithCompletionHandler:^(NSArray *tweets) {
            [self performSelectorOnMainThread:@selector(setTitle:)
                                withObject:title
                                waitUntilDone:NO];

            _tweets = tweets;

            [[self tableView] performSelectorOnMainThread:@selector(reloadData)
                                    withObject:nil
                                    waitUntilDone:NO];

            [self
performSelectorOnMainThread:@selector(scheduleTweetRefresh)
                            withObject:nil
                            waitUntilDone:NO];
        }];
    }];
}
```

Now, we need to cancel the automatic refresh if the user navigates away from this screen. Add an implementation for the viewWillDisappear: method after the viewWillAppear: method and before the viewDidUnload method:

```objc
- (void)viewWillDisappear:(BOOL)animated
{
    [super viewWillDisappear:animated];
```

```
    [NSObject cancelPreviousPerformRequestsWithTarget:self
selector:@selector(reloadTweets)
                                                  object:nil];
}
```

This method will make sure we don't reload the timeline while the timeline isn't visible.

Now, build and run the app. Every 15 seconds or so, it should update your Twitter timeline, without the need to refresh. Now that we've covered using the `performSelector:` family of method to control when your code runs, let's look at an easier way to accomplish automatic reloading: using the `NSTimer` class.

Scheduling Code with Timers

One downside of using `performSelector:withObject:afterDelay:` is that you need to call that method every time you want the selector performed. In our TwitterExample app, for every call to `reloadTweets`, we also called `scheduleTweetRefresh` to enqueue another call to `reloadTweets`. Not only is this tedious, but it causes the refresh interval to be slightly longer than every 15 seconds. For a Twitter app, precise timing is not important, but in some cases it is important to run your code at a specific interval. The `NSTimer` class allows you to schedule code to run, much like the `performSelector:` family of methods, but with the advantage that it can take care of repeating the method at whatever interval you like. You can create a timer using the class method `scheduledTimerWithTimeInterval:target:selector:userInfo:repeats:`, which creates a timer and also schedules it for you. To call a method called `update:` on an object every 30 seconds, the timer creation code would be as follows:

```
NSTimer *timer = [NSTimer scheduledTimerWithTimeInterval:30.0
                                    target:myObject
                                  selector:@selector(update:)
                                  userInfo:nil
                                   repeats:YES];
```

The first three parameters are fairly self-explanatory: how often to repeat the selector (in seconds), the target to call the selector on, and the selector itself. The parameter of this method is a pointer to the `NSTimer` object that fired. The `userInfo` parameter allows you to pass an arbitrary `NSDictionary` along with the timer object, which is useful if you need to pass additional data with your timer. The `repeats` parameter specifies whether the timer should continue to repeat once it fires. While this method is not the only way to create a timer, it does most of the work for you. When we discuss run loops later in this chapter, we'll also cover some additional ways you can create NSTimers. If we wanted to include a string with the timer, we could use the userInfo dictionary as follows:

```
NSDictionary *userInfo = [NSDictionary dictionaryWithObject:@"foo"
forKey:@"myString"];

NSTimer *timer = [NSTimer scheduledTimerWithTimeInterval:30.0
                                    target:myObject
                                    selector:@selector(update:)
                                    userInfo:userInfo
                                    repeats:YES];
```

The corresponding update: method would be able to access the userInfo dictionary as follows:

```
- (void)update:(NSTimer *)timer
{
    NSString *myString = [[timer userInfo] objectForKey:@"myString"];

    ...
}
```

You can add as many objects to the userInfo dictionary as you need, allowing you to pass complex data through your timers.

If you create a timer that repeats, it will continue until receiving the invalidate message, like so:

```
[timer invalidate];
```

If you create a timer that does not repeat, it will invalidate itself immediately following the first time it fires. The first parameter of the method that gets called by the timer must be a pointer to an NSTimer, because the timer will pass itself as the first parameter. Let's modify our TwitterExample project to utilize an NSTimer to facilitate automatic timeline refreshing. We'll create a timer in the viewWillAppear: method, after our timeline is populated with an initial list of tweets. This will remove the need for the scheduleTweetRefresh method and also require that we add an NSTimer parameter to the reloadTweets method. We'll also need an instance variable to store a pointer to the timer. To facilitate this, modify the class extension in LCTTimelineViewController.m as follows:

```
@interface LCTTimelineViewController () {
    NSTimer *_reloadTimer;
    NSArray *_tweets;
}

- (void)reloadButtonPressed:(id)sender;
- (void)reloadTweets:(NSTimer *)reloadTimer;
- (void)scheduleTweetRefresh;
```

```
- (void)tweetButtonPressed:(id)sender;
```

@end

> **NOTE:** We've defined two private instance variables in the class extension:
> _reloadTimer and _tweets. We could also have defined these as properties, and
> you'll hear this approach recommended over accessing instance variables. This
> recommendation comes from before ARC was available, where direct instance
> variable access could lead to memory management issues. With ARC, however, the
> compiler will ensure that you don't under-retain your objects, so direct instance
> variable access is much safer.

You can remove the scheduleTweetRefresh method in its entirety now. Next,
modify the reloadTweets method to add its parameter and remove the call to
scheduleTweetRefresh:

```
- (void)reloadTweets:(NSTimer *)reloadTimer
{
    LCTTwitterController *twitterController = [LCTTwitterController
sharedInstance];

    [twitterController getTweetsInUserTimelineWithCompletionHandler:^(NSArray
*tweets) {
        _tweets = tweets;

        [[self tableView] performSelectorOnMainThread:@selector(reloadData)
                                           withObject:nil
                                        waitUntilDone:NO];

        [self performSelectorOnMainThread:@selector(scheduleTweetRefresh)
                               withObject:nil
                            waitUntilDone:NO];
    }];
}
```

We don't need to re-schedule the update, because the timer we're about to
create will take care of all scheduling for us. We'll create it in the
viewWillAppear: method, as well as removing the old code that called
scheduleTweetRefresh. Modify the method as follows:

```
- (void)viewWillAppear:(BOOL)animated
{
    [super viewWillAppear:animated];

    LCTTwitterController *twitterController = [LCTTwitterController
sharedInstance];
```

```
        NSString *title = [self title];

        [self setTitle:@"Authorizing…"];
        [twitterController authorizeAccountWithCompletionHandler:^{
            [self performSelectorOnMainThread:@selector(setTitle:)
                            withObject:@"Loading Tweets…"
                            waitUntilDone:NO];

            [twitterController
    getTweetsInUserTimelineWithCompletionHandler:^(NSArray *tweets) {
                [self performSelectorOnMainThread:@selector(setTitle:)
                                withObject:title
                                waitUntilDone:NO];

                _tweets = tweets;

                [[self tableView] performSelectorOnMainThread:@selector(reloadData)
                                        withObject:nil
                                        waitUntilDone:NO];

                [self performSelectorOnMainThread:@selector(scheduleTweetRefresh)
                                        withObject:nil
                                        waitUntilDone:NO];

                _reloadTimer = [NSTimer scheduledTimerWithTimeInterval:15.0
                                                    target:self
    selector:@selector(reloadTweets:)
                                                    userInfo:nil
                                                    repeats:YES];
            }];
        }];
    }
```

Finally, we need to invalidate the update timer when our view disappears. At that time, we'll set it to nil, because an invalidated timer cannot be reused. We also need to remove the old code that canceled the selectors we had previously scheduled. Modify viewWillDisappear: as follows:

```
- (void)viewWillDisappear:(BOOL)animated
{
    [super viewWillDisappear:animated];

    [NSObject cancelPreviousPerformRequestsWithTarget:self
                                        selector:@selector(reloadTweets)
                                        object:nil];

    [_reloadTimer invalidate];
```

```
    _reloadTimer = nil;
}
```

Build and run the app. Just like before, it should refresh automatically, but this time it will be nearly exactly every 15 seconds.

Timers are incredibly useful in Cocoa Touch apps. If you have a label that's counting down remaining time, for instance, you would use a timer to update the label's value periodically. Timers are performant enough that you can schedule them to update at very high frequencies. For a UI update, for instance, you could set the time interval to 1/60th of a second, which would cause your UI to update at 60 frames per second; anything faster than that is probably overkill.

One important thing to note about repeating timers is that they don't stack up. The timer schedules code to run, but if it's already scheduled and hasn't yet executed, it won't re-schedule itself; a timer can be scheduled to run next no more than once. For that reason, timers aren't useful for high-performance uses where you need to be absolutely sure that your code runs a certain number of times. We'll discuss this in more detail next, as we cover run loops.

Run Loops

A Cocoa Touch application is a good example of an *event-driven* application. For the most part, the app will start up, performing any actions it needs to initialize itself, and then…*do nothing*—that is, until the user interacts with it. Without user interaction, the app sits there, waiting, with some exceptions, such as if any NSTimer objects fire. How does it do this? Well, if you were writing a system that waited for an event, you might write it like this:

```
BOOL stop = NO;

while (stop == NO) {
    BOOL result = [self eventHappened];

    if (result == YES) {
        [self processEvent];
        stop = YES;
    }
}
```

This code continuously calls the eventHappened method to check to see whether the event happened. If it has, it calls some other code, and if not, it repeats the loop. While this code works, it's horribly inefficient. It will spend 100 percent of its time busy, either calling eventHappened repeatedly or processing an event. A faster processor will simply call eventHappened more times. What's worse, this code will completely block any future execution until stop is set to YES, so we couldn't readily chain multiple loops together. iOS and Mac OS X solve this problem by using a *run loop*, which processes events in a much more efficient manner. The run loop's actions are roughly explained in Figure 8-1.

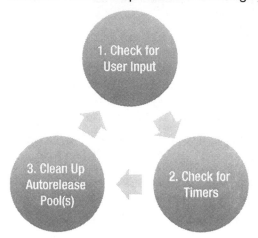

Figure 8-1. *The basic cycle of a run loop*

The run loop loops through these tasks continuously but in a much more efficient way than a simple `while` loop. When it encounters user input or a timer that needs to fire, it will run the code associated with that event and then return to the beginning of the loop. Any autoreleased objects are deallocated at the end of the run loop, and it returns to the beginning.

This diagram covers the important pieces, but other things happen on the run loop, such as network connections receiving data and ports receiving data. For the most part, however, you will only deal with the run loop behavior directly by either adding code to handle events, such as when a button is pressed, or by creating a timer.

You can always get the current run loop by calling [`NSRunLoop currentRunLoop`]. Even if one doesn't yet exist for the current thread, this method will create one. This is useful when creating timers. So far, we've seen convenience methods that automatically schedule timers on the current run loop, but you can do so yourself. Here's how you would create a timer and schedule it on a run loop:

```
NSTimer *timer = [[NSTimer alloc] initWithFireDate:[[NSDate date]
dateByAddingTimeInterval:60.0]
                                  interval:60.0
                                    target:self
                                  selector:@selector(reload:)
                                  userInfo:nil
                                   repeats:YES];
```

```
[[NSRunLoop currentRunLoop] addTimer:timer
                       forMode:NSDefaultRunLoopMode];
```

There are a few new things go over here. First is the use of the NSDate object. An NSDate is simply a representation of a particular time in an object. [NSDate date] returns an NSDate object representing the current time. We used that in the previous example to get the current date and then send it the dateByAddingTimeInterval: method to get a new date that's 60 seconds ahead of the current date. By setting this as the fire date of the timer, we can control when it will first go off.

Next, we get the current run loop with the NSRunLoop class method currentRunLoop and add the timer to it. The mode parameter defines the run loop mode for which we want to add the timer. The run loop always has a mode, which is usually NSDefaultRunLoopMode, but sometimes it will change modes, such as when it's actively processing user input. Usually, you'll want to use NSDefaultRunLoopMode.

A useful method to know on NSRunLoop is the runUntilDate: method. Suppose you're doing a long, complex calculation on the main thread. Doing so will cause the UI to hang, but you don't want that. Since you know that user interactions are processed in the main run loop, you can force it to process those events before continuing. If you needed to do something 1,000 times but wanted your user interface to remain responsive, you could do it like this:

```
for (NSUInteger i = 0; i < 1000; i++) {
    [self performSomeTask];
    [[NSRunLoop currentRunLoop] runUntilDate:[NSDate date]];
}
```

For every trip through this loop, the performSomeTask method is called, and then the run loop runs. At first, passing [NSDate date], which returns the current time, might seem like the run loop will immediately exit, but that isn't the case; rather, it will run through the loop and process everything that happened before the current time. If the user tapped a button or a timer fired during performSomeTask, those events will be processed before the runUntilDate: method returns.

Run loops depend on having either an input source, such as the screen of your iOS device, or the keyboard and mouse on a Mac, to stay alive. If a run loop has no input source(s) or timers, it will exit.

There's a lot more to what makes a run loop, but this is enough for our needs. When you're using Cocoa Touch, run loops will be created and destroyed for you, so as long as you know how to interact with them, that will be enough. A final interesting tidbit is to look at the implementation of main in an iOS program. For any iOS app, you'll find a main.m file that goes something like this:

```
int main(int argc, char *argv[])
{
    @autoreleasepool {
        return UIApplicationMain(argc, argv, nil,
NSStringFromClass([LCTAppDelegate class]));
    }
}
```

The UIApplicationMain function is what begins running your app. It creates a run loop, which starts processing events, and continues until your application exits.

Now that we've talked about run loops, we've covered most of how to control how code runs when one thing is happening at a time. On many devices today, however, there are multiple processor cores, which means you can run multiple pieces of code at the same time! Next, we'll discuss how multithreaded code works, how to write it, and how to do it safely.

Multithreaded Code

When personal computers were first gaining popularity, processor speeds would increase at a fairly predictable rate. Commonly referred to as Moore's law, the speed would typically double every 18 months. As time went on, however, the amount of speed that we could gain from processor advances started to slow down. To make things faster, processor manufacturers began making processors with multiple cores, allowing them to run more than one thing at a time. Instead of simply getting faster, processors now increase the number of cores to allow you to get more done. Beginning with the iPhone 4S and second-generation iPad, even mobile devices offer dual-core processing in iOS, allowing your app to effectively utilize multiple pieces of code concurrently. This ability doesn't come for free, however; in order to take advantage of multiple processor cores, you must write your apps to do so. Otherwise, your app will run on one core, the other sitting idle, unused. You can guess yourself which option provides the best user experience.

Running Code on Another Thread

All Cocoa Touch apps start with one thread: the main thread. This is the thread that UIApplicationMain() is called on, the thread that UI callbacks (e.g., table view data source methods) are called on, and the thread you'll use to configure your app's UI. You'll probably even use the main thread for the majority of your app's code; some things don't benefit much from multithreading.

In cases where you have a long-running task, running on the main thread is not recommended, and in some cases it might get your app killed by the system. The easiest way to avoid that is to call your long-running task on a new thread:

```
[NSThread detachNewThreadSelector:@selector(longRunningTask)
                         toTarget:self
                       withObject:nil];
```

This is the equivalent of calling [self longRunningTask], with the exception that it creates a new thread and runs the longRunningTask method on it. It's important to note that when you create a new thread, a new run loop is created for the thread, because each thread has its own run loop (the main run loop in the application is just the main thread's run loop). As a result, you'll need to create your own autorelease pool before using any methods that autorelease an object. Since you don't know for sure if the system frameworks will ever autorelease an object, it's best to do this immediately. longRunningTask should be implemented like this:

```
- (void)longRunningTask
{
    @autoreleasepool {
        // Task code goes here.
    }
}
```

By wrapping the method's code with the @autoreleasepool directive, we'll catch any autoreleased objects for this thread and deal with them appropriately.

As you can see, creating a new thread is pretty easy. Doing it *right* takes some work.

Thread Safety

Running code on multiple threads can be dangerous if you don't do it right. If you're writing to an integer on one thread and reading it on another, the read might return the old value, the new value, or a garbage value that is neither and might wind up crashing your app or displaying the wrong value. The concept of writing your code to account for these issues is called *thread safety*. One of the easiest things you can do for thread safety is to declare a property as atomic when you declare it. When you do so, by omitting the nonatomic keyword (there is no atomic keyword), you ensure that property access will be thread-safe; if you try to read and write at the same time, one will wait for the other to finish. This isn't enough for true thread safety, but it will prevent you from overwriting a property as you try to read it. You will often see people using nonatomic properties by default, because there is a slight performance gain, but if you're doing anything on multiple threads, you'll want to start by using atomic properties.

One side effect of a writable atomic property is that you can't define your own setter method if you're using a synthesized getter; doing so would undermine the built-in mechanism that provides thread safety. If you need to run code when you set the property, you have two options: use Key-Value Observing (KVO) to observe changes to the code or write the thread-safe code yourself. You can synthesize the accessor methods and use KVO to avoid writing the code yourself. If you need to do write it yourself, however, you can use the NSLock class to create locks that you can use to enforce the proper synchronicity you need for thread safety. Let's consider the hypothetical class ThreadSafeObject with the property name. We want to write our own custom implementation of setName:, so we'll use a lock to restrict access to it. The interface would look like this:

```
@interface ThreadSafeObject : NSObject {
    NSLock *_nameLock;
    NSString *_name;
}

@property (atomic, copy) NSString *name;

@end
```

Before setting or retrieving the value of name, we'll use _nameLock to ensure that we're being thread-safe. Let's walk through the implementation of our ThreadSafeObject class, beginning with the init method:

```
@implementation ThreadSafeObject

- (id)init
{
    self = [super init];

    if (self) {
        _nameLock = [[NSLock alloc] init];
    }

    return self;
}
```

As you can see, creating the _nameLock object is straightforward and needs no special methods; it's just a regular initialization. Next up is the setName: method:

```
- (void)setName:(NSString *)newName
{
```

```
    [_nameLock lock];

    _name = [newName copy];

    [_nameLock unlock];
}
```

When we call the lock method of our lock, the lock method either returns immediately if the lock is unlocked or, if the lock is already locked, waits until it's unlocked and then locks it and returns. If more than one method tries to lock an already-locked lock, they will lock it in a first-come, first-served manner. The upshot is that a lock can be locked at only one point in the code—so be sure to unlock it when you're done, or you won't be able to use it again. Next up is our final method, name:

```
- (NSString *)name
{
    NSString *nameToReturn;

    [_nameLock lock];

    nameToReturn = _name;

    [_nameLock unlock];

    return nameToReturn;
}

@end
```

Notice that we don't want to return before we unlock the lock, so we store the value of _name in a temporary variable, nameToReturn. Using a lock here as well completes our thread safety for the name property, because any combination of calls to name and setName: will succeed without overwriting one another. Thread safety is a complex subject, but locks and atomic properties are a quick and efficient way to get started with it.

Running Lots of Tasks

Spinning off new threads to do something in the background will get you only so far. Suppose you have 1,000 objects in an array and you want to perform a long-running task on each of them. You could of course create one background thread and iterate over the objects in the array on the background thread, but if you're using a dual-core device, you'll want to process two objects at a time to speed things up. A naïve implementation might detach a thread for each object, doing something like this:

```
NSUInteger count = [myArray count];

for (NSUInteger i = 0; i < count; i++) {
    id obj = [myArray objectAtIndex:i];

    [NSThread detachNewThreadSelector:@selector(longRunningTask) toTarget:obj
withObject:nil];
}
```

The problem with this approach is that we'll soon wind up with 1,001 threads running. Each thread carries with it a certain amount of memory cost, so creating 1,000 extra threads gets expensive. With the iPhone's limited resources, your app will get killed before you can spin off that many threads, so that isn't an option.

A slightly less naïve implementation would obtain the count of processor cores in the device, then keep that many threads open, processing the next object in the array each time the task finished. This avoids the too-many-threads problem and ensures that there's always work being done. It doesn't, however, take into account how busy the processors actually *are*. The device might be running some code in the background—checking mail, playing music, and so on—and simply filling the processor with work will hinder those efforts.

When you have individual tasks like this, instead of writing this code yourself, you can use the built-in class NSOperationQueue to enqueue operations, performing them automatically. You could do the previous code using an NSOperationQueue as follows:

```
NSOperationQueue *queue = [[NSOperationQueue alloc] init];
NSUInteger count = [myArray count];

for (NSUInteger i = 0; i < count; i++) {
    id obj = [myArray objectAtIndex:i];

    [queue addOperationWithBlock:^{
        [obj performLongTask];
    }];
}
```

Using an NSOperationQueue will allow the operations to proceed concurrently but while respecting the system and its current tasks. It will automatically scale the operations for the processor, which is less code you need to write.

Example: Twitter Profile Images

Let's take our newfound knowledge and use it in our Twitter example. Our goal will be to load the profile images of users in our timeline. First we'll do it the completely naïve way, loading the images synchronously. Once we've done that, we'll do it with a background thread and then finally an operation queue. Open LCTTimeLineViewController.m, and modify the tableView:cellForRowAtIndexPath: method as follows:

```objc
- (UITableViewCell *)tableView:(UITableView *)tableView
        cellForRowAtIndexPath:(NSIndexPath *)indexPath
{
    static NSString *CellIdentifier = @"Cell";
    UITableViewCell *cell = [tableView
dequeueReusableCellWithIdentifier:CellIdentifier];

    if (cell == nil) {
        cell = [[UITableViewCell alloc]
initWithStyle:UITableViewCellStyleSubtitle
                                    reuseIdentifier:CellIdentifier];
    }

    // Configure the cell...
    NSDictionary *tweet = [_tweets objectAtIndex:[indexPath row]];

    [[cell textLabel] setText:[tweet objectForKey:@"text"]];
    [[cell detailTextLabel] setText:[[tweet objectForKey:@"user"]
objectForKey:@"name"]];

    NSString *profileImageURI = [[tweet objectForKey:@"user"]
objectForKey:@"profile_image_url"];
    NSURL *profileImageURL = [NSURL URLWithString:profileImageURI];

    NSURLRequest *profileImageURLRequest = [NSURLRequest
requestWithURL:profileImageURL];

    NSURLResponse *response = nil;
    NSError *error = nil;

    NSData *imageData = [NSURLConnection
sendSynchronousRequest:profileImageURLRequest
                                    returningResponse:&response
                                                error:&error];

    UIImage *image = [UIImage imageWithData:imageData];

    [[cell imageView] setImage:image];

    return cell;
}
```

Build and run the app. If you're on a fast connection, you might not even notice the slowdown as the app loads a picture for every row, but if you're on a slow connection, you'll definitely notice the hit. Instead of blocking the UI while we wait for the image to download, let's use an NSOperationQueue to queue up the images for downloading. In LCTTimelineViewController.m, add an instance variable for the queue in the class extension at the top of the file:

```
@interface LCTTimelineViewController () {
    NSTimer *_reloadTimer;
    NSArray *_tweets;
    NSOperationQueue *_profileImageQueue;
}

- (void)reloadButtonPressed:(id)sender;
- (void)reloadTweets:(NSTimer *)reloadTimer;
- (void)tweetButtonPressed:(id)sender;

@end
```

Next, let's initialize the queue in the initWithStyle: method:

```
- (id)initWithStyle:(UITableViewStyle)style
{
    self = [super initWithStyle:style];

    if (self) {
        [self setTitle:@"Timeline"];

        UIBarButtonItem *reloadButton =
        [[UIBarButtonItem alloc]
initWithBarButtonSystemItem:UIBarButtonSystemItemRefresh
                                                    target:self
action:@selector(reloadButtonPressed:)];
        [[self navigationItem] setLeftBarButtonItem:reloadButton];

        UIBarButtonItem *tweetButton =
        [[UIBarButtonItem alloc]
initWithBarButtonSystemItem:UIBarButtonSystemItemCompose
                                                    target:self
action:@selector(tweetButtonPressed:)];
        [[self navigationItem] setRightBarButtonItem:tweetButton];

        _profileImageQueue = [[NSOperationQueue alloc] init];
    }

    return self;
}
```

As you can see, there really isn't too much setup code here. Next, let's use the operation queue to download the images. In tableView:cellForRowAtIndexPath:, modify the method as follows:

```objc
- (UITableViewCell *)tableView:(UITableView *)tableView
        cellForRowAtIndexPath:(NSIndexPath *)indexPath
{
    static NSString *CellIdentifier = @"Cell";
    UITableViewCell *cell = [tableView
dequeueReusableCellWithIdentifier:CellIdentifier];

    if (cell == nil) {
        cell = [[UITableViewCell alloc]
initWithStyle:UITableViewCellStyleSubtitle
                                    reuseIdentifier:CellIdentifier];
    }

    // Configure the cell...
    NSDictionary *tweet = [_tweets objectAtIndex:[indexPath row]];

    [[cell textLabel] setText:[tweet objectForKey:@"text"]];
    [[cell detailTextLabel] setText:[[tweet objectForKey:@"user"]
objectForKey:@"name"]];

    NSString *profileImageURI = [[tweet objectForKey:@"user"]
objectForKey:@"profile_image_url"];
    NSURL *profileImageURL = [NSURL URLWithString:profileImageURI];

    NSURLRequest *profileImageURLRequest = [NSURLRequest
requestWithURL:profileImageURL];

    [_profileImageQueue addOperationWithBlock:^{
        NSURLResponse *response = nil;
        NSError *error = nil;

        NSData *imageData = [NSURLConnection
sendSynchronousRequest:profileImageURLRequest
                                          returningResponse:&response
                                                      error:&error];

        UIImage *image = [UIImage imageWithData:imageData];
        [[cell imageView] setImage:image];

        [[cell imageView] performSelectorOnMainThread:@selector(setImage:)
                                           withObject:image
                                        waitUntilDone:NO];

        [cell performSelectorOnMainThread:@selector(setNeedsLayout)
                               withObject:nil
                            waitUntilDone:NO];
    }];

    return cell;
}
```

As you can see, we simply wrap the lines that perform the network requests in a block that we pass to our operation queue. Since this isn't going to run on the main thread, we then set the image in the cell's image view on the main thread, since that is a UI operation. Next, we call `setNeedsLayout` on the cell from the main thread. When the cell is returned from `tableView:cellForRowAtIndexPath:`, its image view won't have an image, so we need to call `setNeedsLayout` to force the cell to adjust its subviews to account for the image.

Build and run the app, and you'll notice your table view cells' content loading asynchronously. This is especially nice for users on a slow connection, because they'll still be able to scroll the table view as they wait for the images to load. Now, as simple as creating your own threads and using operation queues can be, the truth is that it's not the easiest, and it's not the best method for running code concurrently. In Mac OS X Snow Leopard and iOS 4.0, Apple introduced a new low-level framework for managing concurrency called Grand Central Dispatch, which improves on concurrent code in nearly every way imaginable.

> **NOTE:** If you'd like to simulate poor network conditions, Apple provides a tool called the Network Link Conditioner. It isn't part of a default Xcode installation but is an optional developer tool you can use to simulate poor networks on your Mac.

Grand Central Dispatch

Generally speaking, the code you write can be broken down into discrete tasks: download an image from a server, parse a JSON response into model objects, calculate values based on user input, and so on. By breaking down pieces of code into smaller chunks, it's easier to manage them, easier to write good code, and easier to change one piece of how the code works. Apple's Grand Central Dispatch framework helps you manage when your code executes by automatically running your individual tasks based on how busy the system is. Just like with `NSOperationQueue`, you add an individual task to a queue, which then executes its tasks until they're all done. With Grand Central Dispatch, you have much more flexibility than with an operation queue. Instead of manually creating a queue and adding items to it, you can add items to a shared global queue based on priority, as well as a queue that runs its tasks on the main thread. Let's look at the latter case first.

Dispatching Code

In the previous example, when we received an image from Twitter, we had to put it in the table view cell's image view on the main thread and then call setNeedsLayout on the cell, as follows:

```
[[cell imageView] performSelectorOnMainThread:@selector(setImage:)
                              withObject:image
                              waitUntilDone:NO];

[cell performSelectorOnMainThread:@selector(setNeedsLayout)
                     withObject:nil
                     waitUntilDone:NO];
```

With Grand Central Dispatch, we can create a block and schedule it on the main queue, doing the same thing in a much simpler way:

```
dispatch_async(dispatch_get_main_queue(), ^{
    [[cell imageView] setImage:image];
    [cell setNeedsLayout];
});
```

The dispatch_async() function takes a dispatch queue for the first argument and the block to be executed for the second. We'll cover dispatch queues in more detail later, but for now the macro dispatch_get_main_queue() is enough to return the main queue here. In the block, we call these two methods normally, knowing that they'll execute on the main thread.

When you dispatch a task to a queue, there are two ways to do so: synchronously and asynchronously. The asynchronous functions, such as dispatch_async(), return immediately after scheduling the task, while the synchronous functions, such as the corresponding dispatch_sync() function, wait for the task to finish before returning.

> **NOTE:** Take great care with the synchronous functions of Grand Central Dispatch. If you dispatch a task to the main queue synchronously while you're already *on* the main queue, the task will never begin, because the main queue is waiting for the task to finish.

You don't have to use blocks with Grand Central Dispatch. If you'd rather pass a function pointer than a block, the alternative methods dispatch_async_f() and dispatch_sync_f() do the same as their block-based counterparts, albeit with an extra argument: a context pointer that's passed to the function as its first argument. When you're writing new code, you'll usually use blocks, but if you have a lot of compatible C functions, this allows you to use those instead.

There are a couple more locations in the TwitterExample code where we can replace performSelector: methods with Grand Central Dispatch. In LCTTimelineViewController.m, modify the viewWillAppear: method as follows:

```
- (void)viewWillAppear:(BOOL)animated
{
    [super viewWillAppear:animated];

    LCTTwitterController *twitterController = [LCTTwitterController
sharedInstance];

    NSString *title = [self title];

    [self setTitle:@"Authorizing…"];
    [twitterController authorizeAccountWithCompletionHandler:^{
            [self performSelectorOnMainThread:@selector(setTitle:)
                                   withObject:@"Loading Tweets…"
                                waitUntilDone:NO];

        dispatch_async(dispatch_get_main_queue(), ^{
            [self setTitle:@"Loading Tweets…"];
        });

        [twitterController
getTweetsInUserTimelineWithCompletionHandler:^(NSArray *tweets) {
            [self performSelectorOnMainThread:@selector(setTitle:)
                                   withObject:title
                                waitUntilDone:NO];

            _tweets = tweets;

            [[self tableView] performSelectorOnMainThread:@selector(reloadData)
                                               withObject:nil
                                            waitUntilDone:NO];

            dispatch_async(dispatch_get_main_queue(), ^{
                [self setTitle:title];
                [[self tableView] reloadData];
            });
        }];
    }];

    _reloadTimer = [NSTimer scheduledTimerWithTimeInterval:5.0
                                                    target:self

selector:@selector(reloadTweets:)
                                                  userInfo:nil
                                                   repeats:YES];
}
```

Combining the calls to
`performSelectorOnMainThread:withObject:waitUntilDone:` into a single call to
`dispatch_async()` isn't strictly necessary, but in the opinion of yours truly, it
makes the code much more readable.

Using Global Dispatch Queues

We've already seen an example of one dispatch queue: the main queue. You'll
dispatch tasks to this queue for any UI-related methods or anything else that
needs to run on the main thread. For tasks that you'd like to run in the
background, you can get a global queue with the `dispatch_get_global_queue()`
function, which takes two arguments: a queue priority and options. The second
argument is reserved for future use by Apple, so for the time being, just pass 0.
The first argument should be one of four constants, presented here in order of
priority, highest first:

- `DISPATCH_QUEUE_PRIORITY_HIGH`

- `DISPATCH_QUEUE_PRIORITY_DEFAULT`

- `DISPATCH_QUEUE_PRIORITY_LOW`

- `DISPATCH_QUEUE_PRIORITY_BACKGROUND` (available in iOS 5 and
  later)

Once you get a dispatch queue, you use it just like the main queue in the
previous example.

Let's modify our Twitter example to use dispatch queues instead of an
NSOperationQueue. Open `LCTTimelineViewController.m`, and modify the
`tableView:cellForRowAtIndexPath:` method as follows:

```
- (UITableViewCell *)tableView:(UITableView *)tableView
        cellForRowAtIndexPath:(NSIndexPath *)indexPath
{
    static NSString *CellIdentifier = @"Cell";
    UITableViewCell *cell = [tableView
dequeueReusableCellWithIdentifier:CellIdentifier];

    if (cell == nil) {
        cell = [[UITableViewCell alloc]
initWithStyle:UITableViewCellStyleSubtitle
                                    reuseIdentifier:CellIdentifier];
    }

    // Configure the cell...
    NSDictionary *tweet = [_tweets objectAtIndex:[indexPath row]];
```

```
    [[cell textLabel] setText:[tweet objectForKey:@"text"]];
    [[cell detailTextLabel] setText:[[tweet objectForKey:@"user"]
objectForKey:@"name"]];

    NSString *profileImageURI = [[tweet objectForKey:@"user"]
objectForKey:@"profile_image_url"];
    NSURL *profileImageURL = [NSURL URLWithString:profileImageURI];

    NSURLRequest *profileImageURLRequest = [NSURLRequest
requestWithURL:profileImageURL];

    [_profileImageQueue addOperationWithBlock:^{
    dispatch_queue_t dispatchQueue =
    dispatch_get_global_queue(DISPATCH_QUEUE_PRIORITY_DEFAULT, 0);

    dispatch_async(dispatchQueue, ^{
        NSURLResponse *response = nil;
        NSError *error = nil;

        NSData *imageData = [NSURLConnection
sendSynchronousRequest:profileImageURLRequest
                                            returningResponse:&response
                                                        error:&error];

        UIImage *image = [UIImage imageWithData:imageData];

        [[cell imageView] performSelectorOnMainThread:@selector(setImage:)
                                           withObject:image
                                        waitUntilDone:NO];

        [cell performSelectorOnMainThread:@selector(setNeedsLayout)
                               withObject:nil
                            waitUntilDone:NO];

        dispatch_async(dispatch_get_main_queue(), ^{
            [[cell imageView] setImage:image];
            [cell setNeedsLayout];
        });
    });
    }];

    return cell;
}
```

First, we get a global dispatch queue with the default queue priority. Next, we use dispatch_async() to schedule a block of code on this queue. Inside of this block of code, we use dispatch_async() a second time to schedule a block of code on the main queue. Nested calls to dispatch_async() like we have here are not uncommon and are in fact a big strength of Grand Central Dispatch.

Now that we're using these queues, you can remove the NSOperationQueue
variable we created before:

```
@interface LCTTimelineViewController () {
    NSTimer *_reloadTimer;
    NSArray *_tweets;
    NSOperationQueue *_profileImageQueue;
}

- (void)reloadButtonPressed:(id)sender;
- (void)reloadTweets:(NSTimer *)reloadTimer;
- (void)tweetButtonPressed:(id)sender;

@end
```

Similarly, you can remove it from the initWithStyle: method:

```
- (id)initWithStyle:(UITableViewStyle)style
{
    self = [super initWithStyle:style];

    if (self) {
        [self setTitle:@"Timeline"];

        UIBarButtonItem *reloadButton =
        [[UIBarButtonItem alloc]
initWithBarButtonSystemItem:UIBarButtonSystemItemRefresh
                                                    target:self

action:@selector(reloadButtonPressed:)];
        [[self navigationItem] setLeftBarButtonItem:reloadButton];

        UIBarButtonItem *tweetButton =
        [[UIBarButtonItem alloc]
initWithBarButtonSystemItem:UIBarButtonSystemItemCompose
                                                    target:self

action:@selector(tweetButtonPressed:)];
        [[self navigationItem] setRightBarButtonItem:tweetButton];

        _profileImageQueue = [[NSOperationQueue alloc] init];
    }

    return self;
}
```

Great. Now, build and run your code, and you'll see that everything still works as
advertised. If this was all that Grand Central Dispatch could do for you, it would
be a great library. It can do so much more, but before we get too far into what it
can do, let's talk a bit about how it's structured.

Dispatch Objects

Grand Central Dispatch is an object-oriented framework, but it isn't Objective-C. Instead, it's in C, with its own object system. Like Objective-C, it uses reference counting for its memory management, but unfortunately ARC won't be able to help with this code. Creating a dispatch object generally involves a function with this form, where *type* is the kind of dispatch object:

```
dispatch_<type>_create()
```

To create a dispatch queue, for instance, you would call `dispatch_queue_create()`. When you get a queue from this function, it has a retain count of 1, so when you're done with it, you'll need to release it using the `dispatch_release()` function. You don't need to call `dispatch_release()` on global queues or the main queue, since you didn't create them. If you're passing a dispatch object around and need to retain its value, use the `dispatch_retain()` function.

Dispatch Queues

One of the most common types of dispatch objects to be creating is a dispatch queue. There are two types of queues: serial and concurrent. A serial queue runs one task at a time, operating on a first-in, first-out basis. While only one task will be running at a time within a serial queue, Grand Central Dispatch may run tasks from two separate serial queues at the same time. Concurrent queues, as the name suggests, can run multiple tasks at once. One of Grand Central Dispatch's features is that it automatically scales the number of threads active in the app for you, so you don't need to configure how many tasks can run concurrently in a given concurrent queue. Tasks are started in a first-in, first-out order, but the order in which they finish depends on how long they take.

To create a dispatch queue, use the `dispatch_queue_create()` function:

```
dispatch_queue_t myQueue = dispatch_queue_create("com.learncocoatouch.myQueue",
                                    DISPATCH_QUEUE_CONCURRENT);
```

The first argument is a C string that's used as a label for the queue. The set of queues is global to all active apps, so be sure to use a reverse-DNS style label to avoid name collisions. It's also useful when debugging, because you can see which queue a broken piece of code is running on. The second argument is either `DISPATCH_QUEUE_CONCURRENT` or `DISPATCH_QUEUE_SERIAL`, corresponding to the type of dispatch queue you'd like to create. You may also see `NULL` used in code that was written before these constants were available; in that case, the queue is created as a serial queue. You can use this queue to dispatch tasks just like a global queue:

```
dispatch_async(myQueue, ^{ NSLog(@"Hello, World!"); });
```

When you're done with the queue, be sure to release it:

```
dispatch_release(myQueue);
```

When you dispatch a task to a queue, the task retains the queue, so it's OK to release the queue immediately after submitting one or more tasks without worrying about the order in which things will happen.

Another useful function that uses dispatch queues is `dispatch_apply()`. If you need to perform the same task multiple times, you can use `dispatch_apply()` (as well as its function-based counterpart, `dispatch_apply_f()`) to do so. If you use the block-based `dispatch_apply()` function, the block takes one argument, which corresponds to the index of the current iteration. The count will be passed as the second argument to a function if you use `dispatch_apply_f()`. To illustrate, here's how you would use `dispatch_apply()` to iterate through an array:

```
NSUInteger count = [myArray count];

dispatch_apply(count, myQueue, ^(size_t idx) {
    id object = [myArray objectAtIndex:idx];

    [object doSomething];
});
```

Note that the block we passed in as the third argument takes one argument. The `size_t` type is essentially an integer, so we can use it as the index to retrieve the object from the array. When you use `dispatch_apply()`, it dispatches the block to the given queue the given number of times and then waits for them all to finish before returning. Because it waits for the blocks to finish, you can use `dispatch_apply()` as a quick replacement for `for` loops and, when using it in tandem with a concurrent queue, can gain performance as a result.

Dispatch Semaphores

There's a big problem with our Twitter example: since we can display so many cells on the screen at once, we end up with a large number of URL connections all loading at once. Too many simultaneous connections will have an adverse effect on performance. To counteract this, we'll use *dispatch semaphores*, which are counting semaphores that will act as a lock. When you create a semaphore with `dispatch_semaphore_create()`, you pass a number to initialize the value of the semaphore. To use the semaphore, you call `dispatch_semaphore_wait()`, which decrements the current value of the semaphore. If the resulting value is less than 0, the function waits until the value

increases before returning. The value of the semaphore is set in the
dispatch_semaphore_create() method, so to create a semaphore to allow only
one access at a time, you would create it by calling
dispatch_semaphore_create(0);. To increment the value, call
dispatch_semaphore_signal(). It's also possible to specify a maximum wait time
for dispatch_semaphore_wait() to allow you to respond appropriately if you
can't act immediately. If dispatch_semaphore_wait() is called more than once,
the first call to this function to return is determined in a first-in, first-out manner,
similar to a lock.

To limit the number of simultaneous connections in our Twitter app, we'll use a
value of 3 in dispatch_semaphore_create(). We'll also create our own dispatch
queue to handle the requests to help clean things up. Open the TwitterExample
project in Xcode, and navigate to LCTTimelineViewController.m. Add two
variables to the class extension:

```
@interface LCTTimelineViewController () {
    NSTimer * _reloadTimer;
    NSArray * _tweets;
    dispatch_queue_t _profileImageQueue;
    dispatch_semaphore_t _profileImageSemaphore;
}

- (void)reloadButtonPressed:(id)sender;
- (void)reloadTweets:(NSTimer *)reloadTimer;
- (void)tweetButtonPressed:(id)sender;

@end
```

Note that because dispatch objects are not Objective-C objects, they aren't
pointers. We'll initialize them in the initWithStyle: method:

```
- (id)initWithStyle:(UITableViewStyle)style
{
    self = [super initWithStyle:style];

    if (self) {
        [self setTitle:@"Timeline"];

        UIBarButtonItem *reloadButton =
        [[UIBarButtonItem alloc]
initWithBarButtonSystemItem:UIBarButtonSystemItemRefresh
                                                    target:self

action:@selector(reloadButtonPressed:)];
        [[self navigationItem] setLeftBarButtonItem:reloadButton];

        UIBarButtonItem *tweetButton =
```

```
        [[UIBarButtonItem alloc]
initWithBarButtonSystemItem:UIBarButtonSystemItemCompose
                                            target:self

action:@selector(tweetButtonPressed:)];
        [[self navigationItem] setRightBarButtonItem:tweetButton];

        _profileImageQueue =
dispatch_queue_create("com.learncocoatouch.profileImageQueue",

DISPATCH_QUEUE_CONCURRENT);

        _profileImageSemaphore = dispatch_semaphore_create(3);
    }

    return self;
}
```

Even though we're using ARC, we need to release these objects when we're done with them. Add a dealloc method after initWithStyle::

```
- (void)dealloc
{
    dispatch_release(_profileImageQueue);
    dispatch_release(_profileImageSemaphore);
}
```

Next, let's use the queue and semaphore to control the number of concurrent connections. Modify tableView:cellForRowAtIndexPath: as follows:

```
- (UITableViewCell *)tableView:(UITableView *)tableView
        cellForRowAtIndexPath:(NSIndexPath *)indexPath
{
    static NSString *CellIdentifier = @"Cell";
    UITableViewCell *cell = [tableView
dequeueReusableCellWithIdentifier:CellIdentifier];

    if (cell == nil) {
        cell = [[UITableViewCell alloc]
initWithStyle:UITableViewCellStyleSubtitle
                                        reuseIdentifier:CellIdentifier];
    }

    // Configure the cell...
    NSDictionary *tweet = [_tweets objectAtIndex:[indexPath row]];

    [[cell textLabel] setText:[tweet objectForKey:@"text"]];
    [[cell detailTextLabel] setText:[[tweet objectForKey:@"user"]
objectForKey:@"name"]];
```

```
    NSString *profileImageURI = [[tweet objectForKey:@"user"]
objectForKey:@"profile_image_url"];
    NSURL *profileImageURL = [NSURL URLWithString:profileImageURI];

    NSURLRequest *profileImageURLRequest = [NSURLRequest
requestWithURL:profileImageURL];

    dispatch_queue_t dispatchQueue =
    dispatch_get_global_queue(DISPATCH_QUEUE_PRIORITY_DEFAULT, 0ul);
    dispatch_async(dispatchQueue, ^{
    dispatch_async(_profileImageQueue, ^{
        NSURLResponse *response = nil;
        NSError *error = nil;

        dispatch_semaphore_wait(_profileImageSemaphore,
DISPATCH_TIME_FOREVER);

        NSData *imageData = [NSURLConnection
sendSynchronousRequest:profileImageURLRequest
                                              returningResponse:&response
                                                          error:&error];

        dispatch_semaphore_signal(_profileImageSemaphore);

        UIImage *image = [UIImage imageWithData:imageData];

        dispatch_async(dispatch_get_main_queue(), ^{
            [[cell imageView] setImage:image];
            [cell setNeedsLayout];
        });
    });

    return cell;
}
```

As you can see, we wrap the URL connection method in semaphore calls. Once we have the data from the server, we can start a new connection. Build and run the app again, and you should see the images load. Depending on your Internet connection speed, you may notice an improvement.

Dispatch Time

You may have noticed the DISPATCH_TIME_FOREVER macro in the previous code example. That argument in dispatch_semaphore_wait() specifies the maximum amount of time to wait for the semaphore before moving on. Passing DISPATCH_TIME_FOREVER causes the function to wait, well, forever. The return value of dispatch_semaphore_wait() is zero if the semaphore did not time out, and it's nonzero if the timeout did occur. To specify the maximum timeout, you'll need to create a `dispatch_time_t` value. `dispatch_time_t` is not an object, so you don't use a function ending in "create." Instead, use the `dispatch_time()` function to return a new time value. `dispatch_time()` takes two arguments, the first of which is another `dispatch_time_t`; the time you create will be relative to this first argument. Use `DISPATCH_TIME_NOW` to create a time in the near future. The second argument is the number of nanoseconds to add to the first argument in order to get the desired time. You can use the `NSEC_PER_SEC` macro to conveniently calculate the number of nanoseconds to use. To specify a dispatch time 15 seconds from now, you would call the function as follows:

```
dispatch_time_t time = dispatch_time(DISPATCH_TIME_NOW, 15 * NSEC_PER_SEC);
```

To use this time as the timeout for a semaphore, you would call `dispatch_semaphore_wait()` as follows:

```
long success = dispatch_semaphore_wait(mySemaphore, time);

if (success == 0) {
    // The timeout did not occur.
}
else {
    // The timeout occurred.
}
```

Using dispatch semaphores with these timeouts gives you flexible control over resource allocation in your app. Another useful function that uses the `dispatch_time_t` type is `dispatch_after()` (along with its counterpart, `dispatch_after_f()`, that takes a function instead of a block), which schedules the dispatch of a block of code for later. Using `dispatch_after()` is just like using `dispatch_async()`, with one additional argument before the others, a `dispatch_time_t` value specifying when to call the code. If you wanted to schedule a block to run 30 seconds into the future, you could do so as follows:

```
dispatch_time_t time = dispatch_time(DISPATCH_TIME_NOW, 30 * NSEC_PER_SEC);

dispatch_after(time, dispatch_get_main_queue(), ^{
    NSLog(@"Hello, World!");
});
```

Using `dispatch_after()` like this has the same effect as a nonrepeating timer but doesn't have the overhead of creating the `NSTimer` object.

Summary

In this chapter, you learned a few different ways to run your code. The performSelector: family of methods provides you with basic message routing, while timers allow you to repeat code on timed intervals. Run loops are the underpinnings of every thread, processing events in your application. Threads and the thread-safety issues that accompany them allow you to run two pieces of code at once, and NSOperationQueue allows you to enqueue specific chunks of work. Finally, Grand Central Dispatch allows you fine-grained control over how your code runs. Now that you've finished this chapter, you're well on your way toward writing high-performance iOS applications. We've made our Twitter example more responsive with Grand Central Dispatch, but its user interface could use some work. In the next chapter, we'll talk about implementing great iPhone UIs, rendering our own graphics, and animation.

User Interface Design

As of this writing, more than 550,000 apps are available for iOS. Talk about fierce competition. Your app will be in the App Store competing for the eyes—and pockets—of the users of hundreds of millions of devices. With so many products out there, users are often at a loss when trying to compare apps. Here's a quick experiment: fire up the App Store on your iOS device or in iTunes and search for an app. Use the search term "photography." Or "weight loss." How in the heck are users—*your* potential users—going to find your app among all this noise? Primarily, it's through their eyes. One of the most important things you can do for a successful app is to have a great icon. Hire an artist and have them make ridiculously high-resolution graphics for your icon. If your app is good and Apple wants to feature it somewhere, you might be asked for an even higher-resolution version. And if Apple wants to feature your app, you'd better have those graphics at the ready; being featured in the App Store is even more of a path to success than having a great icon.

Once your users see your amazing icon, pause for a moment to weep at its beauty, and decide to purchase your app, they're going to have to use the darn thing. Even if your icon is a couple of stick figures, your users will appreciate knowing that some care went into how the application looks. To that end, this chapter will cover the ways in which you can make your app stand out from the crowd with compelling user interface design. Not only will your apps *look* better, they'll be easier to use. We'll start with high-level—though still quite powerful—frameworks like UIKit, then get more low-level as we progress. By the end of this chapter, you will be able to take an image that your designer gives you and make your app look like your designer's work. To start, let's cover some basic things in UIKit.

UIKit is a very large framework. It covers most of the user interface elements you'll be using to make iPhone apps, from buttons to sliders to labels to image views. Happily, most of what UIKit offers can be customized to fit your needs, whether it's a custom image for a button, a color for a label, or a snappy animation when your app starts up. One of the easiest ways you can make your application stand out is to use custom colors for UI elements; to do that, you'll use the UIColor class.

Coloring Interface Elements with UIColor

You may have already toyed with color when playing with Interface Builder. If so, great. If not, don't worry, because we're about to cover it in depth. Instances of the UIColor class are representations of a specific color. They're used all over UIKit, but one of the easiest demonstrations of how they work is to take a user interface element and add some color to it. To do this, let's use our venerable Twitter example project and add some pizzazz. Open the TwitterExample project in Xcode and navigate to your app delegate's implementation file (LCTAppDelegate.m). Add the following lines in bold to the application:didFinishLaunchingWithOptions: method:

```
- (BOOL)application:(UIApplication *)application
didFinishLaunchingWithOptions:(NSDictionary *)launchOptions
{
    self.window = [[UIWindow alloc] initWithFrame:[[UIScreen mainScreen]
bounds]];
    // Override point for customization after application launch.
    self.window.backgroundColor = [UIColor whiteColor];
    [self.window makeKeyAndVisible];

    LCTTimelineViewController *viewController =
    [[LCTTimelineViewController alloc] initWithStyle:UITableViewStylePlain];

    UINavigationController *navigationController =
    [[UINavigationController alloc] initWithRootViewController:viewController];

    UIColor *navigationBarColor = [UIColor redColor];
    [[navigationController navigationBar] setTintColor:navigationBarColor];

    [[self window] setRootViewController:navigationController];

    return YES;
}
```

NOTE: If you have removed your Twitter account from the device you're using or the iOS Simulator, you'll need to reenter it before using the TwitterExample app.

Build and run the app, and the difference should be quite noticeable. As you can see in Figure 9-1, the navigation bars look quite different already.

Figure 9-1. *The navigation controller with the default tint color on the left and with a red tint color on the right*

Not only does the `tintColor` property affect the color of the navigation bar, it also changes the color of the `UIBarButtonItem` objects displayed on it. Tint colors, which are supported by many UIKit classes, affect the color of the object but not its shape or how it behaves.

You may have also noticed that we simply used the `UIColor` class method `redColor` to get a color. This is provided as a convenience to you, allowing you to create common colors quickly. You can use class methods to make black, dark gray, light gray, gray, white, red, green, blue, cyan, yellow, magenta, orange, purple, and brown color objects. You can also use the `clearColor` convenience method to create a transparent color, which is useful for making the background of a view transparent. You can replace the `redColor` method in the Twitter code to any of those colors, build and run the app, and see the results. Note that for two-word color names, the methods are in camel case, so for dark gray you'd use the `darkGrayColor` method.

The obvious next question is, "Can I use my own colors?" The answer is yes, you can use your own colors. Simply use the `UIColor` class method `colorWithRed:green:blue:alpha:` to create the color. You can create a nice, dark blue slate color with the following line:

```
UIColor *darkBlueSlateColor = [UIColor colorWithRed:0.129f
                                    green:0.278f
                                    blue:0.380f
                                    alpha:1.0f];
```

> **NOTE:** As is the case for all displays, colors on an iOS device's display may not match the same color on another display exactly. Always be sure to test your app on a real device to see what the colors you use actually look like.

Each parameter of this method takes a float in the range from 0 to 1. For the red, green, and blue values, designers are used to giving integer or hex values for colors. For easier modification later, you can use division to get the values between 0 and 1. The previous color could have been written in either of these ways:

```
UIColor *darkBlueSlateColor = [UIColor colorWithRed:(74.0f/255.0f)
                                    green:(82.0f/255.0f)
                                    blue:(90.0f/255.0f)
                                    alpha:1.0f];

UIColor *darkBlueSlateColor = [UIColor colorWithRed:((float)0x4A / (float)0xFF)
                                    green:((float)0x52 / (float)0xFF)
                                    blue:((float)0x5A / (float)0xFF)
                                    alpha:1.0f];
```

In the first example, we use the numerical values divided by 255 to obtain a value between 0 and 1; in the second, we use the hexadecimal value divided by FF to obtain the value. When your designer gives you a specific color to use, you can use the appropriate method to generate the color.

The fourth parameter to this method is the alpha component of the color, which is a measure of how opaque it is. This won't have any effect when setting the tint color on a navigation bar, but it can be used in other situations where you use a UIColor object to add some transparency to the color.

If your designer gives you values for hue, saturation, and brightness, you can create a color with those as well. The same color as shown earlier can be created like so:

```
UIColor *darkBlueSlateColor = [UIColor colorWithHue:(210.0f/359.0f)
                                        saturation:(18.0f/100.0f)
                                        brightness:(35.0f/100.0f)
                                             alpha:1.0f];
```

Colors are useful for more than just tinting UI elements. You can use them to change the text color of a UILabel or the background color of any UIView. If, for instance, you want your table view cells to alternate between gray and a slightly darker shade of gray, you can use a UIColor to do so. Open the TwitterExample project in Xcode, and navigate to the LCTTimelineViewController.m file. Add a new method implementation after tableView:cellForRowAtIndexPath: as follows in bold:

```
- (void)tableView:(UITableView *)tableView
  willDisplayCell:(UITableViewCell *)cell
forRowAtIndexPath:(NSIndexPath *)indexPath
{
    NSUInteger row = [indexPath row];

    if (row % 2) {
        [cell setBackgroundColor:[UIColor grayColor]];
    }
    else {
        [cell setBackgroundColor:[UIColor lightGrayColor]];
    }
}
```

The tableView:willDisplayCell:forRowAtIndexPath: table view delegate method is called just before the cell appears on the screen. Among other things, it's used to set the background color of your table view cell. Build and run the app, and you'll notice that for the gray cells, the user name is invisible, because it's drawing gray text on a gray background. To fix that, let's change the text to be white. Modify tableView:cellForRowAtIndexPath: by adding the following code in bold:

```
- (UITableViewCell *)tableView:(UITableView *)tableView
        cellForRowAtIndexPath:(NSIndexPath *)indexPath
{
    static NSString *CellIdentifier = @"Cell";
    UITableViewCell *cell = [tableView
dequeueReusableCellWithIdentifier:CellIdentifier];
```

```objc
    if (cell == nil) {
        cell = [[UITableViewCell alloc]
initWithStyle:UITableViewCellStyleSubtitle
                                        reuseIdentifier:CellIdentifier];
    }

    // Configure the cell...
    NSDictionary *tweet = [_tweets objectAtIndex:[indexPath row]];

    [[cell textLabel] setText:[tweet objectForKey:@"text"]];
    [[cell detailTextLabel] setText:[[tweet objectForKey:@"user"]
objectForKey:@"name"]];

    NSString *profileImageURI = [[tweet objectForKey:@"user"]
objectForKey:@"profile_image_url"];
    NSURL *profileImageURL = [NSURL URLWithString:profileImageURI];

    NSURLRequest *profileImageURLRequest = [NSURLRequest
requestWithURL:profileImageURL];

    dispatch_async(_profileImageQueue, ^{
        NSURLResponse *response = nil;
        NSError *error = nil;

        dispatch_semaphore_wait(_profileImageSemaphore, DISPATCH_TIME_FOREVER);

        NSData *imageData = [NSURLConnection
sendSynchronousRequest:profileImageURLRequest
                                        returningResponse:&response
                                                    error:&error];

        dispatch_semaphore_signal(_profileImageSemaphore);

        UIImage *image = [UIImage imageWithData:imageData];

        dispatch_async(dispatch_get_main_queue(), ^{
            [[cell imageView] setImage:image];
            [cell setNeedsLayout];
        });
    });

    [[cell textLabel] setTextColor:[UIColor whiteColor]];
    [[cell detailTextLabel] setTextColor:[UIColor whiteColor]];

    return cell;
}
```

Build and run the app again. The text should be visible now, and your app should look like Figure 9-2.

Figure 9-2. *Our Twitter client with a little color*

As you can see, adding just a bit of color—even shades of gray—really makes a difference. As easy as it is, there's no reason to release an app with the plain, default interface. This Twitter interface could still use a bit of sprucing up, however. Most of the tweets are longer than a single line, but they're getting cut off. Let's see what we can do about that.

Fonts and Text Size

The font used to display text in a label is represented by the `UIFont` class. We can also use it to determine how much space we'll need to draw a string. To set a label's font, you can create a font like so:

```
UIFont *myFont = [UIFont boldSystemFontOfSize:17.0f];
```

If you want to use a font with a specific name or a more specific variation of a font, such as bold and italic, you can create a UIFont object using the font's name to represent it:

```
UIFont *myFont = [UIFont fontWithName:@"Helvetica Neue" size:17.0f];
```

The UIFont class method familyNames returns an array of font family names present on the system. To get the names of the fonts in a particular family, use the UIFont class method fontNamesForFamilyName:, which takes a string (the family name) as a parameter and returns an array of font names in the specified family. Use these font names in the fontWithName:size: method.

> **NOTE**: For an up-to-date list of the fonts included with iOS, check out www.iosfonts.com.

To use that font to draw a label's text, set it as the label's font:

```
[myLabel setFont:myFont];
```

For TwitterExample, let's add some style with a custom font. Open your TwitterExample project in Xcode and, if you aren't already there, navigate to the LCTTimelineViewController.m file. Let's add two UIFont instance variables to store the fonts we want to use. We'll add the instance variables to the class extension at the top of the file. Add the following lines in bold:

```
@interface LCTTimelineViewController () {
    NSTimer *_reloadTimer;
    NSArray *_tweets;
    dispatch_queue_t _profileImageQueue;
    dispatch_semaphore_t _profileImageSemaphore;
    UIFont *_tweetFont;
    UIFont *_usernameFont;
}

- (void)reloadButtonPressed:(id)sender;
- (void)reloadTweets:(NSTimer *)reloadTimer;
- (void)tweetButtonPressed:(id)sender;

@end
```

Next, modify the initWithStyle: method to initialize those fonts by adding the lines in bold:

```
- (id)initWithStyle:(UITableViewStyle)style
{
```

```
    self = [super initWithStyle:style];

    if (self) {
        [self setTitle:@"Timeline"];

        UIBarButtonItem *reloadButton =
        [[UIBarButtonItem alloc]
initWithBarButtonSystemItem:UIBarButtonSystemItemRefresh
                                                    target:self

action:@selector(reloadButtonPressed:)];
        [[self navigationItem] setLeftBarButtonItem:reloadButton];

        UIBarButtonItem *tweetButton =
        [[UIBarButtonItem alloc]
initWithBarButtonSystemItem:UIBarButtonSystemItemCompose
                                                    target:self

action:@selector(tweetButtonPressed:)];
        [[self navigationItem] setRightBarButtonItem:tweetButton];

        _profileImageQueue =
dispatch_queue_create("com.learncocoatouch.profileImageQueue",
                                            DISPATCH_QUEUE_CONCURRENT);

        _profileImageSemaphore = dispatch_semaphore_create(3);

        _tweetFont = [UIFont fontWithName:@"HelveticaNeue-CondensedBold"
size:19.0f];
        _usernameFont = [UIFont italicSystemFontOfSize:14.0f];
    }

    return self;
}
```

Finally, let's modify tableView:cellForRowAtIndexPath: to use these fonts. Add the lines in bold (note that I skipped some lines with an ellipsis [...] rather than copy the method in its entirety):

```
- (UITableViewCell *)tableView:(UITableView *)tableView
        cellForRowAtIndexPath:(NSIndexPath *)indexPath
{
    static NSString *CellIdentifier = @"Cell";
    UITableViewCell *cell = [tableView
dequeueReusableCellWithIdentifier:CellIdentifier];

    if (cell == nil) {
        cell = [[UITableViewCell alloc]
initWithStyle:UITableViewCellStyleSubtitle
                                    reuseIdentifier:CellIdentifier];
```

```
    }

    ...

    [[cell textLabel] setTextColor:[UIColor whiteColor]];
    [[cell textLabel] setFont:_tweetFont];
    [[cell detailTextLabel] setTextColor:[UIColor whiteColor]];
    [[cell detailTextLabel] setFont:_usernameFont];

    return cell;
}
```

Build and run the app. You should see the new font in use, as in Figure 9-3.

Figure 9-3. *Our timeline view with custom fonts*

Now, as I mentioned earlier, we can use the font to help determine how large a label needs to be to draw an entire string without truncating it. We can use that knowledge to draw these table view cells at the correct height for the tweet length. First, let's modify the cell to draw its text label with multiple lines. In `tableView:cellForRowAtIndexPath:`, add the lines in bold (again, I've omitted some lines with an ellipsis):

```
- (UITableViewCell *)tableView:(UITableView *)tableView
         cellForRowAtIndexPath:(NSIndexPath *)indexPath
{
    static NSString *CellIdentifier = @"Cell";
    UITableViewCell *cell = [tableView
dequeueReusableCellWithIdentifier:CellIdentifier];

    if (cell == nil) {
        cell = [[UITableViewCell alloc]
initWithStyle:UITableViewCellStyleSubtitle
                                    reuseIdentifier:CellIdentifier];
    }

    ...

    [[cell textLabel] setLineBreakMode:UILineBreakModeWordWrap];
    [[cell textLabel] setNumberOfLines:0];
    [[cell textLabel] setTextColor:[UIColor whiteColor]];
    [[cell textLabel] setFont:[self tweetFont]];
    [[cell detailTextLabel] setTextColor:[UIColor whiteColor]];
    [[cell detailTextLabel] setFont:[self usernameFont]];

    return cell;
}
```

The first line we added sets the line break mode, which controls the label's behavior when the text is too wide for a single line. The next sets the number of lines to 0. This value is 1 by default. Setting the number of lines to more than one will draw the label with that many lines, but setting it to 0 will draw the label with as many lines as it needs and has space for. With this change, we're all set to change the height of the row. Add a new method immediately following `tableView:cellForRowAtIndexPath:` with the following implementation in bold:

```
- (CGFloat)tableView:(UITableView *)tableView
heightForRowAtIndexPath:(NSIndexPath *)indexPath
{
    CGFloat maxWidth = 240.0f;

    NSDictionary *tweet = [_tweets objectAtIndex:[indexPath row]];

    NSString *tweetText = [tweet objectForKey:@"text"];
```

```
    NSString *tweetUsername = [[tweet objectForKey:@"user"]
objectForKey:@"name"];

    // Get the height of the tweet over multiple lines
    CGSize tweetSizeConstraints = CGSizeMake(maxWidth, FLT_MAX);

    CGSize tweetSize = [tweetText sizeWithFont:[self tweetFont]
                            constrainedToSize:tweetSizeConstraints
                                lineBreakMode:UILineBreakModeWordWrap];

    CGFloat tweetHeight = tweetSize.height;

    // Get the height of the username on a single line
    CGSize usernameSize = [tweetUsername sizeWithFont:[self usernameFont]];
    CGFloat usernameHeight = usernameSize.height;

    return tweetHeight + usernameHeight + 8.0f;
}
```

The key methods here, both `NSString` instance methods, are `sizeWithFont:` and `sizeWithFont:constrainedToSize:lineBreakMode:`. The first of those, `sizeWithFont:`, simply returns the size of a string when drawn in a single line in a given font. The second takes a `CGSize` as a constraint, which defines the maximum size for the label, and a `UILineBreakMode` constant, which determines how the text is drawn over multiple lines. A `CGSize` is simply a C struct with two `CGFloat` values, one for `width` and one for `height`. We create a `CGSize` with essentially unlimited height by using `FLT_MAX` and then use it to constrain the tweet text when drawn with our tweet height. The `sizeWithFont:constrainedToSize:lineBreakMode:` method returns another `CGSize`, which is the size needed to draw the text with the given font, size constraints, and line break mode.

By adding these two heights, along with an 8-pixel margin, we can draw the cells at an appropriate height for their contents. The 240-pixel maximum width allows room for margins on either side of the label along with the image. To determine this value, I increased the height of the table views and then took a screenshot of the iPhone Simulator and used an image-editing program to determine its size. This isn't the most scientific way to determine the maximum width, but it works.

Build and run the app. Your table view cells should now be sized according to the tweet they contain, as in Figure 9-4.

Figure 9-4. *Our TwitterExample app drawing the table view cells with the correct height for their content*

Between custom colors and fonts, iOS user interfaces are already extremely customizable. Next up, we'll cover using images in your apps.

Using Images

We've already used the UIImage class a bit, having displayed images in both the TwitterExample and MyStuff sample projects. The UIImage class is used to represent basic images that we've loaded either from remote sources, such as Twitter; from the camera or photo library, as we used in MyStuff; or from the disk.

To use an image in your app, you first need to add it to your app. From Finder, drag it into the list of files in Xcode. You'll see a dialog, as in Figure 9-5. Alternatively, you can select File ➤ Add Files to MyProject… (where MyProject is your project's name), or press ⌘+Option+A. The resulting dialog will be similar to the one you see when dragging files in but with the addition of file selection component at the top with which you select files to add to the project. For either dialog, the checkbox next to your app's name indicates that you'd like to add it to that app. With that checked, when you build and run the app, the image will be included. The top checkbox, if checked, will copy the file into your app's directory. Generally, you'll want to copy files into the same directory as your app to protect against problems if you move the original file or move the project around on your disk. As your app grows to include more and more images, consider adding a group under Supporting Files for them to help organize your app's content. This is how you add any additional file to your app, whether it's an image, a movie, or even code. When you add other files to your target, Xcode will copy them to the application bundle at build time for most types of files, but code will be compiled into your app itself.

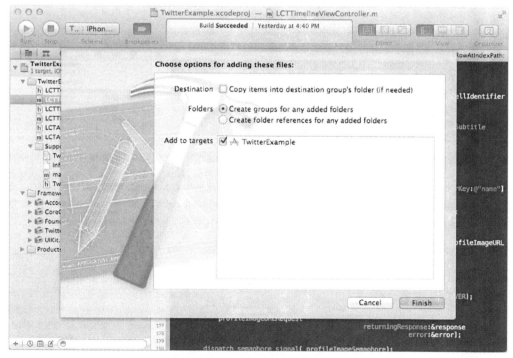

Figure 9-5. *The Add File dialog box in Xcode*

Once the image file has been included in your application's bundle by adding it to the target in Xcode, you can create a `UIImage` object with the `imageNamed:` class method, like so:

```
UIImage *myImage = [UIImage imageNamed:@"myImage"];
```

You don't need to specify a file extension; for any image format that `UIImage` supports, it will find the file in your app bundle and create the image appropriately. For a complete list of image formats supported, refer to the `UIImage` class documentation. To use a `UIImage` object, you can create a `UIImageView` object, which is just a view that draws the image to the screen. You can create a `UIImageView` like so:

```
UIImageView *myImageView = [[UIImageView alloc] initWithImage:myImage];
```

You can also create an image view in Interface Builder by dragging it from the Object Library onto your view.

Beginning with the iPhone 4 and the third-generation iPad, which have Retina displays, the screens have many more pixels—twice as many in each direction. Because of this, when you provide images with your application, you should provide two versions: one at the normal size and one with twice the resolution. If an image in your app is 37 pixels wide by 37 pixels tall, the double-resolution version should be 74 pixels wide and 74 pixels tall. Using the `UIImage` class and creating them with the `imageNamed:` class method will automatically load the correct image for the device, provided that you use the correct naming convention: the double-resolution version should have `@2x` appended to the file name but before the file extension. If your image file, for example, is named `blueButton.png`, then the Retina Display version should be named `blueButton@2x.png` and be twice the size in each dimension. If you don't provide a higher-resolution version of an image, then the system will automatically scale up the normal-resolution version, but that won't look as good and will mar your user experience. We'll talk more about the Retina Display as we cover view layout, but that's what you need to know about it for images.

Being able to create `UIImage` objects and `UIImageView` objects is important, but getting them on-screen makes this knowledge useful. As `UIImageView` is a subclass of `UIView`, it can be involved in the view hierarchy of your application, which is how it'll get on-screen. Next we'll talk about using the `UIView` class to manage a hierarchy of views to present your application's user interface.

View Layout

Up until now, your use of views has been pretty limited. Each view controller you've created has had a view, whether that's been created with Xcode's

Interface Builder or created implicitly by a UITableViewController. The table
views you've used have themselves had child elements, but up until now we
haven't been manipulating them directly too much. Before we do, let's cover
some of the fundamental aspects of the view system in Cocoa Touch.

View Hierarchy

Views in iOS maintain a strict hierarchy. Every view, except for the top-level
view, has a *superview*, and any view may have one or more *subviews*. This
parent-child relationship governs how elements are displayed. The top-level
view on iOS is an instance of the UIWindow class, representing your app's
window. Unlike desktop operating systems like Mac OS X or Windows, your
application may have only one window displayed on a screen at a particular
time—though it is possible to connect your iOS device to another display and
add a window to that display's screen. The Apple TV, for instance, allows you to
use AirPlay to add a TV to your app as a second display. To add a subview to a
view, use the addSubview: method. To add a view called myView to a UIWindow
called myWindow, you would write the following code:

```
[myWindow addSubview:myView];
```

The subviews of a view are arranged in order, which allows you to control which
view will be displayed on top when two views share the same location. You can
manipulate this order with UIView methods, including bringSubviewToFront:,
sendSubviewToBack:, insertSubview:atIndex:, insertSubview:aboveSubview:,
and insertSubview:belowSubview:. To swap two subviews' order, you can use
the exchangeSubviewAtIndex:withSubviewAtIndex: method. To remove a view
from its superview, call its removeFromSuperview method.

View Coordinate Systems

Every view has its own coordinate system. The coordinate system's origin is the
upper-left corner of the view (if you've previously programmed on Mac OS X,
recall that this is different, because Mac OS X's coordinate systems have origins
in the bottom left). The CGRect struct is used to represent the coordinate system
inside of a view, represented with the bounds property. A CGRect has two
members: origin, a CGPoint struct; and size, a CGSize struct. The CGPoint
struct has in turn two members: x and y, both CGFloat values representing a
coordinate in the coordinate system. The CGSize has two members: width and
height, also CGFloat values. Finally, CGFloat values are just regular float values
defined as a type.

The UIWindow object for a typical iPhone app has a **bounds** property whose origin member is the point (0, 0), and whose size member has a **width** value of 320 and a **height** value of 480.

Inside of their superviews, individual UIView objects have a **frame** property, which defines their size and location in the coordinate system of their superview. The **frame** property is also a CGRect and is defined in terms of the parent's coordinate system. A view with a width of 100 and a height of 100, placed in the center of a standard-sized UIWindow on an iPhone, would have a **frame** property whose origin member is the point (110, 190) and whose size member has a **width** value of 100 and a **height** value of 100. Figure 9-6 displays the two views in relation to one another, laid on a coordinate grid with the origin of the superview's **bounds** and the origin of the subview's **frame** displayed.

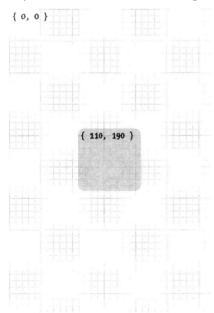

Figure 9-6. *A view inside of another view. The subview, here represented by a gray rounded rectangle, is centered in the view, represented with a coordinate grid.*

It's important to note that a view is always placed inside the coordinate system of its superview according to the origin member of its **frame** property. If we added a subview to the previous gray, rounded rectangle view with the **origin** of (0, 0), it would appear at the upper-left corner of the previous view, *not* at the upper-left corner of the window. In the window's coordinate system, it would be at (110, 190), just like its superview. Similarly, since the **bounds** property represents the internal coordinate system of the view (as opposed to the frame property, which represents the view's location and size in its superview's coordinate system), the previous subview's bounds property would have a size member with a width value of 100 and a height value of 100, but its origin member would be the point (0, 0). In fact, since all views' coordinate systems begin at (0, 0), the bounds property of every UIView object will by default have the same origin. You can change the origin of the bounds property to adjust the portion of the view that will be displayed.

> **NOTE:** Although the UIView class has a center property that returns the center point of the view, you should treat it as a read-only property. If you try to set the center property on a view with odd dimensions, you may wind up with an origin that's not on an even pixel boundary, such as (55.5, 102.5). This will cause your view to appear blurry because of rendering bugs. Similarly, when setting the frame property of a view, always use whole numbers to avoid rendering issues or coerce the values you use to whole numbers with floorf() or roundf().

View Display Properties

The UIView class defines several properties that you can use to customize its appearance and behavior without creating a subclass of UIView. Some are straightforward, such as backgroundColor, a UIColor object representing the background color of the view, and alpha, a CGFloat for the transparency of the object ranging from 0 (fully transparent) to 1 (fully opaque). To give a view a blue background and make it half-transparent, you would set the properties as follows:

```
[myView setAlpha:0.5f];
[myView setBackgroundColor:[UIColor blueColor]];
```

> **NOTE:** One of the properties defined in the UIView class is opaque, a BOOL value that acts as a hint to the rendering engine. If the view completely fills its bounds with opaque content—that is, content without any transparency—then it should be considered opaque, so its opaque property should be set to YES (the default value). For any view that is either semitransparent or doesn't entirely fill its bounds, you should set its opaque property to NO. Properly setting the opaque property can improve drawing performance and avoid unpredictable side effects.

View Autosizing

Other UIView properties are not so straightforward. One of the most important is autoresizingMask. This property is a bitmask that controls how the view behaves when its superview is resized. There are six bits you can set:

- UIViewAutoresizingFlexibleLeftMargin
- UIViewAutoresizingFlexibleWidth
- UIViewAutoresizingFlexibleRightMargin
- UIViewAutoresizingFlexibleTopMargin
- UIViewAutoresizingFlexibleHeight
- UIViewAutoresizingFlexibleBottomMargin

If UIViewAutoresizingFlexibleWidth is set, the view will automatically become wider as its superview becomes wider, and similarly if UIViewAutoresizingFlexibleHeight is set, the view will automatically become taller as its superview becomes taller. The other four, when not set, "anchor" the view to the sides of its superview; for a given side, if the corresponding margin value is not set, the view will remain the same distance from that side no matter what. One of the most common autoresizing masks is simply flexible width and flexible height, which keeps the view the same distance from each side of its superview no matter how its superview changes in dimensions, growing as needed to do so. If you do not want the view to resize at all, use UIViewAutoresizingNone, which is the absence of any of these bits being set.

If you're using Interface Builder to lay out your view, you can set the autoresizing mask visually. Referred to as *springs* and *struts*, you set the values by clicking a virtual map of the view. With the view selected, show the Size Inspector by pressing ⌘+Option+5 or selecting View ➤ Utilities ➤ Show Size Inspector. Figure 9-7 shows the Size Inspector. The bottom portion contains the autoresizing mask, above the Autosizing label. Inside the box are the two springs that represent UIViewAutoresizingFlexibleWidth and UIViewAutoresizingFlexibleHeight as the horizontal and vertical lines, respectively. Click them to toggle the corresponding bit. The outer lines are the struts, which represent the other bit values. Click them to toggle their corresponding bits. The springs and struts are a solid red line if their bit is set or a faded and dashed red line if their bits are not set. To the right is a live preview above the "Example" label that demonstrates the effect your chosen settings will have on a view that is constantly growing and shrinking while your mouse pointer is hovered over the "Autoresizing" section or the preview itself.

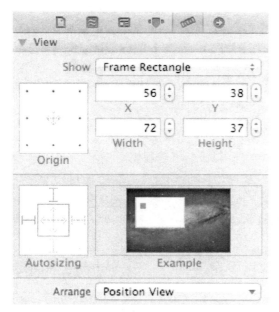

Figure 9-7. *The Size Inspector, with the springs and struts that set the view's autoresizing values*

View Content Modes

Another property of UIView that takes some explaining is the contentMode property. As a view is resized, this property defines how its content is redrawn. By default, a view is not redrawn, but rather its contents are resized, because this is more efficient. The possible values of this property are as follows:

- UIViewContentModeScaleToFill
- UIViewContentModeScaleAspectFit
- UIViewContentModeScaleAspectFill
- UIViewContentModeRedraw
- UIViewContentModeCenter
- UIViewContentModeTop
- UIViewContentModeBottom
- UIViewContentModeLeft
- UIViewContentModeRight
- UIViewContentModeTopLeft

- UIViewContentModeTopRight

- UIViewContentModeBottomLeft

- UIViewContentModeBottomRight

Don't worry, I won't explain each one individually. The first three, ScaleToFill, ScaleAspectFit, and ScaleAspectFill, each scale the original contents. ScaleToFill simply resizes the contents to fit the new view exactly, stretching it if necessary and disregarding its aspect ratio. This is best for content such as gradient or a solid color that doesn't need to maintain its aspect ratio. ScaleAspectFit and ScaleAspectFill both maintain the original aspect ratio of the content. ScaleAspectFit ensures that the original content is displayed in its entirety, making it smaller if it needs to but making it as large as it can without cutting any of it off; any remaining area is filled in with the view's background color. ScaleAspectFill resizes the original content to completely fill the new size, cutting off the top, bottom, or sides as necessary. UIViewContentModeRedraw forces the system to redraw the content for the new size. This is the least-efficient choice but is useful if you need to redraw your content to react to size changes. The rest of the content view modes don't resize the content as the view's size changes but instead anchor it to the specified point.

The content view mode is most useful when dealing with images. Since image content usually has a specific aspect ratio, it's usually best to use either UIViewContentModeScaleAspectFit or UIViewContentModeScaleAspectFill for image views.

View Layout in UIView Subclasses

When you create your own UIView subclasses, they may have subviews of their own. You might, for instance, create a UIView object that contains a UILabel and a UIImage. While the subviews' autoresizing masks go a long way toward customizing this view's behavior, you might want something more customized. You may want, for instance, to display the label underneath the image view if the view is taller than it is wide but to the right of it if the view is wider than it is tall. To accomplish this goal, you would implement the layoutSubviews method in your UIView subclass as follows:

```
- (void)layoutSubviews
{
    [super layoutSubviews];

    CGFloat width = [self bounds].size.width;
```

```
    CGFloat height = [self bounds].size.height;

    CGRect imageFrame;
    CGRect labelFrame;

    if (width > height) {
        imageFrame = CGRectMake(0.0f, 0.0f, height, height);
        labelFrame = CGRectMake(height, 0.0f, width - height, height);
    }
    else {
        imageFrame = CGRectMake(0.0f, 0.0f, width, width);
        labelFrame = CGRectMake(0.0f, width, height - width, width);
    }

    [[self imageView] setFrame:imageFrame];
    [[self label] setFrame:labelFrame];
}
```

This method will, assuming an image view property named `imageView` and a label property named `label`, will make the image square, with the label to its right if the view's width is larger than its height or the label underneath if the view's height is larger than its width.

View Layout on Retina Display Devices

Just as with images, there are some things you need to know for Retina Display–equipped devices when laying out your views. Most of the actual code that you'll write, thankfully, is unchanged, but when dealing with a designer, it will help to know how the Retina Display is handled by the operating system.

Screen dimensions, when drawing and positioning views, are *not* measured in pixels. Instead, they're measured in *points*, an abstract measurement that corresponds to pixels depending on the resolution of the device. On an iPhone, iPhone 3G, or iPhone 3GS, along with their corresponding iPod touch counterparts, the screen is 320 pixels wide and 480 pixels tall and is measured in points at 320 points wide and 480 points tall. The iPhone 4, iPhone 4S, and potentially later iPhone devices, along with *their* iPod touch counterparts, have screens that are 640 pixels wide and 960 pixels tall. In points, however, the measurements are the same: 320 points wide and 480 points tall. So, when you consider the `frame` property of a `UIWindow` on an iPhone 4S, its `size` member's values are 320 and 480, *not* 640 and 960. What this means for developers is that you don't need to do *any* extra work for an existing application to work properly on a Retina Display. If you simply provide double-sized images, the layout is the same.

When you're working with a designer, however, they typically have a dilemma. They'll want to make a Photoshop document that's 640 by 960 pixels large, which they ought to do in order to support a Retina Display iPhone. Inevitably, however, they'll create a button or a title or a logo that's meant for the Retina Display size but has odd dimensions. This presents a problem, because the Retina Display–sized images must be exactly twice the size in each dimension as their non–Retina Display counterparts. The proper thing to do is to *design* user interface elements for a 320-pixel by 480-pixel screen and then generate them at *exactly* twice the size.

Nonimage elements, such as text, should be displayed in the proper size automatically by the system.

View Layout on iPad

Another circumstance that can cause your view layout code to change is running on an iPad. The same app can run on an iPad and iPhone, so there may be times when you need to determine in code which device you're running on. To do that, you can use the UIDevice class, which represents the device the app is running on, like so:

```
BOOL isPad = ([[UIDevice currentDevice] userInterfaceIdiom] ==
UIUserInterfaceIdiomPad);
```

The userInterfaceIdiom method of UIDevice returns either UIUserInterfaceIdiomPad or UIUserInterfaceIdiomPhone, depending on the device (on an iPod touch, it will return the latter). There's a helpful macro defined called UI_USER_INTERFACE_IDIOM(), which replaces the call to UIDevice, as well as wrapping the call in safety checks in case your code needs to run on iOS 3.1.3 or older, which didn't have the userInterfaceIdiom method of UIDevice. The previous line could be written as follows to use the macro:

```
BOOL isPad = (UI_USER_INTERFACE_IDIOM() == UIUserInterfaceIdiomPad);
```

Just as with the iPhone, the Retina Display of the third-generation iPad uses the @2x suffix for high-resolution graphics. As a convention, the suffix ~ipad is often used to denote the iPad version of a file, with the ~iphone suffix (or no suffix) for the iPhone version. A single image, then, might have four variations:

- blueButton~iphone.png
- blueButton~iphone@2x.png
- blueButton~ipad.png
- blueButton~ipad@2x.png

As you can imagine, it's very easy for your image files to multiply in number such that your app's file size is quite large, especially if you have full-sized graphics on both iPhone and iPad.

View Animation

One of the things that makes the iPhone so successful is that using it feels like magic. This might seem like something a marketing department would dream up to say, but the fact is that providing a compelling user interface can make your users feel like they're not interacting with an iPhone or an iPad but rather interacting *directly* with your app. A good way to get this feeling is to increase the interactivity of your app with animations. Some animations are built in, such as when you navigate from one view controller to another in a navigation controller. Others you can create yourself. To animate your views, there are some class methods on `UIView` you can use. For a basic example, here's how you would animate a `UIView` named `myView` from fully opaque (100 percent opacity) to fully transparent (0 percent opacity) over a two-second span:

```
[UIView animateWithDuration:2.0
            animations:^{
                [myView setAlpha:0.0f];
            }];
```

`animateWithDuration:animations:` is the most basic animation method available. The first parameter is an `NSTimeInterval` value, which is really just a `double`, and the second is a block. In this block, simply set the properties of the view you'd like to animate, and the `UIView` class will take care of creating the animation. Many properties are animatable in this manner:

- `frame`
- `bounds`
- `center` (though animating this property has the same drawbacks as setting it directly)
- `transform`
- `alpha`
- `backgroundColor`
- `contentStretch`

To animate a view moving across the screen, you would change its `frame` value to the frame you'd like it to have at the end of the animation. There are also more complicated, but more powerful, animation methods available, the most

powerful of which being
`animateWithDuration:delay:options:animations:completion:`. This mouthful of
a method, along with the other methods with a parameter named `completion`,
allow you to run a block of code when the animation is finished. This code
sample waits five seconds and then animates `myView` to become fully
transparent; when it's done, it removes `myView` from its superview:

```
[UIView animateWithDuration:2.0
                      delay:5.0
                    options:0
                 animations:^{
                     [myView setAlpha:0.0f];
                 }
                 completion:^(BOOL finished) {
                     [myView removeFromSuperview];
                 }];
```

The `completion` parameter takes a block with one argument, a `BOOL` value named
`finished`. If the animation completes successfully, then `finished` will be set to
YES. If it does not, which could happen if, for instance, the superview of `myView`
was removed from the view hierarchy, then `finished` will be set to `NO`.

You can nest animations, as well. The following code would replace `myView` with
`myOtherView`, fading `myView` out and fading `myOtherView` in:

```
[UIView animateWithDuration:2.0
                      delay:5.0
                    options:0
                 animations:^{
                     [myView setAlpha:0.0f];
                 }
                 completion:^(BOOL finished) {
                     [[myView superview] addSubview:myOtherView];
                     [myView removeFromSuperview];

                     [myOtherView setAlpha:0.0f];

                     [UIView animateWithDuration:2.0
                                      animations:^{
                                          [myOtherView setAlpha:1.0f];
                                      }];
                 }];
```

As you can see, before we animate `myOtherView`, we set its `alpha` property to 0.
Since we changed this property *outside* of an animation block, it happens
instantly.

Animations are a great way to add a touch of life to your applications. Great apps use animations in subtle ways, guiding the user through using them. A clever example of animation can be found in Apple's Maps app. When you search for something and the results are displayed on the map as pins, the pins don't just *appear*, instead, they drop down from above, helping the user to see where they're going. The human brain is wired to notice movement; animations can exploit that to gain your user's attention.

Example: Reddit Photo Browser

To demonstrate our newfound user interface skills, let's build a cool photo browser for the social news aggregator Reddit. If you're unfamiliar with Reddit, it organizes its content into subcategories of the site called *subreddits*. Our app, which we'll call RedditPics, will display an animated slideshow of pictures posted to Reddit.

The first question to answer when building an app based on a third-party API is, "How do I get to the data?" For Reddit, the answer is simple: simply append `.json` to any URL to receive the contents of that URL in JSON. We can get the main JSON feed for the front page by loading this URL:

```
http://www.reddit.com/.json
```

The JSON feed will return an array of items, each of which has a URL. We'll inspect the URL for image file extensions—`.png`, `.jpg`, and `.gif`—and download those images for our slideshow. On top of this, we'll make the app universal so it can run on iPhone and iPad. Open Xcode and select "Create a new Xcode project" from the Welcome screen. If the Welcome screen does not appear, select File ➤ New ➤ Project..., or press ⌘+Shift+N. Select Application under iOS on the left column, and then choose the Single View Application template and click Next. For Product Name, use RedditSlideshow. If you don't already have a Company Identifier or Class Prefix set, put them in now; I'll use `com.learncocoatouch` and LCT, respectively. Select iPhone for Device Family. Use Storyboards and Include Unit Tests should be unchecked, while Use Automatic Reference Counting should be checked. Verify that those settings are correct, and click Next. Choose where you'd like to save your project to disk, and click Next again to create the project.

The first thing we'll do is display one image. First, we'll need to load the Reddit site and parse its JSON output. To do this, first we'll declare a method to parse the JSON in our class extension, and while we're at it, we'll declare an array we'll use to store the returned image URLs. Navigate to `LCTViewController.m` (your file name may vary based on your class prefix). If there's a class extension in the `LCTViewController.m` file, then add the line in bold below to it. If not, add the class extension below in its entirety to the top of the file, *before* the @implementation directive, as well as the @synthesize line:

```
@interface LCTViewController ()

@property (strong) NSMutableArray *imageURLs;

- (void)parseJSONData:(NSData *)jsonData;

@end

@implementation LCTViewController

@synthesize imageURLs = _imageURLs;
```

Next, locate the viewDidLoad method. If there is no viewDidLoad method, copy the following code in its entirety between the view controller's @implementation and @end directives; otherwise, just add the lines in bold:

```
- (void)viewDidLoad
{
    [super viewDidLoad];
    // Do any additional setup after loading the view, typically from a nib.

    NSURL *redditURL = [NSURL
URLWithString:@"http://www.reddit.com/r/aww/.json"];
    NSURLRequest *redditURLRequest = [NSURLRequest requestWithURL:redditURL];

    [NSURLConnection sendAsynchronousRequest:redditURLRequest
                                 queue:[NSOperationQueue currentQueue]
                     completionHandler:^(NSURLResponse *response,
                                         NSData *data,
                                         NSError *error) {
                         if (data != nil) {
                             [self parseJSONData:data];
                         }
                         else {
                             NSLog(@"Error loading JSON: %@", error);
                         }
                     }];
}
```

> **NOTE:** Reddit, like many other things on the Internet, consists of user-generated content. It's possible for the content returned from it to be inappropriate for small children, offensive, or culturally insensitive. The URL used earlier points to a portion of the site (called a *subreddit*) reserved for cute pictures, usually of animals, called "aww." Other subreddits may not contain the same type of content; browse at your own risk.

This code loads the Reddit URL and checks to see whether data was returned. If it was, it passes the data to the `parseJSONData:` method. Let's implement that method. If you look at the JSON returned from the web service, its top-level object is a dictionary, followed with a `data` key, which has a key called `children` that maps to an array of child dictionaries. In *those* dictionaries, we'll look at the `url` key to see whether the link is an image. Add the method implementation blow to the class implementation, before the `@end` compiler directive at the end of the file:

```objc
- (void)parseJSONData:(NSData *)jsonData
{
    [self setImageURLs:[NSMutableArray array]];

    NSError *parseError = nil;

    id returnedObject = [NSJSONSerialization JSONObjectWithData:jsonData
                                                       options:0
                                                         error:&parseError];

    if (returnedObject != nil) {
        if ([returnedObject isKindOfClass:[NSDictionary class]]) {
            NSDictionary *data = [returnedObject objectForKey:@"data"];

            NSArray *children = [data objectForKey:@"children"];

            for (NSDictionary *childDict in children) {
                NSString *url = [[childDict objectForKey:@"data"]
objectForKey:@"url"];

                // Is this an image?
                if ([url hasSuffix:@".png"] ||
                    [url hasSuffix:@".jpg"] ||
                    [url hasSuffix:@".jpeg"] ||
                    [url hasSuffix:@".gif"]) {
                    NSURL *imageURL = [NSURL URLWithString:url];
                    [[self imageURLs] addObject:imageURL];
                }
            }
```

```
        }
    }
    else {
        NSLog(@"Error parsing data: %@", parseError);
    }
}
```

This code walks the response, looking for URLs with image extensions and populating the `imageURLs` array with matches. When it's done, the `imageURLs` array is populated with `NSURL` objects, each representing a different image. Once we have the list of URLs, we need to display the images on-screen! First, add an instance variable, a property and two method declarations to the class extension, synthesized accessor methods for the property, as well as a constant we'll use later, by adding the lines in bold to the top of `LCTViewController.m`:

```
static const NSTimeInterval kPictureDisplayTime = 15.0;

@interface LCTViewController () {
    NSUInteger _currentImageIndex;
}

@property (strong) NSMutableArray *imageURLs;
@property (strong) UIImageView *imageView;

- (void)parseJSONData:(NSData *)jsonData;
- (void)startSlideshow;
- (void)loadNextImageInSlideshow;

@end

@implementation LCTViewController

@synthesize imageURLs = _imageURLs;
@synthesize imageView = _imageView;
```

We'll use the `startSlideshow` method to load the first image and the `loadNextImageInSlideshow` method to proceed to the next. So, modify the `viewDidLoad` method to call `startSlideshow` after parsing the data returned from Reddit by adding the line in bold:

```
- (void)viewDidLoad
{
    [super viewDidLoad];
    // Do any additional setup after loading the view, typically from a nib.

    NSURL *redditURL = [NSURL
URLWithString:@"http://www.reddit.com/r/aww/.json"];
    NSURLRequest *redditURLRequest = [NSURLRequest requestWithURL:redditURL];
```

```
[NSURLConnection sendAsynchronousRequest:redditURLRequest
                              queue:[NSOperationQueue currentQueue]
                  completionHandler:^(NSURLResponse *response,
                                      NSData *data,
                                      NSError *error) {
                      if (data != nil) {
                          [self parseJSONData:data];
                          [self startSlideshow];
                      }
                      else {
                          NSLog(@"Error loading JSON: %@", [error
localizedDescription]);
                      }
                  }];
}
```

Next, add the startSlideshow method's implementation, as well as an empty implementation for loadNextImageInSlideshow (so the app doesn't crash if we call it) by inserting the following code in bold after the parseJSONData: method but before the @end directive:

```
- (void)startSlideshow
{
    if ([[self imageURLs] count] == 0) {
        return;
    }

    UIActivityIndicatorView *activityIndicatorView = [[UIActivityIndicatorView
alloc] initWithActivityIndicatorStyle:UIActivityIndicatorViewStyleGray];

    CGRect activityIndicatorFrame = [activityIndicatorView frame];

    activityIndicatorFrame.origin =
    CGPointMake(floorf((CGRectGetWidth([[self view] bounds]) +
                    CGRectGetWidth(activityIndicatorFrame)) / 2.0f),
            floorf((CGRectGetHeight([[self view] bounds]) +
                    CGRectGetHeight(activityIndicatorFrame)) / 2.0f));

    [activityIndicatorView setFrame:activityIndicatorFrame];
    [[self view] addSubview:activityIndicatorView];
    [activityIndicatorView startAnimating];

    // Load the first image
    _currentImageIndex = 0;
    NSURL *firstURL = [[self imageURLs] objectAtIndex:0];
    NSURLRequest *firstImageRequest = [NSURLRequest requestWithURL:firstURL];

    [NSURLConnection sendAsynchronousRequest:firstImageRequest
                              queue:[NSOperationQueue currentQueue]
                  completionHandler:^(NSURLResponse *response,
```

```
                                    NSData *data,
                                    NSError *error) {
                  UIImage *image = [UIImage imageWithData:data];

                  if (image == nil) {
                      return;
                  }

                  UIImageView *imageView =
                  [[UIImageView alloc] initWithImage:image];

                  [imageView
setAutoresizingMask:(UIViewAutoresizingFlexibleWidth|UIViewAutoresizingFlexibleH
eight)];
                  [imageView
setContentMode:UIViewContentModeScaleAspectFit];

                  [imageView setFrame:[[self view] bounds]];
                  [[self view] addSubview:imageView];
                  [activityIndicatorView removeFromSuperview];

                  [self setImageView:imageView];

                  int64_t popTime =
                  kPictureDisplayTime * NSEC_PER_SEC;

                  dispatch_time_t nextPictureLoadDelay =
                  dispatch_time(DISPATCH_TIME_NOW,
                              popTime);

                  dispatch_after(nextPictureLoadDelay,
                              dispatch_get_main_queue(),
                              ^{
                                  [self
loadNextImageInSlideshow];
                              });
                  }];
}

- (void)loadNextImageInSlideshow
{

}
```

This code creates a URL request for the first image and then loads it with an
asynchronous connection. When the data is loaded, it creates a UIImage object
from it and then an image view with which we'll display the image. Next it
creates a dispatch_time_t time representation using the popTime variable and
schedules the loadNextImageInSlideshow after that amount of time.

Build and run the app, and you should see an image appear once it's loaded, before which you should see an activity indicator. Once that's done, the app won't do anything else, because we've left the loadNextImageInSlideshow method blank. Let's fill it in to get our slideshow loading new images! Add the following code in bold to the implementation of loadNextImageInSlideshow:

```
- (void)loadNextImageInSlideshow
{
    _currentImageIndex += 1;

    if (_currentImageIndex >= [[self imageURLs] count]) {
        return;
    }

    NSURL *imageURL = [[self imageURLs] objectAtIndex:_currentImageIndex];
    NSURLRequest *urlRequest = [NSURLRequest requestWithURL:imageURL];

    [NSURLConnection sendAsynchronousRequest:urlRequest
                                queue:[NSOperationQueue currentQueue]
                    completionHandler:^(NSURLResponse *response, NSData
*data, NSError *error) {
                        UIImage *image = [UIImage imageWithData:data];

                        if (image == nil) {
                            return;
                        }

                        UIImageView *nextImageView = [[UIImageView alloc]
initWithImage:image];

                        [nextImageView
setAutoresizingMask:(UIViewAutoresizingFlexibleWidth |

UIViewAutoresizingFlexibleHeight)];
                        [nextImageView
setContentMode:UIViewContentModeScaleAspectFit];

                        [nextImageView setFrame:[[self view] bounds]];
                        [nextImageView setAlpha:0.0f];

                        [[self view] addSubview:nextImageView];

                        [UIView animateWithDuration:1.0
                                        animations:^{
                                            [[self imageView]
setAlpha:0.0f];

                                            [nextImageView
setAlpha:1.0f];
                                        }
```

```
                                        completion:^(BOOL finished) {
                                            [[self imageView]
removeFromSuperview];

                                            [self
setImageView:nextImageView];

                                        }];

                        int64_t popTime =
                        kPictureDisplayTime * NSEC_PER_SEC;

                        dispatch_time_t nextPictureLoadDelay =
                        dispatch_time(DISPATCH_TIME_NOW,
                                        popTime);

                        dispatch_after(nextPictureLoadDelay,
                                        dispatch_get_main_queue(),
                                        ^{
                                            [self
loadNextImageInSlideshow];
                                        });

                }];
}
```

This method is quite similar to the one before it; it fetches the next URL, downloads the image data, and creates an image view. What's new is the animation it uses. The old image view fades out (its `alpha` property animates to 0) as the new image fades in (its `alpha` property animates to 1). Once we've loaded the new image, we schedule the next to load the same way: creating a `dispatch_time_t` time representation and scheduling a block after that amount of time.

Build and run the app again, and there you have it! You should now be seeing a slideshow of Reddit pictures, complete with an animated transition between images!

Summary

This chapter has been all about user interfaces. By now you should be able to create a user interface that's customized to your liking, helping make your app stand out from the crowd. You should be able to use fonts, colors, and images to design your views, as well as lay them out on-screen and animate them. In the next chapter, we'll explore some of the APIs available to interact with hardware components such as the GPS chip and accelerometer, giving you more data to represent on-screen.

Chapter 10

Hardware APIs

One of the debates that comes up frequently in conversations about mobile development is the idea of web apps vs. native apps. So far, we've been writing native apps exclusively; by *native app*, we mean an app written in Objective-C, compiled into a binary executable format, and installed on a device. The alternative, a *web app*, is written in HTML, CSS, and JavaScript; installed onto a server; and accessed via a browser—instead of being compiled into executable binaries, the JavaScript is interpreted at runtime. There are some frameworks available that try to bridge the gap, essentially hiding the web site inside a native app that is no more than a web browser, but it's usually easy to tell the difference between native apps and web apps. Native apps run faster, have smoother user interaction, and can do more on the phone than their web counterparts. This book has been about writing native apps, and this chapter is about them doing more.

The iPhone, iPod touch, and iPad have several hardware sensors you can use to your advantage. Packed into these tiny devices are one or two cameras, one or two microphones, a GPS chip, an accelerometer, a gyroscope, and even a magnetometer! We can use these sensors to our advantage, enabling apps to know where you are, how fast you're moving, and what direction you're facing. The accelerometer can tell us how you're holding the device, and the gyroscope tells us how you're moving it. Put this data into your app, and you can create engaging, immersive experiences. In this chapter, we'll cover using the camera, accelerometer, gyroscope, GPS, and magnetomer, as well as their related frameworks. We'll look at some sample code and extend our Twitter example app to use your current location. First, we'll cover using the camera to take pictures and video.

Using the Camera

We've already used the camera APIs a bit in the MyStuff example project, where we used them to get an image for a possession and save it to disk. In that project, however, we only scratched the surface of what's possible with the camera APIs. There are two ways to use the camera on an iOS device: first, as we did in MyStuff, to use the UIImagePickerController class and its built-in UI to get an image from the camera, and second, to use the AVFoundation framework. The AVFoundation framework is an advanced audiovisual framework created by Apple for iOS and later brought back to Mac OS X. It can be used for many powerful tasks, including audio and video playback, real-time video manipulation, and even video editing! In fact, the iMovie app for iOS was written using AVFoundation using no private APIs, so everything Apple does in that app is possible for you to do in yours.

AVFoundation is a very advanced framework, and as such we won't be covering it here. Plenty of books are available on the subject, and Apple's documentation is helpful as ever.

Using UIImagePickerController for Photos

To accomplish most tasks having to do with photos, we can use the UIImagePickerController class for our needs. As we've seen in MyStuff, creating an image picker controller and displaying it are simple tasks:

```
UIImagePickerController *imagePickerController =
[[UIImagePickerController alloc] init];

[imagePickerController setSourceType:UIImagePickerControllerSourceTypeCamera];

[imagePickerController setDelegate:self];

[self presentModalViewController:imagePickerController animated:YES];
```

This code creates a UIImagePickerController called imagePickerController. Next, it sets its source type to UIImagePickerControllerSourceTypeCamera, which causes it to take a picture; we could have used UIImagePickerControllerSourceTypePhotoLibrary or UIImagePickerControllerSourceTypeSavedPhotosAlbum to use pictures already on the user's device. In the sample code, we have a view controller named myViewController that we set as the delegate for the image picker controller. We then use this view controller to present the image picker controller. It's common to see one view controller do both of these things; since the delegate to the image picker controller is also responsible for removing it from the screen, it makes sense to have it also responsible for displaying the image picker controller in the first place.

An image picker controller presented this way will, by default, show the default controls for taking a picture and either return one picture to its delegate via the imagePickerController:didFinishPickingMediaWithInfo: method or indicate that the user canceled it via the imagePickerControllerDidCancel: method. There are plenty of ways to customize a UIImagePickerController to behave differently. One of the easiest is to add an overlay view to the image preview, which you can use to help line up a photo or just to match your application's UI. Figure 10-1 displays an image picker controller with a custom overlay view.

Figure 10-1. *An image picker controller with a custom overlay view*

This overlay is just a semitransparent image. The code to create an image picker controller and then create an image view to use as an overlay is as follows (the image file is named `Overlay.png`):

```
UIImagePickerController *imagePickerController =
[[UIImagePickerController alloc] init];

[imagePickerController setSourceType:UIImagePickerControllerSourceTypeCamera];

// "self" in this case should be an instance of a subclass of UIViewController
// that conforms to both the UIImagePickerControllerDelegate and
// UINavigationControllerDelegate protocols.
[imagePickerController setDelegate:self];

UIImage *overlayImage = [UIImage imageNamed:@"Overlay"];
UIImageView *overlayView = [[UIImageView alloc] initWithImage:overlayImage];

[imagePickerController setCameraOverlayView:overlayView];

[self presentModalViewController:imagePickerController animated:YES];
```

Any `UIVIew` subclass will do; simply set the `cameraOverlayView` property of the image picker controller to your overlay view.

Custom overlays can do much more than look pretty. In fact, you can completely replace the default chrome of the image picker controller in favor of your own custom UI; just set the `showsCameraControls` property of your image picker controller to `NO`. If you do this, you'll need to implement your own button to take pictures with. That button, which should be a subview of the overlay view, should call the `takePicture` method of the image picker controller, which will result in the image picker controller calling `imagePickerController:didFinishPickingMediaWithInfo:` on its delegate.

If you do implement your own overlay UI with a "take picture" button, you can then use the image picker controller to take multiple pictures, which is something you can't do with the default UI. Every time you call `takePicture` on your image picker controller, it will send another picture to its delegate, but you can't take another picture while the first picture's delegate method is still processing. This can be quite useful if you want to take several pictures in succession.

When you hide the built-in camera UI, you also hide the controls that allow the user to turn on the camera flash. If you'd like to provide your own control to enable or disable the flash, you can control that setting of the image picker controller through its `cameraFlashMode` property. The valid settings are `UIImagePickerControllerCameraFlashModeAuto`, which is the default setting;

UIImagePickerControllerCameraFlashModeOff; and
UIImagePickerControllerCameraFlashModeOn. Note that not all iOS devices with cameras also have a flash, so this setting may be ignored.

Another camera control that the built-in UI provides is a button to switch between the rear-facing camera and the front-facing camera on iOS devices with two cameras. You can control this setting using the image picker controller, as well; simply set the cameraDevice property to either
UIImagePickerControllerCameraDeviceRear or
UIImagePickerControllerCameraDeviceFront. Before doing so, you'll need to make sure that the selected device is available by calling the
UIImagePickerController class method isCameraDeviceAvailable: and passing the desired device as the parameter. You can also use the camera device to determine whether flash is available or not through the
UIImagePickerController class method isFlashAvailableForCameraDevice:.
Through proper use of these methods, you can avoid adding a button to the camera UI to set unavailable options; if, for instance, the user switches the camera from the rear-facing camera that has a flash to the front-facing camera that does not have a flash, then you should remove or disable the flash button you've provided.

Although providing your own UI for an image picker controller can be powerful, there are advantages to using the built-in UI. If you set the allowsEditing property of the image picker controller to YES, then after the user takes a picture, they will be prompted to edit it, allowing them to crop it and move the cropped image around. If you do this, then the image picker controller's delegate can access both the original image and the edited image by using different keys in the dictionary passed as a parameter. Here's how you would get each image:

```
- (void)imagePickerController:(UIImagePickerController *)picker
didFinishPickingMediaWithInfo:(NSDictionary *)info
{
    UIImage *originalImage = [info
objectForKey:UIImagePickerControllerOriginalImage];
    UIImage *editedImage = [info
objectForKey:UIImagePickerControllerEditedImage];
    ...
}
```

When you allow the user the chance to edit the pictures they take with the image picker controller, you should be sure to use the edited image if it exists and to use the original image if it doesn't, which will happen if the user doesn't edit the image at all. If you allow them to edit it, you should not use the original image, because they won't be expecting your app to have received it.

Using UIImagePickerController for Videos

If you'd like the ability to use video in your app, the UIImagePickerController class provides much of the same functionality for videos as it does for photos. To use an image picker controller properly for videos, you first need to tell it what kind of media you'd like via its mediaTypes property. mediaTypes is an NSArray, and by default the only thing in it is kUTTypeImage, which corresponds to images. The alternative is kUTTypeMovie for movies. The available media types for an image picker controller depend on its source type (for example, the camera or photo library). So, to set an image picker controller to give us video only, we would use the following code:

```
[imagePickerController setMediaTypes:[NSArray
arrayWithObject:(id)kUTTypeMovie]];
```

> **NOTE:** To use the kUTTypeMovie constant, you'll need to import the header file that declares it by adding this line at the top of your file:
>
> `#import <MobileCoreServices/UTCoreTypes.h>`
>
> You will also need to link your project against the MobileCoreServices framework.

Since the mediaTypes property is an array, you can create an image picker controller that can select or capture both pictures and videos. To do so, simply set the mediaTypes property to the list of available media types:

```
UIImagePickerControllerSourceType sourceType = [imagePickerController
sourceType];

NSArray *mediaTypes =
[UIImagePickerController availableMediaTypesForSourceType:sourceType];

[imagePickerController setMediaTypes:mediaTypes];
```

You can use the image picker controller this way to obtain videos from the camera as well as the user's photo library.

When a user finishes taking a video or selects a video from their library, objects are provided for different keys in the info dictionary passed to the delegate method imagePickerController:didFinishPickingMediaWithInfo:. Although the image picker controller will pass the raw image data for an image to this method, movies are much too large to remain in memory in their entirety. To this end, the image picker controller will instead pass a file URL to the method with the UIImagePickerControllerMediaURL key. You can access this URL like so:

```
- (void)imagePickerController:(UIImagePickerController *)picker
didFinishPickingMediaWithInfo:(NSDictionary *)info
{
    NSURL *movieURL = [info objectForKey:UIImagePickerControllerMediaURL];
}
```

If you're expecting either photos or videos, then you'll need to look at the object stored with the key UIImagePickerControllerMediaType to determine what type of media the user selected. A complete implementation of this delegate method might look like this:

```
- (void)imagePickerController:(UIImagePickerController *)picker
didFinishPickingMediaWithInfo:(NSDictionary *)info
{
    NSString *mediaType = [info objectForKey:UIImagePickerControllerMediaType];

    if ([mediaType isEqualToString:(NSString *)kUTTypeMovie]) {
        NSURL *movieURL = [info objectForKey:UIImagePickerControllerMediaURL];

        // Handle movie URL here.
    }
    else if ([mediaType isEqualToString:(NSString *)kUTTypeImage]) {
        UIImage *image = [info objectForKey:UIImagePickerControllerEditedImage];

        if (image == nil) {
            image = [info objectForKey:UIImagePickerControllerOriginalImage];
        }

        // Handle image here.
    }

    [self dismissModalViewControllerAnimated:YES];
}
```

Just as with photos, the allowsEditing property of the image picker controller can be set to YES to allow the user to edit their video after recording it. In the case of videos, this allows the user to trim some of the video off at the beginning or end. There are also some video-specific properties of UIImagePickerController that you can set to control its behavior when you're recording video. The videoMaximumDuration property can constrain the length of videos, which can be useful if, for instance, you plan on uploading the video to a service that will accept videos only under a certain length. By default, an image picker controller will constrain videos to ten minutes long.

If you'd like to control the quality of the video returned by an image picker controller, set the videoQuality method to the quality you'd like to receive. By default, the property is set to UIImagePickerControllerQualityTypeMedium, which Apple declares is appropriate for sending the video over Wi-Fi. The quality setting UIImagePickerControllerQualityTypeHigh will prevent the image picker controller from lowering the quality at all; for devices with high-quality cameras, these files can get quite large, so this quality setting is not recommended for transmitting the video file, except over the USB cable. UIImagePickerControllerQualityTypeLow will produce a video with a low enough file size that it can be comfortably transferred over the cellular network. There are also three quality constants for fixed resolutions: UIImagePickerControllerQualityType640x480, UIImagePickerControllerQualityTypeIFrame960x540, and UIImagePickerControllerQualityTypeIFrame1280x720.

No matter what you set the videoQuality property to, the video can be scaled only down, not up. If your source type is the user's photo library and they select a video, the videoQuality property is used to lower the resolution of the video (if needed). When this happens, the info dictionary passed to the delegate in the imagePickerController:didFinishPickingMediaWithinfo: method will contain the original video URL in the UIImagePickerControllerReferenceURL key.

If you set the cameraFlashMode property of an image picker controller to UIImagePickerControllerCameraFlashModeOn, then the flash will remain on while the image picker controller is displaying and set to take videos. This can have an adverse effect on batter life, so be sure to use it only when necessary.

Using UIVideoEditorController for Video

Once you've used a UIImagePickerController to obtain a video's URL, you may want to provide the user with a way to edit it. This is where the UIVideoEditorController class comes in. To use it, simply create an instance of UIVideoEditorController, set its videoPath property to the path of the video, and present it like any other view controller. It has two properties in common with UIImagePickerController, videoMaximumDuration and videoQuality, and they function identically to their image picker controller counterparts, though the default video quality for the image picker controller is UIImagePickerControllerQualityTypeMedium, whereas the default video quality for the video editor controller is UIImagePickerControllerQualityTypeLow. Before you create a video editor controller, verify that it will be able to edit the video by calling the class method canEditVideoAtPath:.

> **NOTE:** The `videoPath` property of `UIVideoEditorController` is an `NSString`, but the `UIImagePickerController` class passes to the delegate method `imagePickerController:didFinishPickingMediaWithInfo:` a dictionary of editing information including the key `UIImagePickerControllerMediaURL`, the value for which is an `NSURL` object. To convert the `NSURL` to the `NSString` path it represents, use its `path` method.

Once the user is done editing their video, the video editor controller calls the delegate method `videoEditorController:didSaveEditedVideoToPath:` with the path (as a string) to the edited video. The delegate will also need to implement `videoEditorControllerDidCancel:`, in case the user cancels the operation, and `videoEditorController:didFailWithError:` in case of any errors.

The `UIImagePickerController` and `UIVideoEditorController` classes give you nearly everything you will ever need for using photos and videos in your apps. For more advanced image manipulation outside the scope of this book, check out the Core Image framework; for more advanced video manipulation, check out the AVFoundation framework. We'll also look at playing audio and video in your app later in this book. Next up in this chapter, let's talk about using another piece of hardware in your iOS app: the accelerometer.

Using the Accelerometer

One way you can respond to user actions is to use the device's accelerometer. This device provides real-time data about the orientation of the device, which lets you know exactly how the user is holding it. The data coming from the accelerometer is extremely verbose—you can receive data as frequently as every ten milliseconds—and for simple tasks, it's definitely overkill. Fortunately, there are some more high-level methods of responding to user motion that don't require you to respond to the raw accelerometer data. We'll cover that, too, just in case you need to use it, but first we'll look at some easier-to-use APIs.

Accelerometer Events

As we saw in Chapter 5, when the user taps the screen, you receive a `UIEvent` object containing one or more `UITouch` objects representing the touch. Similarly, when the user shakes the device, it generates a `UIEvent` representing the motion. This event travels up the responder chain until a responder implements either the `motionBegan:withEvent:` method or the `motionEnded:withEvent:`

method. In those methods, you can respond appropriately to the event. If, for instance, you have a view controller that has an undo method and you'd like to allow the user to shake the phone to call the undo method, first your view controller would need to become the first responder in order to receive the event. To allow an object to become the first responder, implement canBecomeFirstResponder as follows:

```
- (BOOL)canBecomeFirstResponder
{
    return YES;
}
```

You would then tell your view controller to become the first responder when its view appears, as well as resign as the first responder when it disappears:

```
- (void)viewDidAppear:(BOOL)animated
{
    [super viewDidAppear:animated];

    [self becomeFirstResponder];
}

- (void)viewWillDisappear:(BOOL)animated
{
    [super viewWillDisappear:animated];

    [self resignFirstResponder];
}
```

Once your view controller is the first responder, you would implement the touch methods as follows:

```
- (void)motionBegan:(UIEventSubtype)motion withEvent:(UIEvent *)event
{

}

- (void)motionEnded:(UIEventSubtype)motion withEvent:(UIEvent *)event
{
    [self undo];
}

- (void)motionCancelled:(UIEventSubtype)motion withEvent:(UIEvent *)event
{

}
```

As you can see, there isn't much code here. You don't even need to put anything in the motionBegan:withEvent: or motionCancelled:withEvent: methods; they simply need to be present for the application to send motion events to the object. When you're implementing "shake to undo," you'll want to present the user with a choice, but the shake-handling code remains this simple. "Shake to undo" is, in my opinion, a bit obtuse and hard to discover for the user, along with very easy to accidentally trigger, but if you'd like to support it, it isn't very difficult. Usually, you'll use a UIAlertView to present the choice; a typical motionEnded:withEvent: method will be as follows:

```
- (void)motionEnded:(UIEventSubtype)motion withEvent:(UIEvent *)event
{
    // "self" in this case should conform to the UIAlertViewDelegate protocol.
    UIAlertView *alertView =
    [[UIAlertView alloc] initWithTitle:@"Undo"
                               message:@"Would you like to undo?"
                              delegate:self
                     cancelButtonTitle:@"Don't Undo"
                     otherButtonTitles:@"Undo", nil];

    [alertView show];
}
```

Once the user selects either Undo or Don't Undo, your code would either undo or do nothing.

Device Orientation Notifications

Another use of the accelerometer in the device is to determine the device orientation. Most of the time, you don't need to intervene when the orientation of the device changes. If you return the correct value in your view controller's shouldAutorotateToInterfaceOrientation: method, it will automatically rotate its interface to handle device orientation changes. There may be certain situations, however, where you would like to receive notifications of the orientation changing without changing the user interface's orientation. To begin receiving these notifications, you must call the beginGeneratingDeviceOrientationNotifications method on the device, which you can obtain via the currentDevice class method. You can combine the methods and begin generating notifications as follows:

```
[[UIDevice currentDevice] beginGeneratingDeviceOrientationNotifications];
```

Once you've enabled the notifications, you are responsible for telling the device when you're done by calling its endGeneratingDeviceOrientationNotifications method. If you don't, the accelerometer hardware will stay more active than it otherwise would, causing your app to use more battery than it should.

With orientation notifications enabled, the UIDevice object representing the device will post notifications to the default notification center with the name

UIDeviceOrientationDidChangeNotification. Simply add an observer for this notification and then inspect the orientation property of the device to determine its current orientation. The possible values for the orientation are as follows:

- UIDeviceOrientationUnknown

- UIDeviceOrientationPortrait

- UIDeviceOrientationPortraitUpsideDown

- UIDeviceOrientationLandscapeLeft

- UIDeviceOrientationLandscapeRight

- UIDeviceOrientationFaceUp

- UIDeviceOrientationFaceDown

Of particular interest are the last two in this list. If the user holds the phone flat, the device's accelerometer will not be able to determine an interface orientation, just that the device is facing up or down. Be sure to always account for these two values, because your failure to do so may result in unforeseen circumstances.

Using Raw Accelerometer, Gyroscope, and Magnetometer Data with Core Motion

Sometimes, the device orientation is not fine-grained enough for your application. This is often the case with games, which require real-time updates with very fine precision. The accelerometer data is perfectly capable of satisfying these needs. Some iOS devices are also equipped with a gyroscope, which helps provide more accurate motion data. This data is provided to your application via the Core Motion framework. Let's look at a quick sample app that uses device motion to move a dot around the screen.

> **NOTE:** Using Core Motion requires that you test your code on an iOS device, because there is no support for it on the iPhone Simulator. If you have not yet run code on the device, ensure that you have a valid iOS Developer account and read the documentation available at http://developer.apple.com/ios for getting started running your code on the device. This will also be explained in detail in Appendix A.

Open Xcode and create a new project by selecting File ➤ New ➤ Project… or by pressing ⌘+Shift+N. With Application selected under iOS in the left column, select the Single View Application template on the right and click Next. Enter **MotionDot** as the product name, and fill in your company identifier and class prefix. Select iPhone next to Device Family, and ensure that Use Storyboards and Include Unit Tests are unchecked, while Use Automatic Reference Counting is checked. Click Next, choose a location to save the project, and click Create to create your project. There will be one view controller class already created—mine is called LCTViewController. Open its implementation file (LCTViewController.m). First, we'll create a view that we'll move around based on the device motion. Add an instance variable into which we'll store this view by adding the code in bold to the class extension at the top of the file (if there is no class extension, enter this code in its entirety between the #import statements and the @implementation directive):

```
@interface LCTViewController () {
    UIView *_blueDot;
}

@end
```

Modify the viewDidLoad method to create this view and the viewDidUnload method to destroy it by adding the lines in bold:

```
- (void)viewDidLoad
{
    [super viewDidLoad];

    _blueDot = [[UIView alloc] initWithFrame:CGRectMake(0.0f, 0.0f, 20.0f,
20.0f)];
    [_blueDot setBackgroundColor:[UIColor blueColor]];

    [[self view] addSubview:_blueDot];
}

- (void)viewDidUnload
{
    [super viewDidUnload];

    _blueDot = nil;
}
```

We don't want the user interface to rotate, so remove the struck-out line and add the line in bold in the shouldAutorotateToInterfaceOrientation: method:

```
-
(BOOL)shouldAutorotateToInterfaceOrientation:(UIInterfaceOrientation)orientation
{
    return (interfaceOrientation != UIInterfaceOrientationPortraitUpsideDown);
```

```
        return (interfaceOrientation == UIInterfaceOrientationPortrait);
}
```

Next, we'll set up the actual motion-handling methods. First, we need to add the Core Motion framework to the project. Select the project at the top of the file browser, and then select the MotionDot target. In the editing pane, select the Build Phases tab, and then expand the Link Binary With Libraries phase by clicking the arrow to the left of its title. Click the plus (+) sign at the bottom of the expanded list of libraries, select CoreMotion.framework from the list, and click Add. Next, open your view controller's implementation file again (LCTViewController.m) and add an #import statement for the Core Motion headers to the top of the file, as well as an instance variable for a CMMotionManager class in the class extension by adding the lines in bold:

```
#import "LCTViewController.h"

#import <CoreMotion/CoreMotion.h>

@interface LCTViewController () {
    CMMotionManager *_motionManager;
    UIView *_blueDot;
}
```

```
@end
```

Now we're ready to receive motion data. Add method implementations for viewWillAppear: and viewWillDisappear: by adding the following code in bold after the viewDidLoad method:

```
- (void)viewWillAppear:(BOOL)animated
{
    [super viewWillAppear:animated];

    CGRect bounds = [[self view] bounds];
    CGFloat width = CGRectGetWidth(bounds);
    CGFloat height = CGRectGetHeight(bounds);

    CGRect blueDotFrame = [_blueDot frame];
    CGFloat dotWidth = CGRectGetWidth(blueDotFrame);
    CGFloat dotHeight = CGRectGetHeight(blueDotFrame);

    _motionManager = [[CMMotionManager alloc] init];

    if ([_motionManager isAccelerometerAvailable] == NO) {
        return;
    }

    [_motionManager setAccelerometerUpdateInterval:1.0 / 60.0];
```

```objc
    CMAccelerometerHandler accelerometerHandler =
    ^(CMAccelerometerData *accelerometerData, NSError *error) {
        CMAcceleration acceleration = [accelerometerData acceleration];

        CGFloat x = floorf(((width - dotWidth) / 2.0f) + (100 *
acceleration.x));
        CGFloat y = floorf(((height - dotHeight) / 2.0f) + (100 *
acceleration.y));
        CGFloat width = floorf(dotWidth * (20 * acceleration.z));
        CGFloat height = floorf(dotHeight * (20 * acceleration.z));

        [_blueDot setFrame:CGRectMake(x, y, width, height)];
    };

    [_motionManager startAccelerometerUpdatesToQueue:[NSOperationQueue
mainQueue]
                                          withHandler:accelerometerHandler];
}

- (void)viewWillDisappear:(BOOL)animated
{
    [super viewWillDisappear:animated];

    if ([_motionManager isAccelerometerActive]) {
        [_motionManager stopAccelerometerUpdates];
    }
    _motionManager = nil;
}
```

This code works by first checking that the accelerometer is available and then setting the update interval to 60 times per second. The accelerometerHandler variable holds a block that handles returned data from the motion manager, which is in the form of a CMAccelerometerData object. That object, in turn, has a property called acceleration, which is a C struct with x, y, and z, members, which are the actual measurements from the device. We use that data to move the blue dot around. When the view begins disappearing, we check to see whether the accelerometer is active, disabling it if it is.

Build and run this code on a device, and then move it around a bit. You'll notice that the dot is quite jumpy but that you can move it around the screen by moving the device. You're using the accelerometer data now! While serious, business-like applications have little use for this data under normal circumstances; if you're making a driving game, you'll definitely want to look into this.

The Core Motion framework also covers the gyroscope data. The methods look very similar to the accelerometer methods; you'll want to call isGyroAvailable before calling setGyroUpdateInterval: and startGyroUpdatesToQueue:withHandler:. These methods are structured just like their accelerometer counterparts, except that the block passed to startGyroUpdatesToQueue:withHandler: is passed a CMGyroData object, which has the C structure CMRotationRate, which has three members (x, y, and z) and which measures the rate of rotation along each axis measured in radians per second. When you're done receiving gyroscope data, be sure to call stopGyroUpdates.

Another sensor in some iOS devices is the magnetometer, which measures the magnetic field surrounding the device. While this sounds like something straight out of a science-fiction movie, it's now commonplace. The magnetometer methods follow the same pattern as the accelerometer and gyroscope methods: you call isMagnetometerAvailable first, then call setMagnetometerUpdateInterval: and startMagnetometerUpdatesToQueue:withHandler:, and finally call stopMagnetometerUpdates when you're finished. The object passed to the handler is a CMMagnetometerData object with one property, magneticField, which is a struct with three members (x, y, and z), each of which measures the magnetic field in that direction, measured in microteslas. With this information, you'd have enough information to create your very own compass app.

The killer feature of the Core Motion framework is not that it can use any of these three sensors; it's that it can use *all* of them. By combining the accelerometer with the gyroscope, we can filter out gravity, giving us a more pure idea of the user's motion, and we can also calibrate these measurements with the surrounding magnetic fields. These are tough calculations, though, and way beyond the scope of this book. Thankfully, you don't have to figure it out. There is a fourth type of data returned by Core Motion, appropriately called *device motion*. You'll use it just like the others: call isDeviceMotionAvailable, then setDeviceMotionUpdateInterval:, followed by startDeviceMotionUpdatesToQueue:withHandler:, and finally stopDeviceMotionUpdates. The handler receives a CMDeviceMotion object, which has a conglomeration of data from all three sensors in it. The rotationRate property is similar to that returned by the gryroscope, but with the bias—the output from the sensor with no input signal—removed by Core Motion. The accelerometer data is split into gravity and userAcceleration properties, allowing you to measure them separately. The magneticField property stores magnetic field data, also with the bias removed by Core Motion.

When you're using the device motion data in Core Motion, there is a data type not returned by the other kinds of data: the attitude property. This is a CMAttitude object with roll, pitch, and yaw; a quaternion; and a rotation matrix returned. If you know the math behind using these, then you can do so without having to calculate them yourself.

Core Motion is an extremely powerful framework. You probably won't ever need to use it, but if you ever do, you can get a wealth of data out of it. If you need to figure out where the phone *is*, however, you'll be using the GPS chip and the Core Location framework.

Using Location Data

People love searching for local data on their devices. From restaurant reviews to weather to local singles, there are countless opportunities for location data to be useful to your users. That being said, you should also take every opportunity possible to protect your users' privacy and *never* send their location data anywhere they haven't specifically asked you to. This is serious stuff—mess up user privacy and the U.S. Congress might ask Apple about your app.

Using CoreLocation

To get raw location data, you'll use the Core Location framework. You'll create an instance of the CLLocationManager object after checking its availability with the locationServicesEnabled class method. The first time you try to access the user's location, the system will display a prompt asking them to authorize your app to use their location data. If it's not clear *why* your app needs this data, you can set the location manager's purpose property to a string explaining what you'll be doing. You can always check on the authorization status with the authorizationStatus class method, which returns a CLAuthorizationStatus value. If the value is equal to kCLAuthorizationStatusDenied, then the user has declined the authorization prompt or has disabled Location Services entirely. At this point, unless the user opens the Settings app and removes the restriction on your app or reenables Location Services if it had been disabled, you won't be able to use Core Location.

The Core Location framework gets its location data from three sources. The first, available only for devices that communicate with cell networks, is cell tower triangulation. By looking at nearby cell towers and estimating the distance between the device and the tower, the device can get a pretty good idea of roughly where you are. You won't be able to get extremely specific just going off of this information, but if your app just needed to determine which country the user is in, it's probably good enough. Core Location also examines which Wi-Fi networks are nearby and queries a database of locations to help determine the user's location based on which networks are nearby. This is a bit more accurate, because there are more Wi-Fi networks than cell towers. Finally, for devices with a hardware GPS chip, the device can use GPS satellites to accurately pinpoint the user's location. The previous methods of determining the user's location help narrow the GPS search to a rough location, which Core Location can then use to find the correct GPS satellites more quickly.

One of the great things about CoreLocation is that you don't need to manage these different sources of data. Core Location will automatically use them as needed, switching seamlessly from one to the next. All you need to do is ask the CLLocationManager class to start updating the user's location, and it takes over from there.

The CLLocationManager class has many similarities to the CMMotionManager class, but without the modern block-based syntax. You'll call startUpdatingLocation to turn the location manager on, which will then call delegate methods with data. You can shape what it returns with the desiredAccuracy property. If you need to determine street-level accuracy, you'd set desiredAccuracy to kCLLocationAccuracyBest, but if you only need to determine that the user is in a specific geographic region, you'd use the other extreme value, kCLLocationAccuracyThreeKilometers, which is accurate only to three kilometers. In general, you should specify the least-accurate desired accuracy as you can; the more accurate the location manager needs to be, the more likely it is to use the power-hungry communications systems in the device, of which the GPS chip is the worst offender.

The delegate message you'll receive is locationManager:didUpdateToLocation:fromLocation:. You'll receive both the new location and the old location, allowing you to determine whether the location has changed enough to act on. Locations are instances of the CLLocation class. The most important property for user location is the coordinate property, which has latitude and longitude data, as well as the altitude property. There are some other useful properties, such as course and speed.

> **NOTE:** Once you've determined the user's location enough for your needs, be sure to disable location services by calling stopUpdatingLocation on your location manager. The hardware involved is very expensive from a power standpoint, so the less time it spends on, the better.

If you don't need super-frequent updates on the user's location, just to know that they're in a different location; you can instead monitor significant location changes by calling startMonitoringSignificantLocationChanges on your

location manager. This will still result in the location manager calling
`locationManager:didUpdateToLocation:fromLocation:`, but it won't be as
frequent. Be sure to check that this is available with the
`significantLocationChangeMonitoringAvailable` class method.

If what you want to know is when a user enters or leaves a region, you can use
the `startMonitoringForRegion:desiredAccuracy:` method, passing in a
`CLRegion`, which has a center coordinate and a radius in meters. When you're
monitoring a region, the location manager will call the
`locationManager:didEnterRegion:` and `locationManager:didExitRegion:`
methods as appropriate.

Using MapKit

If what you want to do is display a map to the user, then you'll use the MapKit
framework. The centerpiece of MapKit is the `MKMapView` class, which draws a
map that the user can interact with, allowing you to provide your own mapping
data, as well. You can highlight specific points on the map, draw lines over
specific geographic areas, and draw arbitrary shapes over the map. As of iOS
5.1, all of the mapping data used by MapKit is provided by Google, though this
may change in future iOS releases.

The best way to learn how to use MapKit is probably by using it, so let's do just
that. We're going to add a really cool feature to our TwitterExample project: a
map of local tweets. Open the project in Xcode. First, we'll need to add the
CoreLocation and MapKit frameworks to the project. Click the project at the top
of the file browser, then select the TwitterExample target under TARGETS, and
navigate to the Build Phases tab. Expand the Link Binary With Libraries phase,
click the plus button, select `CoreLocation.framework` and `MapKit.framework` (you
can hold ⌘ while clicking to select multiple items), and click Add. Next, we'll
need to add search capabilities to the project.

Open `LCTTwitterController.h`, and add a forward class declaration for the
`CLLocation` class and two new method declarations by adding the lines in bold:

```
#import <Foundation/Foundation.h>

@class CLLocation;

@interface LCTTwitterController : NSObject

+ (id)sharedInstance;

- (void)authorizeAccountWithCompletionHandler:(void(^)(void))handler;
```

```
- (void)getTweetsInUserTimelineWithCompletionHandler:(void(^)(NSArray
*tweets))handler;

- (void)getTweetsNearStreetAddress:(NSString *)streetAddress
                  searchRadius:(NSUInteger)searchRadiusInMeters
             completionHandler:(void(^)(NSArray *tweets))handler;

- (void)getTweetsNearLocation:(CLLocation *)location
                  searchRadius:(NSUInteger)searchRadiusInMeters
             completionHandler:(void(^)(NSArray *tweets))handler;
```

@end

This method we'll call from outside the controller is
getTweetsNearStreetAddress:searchRadius:completionHandler:, which will turn
the street address provided in the first parameter into a CLLocation object and
then call getTweetsNearLocation:searchRadius:completionHandler: to finish
the search, using the Twitter Search API to find tweets near that location, and
then parsing the results into an array of tweets. Navigate to
LCTTwitterController.m and import the Core Location and MapKit headers by
adding the lines in bold to the top of the file:

```
#import "LCTTwitterController.h"

#import <Accounts/Accounts.h>
#import <CoreLocation/CoreLocation.h>
#import <MapKit/MapKit.h>
#import <Twitter/Twitter.h>
```

Next, add the first method to the implementation before the @end directive by
adding the lines in bold:

```
- (void)getTweetsNearStreetAddress:(NSString *)streetAddress
                  searchRadius:(NSUInteger)searchRadiusInMeters
             completionHandler:(void (^)(NSArray *))handler
{
    // Geocode the address
    CLGeocoder *geocoder = [[CLGeocoder alloc] init];

    [geocoder geocodeAddressString:streetAddress
               completionHandler:^(NSArray *placemarks,
                                    NSError *error) {
        if ([placemarks count] > 0) {
            CLPlacemark *placemark = [placemarks objectAtIndex:0];

            CLLocation *location = [placemark location];

            if (location != nil) {
                // Now that we have the address, we can search Twitter.
                [self getTweetsNearLocation:location
```

```
                        searchRadius:searchRadiusInMeters
                   completionHandler:handler];
        }
    }
    else {
        NSLog(@"Error geocoding %@: %@", streetAddress, error);
    }
}];
}
```

The first thing this method does is to create a `CLGeocoder` object, which it uses to geocode the street address into a location. Once it has the location in the form of a `CLLocation` object, it passes it to the next method, along with the search radius and the completion handler. Add that next method after the previous one by adding the lines in bold:

```
- (void)getTweetsNearLocation:(CLLocation *)location
                 searchRadius:(NSUInteger)searchRadiusInMeters
            completionHandler:(void (^)(NSArray *))handler
{
    NSString *searchURI =
    [NSString stringWithFormat:
     @"http://search.twitter.com/search.json?geocode=%f,%f,%fkm",
     [location coordinate].latitude,
     [location coordinate].longitude,
     (float)searchRadiusInMeters / 1000.0f];

    NSURL *searchURL = [NSURL URLWithString:searchURI];

    TWRequest *searchRequest = [[TWRequest alloc] initWithURL:searchURL
                                                   parameters:nil

requestMethod:TWRequestMethodGET];

    [[UIApplication sharedApplication]
setNetworkActivityIndicatorVisible:YES];

    [searchRequest performRequestWithHandler:^(NSData *responseData,
                                               NSHTTPURLResponse *response,
                                               NSError *error) {
        [[UIApplication sharedApplication]
setNetworkActivityIndicatorVisible:NO];

        if (responseData) {
            id topLevelObject = [NSJSONSerialization
JSONObjectWithData:responseData
                                                   options:0

error:NULL];
```

```
            if ([topLevelObject isKindOfClass:[NSDictionary class]]) {
                NSArray *results = [topLevelObject
objectForKey:@"results"];

                if ([results isKindOfClass:[NSArray class]] && [results
count] > 0) {

                    if (handler != NULL) {
                        handler(results);
                    }
                }
                else {
                    NSLog(@"No results.");
                }
            }
        }
        else {
            NSLog(@"Error searching: %@", error);
        }
    }];
}
```

In this method, we create a search URL based on the `coordinate` property of the location and the `searchRadiusInMeters` parameter, which we convert to kilometers for the API. Once we have the URL, searching is just like before: create a `TWRequest` object and execute it.

Since we're going to be displaying tweets on a map, we need a class that implements the `MKAnnotation` protocol. An annotation is a point on the map where we can, for example, drop a pin that the user can click. Since each point on the map corresponds to a tweet, we'll make an `LCTTweet` class that we can use to store tweet information. Click File ➤ New ➤ File… or press Command+N. Select Cocoa Touch in the left column and then Objective-C class on the right. Click Next. Enter **NSObject** for Subclass Of, and then enter **LCTTweet** for Class. Click Next and then Create to save the file to disk. Open `LCTTweet.h` and add the code in bold:

```
#import <Foundation/Foundation.h>
#import <MapKit/MapKit.h>

@interface LCTTweet : NSObject <MKAnnotation>

@property (copy, nonatomic) NSString *text;
@property (copy, nonatomic) NSString *username;
@property (copy, nonatomic) CLLocation *location;

@end
```

Next, open `LCTTweet.m` and add the code in bold:

```
#import "LCTTweet.h"

@implementation LCTTweet

@synthesize text = _text;
@synthesize username = _username;
@synthesize location = _location;

#pragma mark - MKAnnotation Protocol Methods

- (NSString *)title
{
    return [self text];
}

- (NSString *)subtitle
{
    return [self username];
}

- (CLLocationCoordinate2D)coordinate
{
    return [[self location] coordinate];
}

#pragma mark -

@end
```

As you can see, this class is pretty sparse. We'll take care of creating the tweets and filling in their data later; for now, we just need the class to implement the MKAnnotation protocol methods title, subtitle, and coordinate.

We'll parse the tweets into LCTTweet objects in our LCTTwitterController class. Open LCTTwitterController.m and import the header for LCTTweet at the top of the file by adding the line in bold:

```
#import "LCTTwitterController.h"

#import <Accounts/Accounts.h>
#import <CoreLocation/CoreLocation.h>
#import <MapKit/MapKit.h>
#import <Twitter/Twitter.h>

#import "LCTTweet.h"
```

Next, modify the getTweetsNearLocation:searchRadius:completionHandler: method by removing the struck-out lines and adding the bold lines:

```
- (void)getTweetsNearLocation:(CLLocation *)location
```

```objectivec
               searchRadius:(NSUInteger)searchRadiusInMeters
          completionHandler:(void (^)(NSArray *))handler
{
    NSString *searchURI =
    [NSString stringWithFormat:
     @"http://search.twitter.com/search.json?geocode=%f,%f,%fkm",
     [location coordinate].latitude,
     [location coordinate].longitude,
     (float)searchRadiusInMeters / 1000.0f];

    NSURL *searchURL = [NSURL URLWithString:searchURI];

    TWRequest *searchRequest = [[TWRequest alloc] initWithURL:searchURL
                                            parameters:nil

requestMethod:TWRequestMethodGET];

    [[UIApplication sharedApplication] setNetworkActivityIndicatorVisible:YES];

    [searchRequest performRequestWithHandler:^(NSData *responseData,
                                        NSHTTPURLResponse *response,
                                        NSError *error) {
        [[UIApplication sharedApplication]
setNetworkActivityIndicatorVisible:NO];

        if (responseData) {
            id topLevelObject = [NSJSONSerialization
JSONObjectWithData:responseData
                                                        options:0
                                                          error:NULL];

            if ([topLevelObject isKindOfClass:[NSDictionary class]]) {
                NSArray *results = [topLevelObject objectForKey:@"results"];

                if ([results isKindOfClass:[NSArray class]] && [results count] >
0) {

                    NSMutableArray *tweets = [NSMutableArray array];

                    for (NSDictionary *tweetDict in results) {
                        LCTTweet *tweet = [[LCTTweet alloc] init];
                        [tweet setText:[tweetDict objectForKey:@"text"]];

                        [tweet setUsername:
                         [tweetDict objectForKey:@"from_user_name"]];

                        // Not every tweet has an exact location.
                        NSDictionary *geoDict = [tweetDict
objectForKey:@"geo"];
                        if ([geoDict isKindOfClass:[NSDictionary class]]) {
```

```
                        NSArray *coords = [geoDict
objectForKey:@"coordinates"];
                        float latitude = [[coords objectAtIndex:0]
floatValue];
                        float longitude = [[coords objectAtIndex:1]
floatValue];

                        CLLocation *location =
                        [[CLLocation alloc] initWithLatitude:latitude
longitude:longitude];

                        [tweet setLocation:location];
                    }
                    else {
                        // Here, location is the location received from
the geocoder
                        [tweet setLocation:location];
                    }

                    [tweets addObject:tweet];
                }

                if (handler != NULL) {
                    handler(results);
                    handler(tweets);
                }
            }
            else {
                NSLog(@"No results.");
            }
        }
    }
    else {
        NSLog(@"Error searching: %@", error);
    }
}];
}
```

Now that we have the search code written and a class to represent the tweets, let's show some tweets on a map. To do this, we'll need to add a new view controller. Click File ➤ New ➤ File… or press Command+N. Select Cocoa Touch in the left column and then Objective-C class on the right. Click Next. Enter **UIViewController** for Subclass Of, and then enter **LCTTweetMapViewController** for Class. Uncheck Targeted for iPad, but leave "With XIB for user interface" checked (or check it if it isn't checked). Click Next and then Create to save the file to disk and open it.

Open LCTTweetMapViewController.h. We'll be adding a text field and map view, so we'll need to add their delegate protocols to our class. For the map view, we'll also need to import the MapKit headers. Add the lines in bold to the header:

```
#import <UIKit/UIKit.h>
#import <MapKit/MapKit.h>

@interface LCTTweetMapViewController : UIViewController <MKMapViewDelegate,
UITextFieldDelegate>

@property (strong, nonatomic) IBOutlet UITextField *searchTextField;
@property (strong, nonatomic) IBOutlet MKMapView *mapView;

@end
```

Save your work and open LCTTweetMapViewController.xib. From the Object Library, drag a text field and a map view onto the user interface, resizing them to use the view's space, as shown in Figure 10-2. Select the text field and open the Attributes Inspector by selecting View ➤ Utilities ➤ Show Attributes Inspector or by pressing Option+Command+4. Under **Text Field** in the Attributes Inspector, and enter placeholder text that will appear before the user enters their search term. I've used Address (e.g. 10 Main St., Anytown, USA) as my placeholder; the idea is to tell the user what to type into the field. Lower in the Attributes Inspector, select Search next to Return Key, which will change the text on the Return key on the keyboard to Search.

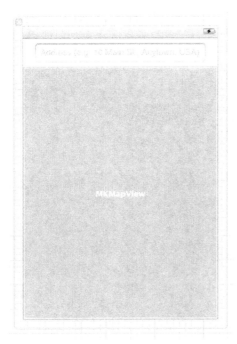

Figure 10-2. *The text field and map view in Xcode, resized to fit the available space.*

Next, in Xcode's editing view, expand the left side if needed by clicking the circle with a triangle in it at the bottom-left of the grid view where the view sits. With the left side expanded, hold Control and drag from File's Owner to the text field. In the Outlets pop-up that appears, select searchTextField. Do the same for the map view, selecting the mapView outlet. Next, from the search text field and then the map view, hold Control and drag to File's Owner, selecting the delegate outlet for each. Now that our user interface is set up, let's put in some search code.

Open the implementation file (LCTTweetMapViewController.m). First, import the Twitter controller and tweet headers and add synthesized accessor methods for the properties we added by adding the lines in bold at the top of the file:

```
#import "LCTTweetMapViewController.h"

#import "LCTTwitterController.h"
#import "LCTTweet.h"


@interface LCTTweetMapViewController ()
```

```
@end
```

```
@implementation LCTTweetMapViewController
```

```
@synthesize searchTextField = _searchTextField;
@synthesize mapView = _mapView;
```

Next, set those properties to nil in the viewDidUnload method:

```
- (void)viewDidUnload
{
    [super viewDidUnload];
    // Release any retained subviews of the main view.
    // e.g. self.myOutlet = nil;

    [self setSearchTextField:nil];
    [self setMapView:nil];
}
```

It's time for some search code. We'll start the search when the user enters some text in the search field and hits Search on the keyboard. Add the following code in bold to LCTTweetMapViewController before the @end compiler directive:

```
- (BOOL)textFieldShouldReturn:(UITextField *)textField
{
    [textField resignFirstResponder];

    NSString *searchText = [textField text];

    if ([searchText length] == 0) {
        return NO;
    }

    LCTTwitterController *twitterController = [LCTTwitterController
sharedInstance];

    void (^completionHandler)(NSArray *) = ^(NSArray *tweets) {
        NSArray *currentAnnotations = [[self mapView] annotations];

        [[self mapView] removeAnnotations:currentAnnotations];
        [[self mapView] addAnnotations:tweets];

        // Get the location from a tweet to center the map
        LCTTweet *tweet = [tweets objectAtIndex:0];
        CLLocationCoordinate2D coordinate = [[tweet location] coordinate];

        [[self mapView] setRegion:MKCoordinateRegionMake(coordinate,

MKCoordinateSpanMake(0.1, 0.1))
                          animated:YES];
```

```
    };

    [twitterController getTweetsNearStreetAddress:searchText
                               searchRadius:1000
                          completionHandler:completionHandler];

    return YES;
}
```

This code triggers our search when the user presses the Search key on the keyboard. To see it in action, we just need to put this view controller on the screen. Open LCTAppDelegate.m, and modify the beginning of the file through the application:didFinishLaunchingWithOptions: method by removing the struck-out lines and adding the lines in bold:

```
#import "LCTAppDelegate.h"

#import "LCTTimelineViewController.h"
#import "LCTTweetMapViewController.h"

@implementation LCTAppDelegate

@synthesize window = _window;

- (BOOL)application:(UIApplication *)application
didFinishLaunchingWithOptions:(NSDictionary *)launchOptions
{
    self.window = [[UIWindow alloc] initWithFrame:[[UIScreen mainScreen]
bounds]];
    // Override point for customization after application launch.
    self.window.backgroundColor = [UIColor whiteColor];
    [self.window makeKeyAndVisible];

    LCTTimelineViewController *viewController =
    [[LCTTimelineViewController alloc] initWithStyle:UITableViewStylePlain];

    UINavigationController *navigationController =
    [[UINavigationController alloc] initWithRootViewController:viewController];

    UIColor *darkBlueSlateColor = [UIColor colorWithRed:(74/255.0f)
                                                  green:(82/255.0f)
                                                   blue:(90/255.0f)
                                                  alpha:1.0f];

    [[navigationController navigationBar] setTintColor:darkBlueSlateColor];

    [[self window] setRootViewController:navigationController];

    LCTTweetMapViewController *viewController =
    [[LCTTweetMapViewController alloc] initWithNibName:nil
```

```
                                              bundle:nil];

   [[self window] setRootViewController:viewController];

   return YES;
}
```

Build and run the app. Enter an address in the search field, press Search, and you should see results, as in Figure 10-3. If you tap them, a pop-up will appear with the tweet text and username. Note that there will be a slight delay as the search is performed.

Figure 10-3. *Our tweet map displaying tweets as pins on the map*

There is a lot more that MapKit can do than what we've covered here—there could easily be an entire book on Core Location and MapKit—but this is a good start. As an exercise to the reader, consider further modifying TwitterExample to integrate maps into the rest of the application's flow.

Bring Your Own Device

If none of the sensors described in this chapter does what you need or if you need greater power than available in the sensors included in your device, it is possible to create a hardware device and use it in your app. Apple has a program, abbreviated MFi, that allows you to license hardware technologies and communicate with iOS devices over the dock connector. I'd love to tell you about it, but to even get the documentation, you need to apply to the program. If you need to create a hardware accessory for an iOS device, look into the program, but expect resources outside of Apple's documentation to be sparse.

There is a glimmer of hope with hardware devices in the form of Bluetooth 4.0. This new Bluetooth standard allows devices to communicate with your apps with much less friction. Implementing Bluetooth hardware is outside the scope of this book, but if you find yourself in need of hardware that communicates with your app, Bluetooth 4.0 may be the way to go with the lease amount of friction.

Requiring Devices in Your App

For certain apps, the absence of a certain sensor renders the app useless. The compass app on your device, for instance, requires a magnetometer, because otherwise a compass is pretty useless. Video-recording apps will require a camera that can take video, and face-to-face video chat apps will require a front-facing camera. To specify what devices are required by your app, you'll modify the `Info.plist` file for your app. By default, this is named after your target, so for TwitterExample, it's `TwitterExample-Info.plist`. You'll need to add a new line for the key "Required device capabilities" if it isn't already there. To do so, right-click in empty space in the editor and select Add Row. Xcode makes the names of keys friendly in your Info plist, but in the file this key is actually `UIRequiredDeviceCapabilities`. The value of this key is either an array or a dictionary; if it's an array, each object inside of it should be a string enumerating a required device capability. If it's a dictionary, each key should be a capability string, and the value should be a Boolean—`YES` if the app requires the capability and `NO` if the device must not have the capability. To change the type of the value, you'll first need to tell Xcode to treat the `Info.plist` file as a regular property list by right-clicking the editor, selecting Property List Type, then selecting None. Once you've done that, right-click the

UIRequiredDeviceCapabilities key, select Value Type, and then select either Array or Dictionary.

Here's a partial list of capability strings covering hardware discussed in this chapter:

- still-camera: The presence of a camera
- front-facing-camera: The presence of a front-facing camera
- camera-flash: The presence of a camera flash (though not necessarily for all cameras on a device)
- video-camera: The presence of a camera that can capture video
- accelerometer: The presence of an accelerometer
- gyroscope: The presence of a gyroscope
- location-services: The availability of Location Services
- gps: The presence of a GPS sensor
- magnetometer: The presence of a magnetomer
- bluetooth-le: The presence of a low-energy Bluetooth chip, used for Bluetooth 4.0 devices

If, for instance, you require a camera for your app to work, then users of devices that don't have a camera will not see your app listed in the App Store. You can see a complete list of the available keys in the Apple document *Information Property List Key Reference* available in the iOS documentation.

Summary

This chapter has been all about taking advantage of the various hardware components of an iOS device. As Apple continues to grow the product line, newer and better hardware components enter their devices. That said, the current line-up is fairly robust. After reading this chapter, you should be able to get photos and videos from the user, determine the device's orientation and acceleration with Core Motion, and determine where the user is with Core Location and show them where they are with MapKit. These hardware sensors enable you to build some really cool functionality into your apps, and if you don't find what you need, you can always make your own!

Media in Your App: Playing Audio and Video

So far in this book, we've covered a lot of ways to control how your app looks and how the user interacts with it. From custom user interfaces design to custom user interactions, what you've learned so far has really been limited to changing how the app appears. In this chapter, we'll introduce media to your app. Being able to play audio and video back from your app allows you to engage users on another dimension, provide instant feedback on their actions, and enrich the content you can provide in your app. For games, being able to play sound effects, ambient noise, and music is essential. Since every iOS device can also play music, the user could be playing music when they start any app, so those that play media should take that into account.

Playing Audio

For the purposes of this section, we'll split audio into three categories: sounds that play by themselves, such as an alert or notification sound; sound effects that play with music or with other sounds, such as game sound effects; and music. The code you write will depend on what you're trying to achieve with the sound. First, let's talk about sounds that play independently as an alert or a notification. For these, you'll use System Sound Services.

System Sound Services

System Sound Services is most basic sound API available on iOS, and with its simplicity comes a few limitations: you can't stop a sound once it starts, you can play only one sound at a time, you can't control the volume of the sound (it plays at the system's current sound level), and sounds are limited to 30 seconds in length. So, for a game, system sounds are right out, but for an app that needs to play a quick sound for a notification or an alert, it's a good fit. System Sound Services is a C API, so you'll be using some lower-level technologies than you're used to using. It's in the AudioToolbox framework, so you'll need to add this framework to the Link Binary With Libraries build phase of any target you'd like to use it with, as well as import the AudioToolbox headers with #import <AudioToolbox/AudioToolbox.h>.

Playing System Sounds

The first thing you need to do to play a system sound is to create a sound ID. The sound ID is stored in the SystemSoundID type. This isn't an Objective-C object, just an identifier that the system associates with your sound. To create an ID, use the AudioServicesCreateSystemSoundID() function, which takes two arguments: a CoreFoundation URL reference (CFURLRef) to the file URL for the sound, and a pointer to the SystemSoundID variable that it will fill in with the correct ID. Since the CoreFoundation class CFURL is "toll-free-bridged" with NSURL, you can convert an NSURL to CFURLRef, and vice versa. This lets you keep the memory management for the URL in Cocoa Touch, allowing ARC to handle it for you. To do so, use the __bridge keyword when casting it, as follows. Creating a system sound for the file mySound.wav in the main bundle would be done like so:

```
NSURL *soundURL = [[NSBundle mainBundle] URLForResource:@"mySound"
                                          withExtension:@"wav"];

SystemSoundID soundID;

OSStatus status = AudioServicesCreateSystemSoundID((__bridge CFURLRef)soundURL,
                                                   &soundID);
```

When the AudioServicesCreateSystemSoundID function returns, the soundID variable will have been initialized with the sound ID, and the status variable will contain the function's return value representing the result code for the operation. If successful, this code will equal kAudioServicesNoError; error codes are listed in the System Sound Services Reference documentation.

Once you've created a sound, there are two different functions you can use to play it. `AudioServicesPlaySystemSound()` will simply play the sound immediately when it's called. Its sole argument is the sound ID. After creating a sound ID with the previous code, you would play it like so:

```
if (status == kAudioServicesNoError) {
    AudioServicesPlaySystemSound(soundID);
}
```

Note that we first checked the value of `status` to make sure that the sound ID was created successfully. The `AudioServicesPlaySystemSound()` function runs asynchronously, so it will return immediately no matter how long the sound is; to run code when the sound completes, you can add a callback to a C function with the `AudioServicesAddSystemSoundCompletion` function. The function you use as a callback must match the `AudioServicesSystemSoundCompletionProc` prototype in the AudioServices header, which is as follows:

```
typedef void (*AudioServicesSystemSoundCompletionProc)(SystemSoundID ssID,
                                                        void *clientData);
```

The function pointer syntax used here is similar to the block declaration syntax but with a pointer (*) instead of a carat (^). If you wanted to create a function called `MySystemSoundCallback()`, you would declare it like so in your header file:

```
void MySystemSoundCallback(SystemSoundID ssID, void *clientData);
```

Then, you would implement the function:

```
void MySystemSoundCallback(SystemSoundID ssID, void *clientData)
{
    // Run callback code
}
```

> **NOTE:** You can use C functions alongside your Objective-C code with no issue. Simply place the function declarations outside of the `@interface` block in the header file, and place the function implementations outside of the `@implementation` block in the implementation file. After the `@end` directive is usually a good place to put C functions, in both your header and implementation files. If you want to keep a C function private to your class, you can put both the declaration and the implementation for it in the class implementation file, so long as your declaration is before the `@implementation` block.

After you've created a C function to use as a callback for your system sounds, you use the `AudioServicesAddSystemSoundCompletion()` function to add the callback. It takes five arguments: the sound ID, which is a `CFRunLoopRef` reference to a CoreFoundation run loop; a `CFStringRef`, which is a Core Foundation string, representing the run loop mode; the function pointer to your function, of type `AudioServicesSystemSoundCompletionProc`; and a `void *` pointer to any additional data you'd like to pass the function, shown earlier in the callback function's implementation as the function argument `clientData`. For the run loop arguments and the client data argument, you can pass `NULL`, which will call your function on the default run loop in the default mode, with no extra data passed. To use our `MySystemSoundCallback` function as a sound callback, the code would be as follows:

```
AudioServicesAddSystemSoundCompletion(soundID,
                                      NULL,
                                      NULL,
                                      &MySystemSoundCallback,
                                      NULL);
```

The `AudioServicesAddSystemSoundCompletion()` function returns an `OSStatus` value as a result code, so if you need to determine that the callback was added successfully, you can use the returned value to do so. You should call `AudioServicesAddSystemSoundCompletion()` *before* calling `AudioServicesPlaySystemSound()` to ensure that the sound doesn't stop playing before your function is added as a callback.

Finally, once you're done with a system sound, you should destroy it to reclaim the resources it used. This is accomplished via the `AudioServicesDisposeSystemSoundID()` function, which takes the system sound ID as its sole argument and reclaims its resources. System sounds are not reference-counted like CoreFoundation or Objective-C objects, so ARC won't be able to help manage their memory; you'll have to call this method yourself. If you call `AudioServicesDisposeSystemSoundID()` immediately after calling `AudioServicesPlaySystemSound()`, the sound will never play. If you need to create a system sound, play it, and then never use it again, you can dispose of it in the callback function.

We now have enough code to play a system sound, which will be adequate for anything like a button click sound. Here it is in its entirety:

```
NSURL *soundURL = [[NSBundle mainBundle] URLForResource:@"mySound"
                                          withExtension:@"wav"];

SystemSoundID soundID;

OSStatus status = AudioServicesCreateSystemSoundID((__bridge CFURLRef)soundURL,
                                                   &soundID);

if (status == kAudioServicesNoError) {
    AudioServicesAddSystemSoundCompletion(soundID,
```

```
                                        NULL,
                                        NULL,
                                        &MySystemSoundCallback,
                                        NULL);

    AudioServicesPlaySystemSound(soundID);
}
```

The corresponding callback function, which should be declared in the header file or before the @implementation block in the implementation file, then destroys the sound ID to reclaim its memory:

```
void MySystemSoundCallback(SystemSoundID ssID, void *clientData)
{
    NSLog(@"System sound finished!");

    AudioServicesDisposeSystemSoundID(ssID);
}
```

This method of playing sounds is simple and adequate for many needs. Earlier, however, I mentioned that there are two ways of playing system sounds. We've just seen one way. The other is to play a system sound as an alert.

Playing Alert Sounds

Playing a system sound as an alert is accomplished using the AudioServicesPlayAlertSound() function. The process is similar to playing it as a system sound, but there are some differences depending on the device. On an iPhone, if the user has configured the device to play a sound and vibrate when they receive a phone call, then the alert sound will also cause the phone to vibrate, unless the app is configured to record audio, in which case the phone will not vibrate, which it does to avoid disturbing the audio. On the original iPod touch, which didn't have a speaker to play sounds without headphones plugged in, playing an alert sound will result in a generic alert sound playing. As with system sounds, alert sounds may not be more than 30 seconds long, or the app will crash with an error. Playing our sound as an alert is pretty straightforward:

```
NSURL *soundURL = [[NSBundle mainBundle] URLForResource:@"mySound"
                                          withExtension:@"wav"];

SystemSoundID soundID;

OSStatus status = AudioServicesCreateSystemSoundID((__bridge CFURLRef)soundURL,
                                        &soundID);

if (status == kAudioServicesNoError) {
    AudioServicesPlayAlertSound(soundID);
}
```

You can add callbacks just as with system sounds. You also still need to call AudioServicesDisposeSystemSoundID() to dispose of the sound when you're done with it, typically in a dealloc method. You should use alert sounds to indicate that the app needs the user's attention, such as when an error occurs. On devices with vibration motors, alert sounds can also be used to trigger vibration, as we'll talk about next.

Triggering Vibration

If you'd like to trigger vibration, you can use the AudioServicesPlayAlertSound() function with a constant sound ID value that indicates vibration:

```
AudioServicesPlayAlertSound(kSystemSoundID_Vibrate);
```

On a device such as an iPhone with a vibration motor, this will trigger a short vibration. On other devices, this will do nothing.

As you can see, System Sound Services is a good fit for short sounds, such as button clicks and alerts. For sounds longer than 30 seconds, music, or playing multiple sounds at once, we'll need to use more advanced audio APIs.

AVAudioPlayer

If you need to play multiple sounds at once, control the playback level of individual sounds, or loop your sounds but you don't need to precisely synchronize two or more sounds with one another, don't need stereo playback, and aren't playing audio from a network stream, then the AVAudioPlayer class is what Apple recommends. Unlike System Sound Services, AVAudioPlayer is written in Objective-C, so you don't need to do any additional memory management for your sounds other than what you would do for any object. You'll create an AVAudioPlayer object for each sound you want to play; they can each play their sound while the others are also playing. You can create an audio player either from a file URL, as with System Sound Services, or with an NSData object if you have the audio bytes in a data buffer.

To play a sound with an audio player, simply call its play method. It doesn't get much easier than this! The .caf extension is the native uncompressed sound format of iOS and is what Apple recommends for short sound effects. You can convert a .wav file to .caf using the afconvert command-line utility; type **man afconvert** at the command line to read its documentation. This step is optional and recommended to save space; a .wav file should work just fine as is.

Assuming that your sound file is named mySound.caf, here's how you would create an AVAudioPlayer for a sound and play it:

```
NSURL *soundURL = [[NSBundle mainBundle] URLForResource:@"mySound"
                                          withExtension:@"caf"];

NSError *error = nil;
AVAudioPlayer *audioPlayer = [[AVAudioPlayer alloc]
initWithContentsOfURL:soundURL

error:&error];

if (audioPlayer != nil) {
    [audioPlayer play];
}
else {
    NSLog(@"Error creating audio player: %@", error);
}
```

> **NOTE:** Since AVAudioPlayer is a part of the AVFoundation framework, be sure to add that framework to the Link Binary With Libraries build phase of your target.

This code is fairly similar to the System Sound Services code. The advantage of AVAudioPlayer, however, is that you can set a number of properties on each player, including but not limited to:

- The volume property, a float value, lets you adjust the playback volume from 0.0 to 1.0 on a linear scale.

- To loop the sound, you can use the numberOfLoops property, an NSInteger value. Setting numberOfLoops to 0 will play the sound once. Setting it to 1 will play the sound two times total (the first time plus 1 loop). Setting it to any value *n* will play the sound *n + 1* times. Setting numberOfLoops to any negative value will loop the sound indefinitely or until you call the audio player's stop method.

- To adjust the stereo position from left to right, set the value of pan, a float, from -1.0 to 1.0, with -1.0 being 100 percent left and 1.0 100 percent right.

- To adjust the playback rate, first set the enableRate property (a BOOL) to YES, then set the rate property, a float. The rate property can range from 0.5 (half-speed) to 2.0 (double-speed).

■ To adjust the playback time, either to seek to a specific point in the sound or to implement fast-forward or rewind functionality, set the currentTime property, an NSTimeInterval value, which is just a double representing seconds.

There are some other considerations to take into account when using an AVAudioPlayer. While an audio player is playing, the audio is loaded into memory and the audio hardware is engaged. To avoid a delay between calling the play method and the audio starting, you can call prepareToPlay, which will preload audio buffers and engage the audio hardware. If you're going to set enableRate to YES, do so before calling prepareToPlay. To stop playback, you can call the pause method of your audio player, which will leave the buffers filled and audio hardware engaged, or call the stop method, which will empty the buffers and disengage the audio hardware. Calling stop will not reset the playback time, however, so if you call stop and then play, the audio will resume where it left off. To stop the audio and reset the playback time, set currentTime to 0.0 after calling stop.

Whereas we used callback functions when using System Sound Services, the AVAudioPlayer class has a delegate property, which conforms to the AVAudioPlayerDelegate protocol. The equivalent of the System Sound Services callback is the audioPlayerDidFinishPlaying:successfully: delegate method, which takes a pointer to the audio player object as its first parameter and a BOOL value indicating whether the playback was successful or not as the second parameter. You can respond to decoding errors during playback using the audioPlayerDecodeErrorDidOccur:error: delegate method.

When the user receives a phone call or the application is otherwise interrupted, playback from your audio player will stop until the interruption is resolved (for instance, if the user declines the call). At the beginning of the interruption, the audioPlayerBeginInterruption: delegate method will be called, giving you a chance to react by, for instance, adjusting your application's UI to reflect that the audio player is not playing. Once the interruption is finished, the audioPlayerEndInterruption: delegate method is called, allowing you to, for instance, resume playback. To receive more information about the interruption, you can instead implement the audioPlayerEndInterruption:withFlags: delegate method, to which the audio player will pass flags containing more information as the second parameter. If you implement both, only the version with the flags will be called. As of iOS 5.1, the only flag is AVAudioSessionInterruptionFlags_ShouldResume, which is set to 1 if the sound should resume. Implementing this delegate method is straightforward:

```
- (void)audioPlayerEndInterruption:(AVAudioPlayer *)player
withFlags:(NSUInteger)flags
```

```
{
    if (flags == AVAudioSessionInterruptionFlags_ShouldResume) {
        [player play];
    }
}
```

This covers pretty much everything you need to know about `AVAudioPlayer`. It has more features, such as audio levels if you'd like to implement that in your application's user interface, but this is the basic interface for playing sound. You can use it to play multiple sound effects at a time at different volumes, such as for a game.

Other Sound APIs

There are other sound APIs available on iOS. If you need to precisely control the synchronization of two or more sounds with one another or load sound from a network buffer, you'll need to use Audio Queue Services. This API gives you a callback method in which you'll fill an audio buffer with sound to play. If, for example, you were making a music app with multiple loops of music playing at the same time, you could use Audio Queue Services to manage the loops and ensure they stay in sync.

If you need to position your sound effects in 3D space, which is most common for a game, then you can use the open source OpenAL framework, which is also available in iOS. While OpenAL is the best choice for games where sounds can be traced to a specific location on-screen, it's also not a bad choice for general-purpose sound playback. For complex audio work such as applying effects in real time, you can use the Core Audio framework, but the relative difficulty level of programming for Core Audio is quite high when compared to the other audio frameworks. Both OpenAL and Core Audio are pretty low-level frameworks, so if you determine that neither System Sound Services nor `AVAudioPlayer` meet your needs, you should investigate these options. To get help with OpenAL, you can visit the web site at OpenAL.org, and for Core Audio, a good resource is the Core Audio mailing list at `https://lists.apple.com/mailman/listinfo/coreaudio-api`.

Example: SoundBoard

Let's make a sample app to test playing sounds. Open Xcode and select File ➤ New ➤ Project…, or press ⌘+Shift+N. Select Application in the leftmost column under the iOS section, and then select Single View Application on the right. Click Next, and then enter **SoundBoard** as the name for the project. Enter your company identifier and class prefix (I'll use **com.learncocoatouch** and **LCT**), select iPhone for Device Family, and ensure that Use Automatic Reference Counting is checked and both Use Storyboards and Include Unit Tests are unchecked. Click Next, and then click Create to save the project to disk.

Before we can play a sound, we'll need a sound to play. You can download a sample audio file named `Trumpet.m4a` that's compatible with iOS from this book's web site at `www.learncocoatouch.com`. Once you've downloaded the file, locate it in Finder, and then drag it into the file browser in Xcode. For organization's sake, let's put it in the Supporting Files section. Check "Copy items into destination group's folder (if needed)," and then next to "Add to targets," check SoundBoard to include the sound in this app's bundle. Click Finish, and then the sound will be added to the project.

The goal of this project will be a view with buttons we can use to play this sound three different ways: as a system sound, as an alert sound, and using an `AVAudioPlayer` object. First, let's create those buttons. Open the main view controller's user interface file (`LCTViewController.xib`) in Xcode. Open the Object Library by selecting View ➤ Utilities ➤ Show Object Library or by pressing Control+Option+⌘+3. Once it's open, drag three Round Rect Buttons onto your project's view, arranging them in a column vertically. Double-click each to set its title; we'll name them Play System Sound, Play Alert Sound, and Play using AVAudioPlayer, respectively. The buttons will automatically resize to fit their text. When you're done, the view will look like Figure 11-1.

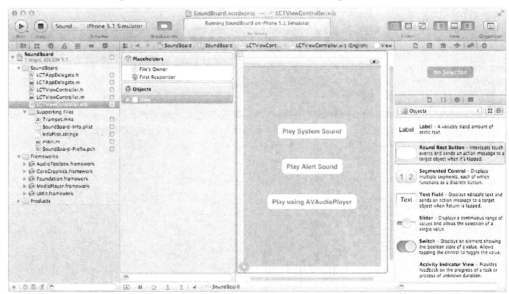

Figure 11-1. *Our view after adding three buttons*

Next, let's add some outlets and actions for these buttons. Open the view controller's header file (LCTViewController.h), and add the lines in bold:

```
#import <UIKit/UIKit.h>

@interface LCTViewController : UIViewController

@property (strong, nonatomic) IBOutlet UIButton *systemSoundButton;
@property (strong, nonatomic) IBOutlet UIButton *alertSoundButton;
@property (strong, nonatomic) IBOutlet UIButton *audioPlayerButton;

- (IBAction)systemSoundButtonPressed:(id)sender;
- (IBAction)alertSoundButtonPressed:(id)sender;
- (IBAction)audioPlayerButtonPressed:(id)sender;

@end
```

As you can see, we've created an IBOutlet and IBAction for each button. Let's connect these to the objects in the view. Open the interface file (LCTViewController.xib) again. Holding Control, click the File's Owner object at the left of the editing pane and drag to the button labeled Play System Sound, and then select systemSoundButton from the pop-up menu. Do the same for the button labeled Play Alert Sound, selecting alertSoundButton; then do the same for the button labeled Play using AVAudioPlayer, selecting audioPlayerButton. Now that we've connected the outlets, let's connect the actions. Holding Control, click the button labeled Play System Sound and drag to the File's Owner object, selecting the systemSoundButtonPressed: method from the list. Do the same for the button labeled Play Alert Sound, selecting alertSoundButtonPressed:, and for the button labeled Play using AVAudioPlayer, selecting audioPlayerButtonPressed:.

Before we implement our view controller, add the AVFoundation and AudioToolbox frameworks to your project and link them to your target. To do this, select the project at the top of the file browser in Xcode, click the SoundBoard target, and then select Build Phases in the editing pane. Expand the Link Binary With Libraries phase by clicking the triangle next to it, and click press the Add button (+) and select AVFoundation.framework. Click the Add button again and select AudioToolbox.framework.

Now that we've added the AVFoundation and AudioToolbox frameworks to the project, we're ready to implement this class. Open the implementation file (LCTViewController.m). First, we'll import the header file for the AVFoundation framework, add private instance variables for the sound ID and audio player, and add @synthesize directives for our properties. We'll implement the dealloc method to properly dispose of the sound ID. Then we'll initialize our sounds in the viewDidLoad method, and finally we'll implement playing the sounds in the

three IBAction methods. To accomplish this, modify the file by adding the lines
in bold:

```
#import "LCTViewController.h"

#import <AVFoundation/AVFoundation.h>
#import <AudioToolbox/AudioToolbox.h>

@interface LCTViewController () {
    AVAudioPlayer *_audioPlayer;
    SystemSoundID _soundID;
}

@end

@implementation LCTViewController

@synthesize systemSoundButton;
@synthesize alertSoundButton;
@synthesize audioPlayerButton;

- (void)dealloc
{
    AudioServicesDisposeSystemSoundID(_soundID);
}

- (void)viewDidLoad
{
    [super viewDidLoad];
    // Do any additional setup after loading the view, typically from a nib.

    NSURL *soundURL = [[NSBundle mainBundle] URLForResource:@"Trumpet"
                                             withExtension:@"m4a"];

    // Create a sound ID used to play the system sound.
    OSStatus status = AudioServicesCreateSystemSoundID((__bridge
CFURLRef)soundURL,
                                                        &_soundID);

    if (status != kAudioServicesNoError) {
        // An error occurred, so let's disable the buttons.
        [[self systemSoundButton] setEnabled:NO];
        [[self alertSoundButton] setEnabled:NO];
    }

    // Initialize the AVAudioPlayer
    NSError *error = nil;
    _audioPlayer = [[AVAudioPlayer alloc] initWithContentsOfURL:soundURL
                                                         error:&error];
```

```objc
    if (_audioPlayer == nil) {
        // An error occured, so let's disable the button and log the error.
        NSLog(@"%@", error);
        [[self audioPlayerButton] setEnabled:NO];
    }
    else {
        [_audioPlayer prepareToPlay];
    }
}

- (void)viewDidUnload
{
    [super viewDidUnload];
    // Release any retained subviews of the main view.
}

-
(BOOL)shouldAutorotateToInterfaceOrientation:(UIInterfaceOrientation)interfaceOr
ientation
{
    return (interfaceOrientation != UIInterfaceOrientationPortraitUpsideDown);
}

- (IBAction)systemSoundButtonPressed:(id)sender
{
    AudioServicesPlaySystemSound(_soundID);
}

- (IBAction)alertSoundButtonPressed:(id)sender
{
    AudioServicesPlayAlertSound(_soundID);
}

- (IBAction)audioPlayerButtonPressed:(id)sender
{
    [_audioPlayer play];
}

@end
```

As you can see in the viewDidLoad method, we use the same NSURL object representing the path to our sound file to create the sound ID and the audio player. If we encounter any errors creating them, we'll disable the relevant buttons. Finally, in the IBAction methods, we play the sound using the appropriate method or function. Now that we're done, build and run the app. You should be able to play the sound by clicking any of the buttons. Just like that, we're playing sounds! Next, let's discuss another type of audio: music.

Playing Music

Every iOS devices supports maintaining a library of music, videos, podcasts, TV shows, and more in its library. Although the iPhone and iPad have this library, it's still referred to in documentation as the iPod library. Your apps are able to search the user's iPod library, play items in it, and even control the built-in music player on the device. One of the most common uses of this is to allow the user to select some of their songs to play while your app is running. To do so, you'll use the MPMediaPickerController class to provide your users with an interface they can use to select media.

Using MPMediaPickerController

Much like the UIImagePickerController class, which allows the user to select an image for use in your app, the MPMediaPickerController allows the user to select media from their iPod library to use in your app, represented by the MPMediaItem class.

> **NOTE:** There is no iPod library on the iPhone Simulator, so using the MPMediaPickerController class is limited to actual devices.

Before you use an MPMediaPickerController, you'll need to add the MediaPlayer framework to your project, link it to your target, and then import the header files for the MediaPlayer framework as follows:

```
#import <MediaPlayer/MediaPlayer.h>
```

As we'll discuss later, you'll need a delegate object for the media picker controller, typically a view controller that displays the media picker controller, that conforms to the MPMediaPickerControllerDelegate protocol. To show an MPMediaPickerController, create one and display it like any other view controller:

```
MPMediaPickerController *mediaPickerController =
[[MPMediaPickerController alloc] initWithMediaTypes:MPMediaTypeAnyAudio];

[mediaPickerController setDelegate:self];
[mediaPickerController setPrompt:@"Choose a song!"];

[self presentModalViewController:mediaPickerController animated:YES];
```

In the initialization method, we specify the type of media we're looking for; in this case, it's any audio. Other media types include podcasts, iTunes U, music videos, audiobooks, and other specific types of media. There is a delegate protocol for `MPMediaPickerController`, and you can probably guess its name: `MPMediaPickerControlerDelegate`. The media picker controller also has a `prompt` property that we can use to display a custom string on top of the picker controller's view. Figure 11-2 shows what a media picker controller's view looks like, with the custom prompt "Choose a song!"

Figure 11-2. *A media picker controller's view. The cloud icon on the right indicates that these artists are in iTunes Match. A cloud icon with a downward-facing arrow in the middle indicates that the song is available in the user's iTunes Match account but is not on the device; tapping this icon will download the song.*

Just as with UIImagePickerController, the MPMediaPickerController returns the selected item or items via its delegate, in this case using the MPMediaPickerControllerDelegate protocol. There are two methods in this protocol: mediaPickerDidCancel: and mediaPicker:didPickMediaItems:. The first is called if the user cancels and does not select any media items, while the second is called with one or more media items that the user has selected. To allow the user to select multiple items, set the allowsPickingMultipleItems property of the MPMediaPickerController to YES. Unlike similar delegate methods, however, the selected items are not returned in an NSArray object; instead, they are returned in an MPMediaItemCollection object. A media item collection behaves like an array of media items but with some extra abilities. Its mediaTypes property contains flags for each of the media types present in the collection. Individual media items, instances of the MPMediaItem class, can be accessed through the items property, which returns an NSArray of the items. When the items all have a shared characteristic—if you select an album by a particular artist, for instance—the representativeItem property will return an MPMediaItem object that has common properties set, in this case, the artist name, album name, release year, and other common metadata.

Accessing these properties of a media item is done not through direct property access but instead through the valueForProperty: method it inherits from MPMediaEntity, an abstract class that sits above both MPMediaItem and MPMediaItemCollection. To access the artist name and title of all media items selected in the MPMediaPickerController, you could implement the delegate method mediaPicker:didPickMediaItems: as follows:

```
- (void)mediaPicker:(MPMediaPickerController *)mediaPicker
  didPickMediaItems:(MPMediaItemCollection *)mediaItemCollection
{
    // Print the artist and title of each item
    for (MPMediaItem *mediaItem in [mediaItemCollection items]) {
        NSString *artist = [mediaItem
valueForProperty:MPMediaItemPropertyArtist];
        NSString *title = [mediaItem valueForProperty:MPMediaItemPropertyTitle];

        NSLog(@"Artist: %@ Title: %@", artist, title);
    }
}
```

Using MPMusicPlayerController

Once you have an MPMediaItemCollection, you probably want to play the music! To do so, you'll use the MPMusicPlayerController class. Instead of creating a music player controller directly, you'll use one of two class methods to access one of two singleton players: applicationMusicPlayer or iPodMusicPlayer. While only one of these can be playing at a time, you'll use them for different scenarios. The application music player is specific to your application; when the user leaves your app, the music stops playing. The iPod music player, on the other hand, is a device-wide music player. When your app starts, it might already be playing music, and when your app quits, it will keep on playing. When your app starts, it's a good idea to determine whether the user is already listening to music. First, as with the MPMediaPickerController class discussed earlier, you'll need to add the MediaPlayer framework to your project, link it with your target, and import its header file. Once you've done this, you can determine whether the user is currently listening to music as follows:

```
BOOL isAlreadyPlaying;
MPMusicPlayerController *iPodPlayer = [MPMusicPlayerController iPodMusicPlayer];

if ([iPodPlayer playbackState] == MPMusicPlaybackStatePlaying) {
    isAlreadyPlaying = YES;
}
else {
    isAlreadyPlaying = NO;
}
```

This code sets isAlreadyPlaying to YES if the user is already listening to music by accessing the playbackState property of the iPod music player controller. Similar to the AVAudioPlayer, the MPMusicPlayerController class has play, pause, and stop methods, though you don't need to prepare it to play before playing. To load the player with the media items that the user selected with the media picker controller, use the setQueueWithItemCollection: method. The following code immediately plays the items that the user selected. (Note that as with UIImagePickerController, you are responsible for dismissing the modal view controller presented by the media picker controller, as it won't dismiss itself automatically.)

```
- (void)mediaPicker:(MPMediaPickerController *)mediaPicker
  didPickMediaItems:(MPMediaItemCollection *)mediaItemCollection
{
    MPMusicPlayerController *iPodPlayer = [MPMusicPlayerController
iPodMusicPlayer];
    [iPodPlayer setQueueWithItemCollection:mediaItemCollection];
    [iPodPlayer play];

    [self dismissModalViewControllerAnimated:YES];
}
```

If you were to press the device's Home button and close the app, music played with the iPod player like this would continue to play.

You may at times need finer-grained control over which media items to play. Suppose you want to build a custom user interface to browse the user's media library or perform advanced searching capabilities. To do so, you can use the MPMediaQuery class, which allows you to search the media library programmatically, giving you finer-grained control than your user has with the search bar in the MPMediaPickerController.

Media Queries

To search the media library, you create an instance of MPMediaQuery using one of several convenience constructors, which are class methods of MPMediaQuery:

- albumsQuery
- artistsQuery
- songsQuery
- playlistsQuery
- podcastsQuery
- audiobooksQuery
- compilationsQuery
- composersQuery
- genresQuery

Media queries can have a grouping type, expressed in the groupingType property. Each of the convenience constructors listed earlier applies a grouping type; the query returned by the albumsQuery method, for instance, has a grouping type of MPMediaGroupingAlbum. The collections property of the query returns media item collections based on the grouping type; for the albums query, the collections property returns a separate MPMediaItemCollection object for each album in the user's library, sorted by album title. You can use the items property to return all of the items returned by the query.

Suppose you want to find all of the user's songs with a title that contains the word *Friday*. To do so, you would create a filter for a media item query. This filter would be a predicate of the MPMediaPropertyPredicate class. First, you would start by creating a query that matches all of the user's songs:

```
MPMediaQuery *query = [MPMediaQuery songsQuery];
```

Then, you would construct a predicate by filtering on the title. Before doing so, you should check to ensure that the property you'd like to use to filter the media items is one that you can use as a predicate. Filtering the query would go as follows:

```
if ([MPMediaItem canFilterByProperty:MPMediaItemPropertyTitle]) {
    MPMediaPropertyPredicate *titlePredicate =
    [MPMediaPropertyPredicate predicateWithValue:@"Friday"
                                     forProperty:MPMediaItemPropertyTitle

comparisonType:MPMediaPredicateComparisonContains];

    [query addFilterPredicate:titlePredicate];
}
```

You can combine multiple filter predicates to zero in on the media items you'd like. With these queries, you can build your own search UI, discover detailed information about the user's media library, and build awesome apps that play the user's music, podcasts, and other items.

With the music player controller and the media library, we've examined several ways to incorporate audio into your app. Whether you're playing a clicking sound when the user taps a button, sound effects for a game, or just some music, there's a framework in iOS that's right for you. Let's put this to work in a sample app.

Example: TitularSongs

The goal of this sample app is simple: find all of the songs in your iTunes library with the same name as the album they appear on. Open Xcode and select File ➤ New ➤ Project..., or press ⌘+Shift+N. Select Application in the leftmost column under the iOS section, and then select Single View Application on the right. Click Next, and then enter **TitularSongs** as the name for the project. Enter your company identifier and class prefix (I'll use **com.learncocoatouch** and **LCT**), select iPhone for Device Family, and ensure that Use Automatic Reference Counting is checked and both Use Storyboards and Include Unit Tests are unchecked. Click Next, and then click Create to save the project to disk.

First, let's add our user interface. This app will be fairly simple: a single table view. Open the main view controller's user interface file (LCTViewController.xib) in Xcode. Open the Object Library by selecting View ➤ Utilities ➤ Show Object Library or by pressing Control+Option+⌘+3. Once it's open, drag a table view out of the library and place it on the view. It should automatically resize itself to the size of the view; if not, resize it to fit the view exactly, looking like Figure 11-3. Next, set your view controller as the table view's delegate and data source by holding Control and dragging from the table view to the File's Owner object at the left of Xcode's editing pane. Do this twice, selecting both `dataSource` and `delegate`.

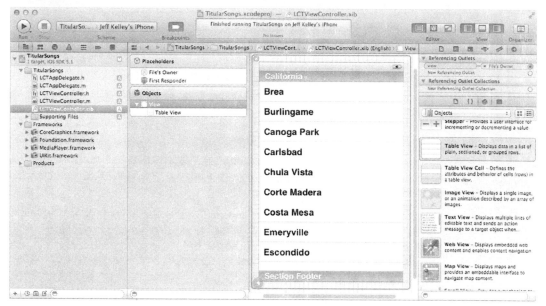

Figure 11-3. *Our view controller's user interface*

Next, let's open the view controller's header file (`LCTViewController.h`). Since we've made it the data source and delegate for the table view, we'll need to conform to the `UITableViewDataSource` and `UITableViewDelegate` protocols. Add the code in bold:

```
#import <UIKit/UIKit.h>

@interface LCTViewController : UIViewController <UITableViewDataSource,
UITableViewDelegate>

@end
```

You may see some warnings in Xcode once you add these protocols to the class declaration. It's OK to ignore those for now; they're simply telling us that we haven't implemented required methods from those protocols, which we're about to do. Before we implement this view controller, add the MediaLibrary framework to your project and link it to your target. To do this, select the project at the top of the file browser in Xcode, click the TitularSongs target, and then select Build Phases in the editing pane. Expand the Link Binary With Libraries phase by clicking the triangle next to it, then press the Add button (+), and finally select `MediaPlayer.framework`.

Now that we've added the MediaPlayer framework to the project, let's implement our view controller. Open the view controller's implementation file (LCTViewController.m). Import the MediaPlayer headers by adding the line in bold at the top of the file:

```
#import "LCTViewController.h"
```

#import <MediaPlayer/MediaPlayer.h>

To store the list of all songs that meet our criteria, we'll use an NSArray object. Add it as a private instance variable by adding it to the class extension with the cold in bold:

```
@interface LCTViewController () {
    NSArray *_songs;
}

@end
```

We'll search the library in the viewDidLoad method. Add the search code (we'll examine it after) by adding the lines in bold:

```
- (void)viewDidLoad
{
    [super viewDidLoad];
    // Do any additional setup after loading the view, typically from a nib.

    MPMediaQuery *mediaQuery = [MPMediaQuery songsQuery];

    // Iterate through songs, figuring out if they share a title with their album. If
    // they do, add them to an array.
    NSMutableArray *matchingSongs = [[NSMutableArray alloc] init];

    // Create a block called on each item; it will add the item to the array if it meets
    // our criteria.
    void (^songBlock)(id, NSUInteger, BOOL *) = ^(id obj, NSUInteger idx,
BOOL *stop) {
        MPMediaItem *song = (MPMediaItem *)obj;
        NSString *songTitle = [song
valueForProperty:MPMediaItemPropertyTitle];
        NSString *albumTitle = [song
valueForProperty:MPMediaItemPropertyAlbumTitle];

        if ([songTitle isEqualToString:albumTitle]) {
            @synchronized(matchingSongs) {
                [matchingSongs addObject:song];
            }
        }
```

```
    };

    // Iterate through the items in the query, calling songBlock with each.
    [[mediaQuery items] enumerateObjectsWithOptions:NSEnumerationConcurrent
                                        usingBlock:songBlock];

    // Now that we have the data, store it in the _songs variable.
    _songs = [NSArray arrayWithArray:matchingSongs];
}
```

The first thing this code does is fetch the list of all songs on the device with the
songsQuery method and store it in the mediaQuery variable. Then, we create a
mutable array to which we'll add the songs as we find them. Next, we create a
block called songBlock that we'll use to enumerate the songs. In it, we'll get the
song title and album title from the song; then, if they're equal, we'll add them to
the matchingSongs array. We use the @synchronized directive to ensure that we
aren't trying to modify the array from multiple threads at once. That this is
important is made clear on the next line: we're enumerating the objects in the
array returned by the items method of our query using the
NSEnumerationConcurrent option, which will result on the block running
concurrently on multiple threads. Finally, once we're done enumerating the
songs, we'll store each matching song in the _songs array. Now that we have the
songs we're looking for, let's implement the table view methods to display our
results. Add the methods in bold before the @end compiler directive in your view
controller's implementation:

```
@implementation LCTViewController

...

- (NSInteger)numberOfSectionsInTableView:(UITableView *)tableView
{
    return 1;
}

- (NSInteger)tableView:(UITableView *)tableView
numberOfRowsInSection:(NSInteger)section
{
    return [_songs count];
}

- (UITableViewCell *)tableView:(UITableView *)tableView
        cellForRowAtIndexPath:(NSIndexPath *)indexPath
{
    NSString *cellIdentifier = @"songCell";

    UITableViewCell *cell = [tableView
dequeueReusableCellWithIdentifier:cellIdentifier];
```

```
    if (cell == nil) {
        cell = [[UITableViewCell alloc]
initWithStyle:UITableViewCellStyleSubtitle
                                        reuseIdentifier:cellIdentifier];
    }

    MPMediaItem *song = [_songs objectAtIndex:[indexPath row]];

    [[cell textLabel] setText:[song
valueForProperty:MPMediaItemPropertyTitle]];
    [[cell detailTextLabel] setText:[song
valueForProperty:MPMediaItemPropertyArtist]];

    MPMediaItemArtwork *albumArt = [song
valueForProperty:MPMediaItemPropertyArtwork];
    CGSize imageSize = CGSizeMake([tableView rowHeight], [tableView
rowHeight]);

    [[cell imageView] setImage:[albumArt imageWithSize:imageSize]];

    return cell;
}
```

@end

Our table view will have one section, with as many rows as we have matching songs. In the tableView:cellForRowAtIndexPath; method, we'll create (or reuse) a cell with the UITableViewCellStyleSubtitle style and then populate it with the song title (which, thanks to the songs we're searching for, is also the album title) and the artist name. Next, we get an MPMediaItemArtwork object representing the album art for the song, and then we'll use it to populate the cell's image view. Build and run the app on an iOS device, and the songs in your media library that match our criteria will appear in your table view. Figure 11-4 shows the app running on my iPhone, displaying the songs in my library that meet this criteria. Note that not all albums may have album art, especially those in iTunes Match.

Figure 11-4. *The TitularSongs sample app*

So far, so good. Let's add one more feature to this app: playing the songs. Add the delegate method `tableView:didSelectRowAtIndexPath:` to the implementation file before the @end directive. Create it with the lines in bold:

```
- (void)tableView:(UITableView *)tableView
didSelectRowAtIndexPath:(NSIndexPath *)indexPath
{
    [tableView deselectRowAtIndexPath:indexPath animated:YES];

    MPMediaItem *song = [_songs objectAtIndex:[indexPath row]];

    NSArray *items = [NSArray arrayWithObject:song];

    MPMediaItemCollection *itemCollection =
```

```
     [MPMediaItemCollection collectionWithItems:items];

     [[MPMusicPlayerController iPodMusicPlayer]
      setQueueWithItemCollection:itemCollection];

     [[MPMusicPlayerController iPodMusicPlayer] play];
}
```

This code creates an MPMediaItemCollection from an array containing only the selected song and then directs the system-wide iPod music player to play it. Build and run the application, and then tap on one of the songs; it'll begin playing. Since we haven't built in any playback controls into this app, you'll need to use the Music app on the device to stop the audio. We used the iPod music player in the app, so clicking Stop in Xcode to stop execution isn't enough, because it hands off control of the audio to the built-in iPod player.

As you can see, the MediaPlayer framework allows us to manipulate the user's iTunes library to perform arbitrary searches and play back the content at will. Next, we'll look at adding another media type to your application: video.

Playing Video

As with playing audio, there are multiple ways to play video on iOS. What you'll use depends on your needs. Some apps simply need to provide videos for their user to consume at their leisure, while other apps may want to play videos with no controls or videos on certain parts of the screen. At a high level, you can use the MPMoviePlayerController class to play video, but if you need more fine-grained control, you can use the AVFoundation framework. Let's first discuss the MPMoviePlayerController class.

Using MPMoviePlayerController

If you have a local video file, you can create an MPMoviePlayerController with the following code:

```
NSURL *movieURL = [[NSBundle mainBundle] URLForResource:@"myMovie"
                                          withExtension:@"mov"];

MPMoviePlayerController *moviePlayerController =
[[MPMoviePlayerController alloc] initWithContentURL:movieURL];
```

It's also possible to play video from a network stream; we'll get into that later. Similar to the AVAudioPlayer class, the MPMoviePlayerController class maintains buffers and engages hardware; to that end, you can call its prepareToPlay instance method to buffer the video and avoid a delay when you call its play method. Unlike the AVAudioPlayer class, however, you aren't done after you call play; because we're talking about video here, we're necessarily talking about UI, and you need a place to put the video as it's displayed to the user.

> **NOTE:** By default, a movie player controller will play the audio of a movie along with the audio in your app. If you'd like to change this behavior and ensure that the movie's audio is not mixed with the other audio in your app, set the useApplicationAudioSession property of your movie player controller to NO.

Using MPMoviePlayerViewController

The easiest way to play video is to not use an MPMoviePlayerController at all but instead to use another class that uses it, the MPMoviePlayerViewController class. This class is a self-contained way to present a full-screen view controller and play a movie in it. It contains its own logic for displaying movie controls but otherwise acts like a normal view controller. Using it is as easy as creating a movie player controller:

```
NSURL *movieURL = [[NSBundle mainBundle] URLForResource:@"myMovie"
                                           withExtension:@"mov"];

MPMoviePlayerViewController *moviePlayerViewController =
[[MPMoviePlayerViewController alloc] initWithContentURL:movieURL];
```

You can access the movie player controller that the movie player view controller uses behind the scenes by accessing its moviePlayer property. This allows you to configure the MPMoviePlayerController properties you need for playback—we'll get to those in a bit. When you want to present a movie player, instead of using presentModalViewController:animated:, you'll use presentMoviePlayerViewControllerAnimated:, a similar method designed for this specific use (and defined in the MediaPlayer framework as a category on UIViewController) that will display the movie player view controller modally. The sole parameter to this method is the movie player view controller; it always displays with an animation. When your video is done, call dismissMoviePlayerViewControllerAnimated to dismiss it. But how do you know that the video is done? For that, you'll need to use the MPMoviePlayerController in the moviePlayer property of the MPMoviePlayerViewController.

One of the things you can do with an MPMoviePlayerController is sign up for notifications it posts at different points in the movie-playing process. The notification in this case, MPMoviePlayerPlaybackDidFinishNotification, is posted when the video finishes, whether it finishes because it played in its entirety or because an error occurred. In the case of an MPMoviePlayerViewController, you might dismiss the view controller when its video has finished. The MPMoviePlayerPlaybackDidFinishNotification notification will not be sent if the user presses the Done button to stop watching the video; in that case, the movie player controller will post the MPMoviePlayerDidExitFullscreenNotification notification. If you don't use a movie player view controller, however, you can do more interesting things with the video by simply using the movie player controller.

Using the MPMoviePlayerController's View

One of the MPMoviePlayerController's properties is the view property. This is a regular UIView and can be placed in your view hierarchy wherever you like. When it appears, it will contain a system-drawn Play button. On an iPhone or iPod touch, because the screen size is limited, the video will automatically play in full=screen. On an iPad, the video will by default play inline right where the movie player controller's view is. You can, of course, play the video without it being full-screen on an iPhone or iPod touch or play the video full-screen on an iPad. Whether or not the video is currently playing and no matter which device you're using, you can call the movie player controller's setFullscreen:animated: method to enter and exit full-screen playback. This generates a notification you can listen for, either MPMoviePlayerDidEnterFullscreenNotification or MPMoviePlayerDidExitFullscreenNotification. When the video is playing in full-screen mode, the system automatically provides a Done button that the user can press to exit the full-screen mode.

The movie controls—the play, pause, rewind, and fast-forward buttons, among others—are provided standard on a movie player controller's view. If you'd like to supply your own, perhaps to use your app's UI style, you can use the movie player controller's controlStyle property. Set this to the MPMovieControlStyleNone constant to remove the built-in controls, and then add your own controls as subviews of the movie player controller's view. Simply call the play, pause, stop, and other methods as appropriate when your custom controls are used.

Playing Network Video

The initialization method for the MPMoviePlayerController class is initWithContentURL:. While you can use a file URL for a file located in your application's bundle or elsewhere in the filesystem, you can also use a remote

URL to play a movie from a server. If the video's URL was
http://www.example.com/myMovie.mp4, the code to create a movie player
controller would be as follows:

```
NSURL *movieURL = [NSURL URLWithString:@"http://www.example.com/myMovie.mp4"];

MPMoviePlayerController *moviePlayerController =
[[MPMoviePlayerController alloc] initWithContentURL:movieURL];
```

If you do this, there are some considerations to keep in mind. Since part of the
remote movie is its metadata such as duration, you can't necessarily access
those immediately. If the movie player controller can't determine the duration of
its movie, it will return 0.0 for its duration property. If that happens, you can
sign up to be notified when the duration is known by registering an observer for
the MPMovieDurationAvailableNotification notification. Assuming you have a
label called durationLabel, here's how you would initialize it with the movie's
duration:

```
MPMoviePlayerController *moviePlayerController =
[[MPMoviePlayerController alloc] initWithContentURL:movieURL];

NSTimeInterval duration = [moviePlayerController duration];

if (duration > 0.0) {
    NSString *durationString =
    [NSString stringWithFormat:@"%f", duration];

    [durationLabel setText:durationString];
}
else {
    [durationLabel setText:nil];

    NSNotificationCenter *notificationCenter = [NSNotificationCenter
defaultCenter];

    [notificationCenter addObserverForName:MPMovieDurationAvailableNotification
                            object:moviePlayerController
                            queue:[NSOperationQueue mainQueue]
                        usingBlock:^(NSNotification *note) {
                            NSString *durationString =
                            [NSString stringWithFormat:@"%f", duration];

                            [durationLabel setText:durationString];
                        }];
}
```

Note that we register for this notification only for the movie player controller in
question; you might have several movie player controllers active at one time, so
you want to be sure you're getting the duration from the right one.

Getting Video Thumbnails

Another item you won't be able to get immediately from a video played over the network is a thumbnail image to use. Ordinarily, you would use the `thumbnailImageAtTime:timeOption:` method to retrieve a thumbnail from a movie player controller. The first parameter to this method is an `NSTimeInterval` value representing the time in the movie, in seconds from its beginning, for which you'd like a thumbnail, which can be useful if, for instance, you're building a UI that navigates between multiple chapters in a movie. The second parameter is an `MPMovieTimeOption` constant, which will be either `MPMovieTimeOptionNearestKeyFrame` or `MPMovieTimeOptionExact`. The former doesn't attempt to get a thumbnail at *exactly* the time specified, instead opting for the nearest keyframe, which can offer better performance, while the second value causes the thumbnail to come from exactly the specified time in the video. Depending on the video compression codec used to compress the video, this can result in the movie player controller compositing several frames of compressed video together to create the desired thumbnail.

The problem with using the `thumbnailImageAtTime:timeOption:` method is that it runs synchronously. For a network video, if you call this method and ask for a thumbnail near the end, this can cause the method to block the current thread for quite some time. To work around this, as well as to offer the ability to request multiple thumbnails at once separately and asynchronously, the `MPMoviePlayerController` class offers the `requestThumbnailImagesAtTimes:timeOption:` method. The first parameter is an NSArray of NSNumber objects representing `NSTimeInterval` values in seconds from the beginning of the video, and the second is the same `MPMovieTimeOption` value as before. When you create the NSNumber objects for use in this array, be sure to use the `numberWithDouble:` class method of NSNumber, because using `numberWithInt:` or other methods that use integers will cause an error. The movie player controller is expecting an `NSTimeInterval` value, which is defined as a double. Once the thumbnails are available, the movie player controller posts a notification with the name `MPMoviePlayerThumbnailImageRequestDidFinishNotification`. Passed with this notification in its `userInfo` dictionary are two objects. One is the NSNumber object representing the time in the movie in seconds from its beginning for which you're requesting the thumbnail, which will be associated with the key `MPMoviePlayerThumbnailTimeKey`. The other object will be either the thumbnail image, represented by a `UIImage` object, or an error, represented by an `NSError` object, associated with one of two keys: `MPMoviePlayerThumbnailImageKey` or `MPMoviePlayerThumbnailErrorKey`, depending on if the operation was successful.

Finally, if you need to cancel thumbnail requests—for instance, if the user leaves a view controller that was to display the thumbnail images—you can call the movie player controller's `cancelAllThumbnailImageRequests` method, which, as the name implies, will cancel all thumbnail image requests currently pending.

AirPlay

AirPlay is Apple's technology for streaming audio and video over a local network. If you have an Apple TV at home and a wireless network, you can use it to receive audio and video from your iOS devices. By default, an `MPMoviePlayerController` will not allow its videos to be streamed to other devices via AirPlay; to allow this, set the `allowsAirPlay` property of the movie player controller to `YES`. Once you do, the controls in the `MPMoviePlayerController`'s view will contain a button to send the currently playing video to another device.

We've covered pretty much everything involved in using the `MPMoviePlayerController` class to play video. You can also use the AVFoundation framework to play video—particularly if you need to play multiple videos at once—but for the vast majority of needs, `MPMoviePlayerController` and `MPMoviePlayerViewController` suffice to handle the playback of video. Let's write a sample app to put this knowledge to use.

Example: CustomPlayer

This sample app will be fairly simple. Our goal is to obtain a video—we'll use a `UIImagePickerController` for that—and then to display the video using custom controls. Open Xcode and select File ➤ New ➤ Project…, or press ⌘+Shift+N. Select Application in the leftmost column under the iOS section, and then select Single View Application on the right. Click Next, and then enter **CustomPlayer** as the name for the project. Enter your company identifier and class prefix (I'll use **com.learncocoatouch** and **LCT**), select iPhone for Device Family, and ensure that Use Automatic Reference Counting is checked and both Use Storyboards and Include Unit Tests are unchecked. Click Next, and then click Create to save the project to disk.

First, let's add our user interface. This app will be fairly simple: a single table view. Open the main view controller's user interface file (`LCTViewController.xib`) in Xcode. Since we'll be embedding this view controller in a navigation controller, select the view and open the Attributes Inspector by selecting View ➤ Utilities ➤ Show Attribute Inspector or by pressing Option+⌘+4. Under Simulated Metrics, select Navigation Bar for the Top Bar setting. You should see a navigation bar appear, indicating the portion of the screen it will take up. Open the Object Library by selecting View ➤ Utilities ➤ Show Object Library or by pressing Control+Option+⌘+3. Once it's open, drag two Round Rect Buttons into your view. Double-click them to change their title; set the title of one to Play and the title of the other to Fullscreen. Drag them down to the bottom of the user interface (a blue guide will appear to show you the appropriate distances from the bottom to use). Next, drag a new View object from the object library into your view, and resize it to fill the space above the buttons, using the blue guides to line it up. When you're done, it should look like Figure 11-5.

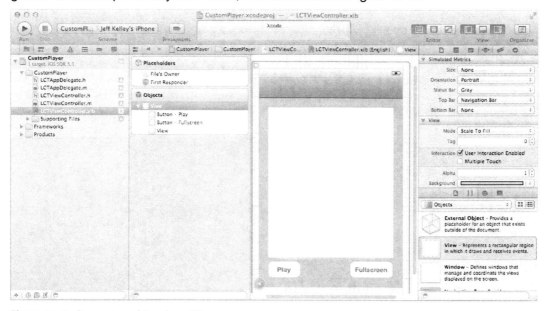

Figure 11-5. *Our custom video player UI*

Since this app is going to support rotation, we'll need to set the autoresizing masks for these views appropriately. We want the Play button to stay in the bottom-left corner, the Fullscreen button to stay in the bottom-right corner, and the view above them to grow with the view. Open the Size Inspector by selecting View ➤ Utilities ➤ Show Size Inspector or by pressing Option+⌘+5. Select the Play button by single-clicking it. In the Size Inspector, adjust the area above the label that reads *Autosizing* to modify the autosizing mask such that the bottom and left struts (the lines outside of the inner box) are selected (indicated by a solid red line) and the other struts and both springs (the arrows inside the inner square) are not selected (indicated by a dashed red line). Next, select the Fullscreen button and set it to the mirror image of the Play button; the only selected springs or struts should be the bottom and right struts. Next, for the view above the two buttons, set the autoresizing mask so that all four struts and both springs are selected; this will allow it to resize with the view.

Our user interface is set up, so let's define some outlets for these objects, as well as some actions for the buttons. We'll also indicate that this view controller conforms to a few of delegate protocols: one for an action sheet, one for a navigation controller, and one for an image picker controller. Open the view controller's header file (LCTViewController.h), and add the code in bold:

```
#import <UIKit/UIKit.h>

@interface LCTViewController : UIViewController <UIActionSheetDelegate,
UIImagePickerControllerDelegate, UINavigationControllerDelegate>

@property (strong, nonatomic) IBOutlet UIView *movieHostingView;
@property (strong, nonatomic) IBOutlet UIButton *playPauseButton;
@property (strong, nonatomic) IBOutlet UIButton *fullscreenButton;

- (IBAction)playPauseButtonPressed:(id)sender;
- (IBAction)fullscreenButtonPressed:(id)sender;

@end
```

Next, let's connect our view objects to these outlets and actions. Open the user interface file (LCTViewController.xib) again. Holding Control, and drag from the File's Owner at the left of Xcode's editing pane to the view above your buttons, selecting movieHostingView from the Outlets pop-up that appears. Do the same for the buttons, selecting the playPauseButton outlet for the button labeled Play and the fullscreenButton outlet for the button labeled Fullscreen. Now let's connect the actions; holding Control, drag from the button labeled Play to the File's Owner object, selecting the playPauseButtonPressed: action from the Sent Events pop-up that appears. Do the same for the button labeled Fullscreen, selecting the fullscreenButtonPressed: action from the pop-up instead. This completes our user interface setup; let's move into the implementation.

Since we're going to embed the view controller in a navigation controller, we'll need to modify the app delegate's implementation. Open its implementation file (LCTAppDelegate.m), and modify the application:didFinishLaunchingWithOptions: method by adding the lines in bold and removing the struck-out line:

```
- (BOOL)application:(UIApplication *)application
didFinishLaunchingWithOptions:(NSDictionary *)launchOptions
{
    self.window = [[UIWindow alloc] initWithFrame:[[UIScreen mainScreen]
bounds]];
    // Override point for customization after application launch.
```

```
    self.viewController = [[LCTViewController alloc]
initWithNibName:@"LCTViewController" bundle:nil];

    UINavigationController *navigationController =
    [[UINavigationController alloc] initWithRootViewController:[self
viewController]];

    self.window.rootViewController = self.viewController;
    self.window.rootViewController = navigationController;
    [self.window makeKeyAndVisible];
    return YES;
}
```

Before we implement our view controller, add the MediaPlayer and MobileCoreServices frameworks to your project and link them to your target. To do this, select the project at the top of the file browser in Xcode, click the CustomPlayer target, and then select Build Phases" in the editing pane. Expand the Link Binary With Libraries phase by clicking the triangle next to it, and then click the Add button (+) and select MediaPlayer.framework. Click the Add button again and select MobileCoreServices.framework.

Now that we've added the MediaPlayer and MobileCoreServices frameworks to the project, let's implement our view controller. Open the view controller's implementation file (LCTViewController.m). Import the MediaPlayer and MobileCoreServices headers by adding the line in bold at the top of the file:

```
#import "LCTViewController.h"

#import <MediaPlayer/MediaPlayer.h>
#import <MobileCoreServices/MobileCoreServices.h>
```

Next, we'll add a private instance variable to store a pointer to an MPMoviePlayerController. We're also going to add a method that will be called by a button on the navigation bar to bring up an image picker controller, and we're going to add a method to show this image picker controller. Modify the class extension by adding the following code in bold:

```
@interface LCTViewController () {
    MPMoviePlayerController *_moviePlayerController;
}

- (void)selectVideoButtonPressed:(id)sender;
-
(void)showImagePickerForSourceType:(UIImagePickerControllerSourceType)sourc
eType;

@end
```

Now we can implement the view controller. The first thing we'll do is add @synthesize directives for our properties. Second, we'll implement the initWithNibName:bundle: method to do some additional setup when our view controller is created. To perform these tasks, add the lines in bold:

```
@implementation LCTViewController

@synthesize movieHostingView;
@synthesize playPauseButton;
@synthesize fullscreenButton;

- (id)initWithNibName:(NSString *)nibNameOrNil bundle:(NSBundle
*)nibBundleOrNil
{
    self = [super initWithNibName:nibNameOrNil bundle:nibBundleOrNil];

    if (self) {
        [self setTitle:@"CustomPlayer"];

        SEL selectVideoSelector = @selector(selectVideoButtonPressed:);
        UIBarButtonItem *selectVideoButton =
        [[UIBarButtonItem alloc]
initWithBarButtonSystemItem:UIBarButtonSystemItemCamera
                                                     target:self

action:selectVideoSelector];

        [[self navigationItem] setRightBarButtonItem:selectVideoButton];
    }

    return self;
}
```

The button we create here will be used to bring up an image picker controller. First, we'll determine whether video is available using the camera, the photo library, or both. Depending on what we find, we'll show either the image picker controller or an action sheet to ask the user which source type to use. We'll implement the selectVideoButtonPressed: method first. Add the lines in bold after the view controller methods from the template but before the @end compiler directive:

```
- (void)selectVideoButtonPressed:(id)sender
{
    // Determine the ways in which we can get a video from an image picker
controller.
    BOOL canUseCamera = NO;

    if ([UIImagePickerController
        isSourceTypeAvailable:UIImagePickerControllerSourceTypeCamera] &&
```

```
        [[UIImagePickerController

availableMediaTypesForSourceType:UIImagePickerControllerSourceTypeCamera]
        containsObject:(NSString *)kUTTypeMovie]) {
        canUseCamera = YES;
    }

    BOOL canUsePhotoLibrary = NO;

    if ([UIImagePickerController

isSourceTypeAvailable:UIImagePickerControllerSourceTypePhotoLibrary] &&
        [[UIImagePickerController

availableMediaTypesForSourceType:UIImagePickerControllerSourceTypePhotoLibr
ary]
        containsObject:(NSString *)kUTTypeMovie]) {
        canUsePhotoLibrary = YES;
    }

    // If we can use both source types, show the user an action sheet to
allow them to
    // decide which to use.
    if (canUseCamera == YES && canUsePhotoLibrary == YES) {
        UIActionSheet *actionSheet =
        [[UIActionSheet alloc] initWithTitle:nil
                                    delegate:self
                           cancelButtonTitle:@"Cancel"
                      destructiveButtonTitle:nil
                           otherButtonTitles:@"Take a Video", @"Use Photo
Library", nil];

        [actionSheet showInView:[self view]];
    }
    else if (canUseCamera == YES && canUsePhotoLibrary == NO) {
        [self
showImagePickerForSourceType:UIImagePickerControllerSourceTypeCamera];
    }
    else if (canUseCamera == NO && canUsePhotoLibrary == YES) {
        [self
showImagePickerForSourceType:UIImagePickerControllerSourceTypePhotoLibrary]
;
    }
    else {
        // Neither the camera or the photo library are available.
        UIAlertView *alertView =
        [[UIAlertView alloc] initWithTitle:@"Error Loading Video"
                                   message:@"No source type is available."
                                  delegate:nil
                         cancelButtonTitle:@"OK"
```

```
                            otherButtonTitles:nil];
        [alertView show];
    }
}
```

In this method, we use `canUseCamera` and `canUsePhotoLibrary` to store whether we can use the camera or photo library, respectively. To determine this, we use the `UIImagePickerController` class method `isSourceTypeAvailable:` to determine whether the source is available and then use `availableMediaTypesForSourceType:` to determine whether the source type can return videos. This is important because some older iOS devices have cameras but are not capable of shooting video, though they can take pictures. If we find that both source types are available and can return video, we create a `UIActionSheet` with both choices and present it to the user. If we find that only one of the source types is available and can return video, we call the `showImagePickerForSourceType:` method on our view controller with that source type. If neither source type is available, we notify the user with a `UIAlertView`. If we present the action sheet, the action sheet delegate method `actionSheet:clickedButtonAtIndex:` is called when the user selects an option. Let's add a `#pragma mark` statement before we implement this method to help us organize the code a bit. Add this code in bold after the previous method you implemented but before the `@end` directive:

```
#pragma mark - UIActionSheetDelegate Protocol Methods

- (void)actionSheet:(UIActionSheet *)actionSheet
clickedButtonAtIndex:(NSInteger)buttonIndex
{
    if (buttonIndex == 0) {
        // The user selected "Take a Video."
        [self
showImagePickerForSourceType:UIImagePickerControllerSourceTypeCamera];
    }
    else if (buttonIndex == 1) {
        // The user selected "Use Photo Library."
        [self
showImagePickerForSourceType:UIImagePickerControllerSourceTypePhotoLibrary]
;
    }
}
```

As you can see, this method simply examines the index of the selected button and calls `showImagePickerForSourceType:` with the source type the user selected. Now that we've added this method, let's implement `showImagePickerForSourceType:`. In keeping with how we're organizing our code, add this method before the `#pragma mark` line you added before by inserting the lines in bold:

```
-
(void)showImagePickerForSourceType:(UIImagePickerControllerSourceType)sourc
eType
{
    UIImagePickerController *imagePicker =
    [[UIImagePickerController alloc] init];

    [imagePicker setDelegate:self];
    [imagePicker setMediaTypes:[NSArray arrayWithObject:(NSString
*)kUTTypeMovie]];
    [imagePicker setSourceType:sourceType];

    [self presentModalViewController:imagePicker animated:YES];
}
```

In this method, we create a UIImagePickerController, set our view controller as
its delegate, set its mediaTypes property to an array including only the
kUTTypeMovie type to prevent the user from selecting images, and finally set the
source type to the given source type. We then present the image picker
controller modally. The user will then either press Cancel, take a video, or select
a video, at which point the image picker controller will call its delegate methods.
Let's implement those now. We'll add a new #pragma mark section for these
methods, so add the following lines in bold after the
actionSheet:clickedButtonAtIndex: method but before the @end directive:

```
#pragma mark - UIImagePickerControllerDelegate Protocol Methods

- (void)imagePickerControllerDidCancel:(UIImagePickerController *)picker
{
    [self dismissModalViewControllerAnimated:YES];
}

- (void)imagePickerController:(UIImagePickerController *)picker
didFinishPickingMediaWithInfo:(NSDictionary *)info
{
    [self dismissModalViewControllerAnimated:YES];

    NSURL *movieURL = [info objectForKey:UIImagePickerControllerMediaURL];

    if (movieURL != nil) {
        _moviePlayerController =
        [[MPMoviePlayerController alloc] initWithContentURL:movieURL];

        [_moviePlayerController setControlStyle:MPMovieControlStyleNone];

        [[_moviePlayerController view]
          setAutoresizingMask:(UIViewAutoresizingFlexibleWidth |
                               UIViewAutoresizingFlexibleHeight)];
```

```
        [[_moviePlayerController view] setClipsToBounds:YES];
        [[_moviePlayerController view] setFrame:[[self movieHostingView]
bounds]];
        [[self movieHostingView] addSubview:[_moviePlayerController view]];
    }
}
```

Whether the user cancels, takes a video, or selects a video, the first thing we do is call dismissModalViewControllerAnimated: on our view controller to get rid of the image picker controller. If the user didn't cancel, we get the movie URL from the info dictionary in the imagePickerController:didFinishPickingMediaWithInfo: method. Here, we create an MPMoviePlayerController pointing to this URL. We set its control style to MPMovieControlStyleNone to remove the built-in controls and then set its view's autoresizing mask to resize along with its containing view. We set the clipsToBounds property of the movie player controller's view to YES in order to prevent it from drawing outside of its frame, then we set its frame to the bounds of the movie hosting view, which will cause it to fill the movie hosting view in its entirety. Finally, we add the movie player controller's view as a subview of the movie hosting view.

Now that we've added this code, if the user of this app were to press the camera button again to choose a new video, our code would add a new movie player controller's view to the movie hosting view. To prevent this, modify the selectVideoButtonPressed: method by adding the lines in bold at the beginning of the method:

```
- (void)selectVideoButtonPressed:(id)sender
{
    // If there is already a movie player controller, clean it up.
    if (_moviePlayerController != nil) {
        [[_moviePlayerController view] removeFromSuperview];
        _moviePlayerController = nil;
    }

    // Determine the ways in which we can get a video from an image picker
controller.
    BOOL canUseCamera = NO;
    ...
```

This will prevent us from having multiple movie player controllers' views in the view hierarchy at once. Next up, let's add methods for our Play and Fullscreen buttons. Add these two methods before the #pragma mark sections, after showImagePickerForSourceType:, by adding the code in bold:

```
- (void)playPauseButtonPressed:(id)sender
{
```

```
    if (_moviePlayerController == nil) {
        return;
    }

    if ([_moviePlayerController playbackState] ==
MPMoviePlaybackStatePlaying) {
        // The video is playing.
        [_moviePlayerController pause];
    }
    else {
        // The video is not playing.
        [_moviePlayerController play];
    }
}

- (void)fullscreenButtonPressed:(id)sender
{
    if (_moviePlayerController == nil) {
        return;
    }

    [_moviePlayerController setControlStyle:MPMovieControlStyleDefault];
    [_moviePlayerController setFullscreen:YES animated:YES];
}
```

In each method, we'll quit immediately by calling return if there isn't a movie player controller. In playPauseButtonPressed:, if the movie player controller is currently playing, we call pause on it; otherwise, we call play. In the fullscreenButtonPressed: method, before we call setFullscreen:animated: on the movie player controller, we set its control style back to MPMovieControlStyleDefault. If we didn't do this, the full-screen movie wouldn't have any playback controls, which would make it hard for us to get back! Now that we've added these methods, build and run the app on a device that supports video recording or that has videos in its media library. Press the camera button, select or take a video, and you can use the Play button to start the video in our view controller's view! If you've selected a video from the library, you may see a progress bar labeled "Compressing Video..." while the video is compressed for playback in your app.

There are a few more things we'll do to improve this app's experience. The movie player controller posts notifications to the default NSNotificationCenter as it plays, which we can take advantage of to modify our user interface. Modify the initWithNibName:bundle: method to listen for these notifications by adding the lines in bold:

```
- (id)initWithNibName:(NSString *)nibNameOrNil bundle:(NSBundle *)nibBundleOrNil
{
    self = [super initWithNibName:nibNameOrNil bundle:nibBundleOrNil];
```

```objc
    if (self) {
        [self setTitle:@"CustomPlayer"];

        SEL selectVideoSelector = @selector(selectVideoButtonPressed:);
        UIBarButtonItem *selectVideoButton =
        [[UIBarButtonItem alloc]
initWithBarButtonSystemItem:UIBarButtonSystemItemCamera
                                                    target:self

action:selectVideoSelector];

        [[self navigationItem] setRightBarButtonItem:selectVideoButton];

        [[NSNotificationCenter defaultCenter]
         addObserverForName:MPMoviePlayerPlaybackStateDidChangeNotification
         object:nil
         queue:[NSOperationQueue mainQueue]
         usingBlock:^(NSNotification *note) {
             MPMoviePlayerController *moviePlayerController = [note
object];

             if ([moviePlayerController playbackState] ==
MPMoviePlaybackStatePlaying) {
                 [[self playPauseButton] setTitle:@"Pause"
                                         forState:UIControlStateNormal];
             }
             else {
                 [[self playPauseButton] setTitle:@"Play"
                                         forState:UIControlStateNormal];
             }
         }];

        [[NSNotificationCenter defaultCenter]
         addObserverForName:MPMoviePlayerDidExitFullscreenNotification
         object:nil
         queue:[NSOperationQueue mainQueue]
         usingBlock:^(NSNotification *note) {
             MPMoviePlayerController *moviePlayerController = [note
object];

             [moviePlayerController
setControlStyle:MPMovieControlStyleNone];
         }];
    }

    return self;
}
```

In this code, we respond to two notifications, MPMoviePlayerPlaybackStateDidChangeNotification and MPMoviePlayerDidExitFullscreenNotification. For the former, we modify the title of the Play/Pause button; if our movie is playing, we set it to Pause, and if not, we set it to Play. For the latter, once the movie player isn't playing full-screen anymore, we set the movie player control style back to None. Since we've registered to receive these notifications, we need to remember to tell the notification center when we no longer need these notifications. To do that, add a dealloc method after initWithNibName:bundle: by adding the lines in bold:

```
- (void)dealloc
{
    [[NSNotificationCenter defaultCenter] removeObserver:self name:nil
object:nil];
}
```

With that, we're done! Any video you select or take using the image picker controller will play in the view controller we've created using our own custom controls. If you have an AirPlay-compatible device, go ahead and test sending the video to it from the full-screen view, too. Using this technique, you can incorporate videos into your app with your own custom UI, so you aren't limited to the built-in style for your app.

Summary

This chapter has been all about media, both audio and video. After reading it, you should be able to play audio and video in your app. For audio, you've learned three different ways to get sound from a file on a disk to your user's ears, and for video, you've learned how to display videos in your own UI or using built-in controls. Using these techniques, you'll be able to make rich apps that use media to gain your users' attention.

Localization and Internationalizion

As we near the end of this book, it's only appropriate that we discuss the process of internationalizing and localizing your app. As you develop the app, you're more than likely developing it in your native tongue. You may already have been thinking about supporting multiple languages in your apps, but in truth that's only part of the story. These processes include thinking about your users' desired language, currency, number formats, date formats, and culture when developing your app. In this chapter, we'll cover the different ways you can localize and internationalize your app, as well as some key considerations to make when doing so. First, though, let's talk about a more important question: *why*?

Many developers create their app in English and then release it worldwide on the App Store. For most of them, this works fairly well; English is spoken enough in countries other than the United States that they'll see sales in those countries, but the majority of their sales will come from English-speaking countries. As of this writing, the App Store is available in more than 120 countries, and iOS supports more than 50 languages. Making the decision to ignore 49 languages and have lackluster sales in 119 countries saves you time, but in the end it will probably cost you money. Localizing your app has an immediate impact, even before your app is downloaded, because you can localize the App Store description of your app. A user is more likely to download your app if she is able to read its description in the App Store. Following this chapter's guidelines, then, can lead to more sales and a much happier user base around the world.

Internationalization

The first thing we'll cover in this chapter is *internationalization*. You're probably already familiar with the concept of localization—translating an app into a different language—but internationalization is a bit more intricate than that. It covers the little things in your app: the way you represent numbers, dates, and currency, for instance. iOS supports your internationalization efforts using *locales*, which encapsulate regional conventions in the NSLocale class. Rather than the user selecting a locale at runtime—or worse, your app trying to determine it automatically—the system keeps track of the locale the user has selected. You can use the currentLocale class method to retrieve the NSLocale for the user. For testing purposes, you can change the selected locale on either an iOS device or the iOS Simulator. Note that this will not affect currently running apps; to test changing the locale in your apps, be sure to quit them before changing the locale. Open the Settings app, select General and then International. You'll see a screen similar to Figure 12-1. The locale can be changed by tapping the Region Format row, here set to United States. Changing the region format does not automatically change the device's language, which is done by tapping the Language row. We'll discuss changing the language later when we discuss localization.

Figure 12-1. *The International section of the General settings section*

Now that we've seen how to change the region format, we can look at how to use the user's selection when presenting data.

Using Numbers

Different areas represent numbers in different ways. A number represented as 1,000.42 in the United States is represented as 1 000,42 in France. The same number will be represented entirely differently in countries that don't use Arabic digits for numbers. Rather than having to write your own code to handle this and then accidentally getting it completely wrong for some countries, thereby angering those users, you can use the NSNumberFormatter class to automatically take the user's selected locale into account when displaying numbers and number strings (for example, one hundred twenty three) to the user.

Let's take a look at how to use `NSNumberFormatter`. If you look at the documentation, there are dozens of instance methods; you can customize the output of a number formatter to your heart's content if you like, but here we're more interested in getting the default behavior for a locale than defining a custom number format. To use the built-in formatting, simply call the `setNumberStyle:` method on your `NSNumberFormatter` object. The possible values include `NSNumberFormatterDecimalStyle`, `NSNumberFormatterCurrencyStyle`, `NSNumberFormatterPercentStyle`, `NSNumberFormatterScientificStyle`, `NSNumberFormatterNoStyle`, and `NSNumberFormatterSpellOutStyle`. To use the decimal style, create a number formatter as follows:

```
NSNumber *number = [NSNumber numberWithDouble:1000.42];
NSNumberFormatter *numberFormatter = [[NSNumberFormatter alloc] init];
[numberFormatter setNumberStyle:NSNumberFormatterDecimalStyle];

NSString *formattedString = [numberFormatter stringFromNumber:number];
```

With your locale set to United States, `formattedString` will be "1,000.42." With a locale set to French ➤ France, it's 1 000,42, and it's 1.000,42 for German ➤ Germany. You should use a number formatter any time you're going to display a number to the user in an internationalized app. By using the number formatters, your users will be able to tell that you've put thought into international versions of your app, which they'll appreciate.

Displaying numbers in the appropriate format isn't enough. If your app uses units of measure, such as for weight, length, or volume, you should use the unit system your user is used to. To support this, you can query the `NSLocale` object to see whether the locale uses the metric system:

```
NSLocale *locale = [NSLocale currentLocale];
NSNumber *usesMetricNumber = [locale objectForKey:NSLocaleUsesMetricSystem];
BOOL usesMetric = [usesMetricNumber boolValue];
```

Once you can determine whether you should use the metric system, you should (if necessary) convert the value to the user's measurement system. It's a small step but one that will make your users like your app better. To demonstrate this, let's make a sample app that uses the locale.

Example: LocaleNumbers

In this sample app, we'll use the current locale to write numbers appropriately for the user. Open Xcode and select File ➤ New ➤ Project…, or press

⌘+Shift+N. Select Application in the leftmost column under the iOS section, and then select Single View Application on the right. Click Next, and then enter **LocaleNumbers** as the name for the project. Enter your company identifier and class prefix (I'll use **com.learncocoatouch** and **LCT**), select iPhone for Device Family, and ensure that Use Automatic Reference Counting is checked and both Use Storyboards and Include Unit Tests are unchecked. Click Next, and then click Create to save the project to disk.

The UI of this project will be fairly simple: just a handful of labels. Open the main view controller's user interface file (`LCTViewController.xib`) in Xcode. Open the Object Library by selecting View ➤ Utilities ➤ Show Object Library or by pressing Control+Option+⌘+3. Once it's open, we'll add two labels for each of the six built-in `NSNumberFormatter` styles, making it 12 in total. Arrange them in six rows with two columns each. To make it easier, you can place two labels next to each other, hold Option, and drag to create duplicate labels, allowing you to create two at a time instead of one at a time. Double-click the labels in the left column to change their text; from top to bottom, set the labels to NoStyle, DecimalStyle, CurrencyStyle, PercentStyle, ScientificStyle, and SpellOutStyle. Let's make these labels bold. To make it easier, you can select them all at once; click underneath them in the view, and then drag to make a rectangle, selecting each view contained inside. Alternatively, you can hold Shift or ⌘ while clicking the labels to select more than one. Once you have all six labels selected, open the Attributes Inspector by selecting View ➤ Utilities ➤ Show Attribute Inspector or by pressing Option+⌘+4. Click the icon with a *T* in it at the right of the Font text box to adjust the labels' font; in the pop-up menu that appears, change System to System Bold. Note that when you do so, the size of the text increases. The labels had automatically sized themselves when you entered text into them. To automatically resize them to accommodate their new size, press ⌘+= with one or more label selected. For the other six labels, let's do two things: first, select them all and open the Attributes Inspector. Next to Alignment, select the rightmost section of the alignment button to set the labels' text to be right-aligned. Second, open the Size Inspector by selecting View ➤ Utilities ➤ Show Size Inspector or by pressing Option+⌘+5. Above Origin, there is a square with nine dots in it. Click the dot in the upper-right corner, which will anchor the labels to that corner of their frame as you change their size. Change the value of the text field above Width to 75, which will expand the labels to be 75 points wide. This will give them enough room to display their content, except for the last one, which corresponds to the "spell out" style. For this label, drag it down below the label to its left and expand it to fill the view horizontally; this should give it enough room. When you're done, the view should look like Figure 12-2.

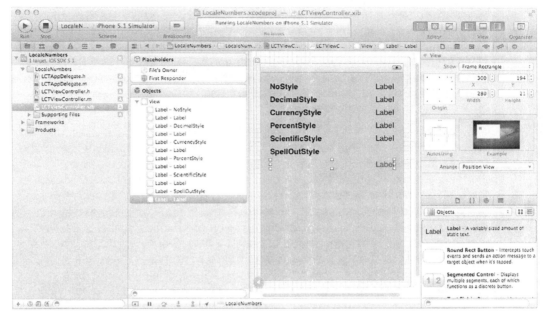

Figure 12-2. *Our sample project's user interface*

Let's define some outlets for these labels. We're going to be changing the labels only on the right, so we'll need only six outlets. Open the view controller's header file (LCTViewController.h), and add the lines in bold:

```
#import <UIKit/UIKit.h>

@interface LCTViewController : UIViewController

@property (weak, nonatomic) IBOutlet UILabel *noStyleLabel;
@property (weak, nonatomic) IBOutlet UILabel *decimalStyleLabel;
@property (weak, nonatomic) IBOutlet UILabel *currencyStyleLabel;
@property (weak, nonatomic) IBOutlet UILabel *percentStyleLabel;
@property (weak, nonatomic) IBOutlet UILabel *scientificStyleLabel;
@property (weak, nonatomic) IBOutlet UILabel *spellOutStyleLabel;

@end
```

Next, switch back to the user interface (LCTViewController.xib) and connect the outlets by holding Control and dragging from the File's Owner object to the left of Xcode's editor pane to each of the labels on the right in turn, selecting the outlet that matches the label to the left for each one. If you make a mistake, it's easy to remove the outlet connection. Click the label you made a mistake with, and open the Connections Inspector by selecting View ➤ Utilities ➤ Show Connections Inspector or by pressing Option+⌘+6. In the Utilities pane at the right of Xcode's window, you'll see a list of all the connected outlets for the selected object. Click the *X* in an outlet to disconnect it. Once your labels are all hooked up properly, let's switch to the implementation file (LCTViewController.m). Add the lines in bold after the @implementation directive to synthesize accessors for our properties:

```
@implementation LCTViewController

@synthesize noStyleLabel;
@synthesize decimalStyleLabel;
@synthesize currencyStyleLabel;
@synthesize percentStyleLabel;
@synthesize scientificStyleLabel;
@synthesize spellOutStyleLabel;
```

Next, we'll modify the viewDidLoad method to fill in these labels. Add the following lines in bold to the viewDidLoad method:

```
- (void)viewDidLoad
{
    [super viewDidLoad];
    // Do any additional setup after loading the view, typically from a nib.

    NSNumber *number = [NSNumber numberWithDouble:1000.42];

    NSNumberFormatter *numberFormatter = [[NSNumberFormatter alloc] init];

    [numberFormatter setNumberStyle:NSNumberFormatterNoStyle];
    [[self noStyleLabel] setText:[numberFormatter
stringFromNumber:number]];

    [numberFormatter setNumberStyle:NSNumberFormatterDecimalStyle];
    [[self decimalStyleLabel] setText:[numberFormatter
stringFromNumber:number]];

    [numberFormatter setNumberStyle:NSNumberFormatterCurrencyStyle];
    [[self currencyStyleLabel] setText:[numberFormatter
stringFromNumber:number]];

    [numberFormatter setNumberStyle:NSNumberFormatterPercentStyle];
    [[self percentStyleLabel] setText:[numberFormatter
stringFromNumber:number]];

    [numberFormatter setNumberStyle:NSNumberFormatterScientificStyle];
    [[self scientificStyleLabel] setText:[numberFormatter
stringFromNumber:number]];

    [numberFormatter setNumberStyle:NSNumberFormatterSpellOutStyle];
    [[self spellOutStyleLabel] setText:[numberFormatter
```

```
stringFromNumber:number]];
}
```

As you can see, for each label, we set a number formatter's style to the appropriate style constant and the value of the label to the same number, formatted with the appropriate style. Build and run the app. You should see the numbers formatted for your locale. Quit the app by clicking the Stop button in Xcode, and then switch back to the iOS Simulator, open Settings, select General ➤ International ➤ Region Format, and select a different locale. Build and run the app again, and you'll see the numbers formatted for the locale you chose. For the United States, French ➤ France, and Chinese ➤ China locales, the app should look like Figure 12-3.

Figure 12-3. *Our example app running in the United States locale (left), French ➤ France locale (center), and Chinese ➤ China (right)*

As you can see, the different number formatter styles have different effects on the numbers displayed in this app. With no region-specific code, however, you can use these styles to display numbers in your users' native format. Next, we'll discuss a similar problem with a similar solution: displaying dates.

Using Dates

Just as we use NSNumberFormatter to present strings from NSNumber objects that represent numbers, we use the NSDateFormatter object to present strings from NSDate objects that represent dates. Using an NSDateFormatter is similar to an NSNumberFormatter:

```
NSDateFormatter *dateFormatter = [[NSDateFormatter alloc] init];
[dateFormatter setDateStyle:NSDateFormatterFullStyle];

NSString *formattedDate = [dateFormatter stringFromDate:[NSDate date]];
```

In the U.S. locale, formattedDate is equal to "Wednesday, April 4, 2012" based on today's date being April 4, 2012. Since the NSDate object also represents time as well as date, we can use the setTimeStyle: instance method of NSDateFormatter to define how the time should be displayed:

```
NSDateFormatter *dateFormatter = [[NSDateFormatter alloc] init];
[dateFormatter setDateStyle:NSDateFormatterFullStyle];
[dateFormatter setTimeStyle:NSDateFormatterFullStyle];

NSString *formattedDate = [dateFormatter stringFromDate:[NSDate date]];
```

In the U.S. locale, formattedDate will now be equal to "Monday, April 16, 2012 12:24:50 AM Eastern Daylight Time," with values for the current date and time, of course, including daylight saving time based on the time zone. This same code, in the France locale, will set formattedDate to "lundi 16 avril 2012 00:24:50 heure avancée de l'Est." In the locale for Irish (Ireland), formattedDate is "Dé Luain 16 Aibreán 2012 00:26:23 GMT-04:00." Now, I don't speak the language nor have I ever been to Ireland, but I can say with confidence that if I need to build an app that displays dates to my users, I can do so no matter where in the world they are (so long as the device supports their locale).

There are a wide variety of date formatter styles you can use for formatting dates. You can set the date and time styles independently to get the format you need. Table 12-1 displays the most commonly used styles, along with U.S. locale examples of their results.

Table 12-1. *Date and Time Formatter Styles Available Using* NSDateFormatter

Date Formatter Style	Formatted Date and Time
NSDateFormatterShortStyle	4/4/12 11:55 PM
NSDateFormatterMediumStyle	Apr 4, 2012 11:55:00 PM

Date Formatter Style	Formatted Date and Time
NSDateFormatterLongStyle	April 4, 2012 11:56:10 PM EDT
NSDateFormatterFullStyle	Wednesday, April 4, 2012 11:56:46 PM Eastern Daylight Time

You can also use NSDateFormatterNoStyle for either the date or time style to omit that portion of the date. You can also mix and match styles; if you want a long date but a short time, you can set the styles accordingly, resulting in a formatted date of "April 4, 2012 11:55 PM."

Using date formatters is much easier than trying to write your own parser for dates. Like number formatters, they allow you to support any locale supported by the device. As iOS devices become available in more countries, Apple's internationalizing and localization teams add more locales and languages to the OS, allowing your apps to take advantage of them automatically.

Calendars, Date Components, and Time Zones

One potential issue you'll run into with the NSDate object is that it represents a single moment in time. It has a day, month, and year, but also a time of day. This can be an issue if you're trying to represent a specific calendar day; midnight in one time zone is the day before in another. To work around this, you can use the NSCalendar class to extract components from a date or create a date from components. If you wanted to represent the current day without including the current time, you could extract the month, day, and year from the date with the following code:

```
NSDate *currentDate = [NSDate date];
NSCalendar *currentCalendar = [NSCalendar currentCalendar];

NSDateComponents *dateComponents =
    [currentCalendar components:(NSYearCalendarUnit |
                                 NSMonthCalendarUnit |
                                 NSDayCalendarUnit)
                       fromDate:currentDate];
```

In this example, the dateComponents object will be created by the currentCalendar object, which will set its year, month, and day values from currentDate. Once you have date components from a date, you can modify these individual values to create a new date. For instance, to create an NSDate five years after currentDate, you could do the following:

```
NSDateComponents *nextDateComponents = [dateComponents copy];
[nextDateComponents setYear:[dateComponents year] + 5];

NSDate *nextDate = [currentCalendar dateFromComponents:nextDateComponents];
```

Again, it's the currentCalendar object that turns the numerical representation of the date specified by the month, day, and year values of the date components into an NSDate object. One thing to note about this example is that it does not preserve the current date's time; the new date will be created at midnight. For most of your users, the currentCalendar class method of NSCalendar will be the Gregorian calendar, but iOS also supports other calendars. As of iOS 5.1, the Japanese and Buddhist calendars can be used as the system calendar, although other calendars can be created as NSCalendar objects and used for date calculations. By using the currentCalendar method, you can ensure that calendar calculations, such as adding a month to the current date, will behave as your users expect. You could calculate a new date by adding the proper number of seconds to an existing date using the NSDate method dateByAddingTimeInterval:, but if you're making assumptions about the user's calendar, you can quickly confuse them.

Dealing with numbers, dates, and the like all attempt to help you display information to the user that's relevant to them based on where they live. Just as critical, however, is to consider the data you're getting from the user.

Processing User Input

Although it may seem obvious, iOS users usually want to write in the same language they read. One of the key advantages to iOS devices' software keyboard is that it can support any written language, even languages composed of complex Asian characters. Figure 12-4 displays several different keyboards available to your users.

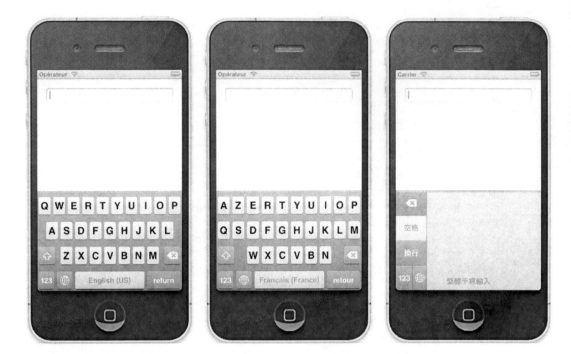

Figure 12-4. *Three different keyboards (from left to right): English, French, and Traditional Chinese in Handwriting mode*

As you can see, the English and French keyboards are very similar, but the Chinese keyboard is in handwriting mode, which allows the user to use their finger to draw characters. When the user has more than one keyboard available, a globe icon appears in the bottom row; tapping this icon will switch between keyboards.

How you react to text provided by the user is up to you, but a general rule is to use UTF encoding for any web services you use rather than ASCII. UTF is designed to accept multilingual input. Even though this may seem like a trivial consideration, if your user has special Unicode characters in their name, they won't appreciate it being garbled by your app.

You should also take special care when dealing with text displayed to the user. Wherever possible, your app should display its content in the user's native language.

Localization

The key difference between internationalization and localization is that internationalization makes the app more generic, able to support whatever locale the user's phone is set to, while localization is about providing alternate content for the user's chosen language. You can provide content for as many or as few languages as you'd like. Any app resource—images, video, text, audio, and more—can be localized. If you localize one resource, however, that doesn't mean you need to localize them all, so if you have a company logo that is the same across all languages, you don't need to do anything to keep it the same.

When any file in your app's bundle is localized, the system moves it to a subfolder of its current location named after the development language of your app. For this chapter, let's assume that's English. To mark a file as localizable, select it in Xcode's Project Navigator, and then open the File Inspector by selecting View ➤ Utilities ➤ Show File Inspector or by pressing ⌘+Option+1. Scrolling if needed, find the Localization group in the File Inspector on the right. By default, it will either be empty or have one language listed, depending on the application template you use. Figure 12-5 shows a sample image with two localizations: English and French. To mark a file as localizable, click the plus underneath the list of localizations; this will move it to a subfolder of the current folder (for English, that folder will be named en.lproj) automatically. You won't see this folder in Xcode's list of files in the Project Navigator, but it's there, created as a subfolder of the folder that contained the now-localized file.

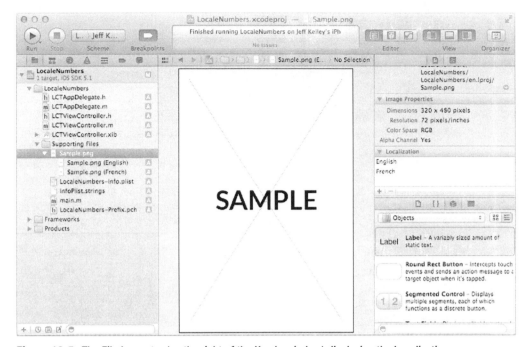

Figure 12-5. *The File Inspector (on the right of the Xcode window) displaying the Localizations group*

To see how Xcode has rearranged things for you, you can right-click the file in Xcode's file browser and select Reveal in Finder. You should notice a folder with a name ending in .lproj that contains your file. To add more languages, click the plus button again; you'll see a list of supported languages appear. Select the language for which you'd like to provide another version of this file, and Xcode will copy the current version to an appropriate folder. Simply modify or replace the copied file to provide a separate resource for that language.

So, how does all this work? For every language and locale setting, iOS builds a list of preferred languages. Let's consider a hypothetical country with two official languages: French and Chinese. Let's also consider an app that supports French and English. For a user whose device is set to French, iOS will automatically load resources from the fr.lproj directory rather than the en.lproj directory. Since our hypothetical country's list of preferred languages includes both French and Chinese, a user whose device is set to Chinese will, if no Chinese resource is found, use the French resource. To get this built-in cultural sensitivity, you don't need to do anything more than provide resources in multiple languages, so long as support for the country is included in iOS.

One of the biggest benefits of using the built-in localization tools in iOS is that you can release one app for your worldwide audience. Instead of releasing an English version, a French version, a Spanish version, a Chinese version, and a German version of your app, you release one version with all of these languages included as localizations. This has a number of advantages: first, if a user switches between languages on their device, perhaps to help learn a second language, your app will switch with them. Second, when it comes time to update the app, you won't be stuck trying to update multiple versions of the app and then waiting for Apple to approve each one. Third, it's much easier to track download figures, use analytics, and troubleshoot problems if you have one app.

When you use Apple's built-in controls, you get some localization for free. Any system buttons that you use, such as the Done button, are automatically translated into the user's language: Done in English is OK in French and Fertig in German, at least according to the Done button. Similarly, specifying different values for the Return key on the on-screen keyboard will result in Apple's translated values being used. While this is great and Apple's translations are, as far as I can tell, top-notch, there is a slight danger here: if you need to translate *done* somewhere else in your app, your translation may not match Apple's, which could confuse users. It's important to have people who speak the language test the app and let you know if translations are off. Also, system buttons won't translate automatically unless you have some localized resources in your application for the target language. An English-only app will display English-only buttons, but if you provide localized text, then the buttons will be localized as well.

Let's look in detail first at the easiest thing to localize: text.

Localizing Text

Localizing text is done through what's known as a *strings file*. This is a special resource you can add to your file that allows your app to load text based on the user's preferred language. To add a strings file to your app in Xcode, select File ➤ New ➤ File… or press ⌘+N, select Resource under iOS in the left column, and then select Strings File from the list on the right. The conventional name for this file is Localizable.strings. In this file, you'll provide a series of strings assigned to keys, which are also strings. In code, you'll refer to these keys, loading the associated string as needed. Consider the following example of creating a button with the title Submit:

```
UIButton *submitButton = [UIButton buttonWithType:UIButtonTypeRoundedRect];
[submitButton setTitle:@"Submit"
            forState:UIControlStateNormal];
```

Notice that the word *Submit* is hard-coded in English. In the localization process, you'd extract this line and place it in the Strings file, perhaps with the title SubmitButtonTitle:

```
"SubmitButtonTitle" = "Submit";
```

Now, when we reference the `SubmitButtonTitle` key in code, we'll get "Submit" back for English. By adding localized versions of the `Localized.strings` file, we'll get the different languages' text instead if the language is selected. To use this in code, you can use the `NSLocalizedString` macro as follows:

```
UIButton *submitButton = [UIButton buttonWithType:UIButtonTypeRoundedRect];
[submitButton setTitle:NSLocalizedString(@"SubmitButtonTitle", NULL)
            forState:UIControlStateNormal];
```

The first argument for the macro is the key to use as an `NSString` object, and the second, here omitted in favor of `NULL`, is an optional comment. The return value will be the string you've put in the strings file, localized for the appropriate language.

The advantage of the strings file is that, most likely, you won't be providing all of the translations yourself. By placing all of your content that needs localization into the same file, you can just give that file to whoever *is* doing the translation and be reasonably sure that they'll be able to understand what to do. Even more, Apple provides the `genstrings` tool to automatically create these strings files based on the comment you use. With this tool available, the best workflow is to always use `NSLocalizedString` in your own code and then use `genstrings` to generate a strings file before localization.

One final consideration when using text of multiple languages is font support. If you provide your own custom fonts for use in your app, be sure that it supports all of the languages your app does.

Example: HelloLocalization

Let's look at how we might localize an app by localizing a simple Hello, World! application. Open Xcode, and select File ➤ New ➤ Project… or press ⌘+Shift+N. Select Application in the leftmost column under the iOS section, and then select Single View Application on the right. Click Next, and then enter **HelloLocalization** as the name for the project. Enter your company identifier and class prefix (I'll use **com.learncocoatouch** and **LCT**), select iPhone for Device Family, and ensure that Use Automatic Reference Counting is checked and both Use Storyboards and Include Unit Tests are unchecked. Click Next, and then click Create to save the project to disk.

The UI of this project will be very simple: a single label. Open the main view controller's user interface file (LCTViewController.xib) in Xcode. Open the Object Library by selecting View ➤ Utilities ➤ Show Object Library or by pressing Control+Option+⌘+3. Once it's open, drag a label into the view and center it. Expand the label to fill the width of the view. Next, add an outlet for this label by opening the view controller's header file (LCTViewController.h) and adding the line in bold:

```
#import <UIKit/UIKit.h>

@interface LCTViewController : UIViewController

@property (weak, nonatomic) IBOutlet UILabel *helloLabel;

@end
```

Go back to the user interface (LCTViewController.xib) and connect the outlet by holding Control, dragging from the File's Owner object to the label, and then selecting helloLabel from the list of outlets that appears. Open the view controller's implementation file (LCTViewController.m) and add an @synthesize directive for the label by adding the line in bold:

```
@implementation LCTViewController

@synthesize helloLabel;
```

Next, set the text of the label by adding the line in bold to the viewDidLoad method:

```
- (void)viewDidLoad
{
    [super viewDidLoad];
    // Do any additional setup after loading the view, typically from a nib.

    [[self helloLabel] setText:NSLocalizedString(@"helloWorld", NULL)];
}
```

If you were to run the app now, the label would read "helloWorld," because we haven't provided any text for this key. We'll use the genstrings command-line utility to create a strings file for the project. Open Terminal and navigate to the directory that contains this project's code files (for me, the command is cd /Users/jeff/Projects/HelloLocalization/HelloLocalization). Next, enter this command:

genstrings -o en.lproj *.m

This will create a subfolder of the current location named en.lproj if it does not already exist and create a file named Localizable.strings inside this folder. As of now, the file's contents should be as follows (it's just a text file, so you can open it in your favorite text editor):

```
/* No comment provided by engineer. */
"helloWorld" = "helloWorld";
```

Open this directory in Finder and drag `Localizable.strings` into your Xcode project under the Supporting Files group. Click Finish, and the strings file appears, already having an English localization. Open this file in Xcode and modify the contents by removing the struck-out line and adding the line in bold:

```
/* No comment provided by engineer. */
"helloWorld" = "helloWorld";
"helloWorld" = "Hello, World!";
```

Build and run the app. The label will now read "Hello, World!" for all languages. To add another language, select `Localizable.strings` in Xcode's Project Navigator, and open the File Inspector by selecting View ➤ Utilities ➤ Show File Inspector or by pressing Option+⌘+1. Under Localization, click the plus button to add a new localization. Let's do French. You may find that if the file doesn't currently have any translations, clicking the plus causes Xcode to select another file; if this happens, simply reselect `Localizable.strings` and click the Plus button again to add a second language. An arrow appears next to `Localizable.strings` in the Project Navigator; click it to expand the file, revealing its translations. Select `Localizable.strings (French)` from the list and modify if by removing the struck-out line and adding the line in bold:

```
/* No comment provided by engineer. */
"helloWorld" = "Hello, World!";
"helloWorld" = "Bonjour, Monde!";
```

Build and run the app. If your language is set to French or French is before English in iOS's list of preferred languages for your region, you'll see "Bonjour, Monde!" appear, but otherwise you'll see the English version. To test this, you can change the language of your device or simulator using the Settings app, but be careful—once you change the language, the Settings app will itself be translated, so you may not be able to read the text to see where to change the language back. If you change it to French and get stuck, know that "Settings" in English is "Réglages" in French and that the path to change the language is Général ➤ International ➤ Langue. Also, once you change the language, any currently running apps are terminated, so you'll need to relaunch your app to continue testing.

As you can see, the `genstrings` command makes generating strings files easy. In general, any text that's going to be displayed to your users should come from `NSLocalizedString()`, allowing you to easily localize your app. Next, let's look at localizing the nontext parts of your app.

Localizing Resources

As we saw earlier, localizing resources is as easy as clicking the plus button. It's easy to get carried away, however. Keep in mind that the App Store has a 50MB limit on downloads over cell networks; if you have full-sized images for each language, your app's size is going to grow quickly, especially if you're providing 2048 x 1536 graphics for the third-generation iPad's Retina display. If you have a large image but only a small part of it, such as a styled title, needs to change, consider splitting it into two images and localizing only the title. The file size savings can be enormous. If your app has bundled video with it, consider removing all text that would need to be localized from the video or hosting the localized video online; users won't want to download several gigabytes of video for languages they don't use.

Another way to limit your download size in the App Store is to avoid providing multiple versions of resources. Wherever possible, render text as text instead of loading it in as an image; your designer will be grateful that she doesn't need to provide 30 different versions of a title image for 30 different languages.

Localizing Nibs

Like any other resource, nibs can be localized. This is especially useful for languages such as German, where words tend to be long. In the event that longer words require you to rearrange your user interface, you can do so for an individual language by changing just its nib and not the others. To localize a nib, simply create another language version using the File Inspector as before, and then replace the English text in it with the text in the appropriate language. Move things around as necessary, save, and you're done.

Localizing nibs can be fraught with peril, however. You should try to do it as late as possible in your development cycle and even consider using localized strings instead. Consider the following scenario: you develop an app and decide to release it in five languages. The app does well, and you begin updating it to fix bugs. In the bug-fixing process, you need to change a property of a view inside a nib. Since you've localized the nib, however, you now have two choices: make the change in each and every nib or delete the others and re-create them using the newly updated nib. Either way, you could be in for a lot of work and should perhaps consider avoiding this altogether in favor of localized strings.

Summary

Localization and internationalization are about more than replacing English text in your app with text in your user's native tongue. It's about being culturally sensitive and recognizing that your users want the app to feel as if someone in their country created it. If you use an idiomatic expression in your app like "her face rang a bell," don't just translate this to another language—and certainly don't use an online translation tool to do it. Similarly, be culturally sensitive about colors, images, and audio played in your app. Red is a sign of good luck in China, so your app might detect a Chinese locale and change how it displays color accordingly.

After reading this chapter, you should be able to take your app from supporting one language and locale to supporting every language and locale that iOS supports. This is a key skill that can take your app from a single-market release to a worldwide phenomenon. It's easy to omit, but it might be the most important feature you add to your app.

Running Code on an iOS Device

Developing for iOS is many things: challenging, fun, rewarding, and exciting. One thing it is *not* is free. To begin, doing any legitimate iOS development requires using Mac OS X, which requires a Mac to be compliant with Apple's license agreement. Once you have a Mac, you can download Xcode for free from the Mac App Store. Using the free version of Xcode, you can write iOS apps to your heart's content and run them in the iOS Simulator. To run your apps on an iOS *device*, however, you need to be a member of the iOS Developer Program.

The iOS Developer Program

Available at http://developer.apple.com/programs/ios, the iOS Developer Program encompasses several aspects of your interaction with Apple as a iOS developer. Not only does enrollment provide you with access to code-level technical support and prerelease versions of the iOS SDK and iOS itself, but it also allows you to test your code on iOS devices. It's also required to submit apps (free or paid) to the App Store. Membership in the iOS Developer Program will set you back $99 USD annually. There's also the iOS Developer Enterprise Program, available at http://developer.apple.com/programs/ios/enterprise/, which costs $299 USD annually. The difference between the two programs is that the iOS Developer Program allows you to run code on up to 100 devices, while the iOS Developer Enterprise Program allows you to run code on an unlimited number of devices. If you're planning on submitting an app to the App Store, you'll need the non-Enterprise version, though you can purchase both.

Why do you need to be a member of the iOS Developer Program to run code on a device? Some might say that this is Apple trying to nickel-and-dime developers, but in the opinion of yours truly, this argument is flawed. Given the number of developers, the $99 annual fee generates so little income for Apple relative to its other ventures that it becomes statistically insignificant. Instead, I view the $99 fee as a deterrent; people who aren't serious enough about developing iOS apps won't purchase the membership and therefore won't make bad apps for the platform. Requiring membership in the iOS Developer Program also allows Apple to enforce much stronger security standards. To understand why you need to jump through these hoops in the course of your development, let's look at the security model of iOS and how that applies to us.

iOS Application Security

Every app on an iOS device must have a valid cryptographic signature to run. This book won't get into the specifics of the cryptography involved, but rest assured that it's industry-standard. This cryptographic signature has two very important features. First, it contains a signature for files in the app bundle; if a nefarious user were somehow able to modify your app's executable code, this would invalidate the signature, and the device would refuse to run the app. Second, the certificate used to create the cryptographic signature, though specific to the individual developer who created the app, is issued by Apple. If a rogue app were to wreak havoc on the iOS user community, Apple could shut it down by revoking the certificate, also resulting in iOS refusing to run the app.

Obtaining a Certificate

So, how do you get your hands on a certificate? In the early days of iOS development, this was a long process involving the iOS Provisioning Portal section of the Developer Program web site. With Xcode 4.3, this process is entirely automated. Open Xcode and open the Organizer window by selecting Window ➤ Organizer or Command+Shift+2. The top band of the organizer window acts as a tab bar; select the Devices section. At the left of the screen underneath the Library heading, select Provisioning Profiles. Click the Refresh button at the bottom of the screen. You'll be prompted to log in to your iOS Developer Program account. If you don't yet have a certificate, Xcode will offer to create one for you. As easy as that, you've created a certificate.

iOS Application Provisioning

The second part to an app running on a device is its *provisioning profile*. The provisioning profile contains two pieces of information needed to determine whether the app can be launched: a list of certificates that are allowed to sign the application and a list of devices allowed to run the app, listed using a unique identifier to the device. If you're provisioning an App Store or Enterprise app, you don't need to specify individual devices, because you won't be limited to the devices your app will run on.

To create a provisioning profile, first you'll need to specify at least one iOS device it can run on. This is another area where Xcode has automated what used to be a tedious process. Connect the iOS device to your Mac with a USB cable. In Xcode's Organizer window, it should appear on the left sidebar under Devices. Select the device by clicking it. If there's a green circle next to it at the right of the sidebar, then it's already configured for development. Otherwise, click the Use for Development button. When you do, Xcode will create a provisioning profile for you to use for generic development and install the provisioning profile on the device. At this point, you should be able to run code on your device! In Xcode with your project open, click the button above Scheme on the toolbar. This opens the Scheme pop-up. If you see the name of your target with a triangle to its right, move your mouse cursor over it to expand the menu. Select the name of your device from the list, hit Run, and your code is compiled for your device and runs! Now that you can run code on your device, you can better test code that takes advantage of hardware APIs such as the camera, GPS chip, and accelerometer.

For more information on further tasks, such as submitting apps to the App Store, refer to Apple's documentation titled "Tools Workflow Guide for iOS," available at the iOS Dev Center at `http://developer.apple.com/ios`.

Index

▪A, B

Blocks
  arrays
    comparison selectors, 199
    NSComparator, 200–201
    sort descriptors, 199–200
  asynchronous callbacks, 193–194
  block-based methods, 192
  code, 201–203
  encapsulated functions, 182
  enumeration
    fast enumeration, 196
    for loops, 194–195
    Mac OS X and iOS 4, 197–198
    NSEnumerator, 195–196
    selectors, 197
  meaning, 181–182
  memory management, 184–185
  objects, 185–186
  parameters to methods, 189–190
  retain objects, 188–189
  scope, 186
  storage qualifier, 187
  TwitterExample code
    activity indicators, 206–208
    completion handler, 203–206
Typedefs, 183
UIView animations, 190–192

▪C, D, E, F

Camera
  types, 278
  UIImagePickerController
    allowsEditing property, 283
    cameraFlashMode, 284
    custom overlay view, 279
    mediaTypes property, 282
    MyStuff, 278–279
    photos, 278–281
    rear-facing and front-facing
      camera, 280–281
    UIView subclass, 280
    videoQuality, 284
    videos, 282–284
  UIVideoEditorController, 284–285

▪G

Grand central dispatch
  code dispatch, 231–233
  dispatch_async() function, 231
  dispatch_sync_f(), 231
  framework, 230
  object-oriented framework, 236
  queues, 233–237
  semaphores, 237–240
  time, 240–241

■H

Handling user touches, 109
   custom views, 111–112
   direct manipulation, 109
   graphical user interfaces, 109
   responder chain, 109–111
   scroll views, 118–119
   UI changes, 120
      action sheet, 134
      drop-down list, 130
      editing mode, 136, 138
      images set, product, 131
      nib, 124
      possessions, 120–132
      table view reordering, 137–139
      table views, 135–137
      UIActionSheet, 132–135
      UIImagePNGRepresentation(), 121
      viewDidLoad method, 126
      viewWillAppear, 125
   UIGestureRecognizer, 112
      built-in gesture recognizers, 113–115
      custom, 115–118
      gesture recognizer life cycle, 113
      target-action methods, 113
Hardware APIs. *See also* Camera
   accelerometer
      CMMotionManager class, 290
      Core Motion, 288–293
      device motion, 292
      device orientation notifications, 287–288
      events, 285–287
      gyroscope data, 291
      magnetometer, 292
      MotionDot, 289
      real-time data, 285
      viewDidLoad method, 290

      viewDidUnload method, 289
   coreLocation, 293–295
   iOS devices, 307
   iPhone, iPod and iPad, 277
   location data, 293
   magnetometer device, 307–308
   MapKit
      CLGeocoder object, 297–298
      CoreLocation headers, 296–297
      framework, 295
      LCTTweet, 298–301
      LCTTweetMapViewController, 301, 304
      LCTTwitterController, 295–296
      text field, 302–303
      triggers, 305
      tweet map, 306
      TWRequest object, 298
      viewDidUnload method, 304
   web apps vs. native apps, 277

■I

Integrating networking and web services. *See also* Twitter
   asynchronous operation
      networking, 152
      NSURLConnection, 148–149
      URL connection delegate methods, 149–152
   data, 141
   download
      Caches directory, 164–165
      files, 162–164
      images, 165
   JSON
      foundation/model objects, 159–162
      JavaScript language, 157–158
      representations, 158
   loading data
      interpretation, 143–145

IoSimpleWeather app, 146
NSURLConnection class, 142
received data, 145–148
URL connection, 142–143
URL request, 142
Xcode editor window, 148
parsing JSON and XML, 153–154
sending data, 165
XML parsers, 154–157
Internationalizion
App Store, 351
calendars, date components and
time zones, 360–361
dates, 359–360
general section, 352–353
LocaleNumbers
app running, 358
LCTViewController, 357
user interface, 354–356
viewDidLoad method, 356–358
NSLocale class, 352
numbers, 353–354
processing user input, 361–362
iOS device, 371
application security, 372
certificate, 372
developer program, 371–372
provisioning profile, 373

■ **J**
JSON
foundation/model objects, 159–
162
JavaScript language, 157–158
representations, 159
web service, 153–154

■ **K**
Key-Value Observing (KVO)
action, 84–88
manual implementations, 83–84
NSObject class, 80
usage, 81–82
working, 82

■ **L**
Localization
built-in tools, 365
file inspector, 363–364
HelloLocalization, 366–368
key difference, 363
languages, 364
nibs, 369
resources, 369
strings file, 365–366
text, 365–366

■ **M**
Media, 309. *See also* Playing audio,
Playing Music, Playing video
Model-View-Controller (MVC), 38–39
Multithreaded code
long-running task, 225–226
processors, 222
thread safety, 223–225
twitter profile images, 226–230
UIApplicationMain(), 222–223

■ **O**
Objective-C
address book creation, 16
categories, 34–35
class extensions, 35–36
code, 28
data, 24–27
forward declaration, 37
function, 18
header and implementation file,
21–22
hyphen (-), 19
implementation, 19
information, 20–21
inherit variables and methods, 16

Objective-C (*cont.*)
  init method, 22
  instance variables, 17
  memory management
    ARC and properties, 33
    automatic reference counting, 32–33
    autorelease pools, 31
    garbage collection, 30
    heap memory, 30
    iOS devices, 29
    reference counting, 30
    stack memory, 29
  method declaration, 18
  Model-View-Controller, 38–39
  new file, 19–20
  object, 16
  parameters, 23
  pointer, 17
  properties, 27–28
  protocols, 36–38
  sayHelloButtonPressed, 24
  square brackets, 18
  tried-and-true methods, 15
  variables, 17

P, Q

Parent and child view controllers
  gesture recognizers, 59
  modal view controllers, 57
  Navigation controllers, 57–58
  page view controllers, 59
  setRootViewController, 57
  split view controllers, 59
  tab bar controllers, 58
Playing audio
  APIs, 317
  Audio Queue Services, 317
  AVAudioPlayer
    advantage, 315–316
    afconvert, 314
    callback functions, 316

    delegate method, 316
  categories, 309
  SoundBoard project
    adding buttons, 318–319
    AVFoundation and AudioToolbox frameworks, 319
    IBOutlet and IBAction, 319–321
    identification and class, 317
  System Sound Services
    alert sounds, 313–314
    AudioServicesCreateSystemSoundID() function, 310
    AudioServicesPlayAlertSound() function, 313–314
    CFURLRef, 310
    limitations, 310
    MySystemSoundCallback function, 312
    system sounds, 310–313
    trigger vibration, 314
Playing music
  media queries, 326–327
  MPMediaPickerController
    delegate method, 324
    initialization method, 323
    MPMediaItem class, 322
    protocols, 324
  MPMusicPlayerController, 324–326
  TitularSongs project
    delegate method, 332–333
    iTunes, 327–328
    MediaPlayer framework, 328–329
    MPMediaItemArtwork object, 331–332
    protocols, 328
    songsQuery method, 330–331
    user interface, 327–328
    viewDidLoad method, 329–330
Playing video

AirPlay, 338
CustomPlayer
  initWithNibName bundle
    method, 342
  LCTViewController, 340
  MediaPlayer, 341
  MobileCoreServices
    frameworks, 341
  notifications, 349
  NSNotificationCenter, 347–348
  outlets and actions, 340–341
  selectVideoButtonPressed,
    346
  showImagePickerForSourceTy
    pe, 344, 346
  UIAlertView, 344
  UIImagePickerController, 338,
    345–346
  video player UI, 338–340
  view controller methods, 342–
    344
MPMoviePlayerController, 333–
  334
MPMoviePlayerController's View,
  335
MPMoviePlayerViewController,
  334–335
network video, 335–336
thumbnails, 337–338

R

Run loops
  convenience methods, 220
  cycle, 220
  event-driven application, 219
  main (), 221–222
  runUntilDate, 221
  UIApplicationMain function, 222

S

Saving content
  file locations, iOS

app bundle, 106
  caches directory, 107
  documents directory, 106–107
moving data
  delegate chains, 80
  Key-Value Observing, 80–88
  MyStuff, 79
  notifications, 88–90
  singletons, 90–92
notifications
  common system, 90
  dealloc method, 89
  post, 89–90
  register, 88–89
NSCoding
  initWithCoder, 101
  modification,
    loadPossessionsFromDisk,
    102
  NSKeyedArchiver, 104
  possessionsArchivePath
    method, 102–103
  savePossesionsToDisk
    method, 101–102
  serialization, 104
NSUserDefaults
  class implementation, 98
  defaults command, 92
  files, 96–97
  loadPossessionsFromDisk
    method, 99
  modification, 98
  mutable array, 94
  possession value, 95–96
  PossessionListViewController.
    m, 94
  property list, 93
  savePossessionsToUserDefault
    s, 94
  synchronize method, 95
  Xcode property lists, 99
persisting data
  core data, 107–108

Saving content, persisting data (*cont.*)
    disadvantage, 92
    file locations, iOS, 106–107
    manual file handling, 104–105
    NSCoding, 100–104
    NSUserDefaults, 92–100
    SQLite databases, 105
  prototypical singleton, 91
Selectors
  background thread, 211
  hood messages, 210
  performSelector, 212
  sending messages, 209
  target-action paradigm, 211
  TwitterExample, 213–215

▪ T

Timer
  dictionary, 216
  LCTTimelineViewController, 216
  NSDictionary, 215
  schedule code, 215
  scheduledTimerWithTimeInterval, 215
  scheduleTweetRefresh, 217
  viewWillDisappear, 218
Twitter
  accounts, 169–170
  authorization, 167
  configuration options, 168
  controller object, 170
  frameworks, 168–169, 179
  function, 166
  implementation file, 171–173
  initWithStyle, 178, 179
  LCTAppDelegate, 177–178
  LCTTwitterController, 174
  OAuth service, 167–168
  pointer, 173
  reloadButtonPressed, 178
  sharedInstance method, 171
  table view, 174–176
  timeline retrieval method, 174
  tweets, 171
  viewWillAppear, 176

▪ U

User interface design, 243
  animation, 266–268
  coloring interface elements
    didFinishLaunchingWithOptions method, 244
    navigation controller, 245
    parameter, 246–247
    tableView, 247–248
    tintColor, 245
    twitter client, 249
    UIColor class, 244
  fonts and text size
    cellForRowAtIndexPath, 253–254
    custom fonts, 252
    images, 255–257
    initWithStyle method, 250
    key methods, 254
    label font, 250
    LCTTimelineViewController, 250
    table view cells, 254–255
    tableView, 251–252
    UIFont class method, 249
  reddit photo browser
    @synthesize image, 269
    JSON, 268
    LCTViewController, 271
    loadNextImageInSlideshow method, 274–275
    parseJSONData method, 270–273
    subreddits, 268
    viewDidLoad method, 268–272
  UIKit framework, 243
  view layout

autosizing values, 261–262
content modes, 262–263
coordinate system, 258–260
display properties, 260
hierarchy, 258
iPad, 265–266
retina display devices, 264–265
superview and subviews, 258
UIView subclasses, 263–264

▪V, W

View controllers. *See also* parent
        and child view controllers
application implementation
        Apple's controls, 47
        clickedButtonAtIndex method,
        49
        didTapButton, 47
        iOS applications, 46
        sliderValueChanged method,
        48
        UIAlertView class, 48–49
        UIButton class, 47
        UISegmentedControl, 47
function, 41
iOS applications, 41
life cycle, 42
        didReceiveMemoryWarning
        methods, 46
        IBAction, 44
        IBOutlets, 45
        Interface Builder, 42–43
        long-winded method, 46
        setTitleLabel, 43–44
        stand-alone application, 42
        viewDidLoad method, 45
nib loading
        .xib file, 54–55
        iPhone and iPad, 56
        table view cell, 55–56
passing data

application, 63–64
connections inspector, 66–67
delegate protocol, 74–78
header, 62
implementation file, 68
init method, 63
modal view Controller, 71–74
MyStuff, 60
page layout, 65–66
parent to child view
        controller, 70–71
possession class, 61–62
PossessionDetailViewControlle
        r, 67
possessions, 64–65
reduce coupling, 60–61
table view
        cell, 50–51
        customized cells, 53–54
        data storage, 52–53
        delegate methods, 52
        delete/insert cell, 53
        editing mode, 53
        header and footer text, 52
        protocol method, 50
        section, 52
        UITableView class, 49–50
UIViewController, 41–42

▪X, Y, Z

Xcode
Cocoa, 1
developer tools, 2–3
Hello, World
        application, 9–10
        Connections, 12
        header file, 10
        implementation file, 12–13
        initial project layout, 7
        iOS app running, 7–8
        method creation, 11

Xcode, Hello, World (*cont.*)
    modification, 12
    object library visible, 8–9
    project creation, 5–6
    templates selection, 4–5
    welcome screen, 3
  installation, 1–2
  simulator and emulator, 3
XML parsers
  array, 156
  connectionDidFinishLoading, 155
  errors, 154–155
  foundation/model objects, 159–162
  NSXMLParserDelegate, 154
  output, 156–157
  sequential parsers, 154
  web service, 153–154

CPSIA information can be obtained at www.ICGtesting.com
Printed in the USA
LVOW110947010712

288382LV00003B/2/P